Edition de la Maison E. Glignan, librairie, literie, Tamatave

Andovoranto - La Rue du Commerce

CARTE POSTALE

Correspondance

Adresse

362 Guadeloupe

Se renseigner à la Poste.

CARTE POSTALE

PARALLEL WORLDS

melanin (melă nin) *n.* Any of the various dark-brown or black ... pigments of animal origin ... as that of negroes' skin —*Webster's New International Dictionary of the English Language,* 2nd edition, unabridged, 1960

PARALLEL WORLDS
PARALLEL WORLDS

The Remarkable
Gibbs-Hunts and
the Enduring
(In)significance
of Melanin

Adele Logan Alexander

University of Virginia Press

Charlottesville and London

University of Virginia Press

© 2010 by the Rector and Visitors of the University of Virginia

All rights reserved

Printed in the United States of America on acid-free paper

First published 2010

9 8 7 6 5 4 3 2 1

Library of Congress Cataloging-in-Publication Data

Alexander, Adele Logan, 1938–

  Parallel worlds : the remarkable Gibbs-Hunts and the enduring (in)significance of melanin / Adele Logan Alexander.

   p. cm.

  Includes bibliographical references and index.

  ISBN 978-0-8139-2887-6 (cloth : alk. paper)

  ISBN 978-0-8139-2978-1 (e-book)

  1. Hunt, William Henry, d. 1951. 2. Hunt, Ida Gibbs. 1862–1957.
3. African Americans — Biography. 4. Married people — United States — Biography. 5. African American diplomats — Biography. 6. African American women civil rights workers — Biography. 7. Hunt, William Henry, d. 1951 — Travel. 8. Hunt, Ida Gibbs. 1862–1957 — Travel. 9. African Americans — Race identity — Case studies. 10. Sex role — United States — Case studies. I. Title.

  E185.96.A474   2010

  323.092 — dc22

  [B]   2009031

End papers: Photograph and postcards from the Gibbs-Hunts' travels. (Hunt Papers, Moorland Spingarn Research Center, Howard University)

What is needed, perhaps, to reverse the picture of the lordly man slaying the lion, is for the lion to turn painter.

—Anna Julia Cooper, *A Voice from the South*, 1892

For members of the Gibbs and Hunt families who remember their antecedents with such respect and affection, and for my own family, especially Jonah, Maya, and Calvin Alexander, and Solomon and Simon Ghebreyesus, who are my beloved keepers of the flame.

Contents

Photographs follow page 104.

PARALLEL WORLDS

Wedding Album
Washington, D.C., 1904

On the evening of Tuesday, April 12, 1904, in the fragrant, garlanded, and music-filled parlor of her gracious Washington, D.C., home, Ida Alexander Gibbs, who originally hailed from British Vancouver, married Consul William Henry Hunt, who claimed New York City as his permanent residence. A chorus of exultant yet relieved relatives and friends, almost all of them Ida's, saluted the newlyweds. According to a vivid report of the nuptials that the capital city's most esteemed newspaper, the *Evening Star,* featured the following day in its prestigious "World of Society" column, "the bride was prettily gowned in duchess lace over white satin, with tulle veil and orange blossoms, and carried a shower bouquet of roses." Both that journal and the newer but almost comparably regarded *Washington Post,* however, chose not to mention that while William said he was only thirty-four years old, his new wife, in fact, was forty-one.

Ida Gibbs was a person of refinement, poise, and acumen. Believing from an early age that knowledge could translate to power, she had graduated from one of the Midwest's premier bastions of higher learning, completing its four-year "gentleman's course" in 1884, then returned a few years later to receive a master of arts degree. More remarkably, her mother, Maria Alexander Gibbs, also had attended college — a rare feat for any woman of her generation. Ida kept abreast of current events and cultural developments

She refused a widower, [and] turned a deaf ear to the solicitations of a clever young lawyer who came to believe that she would suit him better than several younger and prettier girls. . . . At the time of these events [she] had left her thirtieth year well behind, and had quite taken her place as an old maid. . . . Her father would have preferred she should marry, and he once told her that he hoped she would not be too fastidious. "I would like to see you an honest man's wife before I die," he said. — Henry James, *Washington Square,* 1881 as she pursued a successful teaching career and even made a home for two orphaned cousins. She held dear her privileged station, surrounded herself with a galaxy of accomplished, stimulating colleagues, and garnered a modest estate that allowed her to support worthy causes, travel widely, dress well, and otherwise live in comfort.

A few years later, a noted scholar and author with whom, some observers have speculated, Ida Gibbs had enjoyed a bygone liaison, used her as the model for one of his riveting fictional protagonists, a Washington educator he called Caroline Wynn. "She was brilliant and well trained," he wrote of the formidable Miss Wynn. "While not especially pretty," he added, "she was good looking and interesting, and she had . . . the marks and insignia of good breeding."

That portrayal of Caroline Wynn captured Ida Gibbs's essence. With wispy brown hair, close-set hazel eyes, a small, firm mouth and prominent jaw, she was, in truth, "not especially pretty" when judged by orthodox American aesthetics and measures of female desirability. On the other hand, she had the verve and bearing of a woman seriously to be reckoned with, and her brilliance and "good breeding" were undeniable. One antecedent to whom Ida bore more than a passing resemblance was rumored to have been a vice president of the United States, although as a rule she shrugged off or guardedly dodged inquiries into that somehow troublesome family connection.

Ida's father, Judge Mifflin Wistar Gibbs, gave away the bride and presented her with an exquisite pair of etched gold bracelets and his personal check for a thousand dollars — upward of thirty times that amount in current value. In keeping with the judge's overall generosity to his daughter, those were hardly unexpected wedding gifts. In his youth, Gibbs had set forth from Pennsylvania for gold rush California, then emigrated to Vancouver Island, on the booming British colonial northwestern frontier, where his and his wife's children were born; but a decade later, flush with prosperity, they returned to the United States. He moved on to further financial and political successes in Arkansas, and crowned his career as an American consul abroad. The *Evening Star,* well attuned to the particulars of governmental power, readily acknowledged that Judge Gibbs had held "a leading place in the Republican Party . . . for a quarter of a century."

M. W. Gibbs relished his sojourns in Washington, which he called "the American Mecca for political worshipers." "It is here that the patriot and the mercenary, the ambitious and the envious gather, and where unity and divergence hold high carnival," he maintained, and nothing would have pleased him more than presiding over his daughter's wedding in the nation's capital. Ida was the leading lady that day, but her only sister and housemate, Harriet (Hattie) Aletha, attired in a chic ensemble of pastel *point d'esprit,* attended the bride in a key supporting role. Hattie Gibbs, the family's youngest and especially favored child, served as an assistant director of music for the city's public schools, headed a private academy, and was a superb concert pianist who had graduated from an esteemed conservatory then topped off her professional training in Europe.

One of the District's eminent Presbyterian ministers performed the ceremony, a talented trio played the wedding march, and a respected young doctor was William's best man. A septet of Ida's associates augmented the receiving line, while three ruffle-and-ribbon-bedecked flower girls entranced the entire gathering. The guests included local and out-of-town dignitaries — judges, ex-congressmen, and a former governor among them. Other luminaries who could not attend sent gifts, tributes, and congratulatory cables from around the country and the world.

Though scarcely the Gibbses' social equal, William Henry Hunt had made great strides from his humble origins and, in light of Ida's age, was considered a fine catch. In contrast to his patrician bride, William — tall, athletic, and sun bronzed, with luminous gray eyes, cleft chin, tidy mustache, and fashionably pomaded curly hair — epitomized the novelist Horatio Alger's all-American, up-by-the-bootstraps prototype. The Hunts claimed to be able to trace their paternal lineage back to the illustrious Reverend Robert Hunt, who had conducted the first New World Anglican services on the shore at Virginia's Jamestown settlement, but William's branch of the family had endured arduous times. He was born in hardscrabble rural Tennessee, and spent his early life virtually unschooled, impoverished, and scrambling just to survive.

Yet through grit, guile, and hard work supplemented by random strokes of good fortune, William made his way. He toiled in brothels and saloons, hotels and stables, and often spoke of how he developed into a skilled rider under the tutelage of several Derby-winning jockeys, and even crossed paths with the infamous desperado Jesse James. He also told fabulous stories about the transformational, globe-circling odyssey of his youth. That eye-opening, two-year journey as travel companion to a wealthy patron, he said, imbued him with an inextinguishable wanderlust and a nagging itch to overcome the restrictions and assumptions of class and become a diplomat in the service of his country. To prepare for such an apparently improbable career, he cultivated a series of mentors and maneuvered himself through a reputable New

England preparatory academy on a scholarship supplemented by a variety of menial jobs, then into a prestigious college.

At a critical juncture in his early adult life William Henry Hunt met Ida Alexander Gibbs. That chance encounter led Ida to persuade her father, who in 1897 had received a coveted presidential appointment as a United States consul, to take on the young man (by then, William was working at a Wall Street brokerage house) as his clerk. William thenceforth treasured Ida, while M. W. Gibbs became his primary sponsor. When Gibbs retired from his overseas post three years later, the State Department replaced him with the capable, patriotic, and congenial Vice Consul Hunt, who was well respected, already in place, and fully acquainted with the position's demands and minutiae.

The country and the world were poised at the dawn of an extraordinary new "American Century." A surge in the United States' nascent imperialism exemplified by its aggressive stance in foreign relations and trade, and its bold presence throughout the Pacific Basin, conjoined with President Theodore Roosevelt's muscular corollary to the Monroe Doctrine that rationalized his arguably sacred mission to maintain order in Latin America and the Caribbean (his nation's undeclared empire), characterized that era. Thus, with the addition of a peerless helpmate such as Ida, William's advancement in the burgeoning consular service should have been assured.

Ida Alexander Gibbs Hunt, the consul's new wife, was a woman of serious if sometimes thwarted aspirations who maintained an unruffled demeanor but often bristled at limitations that both the law and intransigent societal notions placed on members of her sex. For years she had led an active, independent life as she frustrated the attentions of a series of beaux. And she taught so well and for so long that family and friends must have feared she might forever remain unmarried. As her aforementioned admirer attested about his novel's heroine, "She had many suitors but they had been refused one after another for reasons she could hardly have explained."

But perhaps Ida finally recognized that if she hesitated any longer William could sail off into the sunset alone or with someone else, and with him her final chance to wed. Their deep mutual devotion played a key role in that decision, yet she also probably heeded her sister's and father's advice, or her mother's counsel concerning the pros and cons of men and matrimony. Ida's curiosity about the mysteries and challenges of unfamiliar places and people would have drawn her as well to that particular suitor, whose future seemed destined to take him, and her as his spouse, around the globe. Rather than visiting the St. Louis World's Fair that summer (over a decade before, by contrast, she and her father together had attended the 1893 Chicago World's Columbian Exposition) with a crush of gawking tourists who would marvel at the relocated re-creations of foreign artifacts and rituals, and displays of human exotica such as the recently captured and securely encaged Congolese pygmies, Ida in her reconfigured life would be provided with firsthand opportunities to study, experience, and further appreciate those little known societies herself.

She already was fluent in French and practiced in an array of social skills —undisputed assets for any budding diplomat's wife. By assuming her place at the helm of their matrimonial ship, Ida anticipated that she could steer, mold, and promote her new husband and his incipient career. So she shook off any residual apprehensions, encouraged William's extended epistolary courtship, accepted his earnest proposal, and then, because the District of Columbia denied married women the option of continuing to teach in its public schools, resigned from her job.

Washington's temperature was cooler than predicted that early spring evening during the final year of Theodore Roosevelt's unexpected first presidential term, but the threatened rain showers never materialized to dampen Ida and William's spirits. After the ritual cake cutting and champagne toasts, they boarded the midnight train to New York City. The couple registered at the well-appointed Fifth Avenue Hotel just north of Washington Square, basked in the company of William's associates for several days, then on April 16 embarked for Le Havre, France. They capped that Atlantic voyage with a week in Paris in preparation for the longer leg out of Marseille that would carry them off to his consular post in Tamatave (present-day Toamasina), Madagascar. In contrast to William's solo trip home several months before, this time, when he sailed off to that vast, faraway locale in the southernmost Indian Ocean, Ida stood by his side as he put his old bachelor life behind.

Few Americans frequented the Great Red Island of Madagascar, which was thought of, if at all, in William and Ida's country as the native habitat of eerily contorted baobab trees, sleepy lemurs, and hissing cockroaches — and a fetid incubator for all sorts of tropical pestilence. The small but thriving European (mostly French) government, military, and settlers' communities, as well as a number of Asian merchants, would nonetheless offer warm *bienvenues* to the returning United States consul and his bride. Foremost among that international clique was William Hunt's associate and friend Joseph Simon Gallieni, the acclaimed but still embattled French governor general. Just a few years before, Gallieni had exiled the Malagasy queen Ranavalona III, pacified Madagascar's indigenous population, imposed his own language, and dexterously started reshaping the formerly independent feudal monarchy into a model colony. And a decade later General Gallieni would become a legendary hero during World War I.

But, truth be told, this apparently straightforward story has many complexities and darker undertones. As to the Gibbs-Hunts' wedding, ominous incongruities skewed what was otherwise a dazzling social union reminiscent of a Henry James novel of manners and mores played out against an international backdrop of privilege. In the United States' monumental capital city, Ida Gibbs could teach only in certain overcrowded, underfunded schools. And despite her family's prominence and means, one reason they celebrated the nuptials at her home was that most public facilities would have brusquely denied entry to her, her noteworthy relatives and guests, and the groom — who had, and laudably continued to, represent his country half a world away.

In the ensuing decades, their intelligence and ambitions, supplemented by governmental dicta and the vagaries of fortune, swept Ida and William across oceans and seas, continents and islands. They would participate in some of the new century's critical events and key political and ideological movements, interacting with an epic cast of acclaimed and controversial figures from many nations. Despite several close calls, they survived nature's random assaults as well as the sporadic savagery of men and of war. But the hostile reception they encountered from many fellow Americans limited their professional and personal opportunities, and curtailed their rights as citizens. One factor virtually alone prompted that shabby treatment. The country's idiosyncratic social practices and arcane laws — which with few exceptions determined that even a "drop of colored blood" (the "stain" of melanin) poisoned the genetic pool, ineradicably assigned race, and relegated anyone who possessed that defining and contaminating "drop" to a debased position in society — classified Ida Alexander Gibbs and William Henry Hunt as Negroes.

Deep-seated paranoia about miscegenation, or "amalgamation" as some still called it at the time, meant that in many jurisdictions neither William nor Ida would have been allowed by law to marry a person whose complexion was even a shade or two lighter than his or her own. Washington, D.C.'s statutes did not ban interracial marriages outright, but they were rare, and often disdained by whites — and by some blacks as well. Two decades before, the same clergyman who joined Ida Gibbs and William Hunt in matrimony had also married Frederick Douglass, the Negro titan, to Helen Pitts, a white woman. That earlier union generated rampant controversy.

Most Euro-Americans considered "colored" women inherently impure and wanton. At the snap of a finger they supposedly made themselves sexually available to anyone, anywhere, whereas black men were seen as bestial, insatiable, and hell-bent on ravishing chaste white ladies. Many considered even the least whispers of that sort of venal offense to be ample justification for lynching. Legitimizing an intimate relationship between someone with any trace at all of African ancestry and a white person through the sacred institution of marriage was thus viewed as such a heinous assault on the just and proper order of American society that a few years later a southern congressman sponsored an (ultimately unsuccessful) amendment to the Constitution to ensure that "intermarriage between Negroes . . . and Caucasians is forever prohibited." Its stated intent was to "exterminate now this debasing, ultrademoralizing, un-American and inhuman leprosy." The country's hateful but resilient antimiscegenation laws would only be terminated, at last, as a result of the Supreme Court's 1967 landmark decision in the case of *Loving v. State of Virginia.*

At the dawn of the twentieth century, the District of Columbia was not as wretchedly segregated as many other jurisdictions, but it was a notably sullied citadel of democracy. Federally mandated regulations denied the franchise to all the city's residents and corralled its expanding African American population into separate and decidedly unequal schools, residential enclaves, and, in most cases, places of public accommodation. As Mary Church Terrell, one of Ida's friends, protested, "Indians, Chinese, Filipinos and representatives of other darker races can find reservations. . . . The colored man or woman is the only one thrust out of the hotels of the National Capital like a leper." Church Terrell, the Gibbs-Hunts, and other members of their circle belonged to the small, conscientious, upper-class stratum of Negro society in Washington and elsewhere who honored their racial heritage, held leadership roles in their often autonomous institutions, and struggled to "uplift the race." But wherever they resided, whatever their social or economic standing, all African Americans loathed, condemned, and resisted the virulent (or sometimes subtle) prejudices and discrimination they experienced throughout the United States.

Having emerged only recently from slavery's officially sanctioned atrocities, followed by the violence, indignities, and economic, legal, and political injustices of the Jim Crow years, most late nineteenth- and early twentieth-century members of their race suffered far greater privations than did the Gibbses and Hunts. While those stories of hardship and abuse have roused righteous anger, pity, or sometimes admiration, they are not altogether unfamiliar. With rare exceptions, however, they have been painted on tightly circumscribed geographical canvases. Little known and infrequently told, by contrast, are the significant but stereotype-defying accounts of the few black Americans from that era who adroitly performed on the world stage. Despite predetermined membership in the United States' racially defined lowest caste, they survived, functioned, and sometimes thrived far from home, honorably and skillfully acting on behalf of their country but also — though often hesitantly — challenging its frailties, blunders, and abuses. They refute prevalent perceptions that Negroes were ignorant of or disinterested in international affairs, but their scarcity illustrates how, for so long, arrogant racist and sexist policies have deprived this nation of many of its best and brightest.

In his home country, even a successful African American such as William Hunt was seen and treated (like every "colored" man) as a political, legal, and social inferior, but elsewhere his hard-to-classify physiognomy made him seem racially ambiguous. Members of the international community among whom he lived and worked for decades usually cared little about the "black" racial identity with which his nation indelibly stamped him, but it puzzled them. Seeing firsthand the manifest physical reality of that pale-skinned gentleman in their midst, yet having only a limited grasp of the United States' encompassing definition of Negroes, as well as its storied but predatory relationships with its indigenous people, some of Hunt's *confrères* abroad conjured up images of a *"peau rouge"*— the noble "redskin"— to explain his slightly swarthy complexion and try to pin down his elusive ancestry. In an array of overseas locales, he meanwhile represented and epitomized the United States and its flag as he served for thirty-five years as the first African American to complete a full career with the foreign service. That unusual and elite occupation imbued him with a privileged cachet, but also helped make and sustain him as what he, and many who knew him personally and professionally, considered almost a raceless citizen of the world.

Few Americans of William and Ida Hunt's generation and legally designated race had the combined opportunities and wherewithal to explore the global roads they trod. But by acting on behalf of the United States around the world, Hunt and a handful of his black male predecessors and contemporaries set worthy precedents and helped clear paths and open doors for those who succeeded them. In addition to M. W. Gibbs, they included Frederick

Douglass, Gibbs's mentor in the abolitionist movement and a minister to Haiti; Colonel Charles D. Young, military attaché to four countries; James Weldon Johnson, consul, giant of the Harlem Renaissance, and leader with the National Association for the Advancement of Colored People; and even the little known John Lewis Waller, whose consular tenure in Madagascar sparked a singular international contretemps and cast ominous shadows over both Gibbs and Hunt. Despite some successes, their government erected daunting barriers for such men, and usually posted them only to a few "black" locales. Thanks in large part to those groundbreakers, African American diplomats in the ensuing decades, from Clifton R. Wharton (Sr. and Jr.), Edward Dudley, and Ralph Bunche to Patricia Roberts Harris, Andrew Young, Colin Powell, and Condoleezza Rice, have been able to follow more varied routes, overcoming challenges and controversies with increasing recognition and influence. Those men, and (finally) women too, labored on behalf of their country, bolstering its credibility among the world's vast nonwhite majority and often garnering respect from allies and adversaries alike.

Until recently, significant female African American internationalists have been few. And yet, although their government long denied them — and white women too — opportunities to serve in official capacities with the State Department or in the military, they were not absent. If any women outside her family helped to chart the course that Ida Gibbs Hunt followed, Mary Church Terrell and Anna Julia Cooper were the ones who did so. Because of both race and gender, "colored" women of their era were considered undeserving and incapable of benefiting from higher education, while financial strictures also often thwarted their prospects. So in 1884, when Gibbs, Church, and Cooper graduated from Oberlin (a pioneer in coeducation as well as the academically acclaimed "white" school that, almost alone in the United States, admitted and even welcomed a number of African American students at that time), only two Negroes of their sex before them had *ever* completed the four-year course of study at *any* fully accredited college in the country. A few years later those pioneers relocated to Washington, D.C., where for a brief and sometimes contentious interval, they worked in the same segregated school system. Their challenging, testy, yet enduring relationships with one another would wax and wane for more than seven decades.

Anna Julia Cooper, who bloomed first among them as a public intellectual, articulated a nascent African American feminism soon after finishing college. She attended the 1893 World's Congress of Representative Women from All Lands and seven years later aligned multinational issues with "the

Negro problem in America," the subject of her speech at the seminal Pan-African Conference in London. Mary Church Terrell played significant roles in similar ventures. Ida Gibbs Hunt's critical but little known efforts on behalf of the post–World War I Pan-African Congresses speak to Cooper's and Church Terrell's influence, but more to her own global vision. In contrast to her husband's restraint and the circumspection that his diplomatic career demanded, Gibbs Hunt's outrage at her country's race, gender, and class inequities merged with broader concerns about war, peace, and the tragic past, dismal present, and bleak future of colonial Africa and the Caribbean. Her labors would be directed toward and shaped by those critical issues. Like her onetime classmates, she cast a revelatory light on the common interests as well as the crippling disempowerment that often linked the "darker races."

Ida Gibbs Hunt shuttled in and out of 1920s Paris — a city enthralled both by African "primitivism" and by an array of African American expatriates and sojourners, among them the classical painter Henry Ossawa Tanner, the dynamic boxer Jack Johnson, and the charismatic Josephine Baker — as she toiled away alongside the Pan-African Congresses' otherwise virtually all-male leaders, including the United States' preeminent William Edward Burghardt Du Bois, Senegal's Blaise Diagne, Haiti's Dantès Bellegarde, and Guadeloupe's Gratien Candace. But Gibbs Hunt and most of her circle rejected the spellbinding Jamaican Marcus Mosiah Garvey's separatist "back to Africa" rhetoric and initiatives that, in the same period, captivated legions of often disillusioned, usually poor but aspiring black Americans and West Indians. Rather, she shaped a transoceanic Negro (and feminist) identity as she helped to nourish an embryonic but inclusive though somewhat elitist paradigm for racial commonality among Africans and the diverse people of the African diaspora. Through circuitous routes, pan-Africanism came to fruition with the post–World War II anti-imperial, anticolonial upheavals, and in the civil rights movement and the "black pride, black power" politics of racial identity of the 1950s, '60s, and '70s. Ida Gibbs Hunt also committed herself to global reconciliation through a long association with the predominantly white, left-leaning Women's International League for Peace and Freedom.

All the while, a circle of kin bolstered the Gibbs-Hunts' lives. They repudiate stereotypes attributed to the "dysfunctional" African American family, so often categorically (mis)defined by irresponsible sexual behavior, skewed gender roles, indolence, poverty, and chaos. Ida's parents melded discipline with love as they strove to cloak and overcome the dissonances in their own marriage. They put steel in their daughter's spine and challenged her to achieve. During Ida Gibbs's half century with William Henry Hunt, the Gibbses' higher social and economic status, her seniority, intellect, and superior education, all challenged patriarchal Victorian assumptions about the "proper" hierarchical model for an "appropriately" male-dominated marriage. But the couple rejected those tired formulas as they negotiated and sustained an egalitarian collaboration grounded less on romance or passion than on mutual esteem, firm yet flexible ambitions, and respect for their considerable differences. To date, we have had almost no analyses of any such African American marital partnerships. Because they had few precedents to follow, the Gibbs-Hunts established their own rules of conduct, engagement, and accommodation vis-à-vis William's hidebound, bureaucratic employers. As with all families, they guarded their secrets and even perpetuated a handful of intriguing falsehoods — many of which can now be revealed.

Most studies of African American life and history understandably zero in on race but downplay or even ignore class, gender, and place. This one, however, weaves together those threads and more, into a polychrome, evolving, migratory tapestry. Ida Gibbs and William Hunt emerge from it as fascinating and complex, noteworthy but undeniably imperfect members of the proud, hardworking, often frustrated (and extremely frustrating), sometimes elitist, yet deeply racially conscious Negro leadership contingent that W. E. B. Du Bois called the Talented Tenth. Although many African Americans — owing to marginal economics and lack of education, opportunities, or self-esteem — created or retained few records, ample materials document William's and Ida's lives. In 1902 Ida's father published an autobiography, *Shadow and Light.* It attests to his diverse accomplishments and public personae, but reveals far less about Judge and Consul Gibbs as a parent or husband. The book's laudatory introduction by Booker T. Washington, that era's most powerful American of his race, speaks to Gibbs's prominence and his ties to the black political establishment, but the next year Du Bois's essay "Of Mr. Booker T. Washington and Others," in *The Souls of Black Folk,* swept aside any illusions about ideological unity or uniformity among Negro leaders. The Gibbses invited Washington to Ida and William's wedding, but he did not attend. He could have had a previous commitment, probably had other priorities, or his absence might be attributable to escalating conflicts with Judge Gibbs, or the fact that the Reverend Francis Grimké, who openly aligned himself in the anti-Washington camp, officiated at the ceremony. In any case, several years later, the crafty fellow known as the Wizard of Tuskegee dipped into his bag of tricks and fomented an egregious conspiracy to try to oust William Henry Hunt from his coveted new consular post in Europe.

My unexpected discovery that the "white" *Washington Post* and *Evening Star* featured the Gibbs-Hunt marriage (though they explicitly labeled it a "colored" event) in their society pages, while the "black" *Washington Bee* ignored or snubbed it altogether, further reveals the transience of many such intraracial alliances. Although they shared interests and friends, a simmering tiff between the *Bee*'s cantankerous publisher and editor, W. Calvin Chase, and Judge Gibbs could help to explain that quirky journalistic omission, or Chase may simply have deferred to the rival *Colored American* newspaper, which lauded the wedding as a "brilliant social function." In his autobiography, Gibbs glowingly portrayed Chase, but the editor soon escalated his inexplicable pique to vulgar public name-calling. Such fractious spats highlight the fissures and expose some of the incessant mutations in the African American community's arcane internal power networks.

And M. W. Gibbs was not the only family member who recorded his history. After he retired, William Henry Hunt wrote, yet never published, a lengthy memoir that he titled "From Cabin to Consulate." It provides a riveting and unmatched picture of an African American's life in the foreign service. Hunt's reticence, as well as inbred conventions about maintaining a protective sphere of privacy that were characteristic of his generation and his vocation, however, resulted in a chronicle that, like Gibbs's, shrouds the inner man. Any such account is inherently personal and thus never unbiased, and this one was also transcribed by a novice historian. But even allowing for inaccuracies in transcription and the distorted or smudged lenses of advancing age, it is apparent that Hunt strategically reconfigured at least his early years to transform key chapters — as have many memoirists, including giants of the African American community such as Douglass, Washington, and Du Bois. Du Bois himself wrote about such undertakings, "Memory fails especially in small details, so that it becomes finally but a theory . . . with much forgotten and misconceived, [and] with valuable testimony . . . often less than absolutely true." Whatever Hunt's own memories, theories, or motivations may have been, some of his wily manipulations and dubious truths reconfirm that even the most valued sources must be rigorously challenged.

Manuscript collections, journals, census records, city directories, institutional archives, and interviews have yielded additional bits and pieces about William and Ida Gibbs Hunt. Ida wrote and published selectively, with evidence of brilliance, and saved much of her correspondence, as did her sister, Hattie Gibbs Marshall. An archived body of William Henry Hunt's letters and memorabilia from his years abroad supplement his wife's, and State Department records contain numerous dispatches from, to, and about Consul Hunt in his official capacities. The Gibbs-Hunts are further revealed in W. E. B. Du Bois's voluminous papers, especially those bearing on Ida Gibbs Hunt's indispensable work on behalf of his Pan-African Congresses. A few of those documents suggest, yet also becloud, her ideological, intellectual, political, and personal entanglements with Du Bois. That fascinating relationship infused and contoured much of her adult life. He, in turn, seems to have immortalized Gibbs Hunt (albeit anonymously) as the audacious teacher whom he called Caroline Wynn in *The Quest of the Silver Fleece* (1911), his previously quoted novel.

Ida Gibbs Hunt, however, sometimes chose not to publicly acknowledge authorship of her own essays and letters, as exemplified by a few incendiary pieces that touted feminism and laid out her views on race, miscegenation, and transnational politics. For that work she adopted a pen name: Iola Gibson. Ida's associations with black activists and involvement with pan-Africanism may have deflected the initially ascending arc of her husband's diplomatic career, so in part she probably assumed the pseudonym to cloak her true identity — in order, that is, to avoid causing him further professional hardships, unwarranted exposure, or embarrassment. But Gibbs Hunt's adoption of that nom de plume around 1920 reflects her sense of race and gender solidarity by evoking the fierce black journalist Ida B. Wells, who previously had assumed the briefer alias "Iola," as well as the abolitionist Frances Ellen Watkins Harper's 1893 novel *Iola Leroy, or Shadows Uplifted,* which explores themes of racial (mis)identity, noblesse oblige, and female survival.

The thorny issues that may provoke the use of hidden identities must also be viewed in the context of the times. President Woodrow Wilson, a keen intellectual who was lauded as a global visionary, was, frankly, a bigot when it came to Negro Americans. He promoted the racist blockbuster motion picture *Birth of a Nation,* further segregated his nation's capital, and purged the civil service of many ranking "colored" functionaries. His immediate successors did little to reverse such initiatives. William Henry Hunt never disavowed his full racial heritage, but in contrast to his wife he did lie low, and so for many years he probably retained his consular post in France, to a certain extent, because he was so light skinned that he avoided definitive designation as a Negro — at least for a good long while. But officials back at the State Department were eagle-eyed, persevering, and in some instances perhaps racially biased and vindictive as well when it came to controversial associates (Du Bois, for one), or provocative activities engaged in or espoused by the nation's very few African American diplomats, or in Hunt's case by imprudent and outspoken members of his family.

I also retrieved enticing details about Ida Gibbs Hunt's mother and maternal grandmother and their whispered ties to Richard Mentor Johnson, a once notorious character who is scarcely remembered today. Johnson was a Kentucky colonel, slaveholder, and senator who in 1837 became Martin Van Buren's vice president. As his contemporaries knew and a few biographers have acknowledged, Johnson claimed three or more bondwomen as his sexual partners. Several scraps of evidence suggest that a slave named Lucy Alexander was one of the women who bore his children — Maria Ann Alexander (Gibbs), Ida's mother, among them. Johnson was a public figure, so his bawdy private life raised eyebrows, provided savory grist for the gossip mills, and prompted heated debate and prurient commentary in the slaveholding South and the nation's capital.

In a similar yet usually unspoken narrative, William Hunt's memoir reveals that his own mother, also raised in slavery, was uneducated, overburdened, and died before her time. But he characterized his biological father, whom he knew only by reputation, as "overlord of the county for miles around." Stories like these offer anecdotal though credible confirmation that by wielding their physical, sexual, economic, and emotional powers, such white men have significantly lightened "black" America's collective complexion while, with apparent indifference, they contributed to widespread illegitimacy in that community. They have been among its prevalent but almost always nonsupportive, unacknowledged, and therefore blame-free though delinquent fathers.

The ensuing narrative therefore can be read and interpreted on at least three levels. In the broadest, global sense, it illustrates how an arrogance of power has operated on interlinked, overarching planes to configure but distort world events. For centuries, a hegemonic grid of slavery, colonialism, imperialism, and wealth helped to establish and maintain a viselike grip by a mostly white male minority at the expense of and by abusing, depriving, or neglecting the world's weaker majority — including women, the poor, and the darker races. Money, arms, terror, greed, and ubiquitous patriarchies, reinforced by a panoply of geopolitical, economic, and religious institutions, often still collaborate to perpetuate such sovereignty.

On an intermediary level, this story reveals how certain otherwise disempowered people have made their voices heard and resisted oppression. Those African Americans, both men and women, contested the elitism, racism, and sexism of dominant establishments in our imperfect democracy, primarily, in this case, the State Department and the military. In public and private venues they struggled to establish themselves as enlightened internationalists, and otherwise worked to influence global affairs. Sometimes realistically, but at other times with their heads in the clouds, that flawed cadre tried to stake out and claim their rightfully earned identities as citizens both of their country and of the world. Individually and collectively they often spoke, on behalf of those who could not do so themselves, against abusive male dominion, poverty, violence, unfree labor, and war. They became meaningful, yet in many ways stymied and frequently ignored, figures.

On a third, more intimate plane, the upcoming pages provide examples and gain direction from generations of intertwined friends and families that functioned in different ways, replete with the entangled threads of love and indifference, jealousy, betrayal and anger, support and neglect that characterize any such relationships. On that perhaps most tantalizing level, this story focuses and casts light on Ida Gibbs Hunt and William Henry Hunt, their kin and colleagues — sifting evidence, culling truth from illusions and deceits, and evoking nuanced pictures of their unexpected yet extraordinary lives. These myriad images, which have taken several lifetimes fully to develop, reveal new enigmas even as they bear witness to those sagas. In the 1850s Ida's father, Mifflin Wistar Gibbs, was one of the handful of men who founded and published *Mirror of the Times,* California's first newspaper by, for, and about Negroes. In that same vein, and at its most telling, biography (including this one) can not only reveal and portray a few select individuals but also proffer up broader, lucid reflections of their larger worlds.

Both William Hunt and Ida Gibbs most likely were descended, in some part, from Europeans and Native Americans, but the atypical, *involuntary* African diaspora (sustained by horrendous abuses of power) that engendered the United States' legacy of slavery and debilitating segregation shaped them far more. They and many of those with whom they lived, worked, and otherwise interacted, however, came to epitomize a sizable *voluntary* redispersal of people of African ancestry around the world. Such ongoing quests for a reconfigured and empowering, transnational Negro identity did much to forge the contours and textures of their lives.

This album of sepia portraits from their elegant 1904 wedding has introduced their story. That rite of passage marked the onset of a very long journey together, and shortly preceded a more grievous family milestone: the death of Ida's mother, Maria Alexander Gibbs. Where better to look next, then, than back at Maria, and her shadowy origins in the rapacious antebellum South? Her youth was fraught with peril and intrigue and stratified along predetermined lines of race, class, gender, and condition of servitude, but she let neither those early injustices nor later challenges defeat her. Maria approached her unfolding universe with grit and dignity as she and M. W. Gibbs forged exceptional legacies for their children. That unique heritage helps to explain why, decades later, in one of her manifold letters from remote corners of the globe, their intrepid daughter Ida Alexander Gibbs Hunt would write: "Being an Alexander, I do not worry."

PART I | FAMILY PORTRAITS

The Vice President's Daughters

At least in part, Ida Alexander Gibbs Hunt's legacy leads back to a perplexing white forebear crouched on a shaky branch of her mother's family tree. Yet like some others to whom that illustrious gentleman may be linked, she has never appeared in his official vita; and as told here, their story, while highly credible, cannot be advanced without residual shadows of doubt.

Ida's maternal grandfather was probably Richard Mentor Johnson. He was born in 1780 on the Kentucky frontier in an unremarkable community called Beargrass Station, not far from today's Louisville. During the War of 1812, Johnson's boosters touted him as their hero in the Battle of Lake Erie, where he sustained five bullet wounds. He would bare his hefty torso to display those livid battle scars, and when he reportedly shot the Shawnee chief Tecumseh, his followers deemed him a fearless "redskin" slayer, chanting "Rumpsey Dumpsey, Rumpsey Dumpsey; Colonel Johnson killed Tecumseh." But the paradoxical colonel later facilitated a rudimentary education for some of the Choctaws who lived near his old Kentucky home. That school, he surmised, might help to "civilize" and "socialize" the irksome local Native American population. He also became a lawyer who defended indigent clients and espoused controversial causes, presided over a bustling tavern that served his backwoods community

> "Has not society the right to guard the purity of its blood by the rigid exclusion of an alien race?"
>
> "Excluding it! How?" . . .
>
> "By debarring it from social intercourse."
>
> "Perhaps it has, . . . but should not society have a greater ban for those who, by consorting with an alien race, rob their offspring of a right to their names and to an inheritance in their property, and who fix their social status among an enslaved and outcast race?"—Frances Ellen Watkins Harper, *Iola Leroy, or Shadows Uplifted,* 1892

as well as wayfarers headed out to or back from the western territories, and ruled the roost in several very unusual, evolving households.

R. M. Johnson had first entered politics in 1804 when he went to the Kentucky General Assembly, then a couple of years later the state's white male property owners sent him on to the U.S. House of Representatives. He joined the Senate in 1820 to fill an unexpired seat, and in Washington, D.C., he ultimately became a true-blue Jacksonian Democrat who sponsored federal funding to upgrade the military and for veterans' relief. The Kentucky colonel opposed imprisonment for debt, supported westward exploration and expansion, and backed controversial legislation that advocated annual compensation for all congressmen. He prevailed once, but lost out in two subsequent efforts to have his state's legislature redesignate him as senator, and from 1829 until 1836 he again represented his old congressional district. In all, Johnson's congressional career spanned the administrations of five presidents, from Thomas Jefferson through Andrew Jackson.

In 1836 when no candidate received a majority in the electoral college, the U.S. Senate narrowly selected him as Martin Van Buren's vice president, even though his disgruntled home state representative voted with the opposition and several legislators fumed that Johnson "illustrated abolitionist principles in his own home." Despite his murky reputation (those detractors who claimed that he lined his pockets with government funds probably spoke correctly), Johnson served in that capacity from 1837 until early 1841, yet always considered himself a rustic bumpkin in the nation's capital. After Van Buren's single term, the Whigs' short-lived General William Henry Harrison, with the exuberant John Tyler as his running mate, prevailed in the 1840 election, snapped the Democrats' twelve-year grip on the presidency, and lowered the final curtain on Colonel Johnson's career in national politics.

R. M. Johnson's personal affairs also became intertwined with his public life. According to Leland Meyer, his most authoritative biographer, in his youth Johnson had longed to wed a seamstress, but his mother objected, arguing that the destitute young woman was beneath him. He insisted that his mother would regret her infernal meddling, and as events unfolded, she may have been sorry indeed that she blackballed his first love. From time to time, idle chatter in both Kentucky and Washington suggested that Johnson again was contemplating matrimony, with a suitable lady of means, but those rumors did not materialize and he (apparently) never married.

Johnson maintained his primary residence in rural Kentucky, where, like many prominent white folks, he was a slaveholder, though that circumstance may have unsettled him. Concerning the peculiar institution he once asserted: "No one can more sincerely lament than I the existence of involuntary servitude in the United States, and no one would make greater personal sacrifices, could I discover a way . . . to bring it to an end." Neighbors scoffed that he indulged his slaves, making them "an expense rather than a profit," yet he cared more about class disparities among whites than far more draconian racial inequities. During Johnson's vice presidency, the events concerning the slave ship *Amistad* triggered contentious quarrels due to the mobilization of white abolitionists; the Supreme Court's determination that under the Constitution all Negroes, enslaved or free, retained a core of basic human rights; and the final exoneration, release, and repatriation of the barque's captive Africans. But nothing reveals his position on these bitter debates.

Despite such national discourses, in the 1820s Johnson manumitted four slaves, although in his middle years seventy others remained on his property — as his property. By 1850 he still held seven people in bondage, but he also presided over an atypical household comprising himself (the sole man), several free women of color, and their offspring. Those apparent contradictions notwithstanding, Johnson contended that slavery was a universal institution and an appropriate power relationship that the Congress of the United States should not attempt to contain, control, or end.

Like that of many men of his race and status at that time and place, Johnson's behavior suggests that he believed any enslaved woman belonged to her master in every way, and therefore he could use (or misuse) her for whatever productive or reproductive purposes and personal gratification he might wish. In keeping with that patriarchal dogma, replete with its manifest assumptions of racial supremacy, around 1810 he began an overt, and according to a number of white observers, solicitous sexual relationship with a woman named Julia Chinn, a mulatto slave whom he had inherited through his father's estate. One of Johnson's colleagues further claimed that Chinn served as "chief manager of the domestic concerns of [his] house."

Julia Chinn could have overseen certain aspects of Johnson's domestic life, but calling a woman who became ensnared in any such master-slave relationship a paramour or concubine probably romanticizes and thus misconstrues her situation. Economics and law, custom, race, and gender inevitably converged to reinforce insuperable power imbalances between white men and Negro women. So while Chinn might well have fulfilled some of a "real" wife's more intimate functions, she remained enslaved and subject to her master's will as she learned to read, write, and cipher and maintained her tenuous position in Johnson's domain. They may have cared deeply for one another, although the arrangement could hardly have included more than a modicum of choice on her part, because despite various mitigating circumstances, all manner of coercion penetrated, shaped, and corrupted even the most intimate niches of American slavery.

R. M. Johnson, however, did defy local mores when he asserted that he and Julia Chinn had wed. By today's standards that may create a sympathetic persona for the man, but any such formal union was impossible under the laws of Kentucky and in much of the rest of the country as well. In most jurisdictions slaves were mere chattel, or property, who as such could not marry legally at all, though many of them maintained lasting conjugal partnerships with one another. Such alliances, however, were always subject to the whim of an owner, who might move himself, sell his chattel, or uncouple black families with no consequences or repercussions. Most states banned marriage between the races, so very few women of color, enslaved or free, could become white men's legal wives. Similar regulations made punishable by law all interracial sexual activity, and any sort of extramarital or "unnatural" sexual congress (fornication), but those statutes were enforced almost only in the rare instances when the foolhardy male partner was black.

In the vast majority of cases, according to law Negro women thus bore their children out of wedlock, so the majority of Euro-Americans deemed them inherently promiscuous. Such biased assessments did not see them as victims but instead reinforced the impression that they were lascivious, immoral wenches; created and underlined stark disparities between "decent" white ladies and "lewd" black women; and also effectively protected or salvaged the reputations of licentious male slaveholders and overseers. Yet in Johnson's impermeable realm, he and perhaps Julia too may have believed they were married in God's eyes. However she perceived herself, she lived under his roof for many years as he nimbly clambered up his country's political ladder.

In short order Julia Chinn bore two of Johnson's daughters: Imogene and Adaline. Under the statutory principle *partus sequitur ventrem,* every Negro child's mandated status conformed to that of its mother. That new American doctrine turned on its head the old tradition of English common law that held that a child's condition followed that of its father. It also ensured that regardless of who impregnated her, an enslaved woman's "issue" always belonged to her owner and, much like his livestock's offspring, further enriched him. The United States' participation in the international slave trade had officially ended in 1808, significantly curtailing the further influx of new laborers from

Africa and the Caribbean, so breeding slaves, by any means, replenished that dwindling wellspring and became critical to the peculiar institution's successful repopulation and continuance. Like all the other Negroes on R. M. Johnson's holdings in or around Scott County, Kentucky, Julia Chinn's progeny therefore remained his legal property and augmented his assets — unless he manumitted them, which he never did, since once free, they might well have left him behind to move north, or further west.

Johnson's more-white-than-black daughters grew up in their eminent father's comfortable realm, where he coddled, nurtured — and dominated them. He even hired a tutor for them, and for a few of his other, more biddable slaves as well. Those educational endeavors defied the law, but Johnson loved literature and music and wanted to share those passions with others. Some of his white critics, however, groused that he "tried to force [Adaline and Imogene] into society." They protested that those girls "rode in carriages, and claimed equality." According to several sources, but denied by others, he also gave them his name as a rare acknowledgment of paternity.

Even when it caused him discomfort, Johnson nurtured the two children born of that liaison with Julia Chinn. In law and fact they were his "colored" property, yet in many ways he treated them as if they were both free and white. After assembling persuasive dowries, including substantial homes, ample acreage, and slaves, in 1830 Johnson married off his girls to members of the local white gentry — in blatant defiance of statutes that banned such cross-racial unions. Adaline died just a couple of years later, but Imogene and her father remained an indivisible pair. Imogene's husband, Daniel Pence, had grown up nearby, and after they wed, the couple, and in time their children, resided on property adjoining R. M. Johnson's own. Understanding full well the liabilities inherent in being a Negro in Kentucky, even a mulatto who lived under the aegis of one of the state's more powerful men, for decades thereafter Johnson maintained for his devoted tan-skinned daughter Imogene Johnson Pence a secure and comfortable life as an affluent "white" southern gentlewoman.

His political clout, bolstered by borrowed money or ill-gotten gains, made possible that genetic alchemy, because by statute, even a small amount of "black blood" forever relegated its possessor to the "inferior" race. Yet when it came to the manifest will of an influential white man, not only neighbors but officials and the law often blinked. Julia Chinn, who passed away during an 1833 cholera epidemic, never shed her Negro identity, and Kentuckians surely knew that her surviving child also was "colored," yet even federal census takers reinforced the ruse that R. M. Johnson had created and then sustained.

From 1840 on, they listed his and Julia Chinn's daughter and her offspring as white, while Imogene and her conjugal family benefited from the labor and services of thirty slaves whom her father undoubtedly gave them.

In 1836, several years after Julia Chinn died, when Johnson's name emerged as a leading candidate for national office one critic said, "I do not think ... the nomination of Johnson for the Vice Presidency will be popular in any of the slave holding states ... on account of his former domestic relations." Another fellow observed that Johnson lived "in adultery with a buxom young negro wench," and a political cartoon portrayed a stereotyped yet lavishly dressed black matron spouting the words, "Let ebery good demmicrat vote for my husband," accompanied by the garbled but clearly bawdy, double-entendred caption: "She plucks Dick [Johnson] — Dick plucks you — and Van [Buren] plucks Dick." Many whites feared and loathed R. M. Johnson's supposed belief in and personal perpetuation of racial "amalgamation." Such verbal vilification and trifling slaps on the wrist did not abort his political career, but they may have taught him a lesson, because his ensuing sexual liaisons seem to have been much less cozily familial than the one with Julia. Everybody knew, of course, that he only was doing openly what multitudes of white men did covertly, yet the lewd snickering continued to dog him. A smutty pun whispered in his declining years claimed that if Johnson "expires in his wife's gentle embrace" his epitaph might read: "died in the wool."

Fidelity was never Johnson's forte, and frontier slavery provided him and other men like him with almost unimpeded access to any number of Negro women whom they or their peers owned. A chastening dose of reality therefore must temper any romantic assumptions about his supposedly monogamous relationship with Julia Chinn, because by the late 1820s Richard Mentor Johnson, devilishly called "Old Dick" by friend and foe alike, had appropriated as his sexual consorts at least two more, considerably younger enslaved women. Lucy Alexander, Ida Gibbs Hunt's maternal grandmother, probably succeeded Julia Chinn, and Lucy's nearest relative followed after her.

As early as 1830 a patron at Johnson's tavern commented on the "young Delilah about the complection of Shakespeare's swarthy Othello [who is] said to be his third *wife*." "His second," that observer slyly added, "which he sold for her infidelity, having been the sister of the present lady [who] is some eighteen or nineteen years of age and quite handsome." R. M. Johnson's colleagues claimed that the aforementioned siblings were both Julia Chinn's nieces. If so, those were unsettling, almost incestuous, liaisons indeed! Lucy's original surname was also Chinn, and twenty years later Johnson unquestionably shared his home, and perhaps his bed, with a forty-year-old named Patience Chinn. Patience almost certainly was Lucy's younger sister, and the same "swarthy Delilah" whom the gossipy patron at Johnson's inn had singled out two decades before.

For a while in the 1820s, Richard Mentor Johnson was widely acknowledged to have held in bondage a young woman named Lucy. If white people in the region believed that Lucy was his preferred sexual partner, she quickly would have become a prime object of prurient interest. And if Julia had come to Johnson through his father's estate, he might easily have acquired other Chinn slaves too, with Lucy and Patience among them. Johnson may have lusted after a unique Chinn family visage or demeanor, epitomized first by Julia, then Lucy, and finally by the comely "Delilah" (most likely Patience), whose skin tone supposedly approximated that of Shakespeare's tragic royal Moor.

Other evidence shows that in 1803 a baby named Lucy Chinn was born into slavery in Mason County, and confirms that twenty-three years later a woman known as Lucy Chinn Alexander gave birth to a girl named Maria — the same Maria Alexander who would ultimately become Ida Gibbs's mother. A credible and totally autonomous oral account also contends that an unnamed vice president of the United States fathered Lucy's oldest daughter, and in that era no vice president other than Johnson was even a Kentuckian. Seven members (two adults and five children) of Lucy Chinn Alexander's nuclear family first appear in the 1840 federal census in Mason County, Kentucky, not all that far from Johnson's residence. The next decennial census indicates that Lucy was forty-six, so if Johnson's supposed third "wife," about whom his tavern's customers had idly prattled, was nearly twenty around 1830, her big sister, presumably his previous mistress, was several years older.

But a few years before that, to R. M. Johnson's dismay, his feisty Lucy had run away, encouraged, abetted, and accompanied either by a truant bondman or by an Indian youth from the school that Johnson sponsored. (Descriptions of Lucy Chinn's straight black hair and coppery skin suggest that she may have had Native American forebears as well.) When slave catchers hauled her back to Johnson's bailiwick, he sold her because of that defiance, and also, perhaps, because of what he saw as her perfidious preference for another man. His rage, like that of other cuckolded lovers, suggests that she meant much more to him than just any other fugitive slave. Lucy, in turn, must have been trying to end Johnson's persistent sexual demands, despite the ludicrous statement from one of his white male cronies following her forced return to slavery that she thereby had been properly "restored to the fond embrace of her distracted husband" — Colonel Johnson himself.

As the product of brutal rape, or with Negro women's tacit acquiescence, white "husbands" like Johnson sired any number of mixed-race offspring, and the designations of both Julia Chinn and her nieces Lucy and Patience as mulattoes argue that their mothers before them had borne just such predatory men's children as well. Human bondage in frontier Kentucky was no less abusive, sexually or otherwise, than it was in the Deep South. In 1856 that state's defiant (and widely storied: among other things, she inspired Toni Morrison's 1987 novel, *Beloved*) Margaret Garner, for one, crossed the frozen Ohio River to escape slavery and the molestations of a series of white men who had forced themselves on her mother, then a generation later on her. But Garner was recaptured, and when she slit her own daughter's throat to spare her the horrors of growing up enslaved and thus subject to similar abuse, it unmasked any myths as to the institution's benignity. Ironically, prosecutors in Ohio lost out in their efforts to try Garner on murder charges because federal law took precedence and required that, as property, she instead must promptly be returned to her owner in Kentucky.

Slavery per se did not distress many white Americans at the time, but auctioning off light-skinned young people who shared characteristics of their owners'/fathers' physiognomies unsettled them, because selling one's flesh and blood seemed so sinfully un-Christian. The progeny that resulted when white men sexually exploited and impregnated females slaves reinforced widespread fears of miscegenation. The God-fearing Harriet Beecher Stowe, whose book *Uncle Tom's Cabin* polarized the country in 1853, first became incensed when she saw a tan-complexioned lass being sold on the block — right there in Mason County, Kentucky, where Lucy Chinn Alexander lived. But public auctions were integral and demeaning aspects of slave life everywhere, and female mulattoes often fetched extravagant sums because male bidders prized them as sexual trophies who supposedly combined white ladies' refined grace and loveliness with black women's lasciviously imagined sensuality.

The sale and repurchase of an enslaved woman sometimes cloaked unexpected motives. One source suggests that Henry Alexander, the free Negro considered to be Lucy's husband (though state laws legitimizing marriage usually did not apply to slaves), actually bought her from a white person, then later managed to manumit her. Like more than a few other such well-intentioned southern "colored" men, he might have purchased his spouse to assure her immediate legal and physical security, and further to facilitate her future freedom.

Various data support this version of both Lucy's travails and Maria's paternity, but hard evidence provides few incontestable answers. Nonetheless, Maria certainly was born into slavery in Kentucky, and by 1850 the Alexander household included Lucy, Henry, and five girls, ranging in age from twenty-four (Maria) down to six. Surprisingly, in light of the white South's overall opposition to allowing Negroes any formal education whatever, the Alexander children attended school, though their parents apparently never learned to read or write. To the minor credit of Kentucky's white male legislators, their state was anomalous in that its legal codes did not totally deny non-enslaved blacks access to formal schooling. The Alexanders appear in that year's census as free people of color in Mason County's town of Maysville, situated on the Ohio River's south bank, sixty miles northeast of R. M. Johnson's home in Scott County. Later records pertaining to Lucy's offspring show that her older daughters were born in the village of May's Lick, where the family had lived before moving to Maysville — and it was even closer to Johnson's main locus of operations.

According to *American Slavery As It Is* (1839), a weighty compendium of the peculiar institution's atrocities compiled by the righteous white abolitionist Theodore Dwight Weld, in 1838 a slave owner in Lexington, Kentucky, placed a newspaper advertisement offering a handsome reward for the return of a runaway. He was seeking "a negro girl named Maria . . . of a copper color, between 13 and 14 years of age, bare headed and bare footed." "She is small for her age," the notice continued, and "stated she was going to see her mother in Maysville."

In his wrath over what he considered her blatant infidelity, had R. M. Johnson not only auctioned off his own willful sexual consort but then also sold her (their) child away from Lucy? How likely is it that more than one fourteen-year-old slave "of a copper color" named Maria had a mother in Maysville who, a decade before, had run away from her own master? Could that young Maria have been fleeing a white man's sexual molestations as well, and would she have had the endurance and spunk needed to walk seventy miles "bare footed" to rejoin her beloved mother? It may be just happenstance, but many years later, Ida Gibbs Hunt's longtime friend W. E. B. Du Bois included that insubordinate incident in his feminist essay "On the Damnation of Women." Perhaps he first heard the old family story from Ida, reinforcing the possibility that the runaway with the same name, so close in age and similar in appearance, could indeed have been her own mother, Maria Alexander (Gibbs). This speculative scenario cannot be proven one way or another, but judging from their gumption and propriety, and the steely bonds of kinship that typified the Alexander and then the Gibbs women, the answer could be yes. But in any case, within less than two years, Maria Chinn Alexander was ensconced in Maysville, with her large, non-enslaved "colored" family.

The 1840 census shows that Henry Alexander (only eighty such free people of color lived in Mason County) was engaged in "commerce." A decade later he was listed as a "merchant," with an estate valued at $8,350. Every year that resourceful, hardworking tradesman, perhaps accompanied by his daughter Maria, drove his wagon to Philadelphia, a bastion of abolitionism, to purchase wholesale goods and supplies, then sell them at retail back in frontier Kentucky, thus realizing impressive profits. Maysville's whites may have found it an affront, but the Alexanders became one of their hometown's well-to-do families, although monetary factors alone cannot fully convey the tenuous conditions under which they lived. Henry was industrious, bold, and extremely clever to have achieved such success, yet Lucy may also have retained or renewed her strategic ties to R. M. Johnson — which could help to explain their improving economic status.

Henry Alexander's name first appears in that 1840 census, suggesting that he only arrived in Kentucky after 1830, and that someone else had conceived the older "Alexander" girls. On the other hand, he might not have been listed by name in previous censuses because at that earlier time he still was enslaved himself. Lucy bore her younger children well after her presumed relationship with R. M. Johnson had ended, but whoever their biological father(s) may have been, the community clearly considered all of the children Alexanders. Other circumstances could have contributed to the family's decision to remain so long in a slave state, but their financial status and residence not far from Scott County, combined with the fact that they began a sequential exodus to the North scarcely a year after R. M. Johnson died, argue that his domineering presence influenced them to stay close by until then.

Even if he had sold Lucy in retaliation for her defiance, Johnson's ambivalent paternalism later may have led him to facilitate her manumission and that of her offspring, although he never, in fact, officially freed Julia Chinn or her two children. Maria probably was a half sister to Imogene, the daughter whom R. M. Johnson proudly claimed as his own. And if, as his contemporaries asserted, two of his sexual partners were Julia's nieces, Lucy was also

Imogene's first cousin. Perhaps the "white" Imogene convinced her father that he owed all of his girls serious consideration and encouraged him to facilitate their manumission. On the other hand, she could have been jealous of those "colored" interlopers who might threaten to dilute her singularly privileged role in her father's life.

If the free mulatto named Patience Chinn who lived with R. M. Johnson in 1850 was indeed Lucy's sister, she most likely had been formally manumitted, and she too may have urged Johnson to reestablish his ties with Lucy, though she called him "my dear colonel" and seemingly was more deferential than Lucy. But for whatever reasons — persuasive female intervention, his own compassion or guilt — Johnson could finally have laid aside some of his long-held fury at Lucy Chinn Alexander's long-past betrayal (her attempt to escape with another man), helped to negotiate her freedom, and provided her and her conjugal family with financial aid. Any such support may have required in return that she and her children remain nearby.

In addition, a clear resemblance, suggested by a common paunchiness around the mouths and similarly equine jaws, seems to link Richard Mentor Johnson and Maria Alexander. Maria's coppery skin tone inherited from her mother physically differentiated her from her father, but otherwise the likeness appears evident. And if arguments can be made for inherited interests and skills, Imogene Johnson Pence was a musically gifted "woman of rare intellectual attainments," while similar traits and talents characterized Maria Alexander Gibbs and her children in turn.

These theories cannot be stated with irrefutable certainty, and other data hint at a slightly variant story line. A Bible belonging to Mason County's white Sanford Mitchell family reveals that they once held in slavery a man named Henry Alexander. In addition to the girls, Henry and his "wife" Lucy had a son named Horace, who died young. Years later, Maria Alexander (Gibbs) named one of her own boys Horace — perhaps to memorialize her long-deceased brother. Those same records show that in April 1832, Sanford Mitchell manumitted a twenty-nine-year-old slave named Lucy Alexander, with "black eyes, straight black hair . . . five feet three quarters of an inch high and well set for strength." Nothing indicates when or how the Mitchells first acquired that Lucy, or if her surname was Chinn (though a slave by that name had been born in the county thirty years earlier) before she married Henry Alexander. In lieu of a signature, Henry, by that time a nonliterate free person of color, affixed his "X" to a supplemental legal document, thereby facilitating the emancipation of Lucy's children. This suggests that local authorities deemed Henry to be the father even of Lucy's oldest daughter, Maria. Nothing firmly links R. M. Johnson to the white Mitchells or to the Negro Alexanders. Nonetheless, a masterful manipulator such as Johnson could easily have pulled the strings behind the scenes for all of those manumission transactions, and bedding the resistant spouse of a "colored" man would hardly have fazed him. But if those county records are valid and accurate, the intrepid runaway who in 1838 tried to rejoin her mother Lucy in Maysville may not have been the same Maria.

Lacking genetic evidence such as that which, even for many skeptics, virtually confirms claims about Thomas Jefferson's paternity of several of his slave Sally Hemings's children, little more than custom, marriage, and family resemblance even begin to "prove" who might or might not be any man's child. Yet stories abound, and Hemings's longstanding intimacy with Jefferson was first attested to by her progeny, who quite resembled Jefferson, then retold in the 1853 novel *Clotel, or the President's Daughter,* by the black abolitionist William Wells Brown. More recent literature, scholars, and a number of descendants have reinforced those assumptions. The phrase "mama's baby, papa's maybe" reflects both widespread doubts about paternity and the vulnerability of black women to sexual abuse by white men, especially during the centuries of American slavery. And in many Negro households, possibly including that of the Alexanders in Maysville, Kentucky, some of the young people were known as the children of strangers. But whatever their biological origins, they were accepted, loved, and duly incorporated into the "colored" family circle.

These intimate links between two enslaved women, Julia Chinn and perhaps Lucy Chinn Alexander, and a member of the United States' second-tier political royalty are far less familiar in our ribald national lore than that between Sally Hemings and Thomas Jefferson. Despite some arrogance and even bigotry on President Jefferson's part, including his scurrilous claim that in their continent of origin black women copulated with orangutans (which really are Asian, not African, primates), he was a titan whom Richard Mentor Johnson both admired and in some ways paralleled or emulated in his carnal and domestic habits. And history has not been kind to Johnson. He seems to have been a bombastic, gauche, possibly corrupt populist who certainly never approached the stature of the country's remarkable yet still controversial third president. But if Lucy's oldest daughter Maria was indeed Vice President Johnson's biological child, in contrast to his and Julia Chinn's preferred and pampered offspring, she was raised as an Alexander, and a proud Negro American.

Many sources, including Imogene Johnson Pence's descendants, confirm R. M. Johnson's relationship with Julia Chinn, but his other sexual exploits have been downplayed or trivialized, and any additional children have heretofore remained unreported. Hoping to polish up the white Kentuckian's tarnished reputation, several historians and genealogists have prudishly and blindly insisted that because he never married, Johnson had no progeny at all — but that assertion clearly is not true. Imogene, his daughter with Julia, had children of her own, who without apparent challenge segued over into the white world, where her descendants remain. This portrait of the Alexander-Gibbs family, however, instead examines Johnson's unacknowledged ties to the African American community. And given the vice president's conspicuously lusty appetites and wayward eye, he may have had other, and as yet unrevealed, "colored" offspring as well.

Whatever their kinship with Johnson, the Alexanders left rural May's Lick in the 1830s to resettle in the river port of Maysville, which was part of the slave South but situated just across the broad Ohio River from the free North. Bloody conflicts between the indigenous people and whites characterized Maysville's earliest years, but the relentless settlers prevailed, and secured the waterway for their own lucrative trade and travel. Hemp, used to make wraps and bindings for cotton bales, as well as burley tobacco destined for northern and world markets, rolled in from Kentucky's agricultural hinterlands, while an armada of cargo boats and ferries plied the muddy river headed downstream to Cincinnati and beyond. Maysville also served as a hub for the odious but lucrative business of jailing, trading, and auctioning off slaves, which bolstered the region's economy. Yet at about the same time as the Alexanders arrived there, a white visitor praised the town's friendliness, commercial vibrancy, paved streets, and sturdy brick buildings.

Maysville's more than three thousand residents included slaves, their owners, poor whites, some non-enslaved people of color, and a few abolitionists. No evidence proves that the Alexanders joined those covert insurrectionists, but they may have, since Henry Alexander could have been imbued with antislavery "fever" during his annual trips to Philadelphia, and the cross-river community of Ripley, Ohio, became a hotbed of Underground Railroad activity. A beacon light visible from the Alexanders' hometown in Kentucky shone nightly in the attic window of an abolitionist's riverside abode in Ripley, guiding fugitives to that safe house, while popular fiction such as *Uncle Tom's Cabin* and many slave narratives tell of desperate black mothers with babes in arms who, like Margaret Garner, tried to flee across the Ohio — often mythologized as the "River Jordan."

For many black Americans, including the Alexanders, 1850 was a watershed year, in part because of the draconian Fugitive Slave Act, which reinvigorated an original provision of the U.S. Constitution. That new legislation virtually demanded that citizens cooperate in recapturing fugitives and offered bounties for so doing, required the compliance of law enforcement officers nationwide, and authorized federal marshals to go anywhere in the country to track down, seize, jail, and return runaways such as Garner to their owners. Those men and women had no legal rights and could not testify in court on their own behalf, and their vulnerable children often became kidnapping targets. Free people of color were never fully secure from such threats and injustices, but had advantages over their many brethren held in bondage in that they enjoyed greater freedom of mobility and might reap the fruits of their labors and maintain their families' integrity. Yet even for non-enslaved Negroes (more than ten thousand of whom resided in Kentucky at that time) like the Alexanders, life became more precarious than before, as the fearsome possibility of (re)enslavement loomed large anywhere in the United States, but especially in the South.

Though Henry and Lucy Alexander's girls attended school in Maysville, without a white patron that tenuous privilege could vanish overnight. Lucy must also have resented the blatant disparities between the safe, affluent life that Johnson had created nearby for his older daughter Imogene and her own Maria's insecurity and limited options. And both Lucy and Maria knew from adverse experience that throughout the southern states, where white men's power went almost unchecked, young "colored" women were always vulnerable to their salacious advances.

By 1850 R. M. Johnson suffered from dementia, and though he took his seat in the nearby Kentucky legislature early that November, a powerful stroke felled him, and a week later he died intestate. Lucy and Henry Alexander may also have separated at about the same time. One of their daughters, Rachel, remained a while longer with her father in Maysville, where the two had a minor skirmish with the law when local authorities charged them with "peddling goods, wares, and merchandise without a license." Nothing documents Henry Alexander's presence in Ohio, where the rest of his family gradually took up residence, and Rachel appears there only in 1860, by which point Henry may have died or left Kentucky. But if Lucy Alexander was the same woman who, as early as the 1820s, defied a man of Johnson's authority and stature by running away; and if, as has also been reported, a quarter century after that she and her offspring trekked out to the West Coast and back, traversing arid plains and the daunting Rockies, probably with a Conestoga wagon train subject to climatic assaults as well as attacks from feral animals, Indians, or worse, the slave catchers who preyed on both runaways and free people of color, surely she could have relocated her family to adjacent Ohio in the 1850s — with or without a husband.

No later than early 1852, at least Maria, and soon thereafter others of the Alexanders, set out along a well-trod path to the North. They crossed the river, then continued on to Oberlin, a northern Ohio college town that already included a number of Negro residents, the first of whom had arrived about 1835. By 1860 their "colored" community would increase to four hundred, with three dozen fugitives among them, because most white Oberliners espoused and lived by antislavery ideals. Black people there obeyed the law, enjoyed some civil rights, and earned their community's respect. Prompted by the raw outrages of the Fugitive Slave Act, a few of them became activists for abolitionism. Their children attended school, but interracial male-female friendships were discouraged and perceived as a dangerous route to unseemly intimacy. The men worked as farm laborers, barbers, artisans, and teamsters, and the women as domestic servants, cooks, or seamstresses. But like most white matrons, a handful of Oberlin's more fortunate black women, including Lucy Alexander, stayed at home caring for their own households. Lucy had no stated source of income, raising the possibility that an informal bequest from R. M. Johnson, as well as support from her husband Henry back in Kentucky, contributed to her economic maintenance, because she and her young folks resided in a pleasant neighborhood not far from the school.

Northern Ohio's winters, they soon learned, were harsher than Kentucky's, and July and August simmered, though slavery's absence must have made even the weather feel more tolerable. Spring and fall seemed idyllic, while year round the school dominated the town's sedate moral and social climate as well as its large central green, reminiscent of a New England common. Yet within a short distance, the academic halls, churches, shops, and frame houses with tidy gardens yielded to amber cornfields, and then to dense forests interspersed with isolated hamlets.

John Mercer Langston was Oberlin's first Negro lawyer, and soon chaired its board of education. He later became dean of Howard University's law school, a Reconstruction congressman from Virginia (the state of his birth), then a United States minister in Haiti. Langston arrived nine years before Maria Alexander, who also was a classmate of his wife, Caroline Wall — another southern slaveholder's mulatto daughter. They all remained friends, and one of Maria's sisters later lived with the Walls. The Patterson family arrived in 1856. Henry Patterson worked as a mason, while his spouse cared for several of the school's black students who boarded at their home. In 1862 their oldest girl, Mary Jane, would complete Oberlin's four-year "gentleman's course," and by so doing she more than likely became the country's first female college graduate of her race.

Lucy Alexander and her family — who, like Richard Mentor Johnson, as well as most black Kentuckians, had been Baptists — joined their town's predominantly white First Congregational Church, and her daughters matriculated at Oberlin. Almost alone in the nation, that academy let Negro and white, male and female students study side by side. Its trustees had long insisted that "the education of people of color is a matter of great interest and should be encouraged and sustained at this institution." Nearly 5 percent of its pre–Civil War enrollees were "colored," including one of the slave ship *Amistad*'s West African girls. Until after the war it was the country's only prominent school that routinely admitted and even welcomed female African Americans, several of them sponsored by the white abolitionist writer Harriet Beecher Stowe. They became part of what later was called (in a clever riff on Du Bois's early twentieth-century Talented Tenth) a rare and privileged "Talented One-thousandth." One such pioneer maintained that while Oberlin was "not the pool of Bethesda for the sin of prejudice, [it] came nearer . . . than any other place in the United States." Yet, like most of the older Negroes in that otherwise well-educated Ohio township, Lucy Alexander remained unable to read or write.

Maria had some previous schooling in Kentucky, but was twenty-six (though she began paring nearly a decade off her age) when she resumed her education at Oberlin. She did not let that relative seniority handicap her and studied there from 1852 to 1854, probably completing the college's "ladies' literary course," the choice of almost all young women — race notwithstanding. Three younger sisters soon followed her, and a photograph of an 1855 Oberlin class — featuring primly dressed, serious, but sweet-faced "colored" and white pupils — may include the Alexander girls.

About six years after Maria arrived, the school and town were lauded, yet lambasted too, when an interracial band of students, teachers, and other citizens charged off to nearby Wellington, Ohio, to snatch a black runaway from slave catchers. Two of the rescuers were jailed for their heroic efforts. This was not a singular event. Across the country black men and women became instrumental in liberating such fugitives, and often suffered the consequences. In 1856 a similarly dedicated contingent had tried but failed to spirit off Margaret Garner and her surviving family from Ohio to a sanctuary in Canada.

And soon thereafter, a thirty-six-year-old, brown-skinned, hazel-eyed abolitionist named Mifflin Wistar Gibbs, imbued with steely ambitions and increasing financial assets, called on the Alexanders. Gibbs lived, worked, and had amassed considerable property on Britain's colonial Vancouver Island, but had previously resided in Pennsylvania, then in California. He may have first met Henry Alexander, and perhaps the Alexanders' oldest daughter, Maria, during their trips from Maysville to Philadelphia in the 1840s, and he almost certainly encountered members of the family when Lucy and her offspring later traveled west. Early in 1859 he himself journeyed east, in large part to further court Maria. In Oberlin that March, during the Wellington raiders' widely publicized trial, encircled by friends and kinfolk, Maria Alexander and M. W. Gibbs married.

When Maria Alexander Gibbs set out with her new husband, headed to his distant terra incognita, she cherished Ohio, and would return, but yearned to put Kentucky behind — and leaving the United States guaranteed that their future children could never be enslaved. She must have hoped to forget the place where a beloved brother had died and slavery's tyrannies remained in force. Maria also knew that education could be a vital key in moving beyond such vulnerability, and she probably taught for several years after attending Oberlin. She would also have seen how R. M. Johnson had ensured that Julia Chinn and their offspring had privileges and enjoyed a plethora of assets denied to her. Living with that galling awareness, Lucy Alexander herself had left the slave South and relocated to Oberlin, in large part, she often said, so that her children could be well educated and prepared "for future usefulness."

From their bygone lives, Lucy and her girls understood that men could be worthy fathers, companions, and providers. They might be saviors or tormentors, caretakers or adversaries. A Negro woman could cherish one man but be forced to have sexual relations with another; yet to protect her children, she had to persevere — with no spouse at all if need be. Those were harsh truths for many of the black women who survived in the Old South, where whites revered traditional marriage and embraced ingrained hierarchical assumptions about sex and race, patrimony and property. Slavery's attacks on its victims' dignity were as vicious as grueling, misappropriated labor or physical abuse, and the peculiar institution assaulted and undermined the morality of everyone involved. Its perpetrators cared little about Negro families, yet mother-daughter bonds and a commitment to kinship survived. Family, faith, education, and hard work became keys to survival, and the Alexanders and then the Gibbses adhered to those guiding precepts.

In later years, a number of admirers called Maria Alexander "Lady Gibbs," suggesting that someplace along the way she acquired an aristocratic bearing. Lucy nurtured her children's self-esteem, but her daughter Maria also heard about her own reportedly exceptional paternity. She even may have taken a grudging pride in Vice President Johnson's political accomplishments, educational endeavors, and advocacy of unpopular causes. White men's patriarchal power, however, had uglier faces, and as members of the "inferior" race, sexual partners and even daughters like Maria could easily be cast aside — or worse. Lucy and Henry Alexander maintained their conjugal relationship for many years to ensure their children's "legitimacy," as well as their hard-won physical and economic security. Neither Lucy nor Maria, however, could claim R. M. Johnson's name, assets, or privileged status. If such a man refused to acknowledge his shadow family, his mixed-race offspring knew they must hide both their identities and emotions behind inscrutable masks, never challenge him or speak openly of the unacknowledged kinship without risking severe retaliation.

Daughters even more than sons may have internalized some residual feelings of shame if their mothers had been unable to fend off white men's sexual predations. That forced black women outside the sheltering cocoons that American society constructed to define and circumscribe the lives of virtuous, white Christian ladies. The young country's adherence to the prohibitive premises of "True Womanhood" demanded a premarital commitment to chastity, followed by a lifetime of wedded submissiveness, domesticity, and piety, but few women of Lucy and Maria's heritage could expect, or might want, to live by those restrictive precepts. And for a full century, certainly, just one single whispered account ever spoke to Maria Alexander's reported affiliation with R. M. Johnson. Seven decades after the Civil War another female onetime Kentucky slave still only hesitatingly admitted: "I hate to say these things, but they happened this way . . . the masters were often the fathers." Countless "black" people in the United States shared those often hidden legacies, Maria Alexander Gibbs, arguably the vice president's daughter, among them.

In 1859, as thirty-three-year-old Maria, who claimed to be only twenty-five, prepared to leave Ohio with M. W. Gibbs, she was educated, self-reliant, and attractive, but also, perhaps, conflicted in her relationships with the opposite sex. In certain ways, notably his bravura, independence, ambition, and zest for an unfettered frontier life, her African American spouse resembled the man who was rumored to be her father, but in most respects, especially Johnson's dubious racial ideologies and unrepentant domination of women, the two were vastly different.

Maria Alexander had traveled herself, but if she thought that marrying this worthy man meant that she could domesticate her dashing swain, hold him close to hearth and home, or even keep hearth and home in one place, she was mistaken. She was in love, and probably believed that this was her final chance both to complement her life with a husband of ample means, comparable intellect, and noble motivations and to have children. In many instances, throbbing hearts trump common sense and objectivity, but an unflinching evaluation of M. W. Gibbs's peripatetic route to her front door might have given Maria a more realistic picture of what lay ahead. Forty-three years later, in a disarmingly frank admission, Gibbs would write: "I have had a model wife in all that the term implies, and she has had a husband migratory and uncertain."

2

Mirror of the Times

Reflections on the Lives of M. W. Gibbs

For effective purposes one must not be unduly sensitive or overmodest in writing autobiography —for, being the events and memoirs of his life, written by himself, the ever present pronoun "I" dances in such lively attendance and in such profusion on the pages, that whatever pride he may have in the events they chronicle is somewhat abashed at its repetition. — Mifflin Wistar Gibbs, *Shadow and Light,* 1902

According to his memoir, a self-serving yet reliable account overall, the "migratory and uncertain" Mifflin Wistar Gibbs, second son of a Wesleyan Methodist minister and his Baptist wife, was born in April 1823, in Philadelphia, Pennsylvania. Several decades before, that state had incrementally begun terminating slavery, owing to, roughly in equal parts, the institution's unprofitability there, the American Revolution's contagious, emancipatory ideologies, and pervasive Quaker influences. Many white Philadelphians conceded Negro children's right to an elementary education, so Maria (yes, Mifflin would indeed marry a woman with the same given name as his mother) and the Reverend Jonathan Gibbs enrolled their seven-year-old boy in one of the city's few all-black schools. But soon thereafter the reverend died suddenly, leaving his penniless widow to raise four youngsters by herself, and his surviving kin, who hitherto had occupied a secure niche in the community, found their world starkly changed for the worse.

As a result of her family's financial straits and loss of status, Maria Gibbs went to work as a washerwoman, one of the few occupations open to black women, and withdrew her son Mifflin from his classes. From that point on, although Gibbs's autobiography expresses his devotion to and admiration for his mother, it never again mentions her name.

The overburdened widow most likely had little time, energy, or means to coddle her fatherless brood, so in a few years, rudely thrust into premature adulthood, young Mifflin was hired out to a white lawyer who took him on an expedition around his extensive holdings in nearby rural Maryland. There, the boy first encountered slavery. "I still see that sad and humbled throng," the by then elderly Mifflin Gibbs would write, "as machines they acted, as machines they looked."

"Mifflin," the attorney taunted, "how would you like to be a slave?" Aghast, he replied, "I would not be a slave! I would kill anybody that would make me a slave!" But the white man admonished him: "You must not talk that way down here." "[F]rom my youthful lips had come the 'open sesame to the door of liberty,' 'resistance to oppression,'" he later expounded, "the slogan that has ever heralded the advent of freedom." That episode, M. W. Gibbs declared seventy years thereafter, awakened him to the brutal realities that the vast majority of black people endured in the United States at that time, and started him along challenging pathways.

He and his older brother Jonathan (named for their late father) then were apprenticed to a former slave from whom they learned a medley of building skills, and to support their mother and two younger siblings, they went to work as carpenters. The Gibbs boys also sought out some of Philadelphia's Negro elders to enhance their previously curtailed formal training at community-operated night schools, where they mastered basic academics and progressed so far as to absorb a bit of Latin and Greek. Self-education thus became a central and ongoing part of their lives.

Jonathan attached himself to a group of white Presbyterians who later sponsored his advanced schooling, and by the early 1840s he and Mifflin joined in local efforts on behalf of the Underground Railroad, working with such notables as Robert and Harriet Purvis, the country's wealthiest Negroes, reformers like the neophyte feminist writer Frances Ellen Watkins (Harper), and a mulatto cobbler named Peter Lester, who was among Philadelphia's lesser known black abolitionists. All of them helped to expand Mifflin Gibbs's horizons and infused him with ambitious visions for the advancement of the race. He also may have crossed paths with the Ohio merchant Henry Alexander and his daughter Maria in those years when Henry came to Pennsylvania on his annual trips east, though no hard evidence reinforces that speculation. And Mifflin reminisced about witnessing a ceremonial stopover in his city of the notorious reclaimed slave barque *Amistad,* at which time, he wrote, he saw

Frederick Douglass embrace the ship's rebellious black champion, Cinque. Neither Douglass nor his biographers, however, have made mention of any such historic encounter between those two titans of the African diaspora.

The Gibbs brothers more likely first met Douglass at an antislavery rally a few years later, because in 1849, shortly after Mifflin had addressed such a gathering, the two underemployed Philadelphians accompanied the great abolitionist back to his home in Rochester, New York, in the region called the burned-over district that had been scorched by the fires of reawakening, where fervent revivalism, spiritualism, temperance, and abolitionism often converged. Julia Griffiths, Douglass's worshipful English assistant, had recently arrived there as well. So as an acolyte and apprentice, bodyguard and friend, Mifflin Gibbs worked with Douglass from that June until the following April, traversing upstate New York, western Pennsylvania, and nearby Ohio. Those young men, not far apart in age (Douglass calculated that he was born about 1818), often faced hostile crowds and harsh climatic conditions, but during that crusade Gibbs developed his oratorical skills, came further to value the import of political empowerment and resistance to oppression, and, he later claimed, was inspired and induced by Douglass to enter "the public life."

The whole country throbbed with tales of the fortunes to be made in California, and even Douglass's abolitionist journal published letters touting opportunities for black men in the West. Since Gibbs was more interested in the here and now than in some Promised Land, less than a year after joining Douglass, with limited prospects and a yen to assert his independence, improve his financial status, and have a grand adventure, he heeded the advice of Julia Griffiths, who urged him to "go do some great thing." So he left his brother Jonathan with Douglass in Rochester, and their mother and younger siblings back in Philadelphia, to follow the flood of other disparate Americans who were seeking a new El Dorado in and around California's beckoning goldfields.

Although Philadelphia once was considered a near Utopia for Negroes, its racial divides had stiffened. Streams of fugitive slaves arrived there from the South, swelling the city's black population, which had already topped twelve thousand when Gibbs was born, and in his youth racist assaults had blighted the City of Brotherly Love. One targeted a black church, another an abolitionist hall, and a white mob torched the local "colored" orphanage during a third. (In 1844 nativist arsonists also set fire to a Catholic church serving the city's new immigrants.) Like most northern states, Pennsylvania segregated its schools and denied black men, and all women, the vote, while rising immigration from Europe exacerbated racial tensions owing to the competition between indigenous black workers and aliens — to the former's detriment. Gibbs therefore felt little sense of loss as he left family, friends, and poverty behind in a quest for the Golden West's social fluidity and economic prospects that seemed to promise him many previously undreamed-of opportunities.

Thus, in late spring 1850, for his first venture outside the country, M. W. Gibbs begged or borrowed the money he needed to book as a steerage passenger on a tramp steamer out of New York City bound for Central America. Once there, he engaged a dinghy to navigate the perilous Chagres River halfway across the isthmus, then trekked down to the sultry Pacific Ocean, where, like many other travelers, he fell victim to yellow, or Panama, fever. But he recovered quickly, sailed off again, and after a rocky voyage arrived in San Francisco's congested harbor.

He disembarked that fall in the newly American municipality where the mushrooming population surpassed forty thousand, nearly ten thousand of whom were being ruthlessly corralled into the nation's original Chinatown. In that rowdy, overgrown, largely male city, drinking, whoring, gambling, and major crimes abounded. It bore little resemblance to the glittering metropolis of modern times, and little as well to staid, gray Philadelphia. In its entirety, the new state of California had very few Negroes — less than 1 percent of the population.

Gibbs had hardly a cent when he arrived, but soon he found a rooming house owned by a black man who sometimes boarded newcomers on credit. He took a carpenter's job, accepting lower wages than less skilled whites, yet lost it when those coworkers protested his employment solely on the basis of race. For months he toiled away at menial chores, but somehow became a partner in a modest haberdashery. Outfitting California's fortune seekers could be highly lucrative, and as a diligent, charming huckster Gibbs fared very well. That venture ended in a year, but M. W. Gibbs and Peter Lester, his pal from Philadelphia who had also relocated to the West Coast, soon opened a shop they called the Pioneer Boot and Shoe Emporium. It catered to a flush-or-busted, mostly white clientele, for whom Gibbs and Lester even imported deluxe European footwear. Having cut their teeth on Philadelphia's abolitionist movement, they renewed their efforts in support of the Underground Railroad, enlisted like-minded partisans, and plunged into an array of political endeavors.

In accordance with the contentious Compromise of 1850, California had been admitted to the Union as a non-slave state. Its constitution, however, denied the ballot to "Indians, Africans and the descendants of Africans." Blacks tried to align themselves with other nonwhites (Native Americans, Mexicans, and immigrant Asians), yet those marginalized groups usually chose not to identify themselves with a caste that seemed irrevocably tethered to slavery. Statutes denied black men membership in local militias and banned them from serving on juries or testifying in court against whites, and in 1852 the state enacted a law that quite resembled the onerous federal Fugitive Slave Act. Many of California's pro-slavery sympathizers, including its first governor, went so far as to advocate African Americans' total exclusion from their state.

The political climate galled Gibbs and his associates, who therefore issued a manifesto condemning the "no court testimony by Negroes" laws and their continued disfranchisement, and petitioned the legislature for the vote, but to no avail. The situation called for bolder efforts, so by 1855 a group of activists called into session a Convention of the Colored Citizens of the State of California. Gibbs and Lester became representatives to that assembly and the two that followed, at which delegates addressed their community's concerns and proposed starting their own newspaper. To that end, Gibbs and several cohorts began writing, editing, and publishing *Mirror of the Times*, "the first periodical issued in the State for the advocacy of equal rights for all Americans," he claimed. Adopting the feisty motto "Truth, crushed to earth, will rise again," it came out weekly from 1856 until mid-1858 and, often through Gibbs's zealous editorials, condemned slavery (which covertly survived in California's remote tracts where law enforcement was notoriously lax), disfranchisement, and all manner of state-sanctioned discrimination.

Yet those affiliations and that heightened visibility scarcely bettered the lot of most black Californians, so in 1857 Gibbs and Lester withheld their poll taxes. "We will never willingly pay three dollars as a poll-tax as long as we remain disfranchised, oath-denied, outlawed colored Americans," wrote Gibbs, but local revenue agents found that protest untenable, and seized valuable merchandise from the Pioneer Boot and Shoe Emporium to satisfy the two men's outstanding civic "debts."

Gibbs's life in San Francisco, however, had its rewards. He made money and friends, including several fellows from Oberlin, Ohio, who may have introduced him to the visiting Lucy Alexander and her daughters. Among California's "colored" residents, men outnumbered women by a whopping eleven-to-one ratio, but the intrepid, female-headed Alexander family nonetheless made the arduous journey all the way out to the West Coast, and then back to Ohio.

For a number of black Americans, their long-term or temporary residence in the Gold Rush state was unique in that, often for the first time, no white person, usually a slave owner or trader, had forced them to relocate. And many of them were neither enslaved nor fleeing bondage. Rather, most such settlers there, like Gibbs and Lester, as well as transients such as the Alexanders, belonged to the country's relatively small ranks of free people of color. Archy Lee was different, yet in some respects his tribulations epitomized the adversities that other Negro Californians faced.

An enterprising Mississippian in pursuit of his fortune had brought west with him a slave named Archy Lee. When the white fellow tried to return Lee to the South, he refused to go, arguing that California law disallowed his re-enslavement. His situation quite resembled that of Dred Scott, on whose case the U.S. Supreme Court ruled in 1857. In that recent, venal, landmark decision, justices on the ultimate federal bench determined that Negroes had no citizenship rights at all. Lee's case went up to the highest state appeals court, which exonerated him, but a marshal acting under the authority of the country's Fugitive Slave Act promptly rearrested him. Gibbs spearheaded protests that appeared in both the mainstream press and *Mirror of the Times*. In April 1858 a judicious local commissioner unexpectedly released Archy Lee on the grounds that he was never a fugitive across state lines (a federal offense) but instead properly claimed his freedom within the non-slave jurisdiction of California. That conclusion became a symbolic but rare victory for the state's African Americans, while other circumstances worsened.

State officials again debated banning blacks from California, and violence against them escalated, including an incident in which several white men posing as customers assaulted Peter Lester, Gibbs's partner, in their shop. They taunted the proprietors, who had no legal recourse because of state laws that barred them from testifying against whites in court. And soon Negro children, Lester's daughter Sarah among them, were herded into segregated schools. Before they were so informed, school authorities had not known that the light-skinned Sarah Lester was "colored," but when her race was disclosed, a furor arose, with outraged whites demanding her expulsion.

In that hostile environment, members of the Negro community began discussing the pros and cons of emigration. They faced a quandary about remaining in a country that usually enslaved, demeaned, and discriminated against them. The Californians debated resettling in Mexico, the Sandwich

(Hawaiian) Islands, or Vancouver, knowing that Britain's northern territories often welcomed "colored" runaways. They evaluated the colony's economic conditions, especially the gold boom that Gibbs and others predicted would enhance their opportunities, and were assured that within months of becoming property holders, the men could vote and serve on juries, and within a few years might become British subjects. An exploratory committee shipped off to investigate Vancouver and returned with glowing reports.

As many as nine hundred of California's African Americans resolved to leave the country. Theirs was probably the largest onetime voluntary emigration of Negroes in all of United States history, comprising fully half of San Francisco's black population. To clarify their frustrations and disillusionment, Gibbs's farewell message explained: "I admit the right of a family or nation to say, who from without, shall be a component part of its . . . community; but the application of this principle should work no hardship to a colored man, for he was born in the great American family, and . . . his right to the benefit of just government is as good as that of his pale face brother." So during the summer of 1858 they prepared to embrace the "Queen of the Christian Isles." Mifflin Wistar Gibbs crammed hefty bundles of his cash into satchels. And then he, Archy Lee, who understandably feared the further caprices of American law, the Oberlin men, others from California's Colored Conventions, and soon Peter Lester, all set sail for Vancouver.

Whether Gibbs and his cohorts would remain transients or become expatriates and British subjects was still undetermined. But by opting to depart, they seemed to reject the convictions of many black activists, including Frederick Douglass, who wrote: "Now and always, we expect to insist upon it that we are Americans, that America is our native land; that this is our home; that we are American citizens . . . and that it is the duty of the American people so to recognize us."

The black Californians left the United States for reasons of personal safety, and because of a desire for equal rights and financial opportunities. But more separatist goals motivated other émigrés in that era, such as those bound for independent Haiti or Liberia, who planned to join an all-Negro nation where "Africa's children" might achieve their political and economic potential. The men and women who left San Francisco in 1858, by contrast, wanted to incorporate themselves in every possible way into Vancouver's frontier society. They vowed not to establish autonomous schools, churches, or other institutions, yet also recognized that the residents of England's northerly Pacific Coast colony were not overwhelmingly white. It was populated by quite a few transplanted Anglo-Saxons, but by indigenous people, increasing numbers of Asians, and British West Indians of all hues as well. The Caribbean-born governor even had a mulatto mother.

Once he settled in Victoria, Vancouver's principal port, M. W. Gibbs began speculating in land, mining, rails, and commerce. "On account of the salubrity of its climate and proximity to the spacious land-locked harbor," he marveled, "it is delightful as a place of residence and well adapted to great mercantile and industrial possibilities." He and Peter Lester partnered again to open a store that outfitted prospectors and ultimately expanded to rival the monopolistic Hudson Bay Company. Gibbs designed and built himself a large home in Victoria's best neighborhood. His mother, and his younger brother and sister-in-law, all relocated and joined him there.

Early in 1859, however, Gibbs embarked on a belated but life-altering trip to the United States. His memoir says nothing about prior romances or his courtship of Maria Alexander, but they had met at some earlier date, then inched toward matrimony pursuant to previously made promises followed, no doubt, by an extended epistolary exchange. So as Gibbs prepared at last to put his bachelorhood behind, he journeyed from Vancouver Island all the way to Oberlin, Ohio.

It is hard to determine why such a personable gentleman deferred marriage until thirty-six, but an absence of warmth and the austerity of his mother, the elder Mrs. Maria Gibbs, in his youth could have made him reluctant to dedicate himself to permanent domesticity. On the other hand, Freudian analysis might argue that he actually sought to replicate his only surviving parent when he married a woman with the same given name. Perhaps his previously shaky finances and itinerant life gave him pause, and the stark gender imbalance and lack of "respectable" Negro women in California and then Vancouver probably forestalled his decision as well. Or, as a man of limitless ambition and pride, Gibbs may never before have encountered anyone whom he considered a worthy spouse and partner — a woman who combined the most desired feminine graces with intelligence, education, a degree of independence, and deep racial commitment.

"The ever present pronoun 'I,'" which, Gibbs metaphorically claimed, "dances ... in such profusion on the pages" of all memoirs, permeates his own *Shadow and Light,* but the marital or familial "we" is remarkably absent. He included not a word about love or eternal devotion, saying only: "An important step in a man's life is his marriage. It being the merging of dual lives, it is only by mutual self-abnegation that it can be made a source of contentment and happiness. In 1859, in consummation of promise and purpose, I returned to the United States and was married to Miss Maria A. Alexander, of Kentucky, educated at Oberlin College, Ohio."

Owing to prevailing literary custom, differing priorities, or, more generously, an admirable sense of discretion, Mifflin Wistar Gibbs revealed very little more about his private life with Maria. Complex intersections between the personal and political always intrigued him, and he surely knew about his wife's rumored kinship with Richard Mentor Johnson, the former vice president, but his autobiography says nothing whatsoever concerning that distinctive lineage.

He did, however, share a story about the mixed-race offspring of a "rich planter who died intestate." Gibbs lauded those few southern white men who sent "their colored families [North] to be educated . . . giving them settlement and sustenance, especially that their girls might escape the environments which . . . awaited them at the South." Such rare examples, he continued, appeared "in fine and valuable contradistinction to many cases similarly related, where they were sold on the auction block to the highest bidder." But Gibbs never linked such tales to his wife's parallel history. On a theoretical or impersonal level, he fully grasped the agonizing conflicts that permeated the illicit sexual relations made feasible by the peculiar institution. He acknowledged slavery's enduring impact on casual acquaintances, yet could, or would, not deal with or discuss those issues as they applied to Maria Alexander Gibbs, the woman closest to him.

Leaving Oberlin, the newlyweds visited Mifflin's remaining stateside kinfolk and several abolitionist colleagues, including Frederick Douglass. Maria recalled meeting Douglass on that trip and delighting in his wry anecdote about how while "resisting expulsion from a dining table on a steamboat, he pulled hold of the table cloth and sent all of the dishes crashing to the floor."

During his stay in the United States, Gibbs wrote, he was appalled by the recent Dred Scott decision. The white abolitionist John Brown's plot to raid the federal arsenal at Harpers Ferry, which Douglass knew about but ultimately rejected as unfeasible, exhilarated Gibbs, and less than two years before the Civil War he sensed that the "pulsebeat of the great national heart quickened at impending danger." Soon thereafter, he added, he and his new wife boarded a "steamship for our long journey of 4,000 miles to our intended home in Victoria, Vancouver Island."

The marriage was late in coming, but their many progeny give ample evidence of its early passion. Mifflin wrote of having five children, but Maria, in fact, would bear at least six babies in Vancouver: in 1860 Francis, who died in his early years; Donald in 1861; Ida in 1862; Horace, apparently named for Maria's deceased brother, in 1863; Wendell in 1865; and in 1867 Harriet (Hattie), probably the namesake of her father's friend, Philadelphia's abolitionist Harriet Purvis.

M. W. Gibbs achieved notable successes in Vancouver, but though his wife was arguably the colony's best educated woman and one of its more affluent, elite white ladies did not invite her into their parlors, and few "colored" people of her standing lived nearby. Mifflin was lord of much that he surveyed, and the seemingly aristocratic Maria, ensconced in her stately "English" manor, became known in some quarters as "Lady Gibbs." They joined the Anglican church, yet she never shared Mifflin's pleasures or comfort on the northwestern frontier. Leaving her behind with their houseful of children, he traveled for extended stretches at a time overseeing his diverse investment properties in the colony's outermost reaches, hundreds of miles away.

Vancouver's black male pioneers, Gibbs prominent among them, had left their country of birth and resettled north of the border to escape widespread antipathy toward Negroes and to reap economic rewards. In both respects, a few of them found ample satisfactions. They had raged at being denied the franchise (yet scarcely saw it as an option for women) in the United States, but questions pertaining to their American citizenship remained unanswered. Nonetheless, it presumably would have to be relinquished before they could vote elsewhere. In autumn of 1859, however, soon after the newly married Gibbs returned, Vancouver's attorney general, George Hunter Cary, approached him with a bold and intriguing proposal.

Just two years earlier, Cary argued, the U.S. Supreme Court in its harsh Dred Scott ruling had determined that Negroes had no citizenship rights at all. As a result, he added, American black men had nothing to renounce, and thus should face no barriers to becoming naturalized citizens and exercising the franchise in Vancouver once they fulfilled property requirements and swore allegiance to Queen Victoria. At first, other local officials raised no objections to Cary's rationale, so later that year more than twenty of those former United States residents, but arguably not United States citizens, took the pertinent oath and registered to vote. In January 1860 eighteen of them, including Gibbs, cast their ballots for the first time ever in any civil election. The men unanimously voted for and helped reelect their sponsor, Attorney General Cary, and his cohorts.

But the election's sore losers struck back with an attack that excoriated the newly enfranchised Negroes. Black people "always want a little more liberty than white men," one carped, as he denounced the colony's "niggers." As his community's spokesperson, Gibbs responded in a published letter that concluded with his pithy observation that "a man who pays so little regard to genteel orthography as to spell negro with two g's is not likely to obtain . . . support from colored voters." A colonial court later overturned that first registration of black men on a technicality, but the precedent had been set. In 1861 Gibbs and fifty colleagues applied for British citizenship — although it's unclear whether he ever completed the full naturalization process. He developed into an adept politician, however, accepted the governor's coveted invitations to his annual balls celebrating Queen Victoria's birthday, was elected to Vancouver's Common Council five years later, then represented his colony at the convention that negotiated its upcoming merger with British Columbia and future annexation to the Canadian Confederation.

Back in the United States, by 1861 even Frederick Douglass, the public figure once most vehemently opposed to African American emigration, tempered and shifted his stance a bit. Angered and disappointed by President Abraham Lincoln's sluggish foot-dragging on general emancipation, Douglass better appreciated the complex motivations of men such as Gibbs. That year he mourned in his newsletter: "Whatever the future may have in store for us, it seems plain that the inducements offered to the colored man to remain here are few, feeble and uncertain."

The Civil War's onset, accompanied by an influx of secessionist southerners, brought about increasing strictures on Vancouver's black residents. Yet a few of them, including M. W. Gibbs, continued to prosper, even if the colony no longer seemed their Eden. The theater often served as a diversion for the "colored" newcomers, as it did for others on the frontier, so producers took their stage shows to the far Northwest seeking culture-hungry, free-spending audiences, and the Colonial Opera House became Victoria's favorite venue for such entertainment. When it first opened, the proprietors permitted color-blind seating, but late in 1860, prompted by protests on the part of segregationists from the United States, they attempted to restrict blacks to the balcony because the sight of people of color occupying expensive seats (private boxes or the "parquette") enraged many whites who could not afford such accommodations. A few of the Negroes, in turn, declined to sit where they would have to mingle with the lower classes. The white rabble "rotten egged" darker skinned theatergoers several times, while some Asian immigrants and

Indians aligned themselves with blacks against throngs of irate Caucasian patrons and performers.

The following autumn, with tensions heightened by previous confrontations as well as by increasingly incendiary accounts of the United States Civil War, the Colonial hosted a gala program to benefit the local hospital. That event attracted a few well-to-do "colored" people, including Mifflin Wistar Gibbs and his wife, Maria, who was obviously expecting. Rumor had it that any Negroes who occupied the "prominent seats" might have, instead of rotten eggs, putrid vegetables or flour thrown at them unless they moved to more discreet locations, yet the Gibbses refused to budge. The show began without incident, but then a white man rose and hurled a packet of flour that burst open, spewing a cloud over the Gibbs party. In most instances Mifflin was more restrained, but perhaps because his pregnant wife had been victimized, he leapt into the dusty fray and slugged the assailant. A melee erupted that the constabulary had to quash.

Just a few days later a white thespian from the States publicly asserted that "no sensible person will object to the colored population being admitted to any public place of amusement; but let one part of the house ... be reserved for their particular use." "They form a distinct class and enjoy their full rights as citizens," he added, "but let these 'gentlemen' — *if they claim to be gentlemen* — not force themselves upon white society, where they are not desired." Gibbs, however, retaliated with practiced journalistic fury. "I have taken an oath of allegiance to Her Majesty's Government, paid the other day about $400 yearly taxes into the treasury," he fumed, adding, "am I to be told by you that I shall be degraded on public occasions and proscribed [from] the Box, Parquette, or any other place to please a few Yankees?" When the case went to trial the authorities dropped all charges against the whites because of what they considered inconclusive testimony, but found Gibbs guilty and fined him on one charge of assault. Soon thereafter, the proprietors of Vancouver's public arenas made their discriminatory policies official, a development that angered and bitterly disappointed the colony's Negro population.

Despite the hardships black émigrés came to endure north of the border, most residential neighborhoods, schools, and churches remained unsegregated. The men could vote, hold civic jobs, and testify in court. So the Gibbses and others stayed on, knowing that the discrimination they faced there paled in comparison to what they might encounter in most locales in the hostile nation to their south. But after the Civil War, suffused with nostalgia and increasing optimism, some of the settlers began drifting back to their longed-for families, friends, and former homes in the United States, where they saw that certain aspects of the old order had changed for the better. The black Americans who had lived for years in Vancouver, however, missed the purgative but enlightening traumas of self-emancipation that millions of others experienced during the war.

During that struggle the United States granted diplomatic recognition to the independent nations of Liberia and Haiti — places, along with alternate locales in Latin American, touted by President Lincoln and others, including Harriet Beecher Stowe, as sites for black "repatriation." Of greater domestic import, the Emancipation Proclamation and the postwar ratifications of the Constitution's Thirteenth, Fourteenth, and Fifteenth Amendments (ending slavery, guaranteeing citizenship and equal protection under the law, and universal male suffrage) made their once and future homeland seem far more hospitable, although a fanatic southern actor murdered the country's titanic yet ambivalent president who helped bring about those changes. As Gibbs later wrote, "I had left politically ignoble; I was returning panoplied with the nobility of an American citizen."

At the same time, however, his elusive marital contentment faltered. Maria had returned to Ohio for much of the time between her younger children's births, and relocated there for good by 1868. The following year M. W. Gibbs vacated his mansion in Victoria, extricated himself from business and political ventures alike, left behind colleagues and other family members (although a disastrous fire had destroyed his mother's and his brother and sister-in-law's homes and businesses), and abandoned his self-imposed exile to follow his wife, sons, and daughters back to Oberlin.

Nearly a decade before, Gibbs had set in motion efforts geared toward relinquishing his circumscribed United States citizenship, but nothing confirms whether he actually became a subject of the queen (his memoir adroitly hedges that pivotal question, and certainly a number of Americans, legitimately or not, did hold dual citizenship), although he voted in Victoria, where he also served in several elective offices. He made numerous friends and few enemies, invested wisely and well, succeeded in commerce and industry, and participated in key negotiations concerning the colony's political future. So why did he forsake such notable success for a chancy return to the once hostile nation where he must have become almost a stranger?

Maria had gone back to her mother and sisters in her old hometown, so certainly his altered domestic situation swayed M. W. Gibbs to some degree. But that alone hardly suffices as an explanation, since he had spent as much time away from his nuclear family in Victoria as with them, and freely admitted that "it was not without . . . regret that I anticipated my departure." Rather, several additional factors probably coalesced to lure him back to the United States.

Spurring Gibbs's decision to leave Vancouver was its colonial government's ineptitude. It "sits like a nightmare upon the energies of the people," he moaned, "and is totally unfitted for an intelligent community in the nineteenth century." And for some reason, he had also fallen out with his friend and business partner, Peter Lester. Concurrently tugging at Gibbs to return was what his biographer Tom Dillard calls the "revolutionary change that was sweeping the [United States] in the aftermath of the Civil War," especially the siren song of a booming economy.

Gibbs, who had read law with an English barrister in Victoria, undertook further legal training at Oberlin's Tanner Business College, but his Ohio sojourn proved very short. After nearly two decades in the West, he must have found his wife's hometown's pervasive domesticity and starchy civic idealism more than a bit stifling.

Though Maria and M. W. Gibbs may never have spoken aloud the words that formalized their estrangement, by 1869 or '70 they separated for good. An outsider's conclusions about why the marriage's traditional configuration ended just then can only be speculative, but between the ages of thirty-four and forty-one, Maria had been pregnant at least six times. Perhaps she wanted (and needed) to end her exhaustive, near-annual childbearing and withdrew from further sexual intimacy because abstinence seemed her only effective means of reproductive control. Such a decision may have dismayed Mifflin, and certainly she had no more babies. She must also have missed her family and probably wanted to stay in one place, while his "migratory" propensities wore her down. Maria hoped for a private life, but he aspired to a public one not unlike that of Frederick Douglass, with the burdens, power, and acclaim that accompanied it. And what could it have been like for Maria, no longer Vancouver's "Lady Gibbs," to share her Ohio home with a living legend whom many deferential black people idolized as "Our Moses of the West" when she just wanted a domesticated husband, a father for her children, and a reliable breadwinner?

Maria knew from her mother's example that life without a man in residence need not be intolerable, and may have modeled her marriage on Lucy Alexander's, which also was characterized by a distancing from her spouse after she had borne many babies. But for the nineteenth-century black bourgeoisie, as much as for whites, divorce was almost unthinkable and undoable. So Maria discreetly separated from Mifflin and stayed on with her maternal kin in Oberlin, where she raised two daughters and three sons, whom both parents remained close to and adored. The girls called their usually absent father "pater" or "Pa," and Maria declared him her "duck" — but Mifflin thereafter coolly referred to Maria as "your mother." Although neither Gibbs partner had other known romances, Mifflin spent only one decade of his very long life in conjugal residence with Maria. After 1870 they exchanged visits, corresponded often, and cooperated on a panoply of matters concerning property, finances, and especially their children's well-being, yet lived apart.

After less than a year in Oberlin, M. W. Gibbs set off to join his older brother, Jonathan, in Tallahassee, Florida. Making the most of his inborn talents and singular education in the 1850s at Dartmouth and then at the Princeton Theological Seminary (although the College of New Jersey, later Princeton University, did not knowingly enroll its first male African American students for another century, nor any women until 1969), Jonathan Gibbs thrived in the Reconstruction South. He became Florida's secretary of state, then its superintendent of public education. His son Thomas received a coveted appointment to the U.S. Military Academy, yet stayed only briefly owing to assertions of his unpreparedness in mathematics. Given the ordeals that the handful of other Negro cadets encountered in that era, it is hard to believe that Thomas Gibbs's supposed scholastic shortfall was more than a ruse to justify his expulsion. Only a very few "colored" men, among them Charles Denton Young, who arrived at West Point less than a decade later and ultimately became an acclaimed army officer who served around the world, managed to survive its rigors and bigotry. Dreading unknown perils after the "Ku Klux" threatened his life, Jonathan slept uneasily in his attic — which he outfitted as a bunker and arsenal. Mifflin glimpsed those dire omens in Jonathan's world and resolved not to remain with his brother in Florida.

M. W. Gibbs left there to attend a convention of black businessmen, where he met some Arkansans who urged him to relocate to their state. He decided to give it a try and, lured by sunny prospects, arrived in Little Rock in the spring of 1871. He assessed the situation, liked what he saw, and began using the wealth he had amassed in the Pacific Northwest to reinvest.

Gibbs, who was well-to-do and eager to practice law, joined a firm made up of several white Republicans to complete his legal training (although he was nearing fifty) with a goal of passing the state bar examination, which would allow him to open his own office. After hurdling that barrier, he forged new alliances and partnered sequentially with three of Arkansas's leading "colored" lawyers. During the next quarter century Gibbs and his partners challenged abuses of due process and took on a number of civil rights cases, lobbied for state legislation to protect African American tenant farmers, and defended on appeal and thus saved the lives of a pair of black men who had been summarily convicted of murder and sentenced to hang. Many Arkansans lauded Gibbs as a champion of the race, while his law firms doubled as real estate enterprises through which he invested in residential and commercial, urban and rural properties. Despite his being labeled a "carpetbag Negro," in 1873 white Republicans appointed him as Little Rock's Pulaski County attorney. Later that year Mifflin Wistar Gibbs ran for office, won, and thus became a municipal court judge — the entire United States' very first elected black jurist.

Gibbs did experience a few setbacks, however. He found himself on the losing side in Arkansas's 1874 struggle over gubernatorial succession that put a damper on Negro activism and pretty much crushed Reconstruction in his adopted state. In that repressive racial climate a white Democrat defeated him in his bid for reelection as judge, and Gibbs retreated to his private law practice. Both black and (some) white Arkansans thereafter called him Judge Gibbs, and he participated in a range of Republican activities, but never again served in, or even stood for, elective office.

Mifflin Wistar Gibbs also suffered a shocking and painful personal loss that year. Shortly after he returned home from another sojourn in Florida, his brother Jonathan, a seemingly healthy activist who was just fifty-three years old, died suddenly from "apoplexy" several hours after delivering a rousing speech to legislators at the state capitol. That led many wary black people to suspect that unreconstructed white former secessionists, who resented the power wielded by such a proud and prominent Negro, had resorted to poison to facilitate his premature death. But there was no proof of malfeasance, and no official inquiry into any possible criminal act or conspiracy.

When the Republicans reclaimed a measure of their former power in Arkansas, Gibbs received an appointment as Little Rock's federal land office registrar, and he served as a delegate and presidential elector at several national conventions. The former president Ulysses S. Grant, still a hero to African Americans, visited in 1879, and Gibbs, alone among his city's many Negroes, dined with the honored guest. Two years later he was even rumored to be a candidate for a post in President James Garfield's cabinet. He worked with white and "colored" Republicans throughout the South, including Booker T.

Washington, Alabama's up-and-coming educator and power broker, and he traveled to Kansas to assess the feasibility of further Negro settlement there. But in the same period, another family death, that of his and Maria's teenaged son Wendell, again darkened his life.

As a civic leader, Gibbs honored his commitments and participated in many community and philanthropic efforts. His daughter Ida joined him for several years to oversee his household and to supplement those activities. He championed industrial education, served on the board of visitors for the Little Rock public schools, where a local "colored" institute was (and is still) named in his honor, and gave to the city's charities, especially contributing the land and dollars needed to support the M. W. Gibbs Old Ladies Home for indigent black women.

In 1889 President Benjamin Harrison appointed Gibbs as Little Rock's receiver of public monies. That same year Hattie, his youngest, completed her studies at Oberlin's music conservatory, and he and Ida accompanied her to Minnesota before the girls headed off to Europe. Their "pater" financed many of their endeavors and remained close to his gifted, energetic daughters, whom he seems to have favored over his somewhat less capable sons. His ongoing emotional and financial support gave Ida and Hattie unusual independence, emboldened them, and enhanced their self-esteem.

Yet Judge Gibbs became restless in Arkansas, even with all his acclaim and economic success. In 1889 he wrote Frederick Douglass to assert an interest in serving his country (with which he had such an ambivalent relationship) in a foreign service post, preferably in Haiti, the independent black Caribbean island nation where Negroes sometimes represented the United States. Gibbs implored his revered former comrade to reinforce his own ongoing self-promotion in Washington, especially at the State Department, which Douglass professed himself glad to do.

But soon after visiting with Gibbs and others of Arkansas's leading citizens, Douglass received the very appointment that Gibbs had sought. "I take the first opportunity to congratulate [you] upon your appointment as Minister to Hayti," Gibbs wrote, "which of course I should have liked." Idle gossip suggested that a rift had developed between the two aging brothers-in-arms, but Gibbs reassured Douglass that "we have travelled too long and [are] too near the end of the journey, with mutuality of feeling and purpose, to allow either Carping or Criticism to divide us."

When Douglass returned from Haiti two years later, Gibbs again sought his endorsement for a consular office. "No one that I could apply to for assistance," he pleaded, "would be better acquainted with my . . . experience in business and in politics than yourself, and I feel that I can safely rely upon the character of your commendation." He also expressed grave concerns about "the rumor that our government intend to send a White man as Minister, or that the Haytian government made such a request." Douglass confirmed what Gibbs had heard. Haiti, he responded, clearly emulating the United States' racist bent, "wants white representation from this country and is disposed to resent the appointments of a colored minister while they are not esteemed [enough] to be sent to white nations." Despite that unpromising outlook, Douglass urged Gibbs to "send in your application backed by whatever support and influence you can command." But once again, nothing came of those persistent endeavors.

In a letter to Gibbs written early in 1895, Douglass acknowledged, but unexpectedly challenged, the conventional wisdom that exhorted "eight million" Negroes to always stand together politically because "[i]f we were only united we could shape the policy of government and surround ourselves with favorable conditions." Despite his own oft-quoted credo that "the Republican Party is the ship, all else the sea," Douglass warned Gibbs that such traditional advice might now be ill considered, because "crowding together may break the beams of the building under us and bring us to the ground." But the prophetic Douglass died the next month. Like all black Americans, members of the Gibbs family were profoundly saddened. M. W. Gibbs later reminisced that Douglass "was the grand old man who first took me by the hand and led me into the race struggle for peace and civil rights." On learning of his longtime ally's death, Gibbs sent his grieving widow a cablegram of condolence asserting, "His race, his country and humanity mourn the death of Frederick Douglass" — then briskly set about rekindling his own ambitions.

When William McKinley assumed the presidency in 1897, many influential Republicans knew that Judge Gibbs had served their party effectively for a quarter century, and although he had become one of the wealthiest persons of his race anywhere in the country, he never stopped seeking new worlds to conquer. In that era, few Americans of any age, color, class, or record of accomplishment had such international aspirations, but Gibbs had begun shaping his broad and ambitious global visions as the result of many diverse influences, experiences, and exposures.

In 1845, prodded by State Department officials who probably knew nothing of the man's "colored blood," President James K. Polk had appointed as vice consul in Yerba Buena, Mexico (soon to become San Francisco), an

Antillean-born entrepreneur of African and Danish parentage named William Leidesdorff. Although Leiderdorff had died shortly before Mifflin Wistar Gibbs arrived in that city, he remained a legend for Negro Californians. He held both American and Mexican citizenship, and soon he helped the United States to expedite the forcible annexation of Mexican California.

Gibbs counted several black expatriates among his associates, and he had lived in Vancouver, where he dealt with the white United States consul, a post that a Negro from Kansas named John Lewis Waller (with whom Gibbs almost certainly had crossed paths in various political activities) had sought but failed to secure. Gibbs's cohorts J. Mercer Langston and Frederick Douglass had represented their nation in Haiti, and he must have known about Waller's notorious (mis)adventures. In the early 1890s Waller barely survived a term as consul in Madagascar. And W. E. B. Du Bois, Gibbs's daughter Ida's new friend, had placed black people in a global perspective with his recent Harvard University dissertation analyzing the scope and impact of the Atlantic slave trade. Gibbs read profusely — history, philosophy, geography, current events, and government — and surely he knew how the U. S. Constitution determined that the president "shall nominate and by and with the advice and consent of the Senate, shall appoint ambassadors . . . and consuls."

But throughout the late nineteenth century, the State Department sent just a few American Negroes (businessmen, lawyers, ministers, teachers, or physicians, who were most welcome in the tropics, where up-to-date medical care was scarce) to represent the nation in Haiti and Liberia, the only autonomous black countries with which the United States maintained formal diplomatic relations. Ethiopia would not receive its first ministerial representative, a Caucasian, until 1912. White Americans served as consuls in all but a few "colored" colonial venues. As the United States' designated inferior caste, Negroes were virtually always excluded from such prestigious endeavors as a matter of course. Until recently almost every nation has reserved all significant diplomatic efforts for its elite men.

The first appointment of an American Negro as minister resident and consul general in Port-au-Prince, Haiti, went to Ebenezer Don Carlos Bassett in 1869. He stayed until 1877, then returned twelve years later as Frederick Douglass's clerk. John Mercer Langston, a onetime Virginia congressman and the Alexander-Gibbses' Oberlin friend, succeeded Bassett. John Terres, John E. W. Thompson (a Yale graduate who was the son of Haitian parents), Douglass, and John S. Durham, who served sequentially in the 1880s to early 1890s, held joint credentials to Santo Domingo, the mestizo Spanish protectorate that shared the island of Hispaniola. In that era, as Douglass had predicted, the State Department dispatched several white men to Haiti as well, but also posted two African Americans, Archibald Grimké (a Boston lawyer, Harvard graduate, and the brother of Ida Gibbs's pastor in Washington) and then Campbell Maxwell, as consuls in Santo Domingo alone. William F. Powell took charge of the Port-au-Prince consulate in 1897.

Following the appointments of two white men after the Civil War, the Liberian leg of the black diplomatic loop began with J. Milton Turner, named minister resident and consul general in 1871. The next consuls, Henry Highland Garnet and Moses Hopkins, both succumbed to "Africa fever" and died. Charles H. J. Taylor went in 1887 and did such a fine job that President Harrison soon broke with tradition and nominated him as a consul to Bolivia. The Senate, however, apparently refused to confirm a "colored" man to that post, so Taylor discreetly declined the appointment. Ezekiel Smith followed Taylor in 1888, and was succeeded by Alexander Clark (some accounts have incorrectly called Consul Clark an ambassador) and William McCoy, both of whom passed away in pestilent Liberia. The Reverend William Heard, an African Methodist Episcopal minister, went there in 1895, survived his tenure, then returned home to become a leading bishop in his church.

Reflecting the disdain with which the State Department considered Liberia (founded and funded in 1822 by whites as an African "homeland" for emancipated American slaves, and since 1847 an independent republic austerely governed by Negro Americo-Liberian politicians), the top diplomatic position there was designated commissioner, or minister resident and consul general, until 1930, then linguistically upgraded to envoy extraordinary or minister plenipotentiary. The United States granted it an ambassador only in 1949, in some part because doing so portended the reciprocal appointment of a "colored" man of equal rank who could hardly be expected to participate in Washington, D.C.'s racially segregated diplomatic social life. And not until the 1960s did the government assign more than a handful of black Americans to foreign service posts beyond what some State Department officials disparagingly came to call the "Liberia-Madagascar-Azores circuit."

The few exceptions in that minor pantheon of African Americans approached early on to serve their nation overseas included Blanche K. Bruce, John Quarles, William Hannibal Thomas, and Henry Francis Downing. Bruce, a Reconstruction senator from Mississippi, declined the offer of a position as an envoy to Brazil because that country still sanctioned slavery. In 1870 President Grant appointed Quarles as consul on the Mediterranean island of

Minorca, and a decade later he was transferred to Malaga, Spain. After failing to snare an appointment to either Liberia or Haiti, but still bruiting his Republican credentials, Will Thomas, a disreputable reprobate indeed, was named consul to Luanda, in Portugal's Angola, in 1878, but he never, in fact, even left the United States. In 1887 Henry F. Downing served for a while in that same Portuguese colony before becoming a prolific expatriate writer and an astute private sector observer of African affairs from London.

By the mid-1890s, Republicans in Washington, yielding to a rising tide of government-sanctioned bigotry and pressure from their party's most racist factions, offered Negro Americans ever fewer patronage positions in the Jim Crow South. Sending them instead to minor hardship posts abroad in remote, unhealthy, and reputedly inferior "colored" locales where white Americans often refused to go seemed a politically savvy way to assuage the Negroes' ambitions and maintain their loyalty to the Grand Old Party without offending more valued white voters. During the few years when they occupied the White House in the late nineteenth century, Democrats made similar overtures to the rare black men affiliated with their still suspect party.

Even at seventy-four, M. W. Gibbs remained energetic and ambitious. His quest to reinvent himself again and serve his country abroad began in 1889, but for eight years he failed to snare an assignment to Haiti or to his second choice, Venezuela, which would not receive its first "colored" consul until 1904. And Gibbs was hardly alone. Following McKinley's election, African Americans seeking federal appointments often queued up alongside white men outside the White House (at that time the State Department was located just across the street), and most, but not all, aspirants for the very limited number of overseas posts earmarked for their race were shunted aside. Anglo-Americans sometimes sought consular positions to enrich themselves, but that motivation seemed rare among the Negro minority, who wanted decent jobs, hoped to serve and represent their nation, and succumbed to a zest for international adventure.

Early in November 1897, only a few weeks after Gibbs learned of the death of another friend, the former consul and congressman J. Mercer Langston, President McKinley's proclamations included the confirmation of Arkansas's Judge Gibbs as his consul in Tamatave, Madagascar. At much the same time, McKinley appointed several other "colored" men to minor overseas posts. He sent George H. Jackson, a medical missionary, to La Rochelle, France, and asked Richard T. Greener (a henchman of Booker T. Washington, and Harvard's first black graduate) to represent him in India. But Greener declined owing to an outbreak there of bubonic plague, though he soon headed off for seven years as a commercial agent and consul in Russian Siberia's far-east city of Vladivostok. John N. Ruffin went to Asunción, Paraguay, while Owen Lun West Smith replaced the Reverend Heard as minister in Liberia. Mahlon Van Horne was sent to the Danish Virgin Islands, and Dr. John T. Williams to Britain's West African colony of Sierra Leone. How much, if anything, the president's advisers knew about Gibbs's putative and transient embrace of British Canadian citizenship in the 1860s remains a mystery. Gibbs successfully beclouded his own previous emigrationist endeavors and presented himself as an unceasingly loyal American citizen, and of course, a stalwart and affluent Republican partisan.

Judge Gibbs never sought the position in Tamatave, and at first he was disinclined to accept it. "Madagascar had not come within my purview," he later wrote, adding, "its distance had not 'lent enchantment to the view.'" But like a number of other Americans in that era who had energy and missionary zeal, he came to see the unexpected appointment (in an ironic twist on the "white man's burden") as a preordained opportunity to bring spiritual and moral enlightenment, "civilization," and his splendid organizational and entrepreneurial skills to "darkest Africa." He also hoped to improve diplomatic relations and stimulate trade with the United States. Although France's Indian Ocean island colony of Madagascar was geographically, historically, culturally, and racially almost as far from Liberia as Liberia and the rest of West Africa were removed from Arkansas, perhaps Gibbs also felt some sort of nascent, overarching pan-African identity. And certainly, the opportunity to experience the prestige and wield the power implicit in the consul's role as a virtual embodiment of the United States of America motivated him as well.

The Tamatave post nonetheless must have been hard to fill. The pay was poor and living conditions precarious. The few Americans who went to Madagascar often experienced serious consequences to their health, and even survival, capped by the 1888 murder of Consul Victor F. W. Stanwood. In the mid-1890s Consul John Lewis Waller, a black Kansan, plunged hip-deep into diplomatic and legal hot water there, while his white southern successor, Edward Telfair Wetter, was ultimately exposed as both a bigot and a sleazy libertine. Nonetheless, Judge Gibbs shouldered the new challenge, put his affairs in order, shuttled to and from Washington, D.C., and that Christmas Day, Little Rock's Negro elite feted him at a bittersweet gala farewell dinner.

Gibbs wanted an aide to accompany him. Many "colored" men sought him out as a mentor and he received numerous recommendations, but the entreaty that most influenced him came from his canny daughter Ida (though she herself was better qualified for the position than the ambitious fellow whom she endorsed), the woman whose judgment he most respected and valued. Either in a letter sent to him in Little Rock, or in person when he went to receive his credentials in the District of Columbia, where she had recently moved, Ida Gibbs persuaded her father to take along as his consular clerk a friend and correspondent of hers named William Henry Hunt. Hunt longed to serve his country, travel, and see and learn what he could of the world.

Gibbs let his tender paternal heart guide him when he offered the position to a young man whom he had met only once before, and on New Year's Day 1898, they set sail from New York's teeming but glacial Manhattan Island headed first for France, then on to a remote tropic isle that they could scarcely even envision. At dockside, Ida bade them adieu. She had studied for years, taught, traveled, and was an accomplished linguist, but neither M. W. Gibbs nor W. H. Hunt spoke or understood any of Madagascar's indigenous languages, or more than a few phrases of the French imposed as a formidable instrument of empire by the recently established colonial government. To impress his deservedly self-important sponsor, the enterprising Mr. Hunt had committed to memory copious details about Judge (by then, U.S. Consul Designate) Gibbs's public life, yet weeks at sea and many more in Madagascar itself would pass before Gibbs gleaned even the sparest history of Hunt. Nor would Gibbs have fully realized how permanently or intimately his ardent new assistant and his thirty-five-year-old daughter, who had grown up both with and without him, would be bound together.

Ida Alexander Gibbs's Pictures from a Well-Spent Youth

3

Ida Gibbs, a child of affluent, urbane parents, and arguably the granddaughter of a vice president of the United States and the defiant woman he had held in bondage, was thirty-five years old in January 1898 when she said good-bye to her father and William Henry Hunt as they left New York City bound to Madagascar. She had not yet been anywhere near that remote colonial island, but neither geographic nor cultural barriers ever circumscribed her world.

Ida had been born in 1862 in the northwest British Canadian colony of Vancouver, where the immediate family included her brothers Donald, Horace, and Wendell (Francis, the oldest, had died), and a younger sister, Hattie, who became her closest ally. In Ida's early childhood she made several trips to and from the United States with her mother, but in 1868 all of them, except her father, relocated to Oberlin, Maria Alexander Gibbs's old hometown. Mifflin Wistar Gibbs later joined them there, though he stayed only briefly. After his invigorating interludes in California and Vancouver, he needed a full year to reorient himself, but soon he settled down in Arkansas, while Maria and the five children remained with her kinfolk in Ohio.

Over time, the Alexanders, who had been Oberlin residents since the 1850s, and then the Gibbses joined the First Congregational Church. Spiritual, educational, and civic ideologies and interests were nearly indivisible in that righteous community

[F]riends and schoolmates urged me not to select the "gentlemen's course," because ... it might ruin my chances of getting a husband, since men were notoriously shy of women who knew too much. "Where," inquired some of my friends sarcastically, "will you find a colored man who has studied Greek?"
— Mary Church Terrell, *A Colored Woman in a White World*, 1940

where most residents lived by what John Mercer Langston, a leading lawyer and the Alexander-Gibbses' neighbor and friend, characterized as "principles of religious faith and life, as inculcated in the severest teachings of Jesus Christ and the Apostles, . . . accepted and pressed as indispensable to the individual and popular obligation."

Langston recalled how Oberlin's "well-regulated streets, its public grounds, its college buildings and private residences . . . constitute a town of rare New England character and beauty." He and his wife had known Maria Alexander (later Gibbs) for years, and the Langstons became the first of their race to settle in Oberlin's best neighborhood — on the same block as the school's president, James Fairchild. They initially faced resistance from a few whites who lived nearby, but soon they, and then the Gibbses (when the Langstons left Ohio in 1871 the Gibbses bought their large two-story home with its diverse outbuildings, many bedchambers, and a parlor that opened onto a broad veranda facing the town's main thoroughfare), wrote Langston, "spent the time of their residence there in happy . . . accord . . . and cordial neighborly treatment."

Ida and her siblings first attended the local public elementary school. The girls studied at Oberlin's music conservatory and then enrolled in its preparatory academy, where in the mid-1870s Ida Gibbs met Mary Eliza Church. Although they soon became fast friends, Mary — usually called Mollie — was a year younger, more vivacious and extroverted than Ida. They had another point of commonality in that both sets of their parents had separated. Despite daunting legal barriers augmented by widespread social opprobrium in their dignified, upper-class African American community, which strove to cast off demeaning images of the race perpetrated during and by centuries of slavery, the Churches actually divorced. But Ida and Mollie always remained close to their fathers, whose affluence and influence provided them with resources and advantages undreamed of by the vast majority of Negro Americans. Bolstered, in good part, by that paternal support and unconditional love, the girls developed into self-assured young women.

Another "colored" student, Anna Julia Haywood Cooper, older, married while young but recently widowed, came to Oberlin in 1881. She, however, was the product of a different, yet more typical, upbringing. She was born in 1858 or 1859 to an enslaved mother who had been impregnated by a white man, and raised in poverty in an environment where whites tyrannized Negroes and most people presumed that girls were less intelligent and less deserving than boys. Nothing was given freely to Anna, and her life never lacked struggle, yet she, Ida, and Mollie all benefited from Oberlin's many strengths. Langston observed that Oberlin was "the first institution of learning in the world to give woman equal educational opportunities and advantages with man." "To it, too," he added, "belongs the honor of being the first college in the United States to accept the negro student and give him equal educational opportunities and advantages with the white."

On one occasion when Langston lauded his own first-rate education, a listener taunted, "You learned another thing at Oberlin! You learned to walk with white women there!" Mollie Church similarly commented, "It was predicted that if white and colored students were allowed to associate with each other on terms of 'social equality,' . . . [t]here would be intermarriages galore . . . and the whole tone of the school would be low." Oberlin's "tone," nonetheless, remained elevated, while its commitment to racial, gender, and "social equality" was among the blessings, yet also the controversies, to which Ida Gibbs, her family, and colleagues became heirs. Away from their school and town, however, they often faced ruder realities.

Elsewhere during her college years, Mollie met a white woman who said, "I observe you are quite swarthy. . . . What is your nationality?" "I am a colored girl," Mollie replied. She added that "if I had told [her] I was a gorilla in human form, she could not have been more greatly shocked." In most instances, African Americans of any skin tone could feel at ease in Oberlin, but lighter-complexioned ones such as the Langstons, Mollie, Ida, and Anna, though they sometimes enjoyed greater privileges, at other times endured similarly awkward situations.

Mollie later recounted that she and Ida were "classmates from the eighth grade in the public schools of Oberlin through the high school, the Oberlin Academy and Oberlin College, nine years all together." They roomed together in a dormitory, while Anna Julia Cooper boarded with a professor's family, so Ida and Mollie's relationship with Mrs. Cooper was cordial, yet never equally close. All three knew they had unique advantages and therefore bore unique responsibilities. Rebutting mainstream assumptions, Cooper would argue that "if there is an ambitious girl with pluck and brains [for] higher education, encourage her to make the most of it." Mollie, however, wrote with humor about the widespread prejudices against any such advanced training for members of her sex: "College-bred women had a bad reputation for neatness both as to personal appearance and in the home. . . . Women who had studied higher mathematics, the sciences, and Greek had so violated the laws of nature that it was never possible for them to learn afterwards to do well the work which the Creator had ordained they should do."

Most contemporaries agreed that the Creator's preordained role for women was not to study and pursue a career, but rather to marry early, yield to the will of a "superior" man, and then bear his children. Undeterred by such biases, Ida, Mollie, and Anna hit the books. Against ample advice, though at least for Ida with family support, they tackled Oberlin's "gentlemen's course." Ida majored in English, but completed the rigorous curriculum that included history, philosophy, government, economics, laboratory sciences, higher mathematics, French and German, Latin and Greek. She and Mollie also enjoyed playing the piano, social dancing, horseback riding, sailing, and swimming, while all three became committed to the radical notion that women should be allowed to vote, though most Americans (black, brown, or white) of both sexes disagreed and still believed that espousing such political heresy undercut a young woman's chance to marry.

Oberlin had no Negro instructors, but it did have one white female professor — almost unheard of in the country's few elite coeducational "white" colleges — who served as a model for her students. As Anna wrote about the school's influence on her: "Teaching had always seemed to me the noblest of callings, . . . if I were white I should still want to teach those whose need presents a stronger appeal than money." Her statement reflected Oberlin's philosophy that education stimulated personal growth and inspired a lifetime dedicated to uplifting others, a credo that shaped Ida's and Mollie's lives too. In June 1884 the three women donned austere black dresses, families and friends assembled, and President Fairchild signed and bestowed their beribboned parchment diplomas as the scholars joined their senior class of seventy-five gentlemen and three other ladies and prepared to march out, face, and tackle the world. Almost certainly, only two Negro women before them (both of whom had also graduated from Oberlin) had ever completed the four-year bachelor's degree program at any fully accredited college in the United States.

Of that trio, only Cooper really had to support herself, so she took an academic position at Wilberforce College, a small "colored" school nearby. Despite her father's objections and his contention that "'real ladies' did not work," Mollie Church also planned to teach, and joined Cooper at Wilberforce. Ida Gibbs, however, remained for another year at Oberlin, pursuing music studies at the conservatory and dealing with pressing domestic matters. During that period her brother Wendell died, then her slave-born grandmother, Lucy Chinn Alexander, passed away in August 1885. Lucy, who lived with the Gibbs family, had spent the previous eight years in failing health, but nonetheless proudly persevered to see her oldest granddaughter graduate from college.

Soon afterward, Ida departed from Ohio to take a position in Huntsville, as an instructor in Latin and mathematics at the "colored" Alabama State Agricultural and Normal School. Then she spent a two-year stretch with her father in Little Rock, where she taught as a missionary in the city's needy African American community. In 1888 Ida left Arkansas to travel, perhaps with Mollie Church, who later wrote about how she shared quarters in Europe with an unnamed "Oberlin friend." Mollie boarded for a while in a *pension* with some white Americans, though her presence riled them. They told their ill-informed continental proprietress that "[i]f an individual has only a single drop of African blood in his veins . . . white people in the United States consider him a Negro," but Mollie packed up and left before she could be evicted.

Back in the United States, shortly after Hattie's 1889 completion of the music conservatory's curriculum at Oberlin, Ida and their father went to Minnesota to hear Hattie perform, and Judge Gibbs addressed St. Paul's civic Afro-American League. Either through that group or at Hattie's concert, the sisters met a personable but barely educated contemporary named William Henry Hunt, who worked as a porter at a deluxe local hotel and involved himself in Republican ward politics. As Mollie Church later cautioned, men such as that often were "shy of women who knew too much," but Hunt overcame any such reluctance and shared colorful anecdotes about his early life. Ida was immediately attracted to that diamond in the rough, and the Gibbs ladies must have advised him that education would provide the key to his career advancement. They corresponded often thereafter, but rarely saw each other for some time to come. Ida nonetheless prodded William to gain knowledge, experience, and polish, while he extolled her as his "guiding star."

That fall Hattie Gibbs set off for Paris to pursue her musical instruction with an internationally renowned composer and pianist, and Ida accompanied her for several months. Hattie was the first "colored" person to complete the curriculum at Oberlin's conservatory. She had studied composition, voice, organ, and violin there, but the piano was her forte. Returning from Europe a year later, she continued her advanced private training, gave more concerts, then moved to Eckstein-Norton University, a school for "colored" students in rural Kentucky (not far from her mother's childhood home), developed along the lines of Booker T. Washington's Tuskegee Institute. There she founded, funded, and ran a program for talented, needy boys and girls, and named her newly erected music building in honor of its major donor: Judge Mifflin Wistar Gibbs.

Hattie aspired to preserve the splendid but endangered heritage of her people's music and to develop youngsters' skills in an environment similar to that which she had been singularly privileged to enjoy at Oberlin. She later contended that "Negro melodies were the only true American music." "With true race pride" she urged African Americans to "feel rich in the thought that the garden is your own." "Everyone should study music," she insisted, "as everyone should study literature, . . . to become familiar with . . . the highest forms of human intelligence." However, she added, "we must . . . realize that brains and hard work are essential to produce true art." Ida often joined her sister in rural Kentucky, and lectured for her there at Eckstein-Norton.

An extended bout of poor health took Ida Gibbs back to her mother and their longtime home in Oberlin, but she made productive use of that hiatus, and in 1892 officials at the school solemnly laid its crimson-and-gold-bordered hood across her shoulders and granted her a prestigious and rare master's degree. Anna Julia Cooper and Mollie Church had received the same acclamation from their common alma mater a couple of years earlier, as would Hattie Gibbs in 1906.

For the next three years, Ida headed the preparatory division at the Florida State Normal School (later Florida A & M) in Tallahassee, as one of eight teachers led by her cousin Thomas Gibbs. After leaving the U.S. Military Academy under an unwarranted academic cloud, Thomas had attended Oberlin, received his degree from a college in Boston, then followed along the path in education laid down by his late father, Ida's distinguished uncle Jonathan.

Women of their ilk faced daunting attitudinal, legal, and economic barriers, but in 1892 the impassioned Anna Julia Cooper completed her book *A Voice from the South.* Its essays lay out the challenges faced by African American women through a seminal evocation of black feminism. The very next year, M. W. Gibbs's former abolitionist colleague Frances Ellen Watkins Harper published *Iola Leroy, or Shadows Uplifted,* a story that explores the intricacies of racial identity. Harper affirmed privileged "colored" people's obligations to succor the less advantaged through Iola, her almost-white protagonist, who embraces other Negroes and then emerges as a spokesperson for disempowered members of her legally defined race. *Iola Leroy* was among the few early novels written by a black woman, and it spoke urgently to people such as Ida Gibbs.

Like many others that summer of 1893, Cooper, Harper, and the recently married Mollie Church Terrell, as well as Ida Gibbs and her father, went to the World's Columbian Exposition commemorating the quadricentennial of Columbus's "discovery" of the Americas. The Exposition drew millions of visitors to Chicago, where civic leaders were determined to outdo the recent Paris Exposition Universelle and prove that their bumptious Midwest burg could be much more than just its country's reeking, hog-slaughtering hub. The edifices that made up the glistening "White City" clustered around a lavish complex of gardens, lagoons, and fountains festooned along the city's lakefront. In its entirety, that urban extravaganza, sparkling and "electrified" beyond anything that had preceded it, was dedicated to enlightenment, entertainment, and ravenous consumption.

George W. G. Ferris's gigantic revolving wheel, a filigreed iron phenomenon more splendid, some said, than the Eiffel Tower, could carry two thousand riders at a time, lofting them nearly three hundred feet above the city. High-brow and honky-tonk amusements and exhibits from around the world showcased their countries' cultures, sciences, and industries. At Buffalo Bill's Wild West Show, manly white cowboys "killed" droves of bloodthirsty Indians, while George Pullman's railroad town, as well as ersatz Zulu and Dahomey African villages (populated by almost naked, spear-wielding "cannibals"), stretched incongruously by Lake Michigan's shore. Fairgoers searched in vain for Thomas Alva Edison's promised "moving pictures," while they loaded, focused, and clicked George Eastman's portable cameras, captured on celluloid every spectacle they saw, and bought innovative products such as Shredded Wheat and the new, all-purpose baking mix sold under the trade name Aunt Jemima and doled out of the world's largest flour barrel by an obese, bandana-ed black woman.

The gala displays that occupied a place of honor on the glittering Midway reflected the organizers' conviction that human development was easily separable into three sequential stages. Blacks (mostly Africans) represented the lowest, or "savage," phase of societal evolution, Asians constituted an intermediary caste and a period called "barbarism," while northern Europeans and white North Americans epitomized the triumphs of modern "civilization." The only acknowledgment of Africa's contributions to that "civilized" world was a gold medal awarded to the Republic of Liberia for its aromatic coffee.

A large pavilion showcased Euro-American women's domestic and artistic achievements in a congenial if condescending fashion, and included a hard-to-find exhibit devoted to African Americans prepared by Hampton Institute (Booker T. Washington was its most renowned graduate), the Virginia industrial school that educated both Negroes and Native Americans. Black participation in the "White City" was, nonetheless, rare and fractious.

The suffragist Susan B. Anthony attended the fair, and when Ida Gibbs went sightseeing with her father and Mollie Church Terrell, they crossed paths with the rising Negro poets James Weldon Johnson and Paul Laurence Dunbar. The latter worked there under Frederick Douglass's aegis. The young ladies conversed with the country's black elder statesman, and Ida later wrote about his keynote speech on the Exposition's "Colored Jubilee Day" (Douglass was appalled when white vendors offered free watermelon to all black attendees) that "his fiery eloquence and . . . commanding figure impressed me greatly." Anna Julia Cooper addressed an interracial group of well-educated women, while Ida A. Gibbs may have met Ida B. Wells, who shared her given name and age — both were born in 1862 — and must have roused her political instincts. Wells, a fierce antilynching protagonist whose journalism had become so controversial that she sometimes concealed her identity by adopting the pseudonym "Iola," addressed a generic "seeker after truth" in her pamphlet titled "The Reason Why the Colored American Is Not in the World's Columbian Exposition," distributed from the Haitian Pavilion, where Douglass presided after his recent return from a two-year ministerial assignment in that Caribbean island nation.

"The Reason Why" describes how African Americans protested throughout the contentious period leading up to the fair's opening, arguing that they were led to "understand that they were *persona non grata,* so far as participation in the directive energy of the Exposition." Wells's booklet includes essays detailing slavery's history, explaining how its legacy still distorted current events and perceptions, and condemning lynching. It reveals that from President Benjamin Harrison on down, the Exposition's sponsors had included virtually no black people on any planning committees, nor allocated the funds needed to develop a significant exhibit that "would tell to the world" what the country's millions of Negroes had accomplished. Controversies over whether their contributions would or should be incorporated into the United States exhibits as a whole, or separated in a peripheral "colored" display, sharply divided the "race women" with whom Ida Gibbs identified. But whatever her impressions of the Exposition may have been, she preserved a colorful, embroidered silk streamer as a treasured memento.

Soon afterward her life took a critical new tack. In her 1940 autobiography, Mary (Mollie) Church Terrell said that in a letter of recommendation Oberlin's dean of women had written "so enthusiastically about the three colored women who had graduated in the class of 1884, that [the only Negro member of the District of Columbia's Board of Education] sent for one of the others [Cooper] and for me to come immediately." "The third member of the class" — Ida Alexander Gibbs — Church Terrell added, "came to teach [in Washington] several years later."

Education in the nation's capital was segregated by race, but its schools (at least a few of them) for African Americans were among the country's best, and its teachers the best paid. That, combined with the myriad attractions of Howard University, the "capstone" of Negro academe, made the city a magnet for "colored" intellectuals. Early in 1895, Ida arrived to teach English at the M Street School — officially the Washington Colored High School. Twenty years before, Mary Jane Patterson, the country's first female Negro college graduate, also from Oberlin, had been its principal, and that same college's Richard T. Greener, who went on to become a United States consul in Siberia, followed Patterson. Anna Julia Cooper started working there in 1890, and, unlike her two classmates, she stayed for decades thereafter, though not without contentious interruptions.

Robert Heberton Terrell, a graduate of Lawrence Academy, Harvard College, and Howard Law School, also taught at M Street, and soon he began courting Miss Mollie Church. Their students relished the budding romance, and one scribbled on a chalkboard: "Mr. Terrell . . . used to go to dances, but now he goes to *Church*." The relationship blossomed and they married in 1891, but Washington's public school regulations required that the new Mrs. Terrell, like all other married women, relinquish her teaching position. Mollie Church Terrell was good looking, well spoken, energetic — and ambitious. She remained committed to education and soon snagged an appointment as the first female African American member of the District of Columbia's (or any major American city's) school board.

In one of her definitive biographical studies of Anna Julia Cooper, Louise Hutchinson claims that when Ida Gibbs first arrived in the city, she and Cooper roomed together at the home of the Reverend Alexander Crummell, an early pan-Africanist and the dean of Washington's black clergy. But Ida soon moved on to reside with Robert and Mollie Terrell in their new house (Mollie's wealthy father purchased it for the newlyweds) on Fourth Street N.W. By then, Mollie sat on the school board, and within a short time her lawyer husband was named principal of the M Street High School. Living with a married couple provided the requisite respectability for any single woman, while Ida's residence with the prominent Church-Terrells, combined with Judge Gibbs's affluence and renown and her own academic appointment, gave her credibility with and fully incorporated her into the District's small "colored" upper class.

In some ways the mid-1890s were grueling for the Church-Terrells, and because she shared their home, for Ida too. "In five years [I] lost three babies," Mollie wrote in her autobiography. "I literally sank down into the very depths of despair." As a result of one stillbirth, she wrote, "I came near losing my life." Only after seven years would she see a single pregnancy to successful completion and bear a daughter, Phyllis, who always remained devoted to her "Aunt Ida."

But there were other obligations, distractions, and rewards as well. Ida, Anna, and Mollie became charter members of the new National Association of Colored Women (NACW), with the latter elected that umbrella service organization's president several times. "Lifting as We Climb," the NACW's credo, exemplified, as did F. E. W. Harper's recent novel *Iola Leroy,* the responsibilities that such women believed they bore for others of their race.

In an article Ida Gibbs (Hunt) wrote years later, she recalled a gala reception early in 1895 at Frederick Douglass's Washington home, and she and Mollie Church Terrell saw him again just a few weeks later when they attended the National American Woman Suffrage Association's convention. Mollie prominently involved herself in the suffrage movement, but Ida quietly insisted, "[W]e both believed that women needed the ballot to correct many of the injustices to which women of that day were subjected." And both of them recalled how Susan B. Anthony escorted Douglass to the podium that afternoon, and the entire almost all-white assemblage arose and waved their snowy handkerchiefs to salute his efforts on behalf of women's rights.

The District of Columbia's residents were stunned to learn that the distinguished old man died that evening. "His funeral was one of the largest ever held in Washington," Ida later recalled. As a teacher and a longtime admirer of Frederick Douglass (her father's mentor and former colleague), she was touched when the city's "schools were dismissed and children with their parents passed by to have a last look or cast flowers on his bier." And as a member of the board of education, Mollie Church Terrell negotiated the passage of a resolution making February 18, when Douglass celebrated his birth, an official local day of remembrance.

After almost a decade during which she had struggled to raise funds in an ultimately futile effort to sustain her music school in Kentucky, Hattie Gibbs also relocated to Washington. She and Ida briefly moved into the Church-Terrells' elegant new four-story, red-brick house on T Street, close to their former abode and just a few blocks from Howard University, in the city's pleasant Le Droit Park neighborhood. Until recently, it had been a fenced-in, exclusively white enclave, but as Washington's *Colored American* newspaper acidly commented at the time, "[I]t is rumored that Le Droit Park is rapidly being Africanized." Soon after, however, Maria Alexander Gibbs left Ohio to join her daughters, and the three women settled down together in a nearby home of their own purchased for them by the ever solicitous, well-to-do Judge Gibbs.

An intriguing speculation about Ida Gibbs in this period concerns her in-volvement with W. E. B. Du Bois. No documents provide any solid proof, but several scholars have conjectured about their personal relationship. David Levering Lewis, Du Bois's peerless biographer, believes that Du Bois and Gibbs enjoyed a liaison that long predated their mutual association with the post–World War I Pan-African Congresses. He bases that hypothesis on a number of factors. First, Du Bois was an incorrigible philanderer. Second, their correspondence suggests to Lewis the testiness of one-time intimates, accustomed to spats and reconciliations. (He mentions the "presumptuous" nature of Gibbs's letters to Du Bois.) A third clue lies in Du Bois's admir-ing and artful depiction of Caroline Wynn, a leading protagonist in his first novel, *The Quest of the Silver Fleece.* His delineation of Wynn's family, educa-tion, intellect, international and civic concerns, and her career, demeanor, and personality, shows an uncanny likeness to Ida Gibbs.

In his novel, set around 1900, Du Bois described Caroline Wynn as a ma-ture, articulate, politically savvy teacher in the nation's capital. In addition to being "brilliant and well-trained," he wrote, "she was sprung from respect-able mulattoes who had left a little competence which yielded her three or four hundred dollars a year." Du Bois scarcely mentioned Wynn's physical attributes, but stressed her dignity, acumen, and intellect. "She was unusu-ally presentable and always well-gowned and pleasant of speech," he added, yet "found nearly all careers closed to her." For Gibbs too, although teaching was a mission, honor, and pleasure, it was also probably seen as her sole fully respectable career option. "She attributed [those barriers] to her sex," Du Bois concluded about Wynn, but "was sure that, beyond chance and womanhood, it was the color line that was hemming her in."

Just as Ida Alexander Gibbs nurtured and groomed the naive, undereducated William Henry Hunt for years after they first met in Minnesota, Caroline Wynn, Du Bois's supposedly fictitious leading lady, also cultivated an unsophisticated suitor whom over time she made "thoroughly presentable according to the strictest Washington standards." Du Bois added, "Whether or not Caroline Wynn would ever marry him was a perennial subject of speculation among her friends and it usually ended in the verdict that she could not afford it."

Questions concerning race infused Ida Gibbs's world much as they did that of Du Bois's heroine. "We're talking of it all the time," his Miss Wynn asserts. "We veil it a little . . . but there is only one thought in this room." "We don't just blurt into the Negro Problem; that's voted bad form," she adds. "We saunter to it sideways, touch it delicately, because, you see, it hurts."

Between 1897, when Du Bois, a precocious new PhD from Harvard, addressed a group of Washington's intelligentsia and probably first met Ida Gibbs, and 1911, when he published *The Quest of the Silver Fleece,* Ida resembled Caroline Wynn more than did any other woman in the nation's capital. Her acumen, wit, worldliness, background, and vocation, and similarly unpolished beau, combine to make Du Bois's fictitious Caroline a dead ringer for Ida. But all that provides no proof whatsoever that she and he engaged in even so much as a lively flirtation.

Yet W. E. B. Du Bois did attract many women of Ida Gibbs's ilk. He was widely traveled and dapper, and his intellect, vigor, confidence, and sensuality were compelling, though he was balding early, shorter than most, and hardly an Adonis. He had wed in 1895 and stayed with his first spouse until she died, but was demonstrably untrue to her in later years, so there is little reason to think that he was more faithful in his virile youth. He justified his recurrent infidelities by saying that "my wife's life-long training as a virgin, made it almost impossible for her ever to regard sexual intercourse as not fundamentally indecent." Ida Gibbs also resembled (and became friends with) several of the spirited, accomplished Negro women with whom Du Bois had his well-documented later romances. But if the younger but mature-beyond-his-years Du Bois even aspired to embark on an intimate friendship with Ida, how, when, and where could it have evolved, given her clear moral rectitude and the Negro bourgeoisie's condemnation and rigid disapproval of such relationships?

They probably initially met at a social event when Du Bois came to the District of Columbia in April 1897 for the first sessions of the American Negro Academy under Alexander Crummell's leadership. Anna Julia Cooper, Ida Gibbs's fellow alumna and teacher, was living with the Crummells and was (albeit briefly) the only female invited to join that society. Even its otherwise enlightened members such as Du Bois, the Reverend Francis Grimké, and Crummell himself took for granted most of that era's ingrained assumptions of male superiority.

If a relationship began then, it could have been rekindled during Du Bois's subsequent trips to Washington, then at the Pan-African Conference in London three years later (the occasion when he first uttered his prophetic phrase, "The problem of the Twentieth Century is the problem of the color line"), where Cooper also spoke, or at the Paris Exposition that followed. No evidence has been found that Ida Gibbs even went to Europe that summer, but she and her sister often journeyed abroad during their holidays, and could have done so in 1900. When members of the "colored" elite traveled — a number of Ida's friends, including Cooper and Du Bois, did go to Paris that July or August — they coordinated their schedules to meet, shop, dine, enjoy the sights, and cavort with one another as they widened their cultural horizons, largely free from the societal confines and racism they encountered at home. Du Bois resided and taught in Atlanta at the time, but often went up to the District of Columbia, where in 1902 he delivered a controversial address to a group of Negro educators, Ida Gibbs surely among them. On that occasion he endorsed rigorous academics for black students and also challenged Booker T. Washington's pragmatic orthodoxy that promoted mechanical and industrial training for most "colored" youths. The next year Du Bois's fractious essay "Of Mr. Booker T. Washington and Others," in his powerful anthology *The Souls of Black Folk,* exacerbated that widening schism.

But even if Du Bois became a distraction for Ida Gibbs, William Henry Hunt, whom she first had met in 1889, was her true and steady, if usually distant, beau, and they corresponded through the ensuing years. When M. W. Gibbs received his appointment as United States consul to Madagascar late in 1897, Ida served as the intermediary who exhorted her father to take Hunt along as his aide. Out of loyalty, and also as an interventionist paternal act aimed at locking in Hunt's commitment to his mature and as yet unmarried daughter, Judge Gibbs quickly agreed.

About the final tender meeting with William in her New York City hotel just before his departure for Madagascar, Ida wrote her sister and most trusted confidante, "He isn't so bad as a lover, after all, when he gets started, I find. Bless his dear old heart!" — raising questions as to whom, if anyone, she might have been comparing him. If Ida and "dear old" William became even informally engaged during that holiday season, it would have given them greater license to become increasingly intimate with one another, in accordance with the straitlaced "colored" upper class's restrictive behavioral mores. On the other hand, despite her candor with Hattie about the evening's clearly romantic content, Ida may well not have been referring to him as her "lover" in its explicitly erotic modern sense.

After Hunt and Judge Gibbs set sail for Madagascar, Ida and Hattie Gibbs both continued teaching. But with her talent, drive, and credentials, Hattie quickly advanced to become assistant director of music for the District's "colored" schools, a new position that their friend Mollie Church Terrell maneuvered into existence through her post on the city's board of education. Hattie's career clearly vaulted over those of many other Washington, D.C., educators, because amid carping, gossip, and charges of favoritism, the *Colored American* sprang to her defense, insisting that "there is no need of any kick over Miss Gibbs's appointment as musical directress, as she won her way fairly." In addition, Hattie Gibbs established a private lyceum, the Washington Conservatory of Music and School of Expression, where she employed a number of accomplished black musicians, created an administrative position briefly filled by her brother Donald, and even procured scholarship support from leading members of the race such as Booker T. Washington. By early 1904 Hattie moved her operation into larger quarters in an imposing building that Judge Gibbs again purchased to fulfill his daughter's dreams, but in a letter to his protégé William Hunt in Madagascar, Gibbs jokingly claimed that it was "such a *high toned place,* that I am afraid to go there lest I break something, and thereby bring my raising into disrepute."

"Although seventy-eight years old, [Gibbs] is hale and hearty and looks like a man thirty years younger," the *Colored American* applauded in 1901, but early that year, the judge left the distant consulate in Hunt's capable hands and returned home to Little Rock. There he wrote and published his autobiography, re-involved himself in civic and political affairs, and started a bank. Maria Alexander Gibbs meanwhile remained comfortably ensconced with her daughters in the District of Columbia, where the three women conducted an active community and social life.

Ida Gibbs founded the Book Lovers' Club, which William Hunt described as a group of "brainy . . . charming . . . talented" women. She, Anna Julia

Cooper, and several other teachers and friends also started a modest endeavor they called Le Cercle Français, dedicated to studying and reveling in all aspects of French culture. In addition, Ida became an officer of the Bethel Literary Society, "colored" D.C.'s foremost intellectual and political forum, where that same winter the *Washington Bee* noted her attendance at a public lecture advertised as "The Negro Woman and her Influence Upon the Political, Social and Economic Advancement of the Race." An admiring reporter wrote that the outspoken "Miss Gibbs" generated "great applause [when she] paid the essayist a glowing compliment," then turned on some misogynist critics and added, "[I]f you learned gentlemen will come down out of the clouds, I think you would [not] be able to dismiss this vital subject."

Soon thereafter, "Mrs. Mifflin Wistar Gibbs," a respected matron (the black press and members of their social set turned a blind eye on Maria's thirty-year marital separation from the judge), celebrated at one of President William McKinley's 1901 "colored" inaugural balls, while Hattie and Ida attended another such event along with key representatives of Washington's Negro society. That summer the sisters traveled to London, Antwerp, Berlin, and Paris, where they met up with William Hunt, who had written Ida from Tamatave, Madagascar: "I thought we would carry out our intentions that we have too long delayed, and then take a steamer for France or England." Hopefully, he continued, they "could . . . spend some time in the Midi de la France."

In all, Ida Gibbs and Consul William Hunt carried on their transoceanic courtship for six years. On one occasion he cajoled that "if I had her here this moment she would not doubt my love for her." He reminded his "dear girl" of that long past evening in Minnesota, when "I first met and learned to love you so fondly and dearly." But, he grumbled, "I think you are not fond of such sweet nothings." In another letter to "Ma chere Ida," he sulked because she had failed to respond promptly enough to a previous missive. William also confessed to flirting and carousing a bit during his bachelor years in Madagascar, perhaps doing so to make Ida feel a trifle jealous. "For some unaccountable reason," he teased, "I am quite popular with the French people, especially the women." His memoir even mentions a few "Bacchanalian jamborees," but nonetheless he swore that he aimed to avoid "the very appearance of mischief." Though hardly a passionate avowal, if anything can be construed as Hunt's formal proposal, these words can: "We are not growing any younger, and we ought not to lose many more of our precious years apart from each other in the future as in the past. It is not just to you, nor good for me. I, at any rate, am very tired of my life of single blessedness and willing to change it as soon as I am prepared to furnish the salt and water for *that girl*." As usual, he closed with, "Toujours, ton beau devoté, Guillaume."

Once back from Madagascar, Judge Gibbs often visited his daughters in the nation's capital, where in 1902 he came to promote his autobiography, *Shadow and Light*. Gibbs, who was said "to be worth seventy-five thousand dollars" (easily the equivalent of more than a million a century later), became a supporter and the first lifetime member of Booker T. Washington's vigorous new National Negro Business League, and Washington wrote the introduction for Gibbs's memoir, "giving it a good send off."

In a note to B. T. Washington that January, M. W. Gibbs reported that he was delivering copies of his book to the White House for President Theodore Roosevelt (McKinley had been assassinated the previous fall) and other federal officials. But Gibbs also complained that "there is much dissatisfaction in my state of Ark. with the conduct of the present Republican Office holders," adding that "a white man of no political repute" had offended Little Rock's loyal black partisans. He implored Washington to write the president a letter recommending him as a replacement for the ill-suited white fellow, but without better cause, the Alabaman would not put himself on the line for Gibbs, whom he may have begun to see as something of a loose cannon. He did not condone political boat rocking, and this may have marked the onset of a rift between the two men who had so recently been close allies. Mostly, Gibbs wanted to return home, writing that "my affairs [are] needed at the Rock." "I have been for the last week dancing attendance at the White House," he concluded. "I am tired of Washington [D.C.] and want to get away."

The patriarchal Judge Gibbs also insinuated himself into his older daughter's and Hunt's affairs. "I have your & Ida's letters!" he pointedly noted in 1903 to the diligent Consul Hunt, who remained on duty in Madagascar. At last, however, the couple set a firm wedding date for the following spring, as Hunt prepared to return for a pivotal respite in the land of his birth.

He arrived back in the United States the next February and wrote Ida Gibbs from New York detailing his "tempest tossed" voyage from France. During his years abroad, Hunt had become a respected junior diplomat, and arguably a bona fide new member of the group that Du Bois designated the Talented Tenth. While staying at one of the city's urbane hotels he avoided any possibility of being snubbed in a domestic locale where he might, once again, be taken for and abusively (mis)treated as just another Negro American. Hunt's letter to his fiancée confided that "here I speak only French," and thus he slyly passed himself off as a becomingly suntanned European. But what he most wanted, he concluded, was to "see your own dear self."

Delayed matrimony was one thing, but forty-one was very late for Ida to consider bearing children. Perhaps her grandmother's and mother's truncated marriages following their many pregnancies convinced the younger woman to limit her sexual contacts and delay any marital commitment. The agonies of Mollie Church Terrell, who experienced the tragedies of miscarriages and stillbirths while Ida was living with her, may have reinforced those trepidations. Ida also experienced both the delights and trials of parenthood when two orphaned cousins resided with her and Hattie in their Washington home. Complacency or inertia, an adoring father, her antecedents' and several acquaintances' marital woes, a rewarding career and financial independence, all coalesced to make Ida less than eager to marry in haste.

Many "colored" Washingtonians had successful marriages, but others did not. According to Eleanor Alexander's disturbing dual biography *Lyrics of Sunshine and Shadow* (2001), the Terrells' and Gibbses' neighbors, the poet Paul Laurence Dunbar and his wife, Alice, also a gifted writer, captivated people in their clique, but they were troubled by his domestic violence and other excesses, which they assiduously tried to ignore.

The couple had eloped in 1898. "When Paul Dunbar married, he brought his wife . . . to live in my father's house, which was next door to ours," wrote Mollie Church Terrell, idealizing the black bard even as she shut her eyes to his marital misbehavior. "I can see [him] beckoning me as I walked by," she sighed, "when he wanted to read me a poem [or] discuss a word or a subject on which he had not fully decided." But she did not mention the name of Paul's spouse or his abominable conduct, which precipitated his wife's scandalous midnight flight in 1902. Paul, a splendid lyric poet, master of the vernacular, and member of the elite American Negro Academy, nonetheless was a bitter alcoholic who probably suffered from and infected Alice with gonorrhea. He assaulted her emotionally, physically, and verbally before and during their brief marriage. In their circle, however, virtually the entire blame for the marriage's discord and ultimate failure fell on his wife, who admittedly tolerated his brutality for several years in exchange for the "honor" of being Mrs. Paul Laurence Dunbar. On one occasion, the Reverend Francis Grimké — Ida's friend and pastor — witnessed Paul abusing Alice, but even he declined to intervene. As for Americans of any racial background at that time, the semblance of moral rectitude, manifested in and by a stifling, patriarchal domestic tranquility, seemed so crucial for members of the Negro so-called Talented Tenth that they looked away from even such abhorrent behavior.

As Mollie Church Terrell's unsolicited advisers warned, it was next to impossible for a woman such as Ida Gibbs to find and secure as her husband "a colored man who has studied Greek." Yet due to his "classical course" in secondary school, William Henry Hunt had hurdled, barely, that artificial barrier. Presumably further limiting any chance at matrimony, Ida was not, by traditional standards, especially pretty. She also was a forthright feminist (another supposed impediment), and had reached an age when the belittling words "old maid" or "spinster" might be murmured in conjunction with her name. In November 1902, when Ida celebrated her fortieth birthday, the *Colored American* staunchly insisted that M. W. Gibbs's older daughter was five years younger. A nubile, single miss might be a shining star and a distinct social asset, but the luster and appeal of an unmarried woman in her middle years purportedly withered like a rose.

In addition, Ida Gibbs's three closest female associates had surpassed her in public repute. Mollie Church Terrell had become a much-in-demand lecturer, and Anna Julia Cooper had succeeded Robert Terrell as principal of the M Street High School, where for several years she garnered enthusiastic kudos. Hattie Gibbs received plaudits for her musical endeavors, while laudatory articles and her winsome picture often graced the *Colored American*'s pages. It must have been difficult, even for Ida, a hardworking and gracious person, when the women contemporaries nearest and dearest to her so thoroughly eclipsed her in acclaim. Others of her Washington friends also appeared in the "colored" press during those months in rhapsodic paragraphs headed "Orange Blossoms" or "Wedding Bells," but never Ida. A chatty news item even predicted that an up-and-coming lawyer named Napoleon Bonaparte Marshall "will be united in marriage to a Washington Miss some time in June." Hattie Gibbs was Nap Marshall's unnamed sweetheart. But almost fifteen years before, Ida had met the charming but callow fellow whose career she adroitly jump-started, and whom she prodded, cajoled, and otherwise helped mold into a mature and successful gentleman, and she still had an opportunity to play the lead role in a gala matrimonial production of her own design and execution. Further, in 1902 the city's foremost "colored" journal had rued the "alarming growth of color prejudice in Washington," by then a city of 300,000, so Ida may have been ready, willing, even eager to leave town.

Their April wedding would have to be meticulously orchestrated; Ida Alexander Gibbs and William Henry Hunt would never embarrass her family by furtively eloping, as had the ill-fated Alice Moore and Paul Laurence Dunbar. Ida found Mollie's involvement essential in planning her wedding, and Mollie must have been pleased to learn that William had graduated from the same preparatory school as had her husband, Robert.

Associates and family members rallied to Ida's side as she compiled an extensive guest list, decided on the music, refreshments, and tasteful adornment of her home, attendants, and, of course, herself. She ordered, purchased, addressed, stamped, and mailed boxloads of engraved invitations, printed on the finest heavy ivory-colored card stock, in which "Mr. and Mrs. Mifflin W. Gibbs request[ed] the honor of" select relatives', friends', and colleagues' attendance "at the wedding reception of their daughter Ida Alexander." Ida and Hattie also prepared press notices and provided photographs for the *Washington Post, Evening Star,* and *Colored American.*

William Henry Hunt, while respectably and gainfully employed, was little known among the Gibbses' social set, though three years before, the *Colored American* had acknowledged his professional achievements by observing that "the appointment of Mr. Hunt keeps the consulship among the few good places allotted the colored voters." Nonetheless, the upcoming nuptials of Ida and William would be almost exclusively, by, for, and about the bride and her prominent, esteemed, well-heeled family.

Maria Gibbs's health declined precipitously early in 1904, and Ida must have believed that her mother hoped to see her married before she died. M. W. Gibbs prepared to "give away" his older daughter, and to give her an ample check as well. The laudatory *Colored American* noted that "the present of $1,000 to the bride was a repetition of a like gift which he made to both of his daughters a few years ago," and it equaled the amount that Mollie Church Terrell's father had given his daughter when she married. Hattie, of course, served as Ida's maid of honor, while their two young cousins-in-residence and the Terrells' daughter, Phyllis, made an angelic trio of junior bridesmaids. Mollie and six others of Ida's colleagues, who numbered among the city's most accomplished and socially prominent Negro women, were genial hostesses who supplemented the receiving line and "presented . . . hundreds of friends to the bride and groom."

Members of the country's "colored" elite, including P. B. S. Pinchback (who had briefly served as Louisiana's Reconstruction governor and was twice elected, but twice denied, a seat in Congress), George White (North Carolina's former congressman), the newly appointed federal judge Robert Heberton Terrell, the Treasury Department's registrar, the District's recorder of deeds, and local lawyers, physicians, and educators with their families, along with guests from Boston, Chicago, Cincinnati, and Little Rock, all arrived bearing "numerous and costly" gifts. The fawning press noted that Booker T. Washington, a former governor of Massachusetts, "Prince Boris of Bulgaria, ... the Right Honorable Lord [J. P. D.] French" (a British hero of South Africa's recent Boer War), and Joseph Simon Gallieni, Madagascar's governor general, had also received invitations. The latter luminaries could not attend but sent hearty congratulations to the couple, although the presence of the invalid Maria Alexander Gibbs — who had only a brief opportunity earlier that week to meet William Henry Hunt — if indeed her failing health allowed her to participate, was not mentioned. Similarly, the names of Ida's good friends W. E. B. Du Bois and Anna Julia Cooper, as well as those of any of the groom's relatives, were notable only in their absence.

Faith and religion were important to Ida Gibbs, but she maintained no exclusive allegiance to any single Christian denomination. She had been born in British Vancouver, where her family belonged to the Anglican Church, and in Oberlin they had joined the Congregationalists. Through Cooper, Ida had met and probably boarded with the Reverend Alexander Crummell, a Baptist, as were her grandparents. But she also admired the Reverend Francis Grimké (like her late uncle Jonathan Gibbs, he had attended Princeton's seminary), minister of Washington's Fifteenth Street Presbyterian Church, where he shepherded many of the District's "colored four hundred." Reverend Grimké performed the Gibbs-Hunt marriage. Angelina Weld Grimké, an accomplished poet who taught English in the District's "colored" schools, accompanied both her uncle Francis and her canny, outspoken father, Archibald, who came down from Boston. The cerebral Grimké brothers had planted themselves solidly and visibly in the anti–Booker T. Washington camp. Ida may not have realized, or cared, that her affiliations with the Grimkés — not to mention other apostates such as Du Bois and Cooper — might shift her and her family outside the powerful and manipulative Mr. Washington's approved and unfalteringly loyal circle.

Judge Gibbs did not equal Booker T. Washington's singular muscle or renown, but most Negroes, as well as many observant and informed white people, knew his name and admired his acumen and wealth, as well as his noteworthy public achievements. And over the previous decade, Ida Gibbs had become a respected teacher and an outspoken civic activist. So in 1904 the *Colored American,* which had increasingly ignored her as a no longer young, but still unmarried woman, applauded her April wedding as "the most brilliant social function of the season."

As the newlyweds set off for their honeymoon in New York City — where the patriarchal and peripatetic, ever attentive Judge M. W. Gibbs doggedly accompanied them — and then Paris, Ida Alexander Gibbs Hunt's fine education, social and linguistic skills, and firsthand knowledge of the world had thoroughly prepared her for her upcoming life as a diplomat's wife, yet those same factors also made her reluctant to settle for any subservient or compliant conjugal role. If in many ways unconventional, their marriage would always be one of remarkable parity.

Ida filled her commodious steamer trunks with books, magazines, journals, fountain pens and stationery, talcs, brushes, combs, hats and silk parasols, pale linen and organdy frocks for the tropics, as well as precious mementoes such as the pair of gold bracelets given to her by her father, and a small gallery of photographs of friends and family, one of which was signed "Bon Voyage — Your old College Mate — Mollie." Mollie Church Terrell was herself heading off to Berlin for a conference of the International Council of Women, where she delivered her address in exemplary French and German as well as English. The new Mrs. Hunt, of course, also had to relinquish her teaching position, because, as Mrs. Terrell knew so well from her own experience, the "marriage of a woman teacher automatically severed her connection with the school system." While Ida never shut the doors on her past, that spring she opened a whole new chapter in the long, convoluted book of her life.

Yet her loving relatives and colleagues may have wondered: whence came her good-looking, little known, and reportedly much younger husband, William Henry Hunt, a man who not only tolerated and respected but had the wherewithal to adore such a mature, independent, and gifted woman? After a predominantly long-distance friendship that had spanned fifteen years, William and Ida finally wed. She was forty-one, and he was — well, just how old was he?

4

"From Cabin to Consulate"

Billy Hunt's Memory Book

By April 1904, when Ida Alexander Gibbs and William Henry Hunt married, he, like Horatio Alger Jr.'s fictional Harry Walton, had "risen from the ranks" and started along an uncertain path toward success. Hunt claimed to be thirty-four, but like some other assertions about his life prior to their nuptials, that self-declared age diverges a good deal from the unvarnished truth.

William (usually called Billy) Hunt may have read Alger's wildly popular contemporary fiction in his youth, and certainly he should have, because in many ways he embodied the same optimism, opportunism, gumption, and all-American upward mobility that the Alger boys so famously epitomized. Billy's early years, however, were quite unlike Ida's, despite their mutual ties to the Midwest, five siblings, and similarly mixed racial ancestry.

By his own intermittently verifiable accounts, Billy Hunt worked hard as a youngster. He finagled his way out of fixes, struggled to succeed, cultivated useful mentors, and despite many deterrents and detours, remained confident. Horatio Alger wrote, "Youth is hopeful, and can find enjoyment under the most unpropitious circumstances," while Hunt maintained that "the life history of an ordinary boy, youth, and man who always looked for the silver lining in the blackest clouds, is always interesting, whether he made a mess or a success of his limited chances." Though he was a known pedophile in private, Alger publicly authored inspiring formulas for avid young readers. For his part, Hunt artfully crafted, then recounted, his intriguing but obscure "life history" as, step by step, he ventured out into a larger, more complex world than he first foresaw.

A major difference between Horatio Alger's protagonists and Billy Hunt, however, lies in race: Alger's heroes were poor but white. Given the United States' hostile racial history, it is hard to believe that Alger could have envisioned or portrayed his Harry Walton as "colored," or as a bastard. Hunt glossed over his own illegitimate birth, but he was a realist who understood race's economic, legal, and social import, writing in later years that "an American colored youth, however well equipped he may be, often has a . . . slim chance at best in the game of life, and had one infinitely more difficult in those years I am trying to describe."

"From Cabin to Consulate," Hunt's engaging but sometimes disputable memoir, evokes earlier African American rags-to-riches texts with which he would have made himself familiar, by men such as Frederick Douglass, Booker T. Washington, John Mercer Langston, and Mifflin Wistar Gibbs. In his autobiography, Hunt claimed that he was born on June 29, 1869, and several subsequent, albeit brief, accounts of his life have reaffirmed that as the year of his birth. June 29 may be the right date, but he was born, not in 1869, but six years earlier. It is tough, yet hardly impossible, successfully to falsify one's age by that much, but the assertion raises more pertinent questions as to when and why Billy Hunt chose to, or decided that he needed to, reconfigure the truth.

One reason may have been that he, and perhaps his mother too, wanted to eradicate any stigma that society might attach to his unfree and out-of-wedlock nativity. She gave birth to Billy in 1863, in Hunt's Station, Tennessee, a small hamlet located on the Cumberland Plateau's western escarpment just north of the Georgia-Alabama border — and he was born into slavery. Regardless of his or her paternity, under law in all the southern states, any child of a woman held in bondage also was enslaved. Billy never knew the person responsible for his conception, but his pale skin and light eyes gave clear evidence of a primarily Caucasian biological heritage. The main onus for such illegitimacy should have fallen on some predatory man, and in a larger sense on the peculiar institution, but Negro women usually bore the full burden of guilt.

The white Hunts, whom Billy described as proprietors and residents of the nearby "big house," often asserted that their family could trace its roots back to the Reverend Robert Hunt, a member of Captain John Smith's intrepid band who had established the Jamestown Colony in 1607. Other Anglo-Americans with that surname similarly have laid claim to the same revered though contestable lineage. In any event, early in the 1800s, two centuries after the first English colonists reached the place they called Virginia, several yeomen named Hunt, with slaves in tow, arrived in southern Tennessee. In time, Billy wrote, the Hunts' leader in that region came to be considered the "overlord of the county for miles around." William B. Hunt, the white man to whom all evidence points as Billy's biological father, hardly merited "overlord" status, but he nonetheless was a prosperous farmer, and by 1860 the federal census valued his assets at a sizable sixteen thousand dollars.

Billy's mother disclosed, and probably knew, little about her own ancestry. The diverse dislocations generated by slavery make it impossible to discern her African and (possibly) Native American progenitors. And like many disempowered and therefore cautious women of color who bore white men's children, she never shared his white father's identity with her son, but she did provide solid clues as to who he was. Billy, it seems, did not further investigate his paternity. More surprisingly, his memoir never provides his mother's name, though he clearly loved her and lived with her until he was past twenty. Perhaps her illiteracy and former enslavement embarrassed him or represented a hated reality he wanted to expunge, but by 1870 she can be identified in both Nashville's city directory and the United States census as Sophia Hunt. Soon thereafter, Sophia claimed to be the widow of "William Hunt," for whom she, like many more-privileged women, had named her firstborn male child. Most members of the country's white majority believed that marrying any man of their "superior" race was unthinkable for a "colored girl." In most jurisdictions it was also flat-out disallowed both by law and in practice, but except for a different middle initial, Sophia's eldest son always bore his father's full name.

Juxtaposing Billy Hunt's memoir with federal census records, either William B. Hunt or his brother Clinton, who lived on the next farm, had owned Sophia and all but her two youngest children, who were born after 1865. President Abraham Lincoln issued the Emancipation Proclamation in January 1863, six months before Billy's birth, but the decree had limited impact in the eleven slave states that had seceded to form the Confederacy. After the Yankees resecured Tennessee's Mississippi River ports, but not the state's remote midsection, where the Hunts lived, wayward Tennessee pragmatically returned to the Union fold. Its slave owners, however, kept their human chattel for several more years. Very few white southerners saw any reason to free the myriad Negroes whom they considered legal property in order to meet the demands of a president whom they despised, and in many instances refused even to recognize.

William B. Hunt had been married, and by 1860 he had four children by his recently deceased wife. She had died a year or so before, possibly in childbirth, as was often the case in places where medical care was chancy and hard to come by. The time of her death can be approximated by the age of W. B.'s youngest white child, who was less than two years old that summer. W. B., in turn, was fifty, with a sizable farm to manage, a houseful of his motherless offspring, and for the first time in his adult life, no woman with whom to have sexual relations under the respectable shelter of matrimony. But appropriating the services of female slaves for carnal purposes was both common and widely tolerated throughout the South, especially to initiate white youths or to assuage the libidinous hankerings of bachelors or widowers such as W. B. Hunt.

The 1860 southern slave states' census listings of non-free persons include owners' names, and the ages, sex, and sometimes color ("black" or "mulatto") of the people whom they held in bondage, yet rarely stipulate the relationships between or names of those individuals themselves. The record for Franklin County, Tennessee, shows that, with the exception of an infant who was probably Sophia Hunt's first daughter, all of W. B.'s six slaves were male, though his brother Clinton owned a twenty-two-year-old woman. Estimates of slaves' dates of birth were often inaccurate, but that closely conforms with Sophia's age as it appears in later censuses. Just before the Civil War, the white Hunt brothers held fourteen people — eleven males and three females — in bondage on their adjoining farms. The only female Negro of childbearing age at either place apparently was Sophia, and the older enslaved woman living there was probably Sophia's mother, Annekee.

Years later, in his memoir, Billy Hunt made fond mention of Annekee, his beloved maternal grandmother, as well as his older sisters, Elizabeth, Margaret (Maggie), and Frances (Fannie), whom Sophia had borne between 1860 and 1862. After Billy's birth, and after the war, Sophia had two freeborn sons, John and Daniel. The 1870 census labels Sophia "M" for mulatto, and her pale-skinned children suggest that a generation before, some other white man, perhaps an earlier Hunt who had been Annekee's master, or an overseer or neighbor, had sired Sophia.

Together, the Hunt brothers' homesteads included seven hundred acres, and they owned twenty-two horses, seventy cows and cattle, many sheep and swine. As the region's soil became depleted, grains often replaced the cotton that had dominated in the 1820s and '30s, so the Hunts' slaves annually raised several hundred bushels each of wheat, rye, oats, and corn, as well as field peas and Irish and sweet potatoes. Sophia probably tended to the poultry, milked, churned, cleaned, cooked, sewed, and laundered for the "big house," while she cared for her own (mulatto) as well as W. B. Hunt's four older (white) children — and also complied with his sexual demands.

During the Civil War, waves of Union troops rampaged through Franklin County. Neither war (W. B. Hunt was too old to be called up by the draft) nor the ensuing peace curtailed Sophia Hunt's childbearing, but within a few years she left the area, perhaps when W. B. died. In any case, after 1869 she gave birth to no more children. And Sophia was wise to depart. The derelict rural county provided little schooling for its former slaves, only the most arduous, poorly paid work was available to them, and a spate of extralegal hangings — lynchings, in fact — of black youths occurred near Hunt's Station as the egregious Ku Klux Klan swept into the region. Billy recalled that his "attachment to the straggling village and home town was not very deep . . . and therefore no tears were shed on bidding farewell to my birthplace."

Sophia packed up her sons, aged seven, four, and one, and set off for Nashville, Tennessee's capital, eighty miles northwest. She and the boys first appear there in 1870, so Billy would not have remembered Franklin County at all if, as he maintained, he had been born just the previous year. His grandmother, Annekee, and his oldest sister, Elizabeth, he wrote, died around that time, and the two surviving girls, Fannie and Maggie, though still quite young, moved elsewhere to work for white families as maids, cooks, or laundresses. Of all the siblings, Billy claimed years later in his memoir (though perhaps incorrectly), Fannie alone had children and grandchildren.

In Nashville, at an inn called the Sumner House, Sophia Hunt engaged in much the same labor that she had performed in slavery. She and her boys boarded with Charlotte Sumner (other members of her white family lived nearby), a widow in whose home the 1870 census lists Sophia as a servant. Four other African Americans, two women and their children, dwelled there as well. Those Negroes — poor, illiterate, and prepared for little else — probably cleaned the Sumners' residences, and laundered clothes and linens for the white clan and their commercial ventures.

Billy entered a classroom only briefly, first at the McKee School, whose strict principal-teacher, a member of Nashville's starchy "colored" gentry whose "ever-ready rattan cane" Billy never forgot, then at the Bellevue Academy, run by a transplanted white New Englander who became his enthusiastic booster. Billy wrote that "she spared no pains to encourage me with my studies" and recalled "the thrill I experienced when I commenced to read and write and cipher." But unlike many former slaves, he added, Christianity gave him no comfort, because he insisted that he never even saw a Bible until he was much older. Yet he became swept up in Reconstruction's optimism and hungered for an education, even though his white father had not acknowledged, supported, or motivated him, his mother could not read or write at all, and even among Nashville's poorest Negroes, he was so ragged that classmates, he said, ridiculed him. Billy probably had no personal contacts with nearby Fisk University's more fortunate African Americans, most of them former slaves as well, who studied at that acclaimed new school to become their struggling community's educators, ministers, medical practitioners, and lawyers.

Soon, however, Sophia had to tell her eldest son that she "found it quite impossible to keep the 'home pot boiling' on her meagre earnings, and that [as] I was the 'man of the family,' I must leave school and start on the hunt for a job." Billy felt numb: "It was like passing sentence on my hopes and aspirations and the memory of it remains as the unhappiest incident of my boyhood." Around the age of ten, he therefore grudgingly set schooling aside and turned to full-time employment.

On one early job, Billy marched around town bearing a placard for the "Great Magician Heller," but that ended when some "gay blades . . . on mischief bent" covered two letters on the billboard so that it read: "Go To Hell[ ] To-night and See Wonders." Heller "did not see the joke at all, and discharged me at once," Billy recalled, but he found new work and learned to cook with Cal, a fondly remembered chef at "Frau and Herr Dornbusch's" restaurant. During those years he also remembered watching in horror the hanging of a Negro named Bill Kelly (who, wrote Billy Hunt, had been summarily tried and condemned to death following trumped-up charges of raping a white woman), and hitching a ride with a charismatic stranger who, he insisted, was the legendary desperado Jesse James. But hard labor more than anything defined Billy's childhood. Moving on from Cal's tutelage, he toiled as a janitor in a series of saloons.

Then he went to work as a "night porter and handy man in a gambling house [for] 'Spot' McCarthy, a well known sportsman and breeder of race horses," who introduced him to "life on the race tracks." Whether that actually happened is unknown, but Billy did become an accomplished equestrian. "After biting the dust many times," he wrote, "we . . . learned to stick in the saddle, and were eventually allowed the much coveted privilege of exercising the high steppers over the track at day break." "In a year or so," he continued, "I blossomed out as a fairly good jockey, . . . mounting in quite a number of flat, hurdle, and steeple chase events." Among his most "intimate comrades," he claimed the great Isaac Murphy, who captured the roses at several Kentucky Derbies, and Link Jones, another celebrated black rider who proudly wore the silks in those years before members of their race were brusquely expelled from the sport of kings.

Billy Hunt hoped to gain fame and fortune as a jockey until he witnessed a spat between two trainers that spiraled out of control. The stronger man "knocked the other down . . . pinioned the poor chap's arms under his knees, then with an inconceivable calmness, drew out a knife and cold-bloodedly cut his rival's throat from ear to ear." The authorities did not investigate, but Billy "could not banish that tragedy from my memory." Concluding "that life was considered too cheap in such surroundings," he sought other career paths, but his love of riding never flagged.

The nagging problem with those gritty and animated horse tales is that, like a number of others from Billy Hunt's youth, they cannot be substantiated. No one resembling "Spot" McCarthy appears in Nashville's annual directories, nor do the famous aforementioned jockeys, although they may well have passed through Tennessee's capital city as they galloped around the southern racing circuit. Perhaps his colorful stories were true, but some of them may instead represent Billy's later-in-life attempts to embellish and dramatize his arduous and dreary youth.

It seems inarguable, however, that Billy had little money or idle time. He had few buddies, which he credited with keeping him out of trouble, but such was not the case for his brother John, who began consorting with an unsavory crowd. In an effort to realign the trajectory of his life, Billy wrote, John was apprenticed to and moved in with a white bachelor named Lewis Winters, who "had no children, and was attracted to John." Winters claimed that he wanted to "adopt" the boy and send him on to college one day, but Billy also remembered that "for some reason, John and his new Papa did not hit it off very well." Young John Hunt, Billy added, vented his fury by torturing and then ruthlessly garotting Winters's "favorite cat and dog." One can only wonder what favors "Papa" Winters (like Horatio Alger, perhaps) may have demanded in return for his supposed benevolence toward a handsome but fatherless and already troubled "colored" youth.

The Hunts extricated John from Lewis Winters's command, and in 1883 they moved on to St. Louis, Missouri, to live near Billy's sister Fannie. There, Sophia Hunt, identified as a laundress, specifically called herself William Hunt's "widow" in an apparent attempt to garner a modicum of respectability for herself and her children. The ploy gained new urgency when Fannie got Billy a job in "a house of ill fame, operated by a well known harlot." Loathing that sordid "moral and social environment," he soon found other work as a janitor at a railroad depot. With his vulnerable, illiterate family and servile employment, Billy might have observed from a distance but had no social intercourse with the more successful members of St. Louis's small, middle-class African American community.

Sophia Hunt died a year or two later, thus at twenty-one (though he later insisted he was orphaned at fifteen), Billy wrote, it "devolved upon me to look after my brothers the best I knew how." He had almost no education, but his amiability and robust ambition served him well. His memoir claims that he soon gained "the esteem, and in some instances, the friendship of . . . the oldest and most prominent [white] families in the city." He further asserted that he became involved in politics, even being selected as "a delegate to the Republican State Convention from my Ward." If true, his political activity proves that Billy had reached his majority (twenty-one) by that time. That also, he wrote, was when "the *Wanderlust* claimed me for its very own." Like many other "colored" men, Billy Hunt found work "wielding the broom, scrub brush, bucket, mop and feather duster, and spreading sheets for 'Uncle George'" (George Mortimer Pullman, the railroad mogul) as a sleeping car porter shuttling around the Midwest. Those jobs, created in conjunction with the demands of burgeoning post–Civil War long-distance rail travel, were allocated to former slaves, who purportedly were best suited for such service. But Hunt soon decided that such an occupation never would get "me where I wanted to go."

Billy Hunt spun a truly wondrous tale about the next chapter of his life. In 1886, when he said he was a mere seventeen, he secured a porter's job at the Lindell, one of St. Louis's finest hotels. There he met a recent honors graduate (in contrast to most of the other characters who populate Hunt's stories, this fellow remains nameless) of the city's renowned Washington University who had contracted tuberculosis and did not have long to live. In the little time left to him, "Mr. X" yearned to travel, especially to Siam (now Thailand), where his uncle served as the United States minister — until 1893 the country's topmost designation for any American diplomat serving overseas. Because he was so ill, the young man, whose affluent family resided at the Lindell, needed a traveling companion, and chose Hunt. Even Hunt conceded his saga's pre-posterousness and admitted that what "staggered me beyond all else, was the responsibility entrusted to the discretion of a youth as unsophisticated as I was at that time." With limitless funds, unqualified support from his sponsor's parents, and their instructions to "indulge every whim and fancy of my companion," the two of them, Billy Hunt later claimed, started out to see the world. If this account is true, he also negligently abandoned his orphaned and vulnerable younger brother, Daniel.

Hunt offers many improbable details about the ensuing interval. According to his tale, they set off by rail early in 1887, headed to Vancouver (a telling, if dubious, link to Ida Gibbs's childhood), where they boarded the SS *Empress of Japan*. This is one of the first and most easily refutable components of his account, since the *Empress of Japan* took its maiden voyage only in April 1891. If the youths made any Pacific Ocean crossing at all, that was not their ship.

They supposedly sailed to and spent several weeks in the Sandwich (soon the Hawaiian) Islands, then journeyed on to Japan, where Billy's descriptions of Mount Fuji, he freely admitted, closely resembled the scenes on commercial picture postcards. He further claimed that, until this juncture, Gilbert and Sullivan's *The Mikado* had shaped his mental images of Japan, but it seems unlikely that a struggling, uneducated hotel bellman in the Midwest would have been familiar with an operetta that had premiered in London only two years before — although it did play in a select few American cities in 1886. The peripatetic pair, Billy Hunt continued, went from Japan to Korea and China, then on to bask at length in Hong Kong's "slothful atmosphere."

Their next and primary port of call was said to have been Bangkok, imperial city of Siam, widely known at that time as the "Kingdom of the White Elephant." Once ashore, the travelers "entered a luxurious carriage which conveyed us to the Legation where we were comfortably lodged beneath the Stars and Stripes." Hunt described the "gala dinner" organized and staged by their gracious and welcoming host, the minister (Jacob T. Child, supposedly his companion's uncle, though Hunt's manuscript never gives his name either), which he and his young employer attended. On that magnificent ceremonial occasion, Hunt contended, Child's illustrious guests included both members of the Siamese royal family and the top diplomatic envoys from Europe.

In 1892 Jacob Child published a memoir, *The Pearl of Asia: Reminiscences of the Court of a Supreme Monarch, or Five Years in Siam*. The book provides profuse details about his official and social life in Bangkok, some of them much like those in Hunt's travelogue, but it makes no mention of a four-month visit from Child's only beloved nephew — if, indeed, he had one. But *The Pearl of Asia* could have provided Hunt with useful specifics about the minister's quarters and activities which he later included in his own account. He also confessed that "the data which I gathered about Siam certainly could be found in any public library," adding that he never "dream[ed] that I would some day enter the Foreign Service of my country."

If Hunt's story were true, this link to Jacob Child should provide clues to his companion's identity, and Minister Child was indeed a Missourian who had one brother. Although several people with that surname lived in St. Louis at the time, none of them fit the many intricate criteria that Hunt laid out for his "friend's" family. And no one at all named Child graduated from Washington University during the period in question. His unidentified travel mate could have been related to his "uncle," Minister Child, through the envoy's wife, and if so, he would have had a different surname. So that alone provides no definitive proof that Billy Hunt created his narrative out of whole cloth, but he did suggestively characterize the entire trip as "a veritable phantasmagoria."

Hunt continued his saga with reports of their exploits in French Indo-China, Singapore, Java, and Borneo, followed by more than a month in "British India" and Ceylon. He and his consumptive "beloved companion," Hunt later wrote, sailed the Indian Ocean to Aden, crossed the Red Sea, slipped through the Suez Canal, then boarded a train bound for Cairo, where they supposedly booked for several weeks at the fabled, and therefore widely photographed and chronicled, Shepherd's Hotel. From there, they journeyed to Jerusalem. Hunt's account of their evening by the river Jordan is a notably romantic vignette in his long, often novelistic memoir:

> We dined together under the big tent, one side of which was raised so that we could see the wild countryside by moon light. It was a beautiful night and a deep silence pervaded the land, broken only by the cries of the jackals. When we had finished dinner, the night had grown cooler and the boys lighted a big fire around which we were all seated, when suddenly the silence was broken by a band of some twenty Bedouins who wished to entertain us with some of their folk songs and war dances which lasted until a late hour.

From Syria the pair headed off to Greece, since Hunt's co-voyager purportedly had been a classics major in college. They toured Cyprus, Crete, and Rhodes, circled the Cyclades, and sailed on to Malta and Italy. Then they meandered through Switzerland, Hungary, and Austria — a "dreamland of waltz and song." Exquisite Paris followed, and in his nostalgic account, Hunt mused, "[N]ot in my wildest dreams did it ever occur to me that in later years I was destined to live in France." They continued by rail to Belgium and the Netherlands, ferried across the English Channel to Gravesend, then relaxed in London for weeks on end. No tour of England, of course, would be complete without paying a lengthy tribute to the Bard at Stratford-upon-Avon. The travelers eased their way north to Edinburgh (as a deft fabulist, might Hunt have recalled that city's Sir Walter Scott's familiar couplet, "Oh, what a tangled web we weave/When first we practice to deceive"?) and hence on to Ireland to kiss the Blarney Stone, before sailing the Atlantic Ocean west to the United States.

A further example of the unreliability of Billy Hunt's story lies in his assertion that he and his mentor returned to New York from Southampton on the SS *Baltic*. According to his timeline, that would have been in autumn of 1888. First, the *Baltic* always sailed from Liverpool, not Southampton, yet an error such as that could have been due to faulty memory. But all that year the ship never once docked in New York. To give him further benefit of the doubt, perhaps they traveled a year or two earlier than he recalled, but the passenger lists for the ship's many arrivals in 1886 and 1887 reveal no Mr. Hunt with a remotely similar age, first name, or initials on any of the SS *Baltic*'s meticulous rosters — and no one with the surname Child arrived on that liner at all.

Could Hunt's epic have been just a strategic figment of his imagination? Another reason to believe so is that his name appears in the St. Louis city directory through 1887, and the next year in the Minneapolis directory. Such listings, though hardly infallible, are more apt to overlook those who are present than include those who are absent. One more clue suggesting a concerted deception is that at some point Hunt altered his age. Even he admitted that it seemed unlikely for an affluent white family blithely to send off their only, dying, tubercular son with an uneducated, "colored" seventeen-year-old hotel porter whom they scarcely knew. By 1887, however, Hunt was no teenager, but well into his twenties, so one aspect of his convoluted story belies another.

He carefully explained, and rightly so, that United States citizens often did not need passports at the time, and indeed, a survey of those records from the mid-1880s yielded no such document issued to a William, W. H., Bill, or Billy Hunt. Further smudging his tracks, he added that his anonymous benefactor died (Hunt mournfully claimed that he was "unable to reach his bedside in time to give him my last embrace") not long after their supposed return to St. Louis.

Can all of this apparent disinformation be racked up to Hunt's advanced age and murky recollections when he compiled his splendid book of memories? It's possible, yet unlikely. It is more critical to determine how, when, and especially why he chose to create such an untraceable tale that would be embroidered over time and repeated so often, perhaps, that even its creator came to believe it. Jacob Child's published account of his ministry in Siam may have provided details and substance. Billy Hunt's global travels and career, starting in 1898, gave his stories credence, and the countless picture postcards he preserved from around the world offered him similar images of scenic splendors and tourist attractions. Throughout the ensuing years he must have embellished, refined, and retold this saga many times over for relatives, friends, and wide-eyed youngsters. It was a glorious and engaging adventure in which Billy starred as the picaresque hero. Even if not a single scrap of it ever happened, it provided endless magical entertainment for his rapt listeners. And in truth, who did (and does) such a marvelous fiction really harm?

In a letter written in the 1890s, Billy Hunt revealed his fascination with the late 1700s Baron Friedrich Hieronymous von Munchausen, whose name became synonymous with preposterous sagas cunningly told, and certainly the crafty, trickster storyteller looms large in folklore throughout the African diaspora. But the specific genesis of Hunt's narrative may in fact be found in one of the late nineteenth century's most popular tales, Jules Verne's *Around the World in Eighty Days*. That charming fantasy, published in French in 1872 and in English the following year, enjoyed a wide audience in the United States. In *Around the World,* Phileas Fogg, a wealthy, adventurous Englishman, circles the globe accompanied by his intrepid, loyal servant, Passepartout, a man, like Hunt, of ambiguous race and shadowy origins. Such a tale would have appealed to and provided the inspirational magic carpet for an ambitious and inventive travel-smitten young reader such as Billy Hunt. Unlike the fictional Fogg and Passepartout, Billy Hunt and his anonymous friend probably did not circumnavigate the globe at all, yet Hunt most assuredly did so, as Verne wrote about Fogg's travels, "in the spirit."

The trip that Hunt lovingly described supposedly spanned nearly two years, not eighty days. Verne's daring duo "employed every means of conveyance — steamers, railways, carriages, yachts, trading-vessels, sledges, elephants." Hunt's purported travels lacked the sledges and elephant rides (though he did claim to have fed sugarcane to Bangkok's legendary albino pachyderms), but he cited rickshaws, gondolas, mules, camels, and other modes of transportation precisely like those of Verne's adventurers.

Yet how could Billy hope to get away with such a labyrinthine fabrication? Actually, it would have been easy. His mother, oldest sister, and brother John had passed away. Best estimates indicated by the year when John Hunt's name disappears from the St. Louis city directory suggest that he died — Billy blamed a smallpox outbreak — in 1887. His surviving sisters were absent from his life at that point, Fannie having married a man surnamed Murray and moved to Colorado, while his brother Daniel vanishes altogether from the memoir. A "white" farmer named Daniel P. Hunt (married with one son), however, born the same year as Billy's youngest sibling, appears in the 1900 federal census, living in Tennessee. Nothing guarantees it, but that Daniel Hunt probably was Billy's youngest brother, who permanently and irrevocably passed over into the white world, at which time he severed all links to his "colored" family, as did a good number of light-skinned Negroes who sought to avoid segregation and the many other ugly vicissitudes of race prejudice. As for Billy himself, by 1888 he had left St. Louis for good, so no neighbor, colleague, or former employer there could attest either to his actual age or to previous experiences — or question the veracity of such a splendid journey.

Soon after that unlikely mystery tour, Billy relocated northward up the Mississippi River to Minneapolis, where despite the absence of rigid segregation, he had little opportunity but to continue his menial and perhaps futureless employment. The city directories confirm that he worked and lived at the West Hotel, which advertised itself as the "Most Magnificent Hotel in the World." At that point, if his account in this instance can be believed, he used his energy, wits, and charm to ingratiate and involve himself with members of Minnesota's Republican Party.

In 1889 some politicians in the Twin Cities invited Judge Mifflin Wistar Gibbs to speak there, and Hattie Gibbs, newly graduated from Oberlin, came at the same time to give a concert. Newspapers confirm that Ida Gibbs joined them there, so one chance meeting that autumn altered forever the course of Billy Hunt's life. In contrast to his intricate account of a probably fictitious odyssey, Hunt's assertion that he first met Ida Gibbs in Minnesota can easily be corroborated, yet he shrugged off that pivotal encounter with but a single line in his memoir, saying only, "[D]uring my residence in the Northwest, I [met] Ida at a party in St. Paul."

Billy was a bright, handsome, and engaging survivor, but he was also uneducated, while Ida was clearly affluent, and one of barely a dozen Negro women in the entire country who had earned four-year college degrees. The Gibbs ladies were elegant, well dressed, and well traveled, and they were headed to Paris, the world's most fascinating city. How they must have dazzled Billy Hunt, and how he must have yearned to impress them! On the Pullman cars, and in the hotels where he worked in St. Louis and Minneapolis, he had encountered a number of wealthy and sophisticated white women, but his late mother and surviving sisters were nearly penniless, naive, and scarcely literate. He never had known (yet surely might have dreamed of) "colored" women such as these. Flat-out moonstruck, the ambitious young man responded in several ways.

To impress Ida and Hattie Gibbs, Billy Hunt most likely conjured up a vestigial and untraceable curriculum vita in which, like them, he too became a world traveler. Once he had added that shrewdly contrived, embryonic fiction to his "résumé," he stuck (and was stuck) with it. He also vowed to keep in touch with the Gibbses, and did so. Lastly, as much as they relished and valued their education, Billy knew that if he was going to progress beyond his lowly origins and have a chance to woo and win a lass such as Ida Gibbs, he must return to school. She and Hattie probably urged him to do just that. He had enjoyed classroom learning during his onerous early years and believed he was capable of much more. Billy Hunt was enterprising as well, and contended that "the school-maggot was constantly giving loose rein to my imagination."

Hunt may have asked himself how, at twenty-six, his true age in 1889, he might convince anyone to help him resume his formal education. But with members of his family deceased or at a convenient distance, and no birth certificate or Social Security credentials to blow his cover, he could remake himself into a much younger lad — with little chance of discovery. Six years may have been a stretch, but it seemed doable. Instead of 1863, his actual year of birth, the youthful-looking Hunt claimed, and always thereafter reaffirmed, that he had been born in 1869, though the Gibbses surely knew better. At twenty-seven, Ida Gibbs would hardly have entertained romantic notions about a callow youth that much her junior, and in fact she may have been the first one to suggest the pragmatic age adjustment. Her mother, Maria Alexander, seems to have similarly moved up her own birth date by eight years when she entered Oberlin in 1852. So virtually overnight, Billy Hunt became a rejuvenated nineteen- or twenty-year-old eagerly seeking an education. Assuming Ida knew that she and he were about the same age (a mere seven months actually separated them), she forever thereafter guarded his secret and, reluctantly or not, suppressed her own vanity and reconciled herself later in life to being seen as the considerably older wife of a vibrant, attractive man who, at least in the public eye, was seven years her junior.

After the Gibbses left Minnesota, Hunt described yet another journey (one that, though undocumented, probably did take place), from Minneapolis through the Canadian Northwest and back. For that venture he worked as a porter in an elegant private coach on the Canadian Pacific Railroad. Sir William Van Horne, the railway's president, Hunt asserted, hosted the excursion.

Following that jaunt, Sir William reportedly rewarded Billy Hunt with a letter of recommendation through which he was reemployed as a Pullman porter. On one of his very next trips, Hunt waited on and met Alfred Oren Tower, the headmaster of Lawrence Academy, a respected, century-old New England preparatory school. After Hunt had "explained fully my situation economically and otherwise" to the benevolent educator, he was admitted to the school, granted a scholarship, and provided a place to live and work with "one of the prominent families" in Groton, Massachusetts. He wrote that he entered Lawrence in the fall of 1890, but school records suggest it was a semester, or even more, earlier. Hunt admitted that he was older than any of the other students in his class ("those boys and girls," he later insisted, "had never come in contact with a classmate my age"), yet most likely passed himself off as no more than twenty.

During the ensuing years he lived with Michael Sheedy, the Irish American owner of a successful general store, his wife, and their children. For decades afterward, Hunt stayed in close touch with the Sheedys, whom he came to consider his adoptive parents. Every weekday he rose "with the lark," fed, watered, and curried the horses, cleaned the stables, drove his proprietor to work in the buggy, and then returned home, all before trudging off for morning classes. At first, he took his meals in the kitchen, but soon the family invited him to join them in the dining room, over the protests of their white housemaid, who "heard it said that I had colored blood in my veins." That woman, he explained, "had been frightened by a black man once when a little girl; which was enough to prejudice [her] against the race for all time," but even she finally came to accept him.

Billy Hunt was the only African American at Lawrence Academy at that juncture, but a decade earlier Robert Heberton Terrell (who later described Lawrence as "a place where we were taught to think for ourselves and where our ambitions and aspirations began to sprout wings and grow") had been the school's first graduate of his race. Terrell headed from there straight on to Harvard College, then to Washington, D.C., where he completed Howard Law School, taught, and in 1891 married Ida Gibbs's best friend, Mollie Church. Another black youth, John E. W. Thompson, followed Terrell at Lawrence, finishing in 1883. He went on to Yale Medical College, and soon became a United States consul in Haiti. Despite having no other "colored" youngsters or teachers around as friends or mentors, the light-complexioned Billy Hunt said that he faced little race prejudice at the school itself, or in the town of Groton.

During several of those summers Billy worked on a nearby farm, and then for a wholesale grocer in Boston. In that city, for the first time except for his brief encounter with the Gibbses, he met several members of the more comfortably situated Negro intelligentsia, among them the brilliant Harvard PhD candidate W. E. B. Du Bois and the activist, politically independent attorney Archibald H. Grimké, who often lectured about diverse people of color in their global contexts. Just as Hunt very belatedly finished secondary school in 1894, President Grover Cleveland appointed Grimké to head the United States diplomatic legation in Santo Domingo.

Billy Hunt became a hero at Lawrence Academy when, one rainy night, he mounted the Sheedys' horse, rode to summon a doctor, and thus helped save the life of Headmaster Tower's critically ill son. He succeeded scholastically in the "classical course," became an editor of the school newspaper, and won a few debate prizes. The subject of his oratory, Massachusetts's late Senator Charles Sumner (was it mere coincidence that the Hunt family had lived in Nashville with a woman named Charlotte Sumner?), a staunch champion of Negroes' rights during Reconstruction, suggests Billy Hunt's knowledge of and even pride in his African American heritage.

He also observed a number of disparities between his own middle-class, coeducational institution and the nearby all-male "swanky and aristocratic Groton School." Hunt maintained that, as a result of the two academies' proximity, he came to know several of Groton's "Economic Royalists" (as he called them), including Theodore and Franklin Delano Roosevelt, both future presidents of the United States. That assertion, however, is yet another instance of Hunt's attempts to embellish his life story by claiming to have rubbed shoulders with members of the powerful upper class, because Teddy Roosevelt left Groton for Harvard in 1876, while FDR arrived there only in 1896, two years after Hunt had moved on from Lawrence Academy.

After four or more years, Hunt graduated at age thirty-one. His only regret, he said, was that no family members were present to share his success.

He garnered a scholarship, and matriculated in fall 1894 at western Massachusetts's Williams College. As a member of the "Little Ivy League," Williams was among the United States' finest institutions of higher learning. Few Americans had the means, opportunity, and preparation needed to attend such a school, and again Hunt was his class's sole Negro. (The two "colored" men enrolled concurrently with Hunt belonged to the class of 1897.) Three years before, Gaius Charles Bolin had become Williams's first black graduate. Gaius was followed at Williams by his brother Livingsworth Bolin; George Lightfoot, later a Howard University professor; and Edward Everett Wilson, another attorney and a gifted essayist who penned minor classics of journalistic satire such as "The Joys of Being a Negro" (1906) for the *Atlantic Monthly.*

Although the Sheedys and Headmaster Tower had urged him to do so, Hunt went to Williams only reluctantly, fearing that it might already be too late. "On completion of the four year's college course," he rationalized, "I would have grown too old to spend the supplementary years preparing for a professional career," and an unfortunate encounter soon reinforced his apprehension. "Before I had a chance to hear President [Franklin] Carter's address of welcome to the Freshman Class," Hunt claimed, "I ran squarely into the hydra monster, race prejudice, for the first time since I was old enough to feel its sting." The registrar had assigned him to share dormitory quarters with a student named Thorpe, who "got wind of the fact that his room-mate belonged to the colored race [and] became alarmed at the possibility of being contaminated." Thorpe, Hunt added, left Williams "without a word of explanation." The faculty secretary, Eben Parsons — amusingly, given his pious surname, a former chaplain with the U.S. Colored Troops during the Civil War — summoned Hunt to his office and "hauled me over the coals because I did not report that I was colored." Hunt protested that he "hadn't the remotest idea that such a step was obligatory in a New England college." Such mix-ups reconfirm how his pale complexion could flummox white people. Hunt added that his anger never abated, since "by his lack of Christian charity, intelligence and tact, [Parsons] missed an excellent opportunity to show some back bone and measure up to his position, instead of showing himself nothing but an old duffer." As a result, "I cordially detested everything connected with Williams." Before classes even started, he mourned, "I no longer heard the song of the Sirens."

Three documents verify Billy Hunt's attendance at Williams, and suggest that others there may have felt as uncomfortable with him as he himself did at the college. First, he appears in a freshman class photo wearing a jaunty cap, positioned at the group's edge, angled slightly away from his classmates. Despite the aloofness that his posture suggests, his skin seems no darker and his features no more typically Negroid than those of the nearby white students. Second, his name is included on a roster of thirty "sometime members" from the class of 1898. Third, a "Freshman Editorial" in the 1894–95 yearbook includes a bizarre and uncharacteristic anecdote that targets Billy Hunt for his inappropriate behavior. "It is to be noted that [among the freshmen] there are a number . . . who have abnormally large heads," the curious tale begins:

> If Hunt could be made to realize that he was not a Senior and was progressing too rapidly to insure permanent success, it would be a fine thing for the class. Such officiousness as he assumed at the Sophomore-Freshman foot-ball game, when he waved a stick in the faces of Professors, Seniors and Juniors, and shouted in tones more repulsive than persuasive, "Keep back!" created an impression that his condition should be regarded by his class with remorse, [and] by others with pity and anxiety.

Williams's lowly freshmen were *not* supposed to accost professors or upperclassmen! The editorial concludes on a cautionary note, pontificating for all the novices' benefit: "What you are as Sophomores depends upon your conduct this year. . . . Meekness has a rich reward. Humility this year reveals the heavenly lights of the remaining years of your course." Billy Hunt, it seems, had neither the "meekness" nor the "humility" needed to allow the college's "heavenly lights" successfully to illuminate him. The only other misfit from the class of 1898 similarly singled out for censure in that same acerbic yearbook account soon left Williams altogether.

Yet Williams College did have a high rate of attrition. Fifty-eight students appear in the freshman picture taken in 1894 or 1895, but the "sometime members" list suggests that thirty youths from the original class of 1898 did not graduate on time. A tenth reunion snapshot found among Billy Hunt's correspondence shows twenty-eight "alumni," but even if it includes several nongraduates, less than half of their entering class (all of them white, except Hunt, and most from privileged backgrounds) stayed straight on through the predetermined four years. Since Hunt received and saved that reunion picture, he must have kept in touch with at least a few of his onetime classmates, despite his wretched and abbreviated college experience. So he left Williams for reasons of his own, generated by insensitivity at least or institutional racism at worst, though he later chastised himself by saying, "I have realized since then that it bordered upon stupidity to be so thin-skinned about such a trifling thing as racial discrimination." Attempting to participate in undergraduate athletics, he wrote, also made him painfully aware of his comparatively advanced age, but he collected his academic credits for two semesters before deciding that it was "impossible to attempt to stick it out three years longer."

Six years before, he had most likely promised the Gibbs ladies that he would acquire an education, and to some extent he had fulfilled that vow. But at thirty-two, he not only despised Williams but was restless in those bucolic surroundings with fellows who were at least a decade younger than he. He was anxious to get on with the serious business of his adult life and career. More advantageous opportunities, he believed, awaited him in cosmopolitan New York City.

The only person whom Hunt recalled fondly at Williams College was the school's rector, Theodore Sedgwick. Since Hunt knew no one at all in the New York metropolitan area (save his recently married sister Maggie, whose husband, Dallas Hughes, was a genial if uninfluential Pullman car porter), Sedgwick wrote him a letter of introduction to Frank Nelson, an assistant minister at the renowned St. George's Episcopal Church on Manhattan's Stuyvesant Square. Reverend Nelson, in turn, found him solid though menial work at the laboratory of a white man named William Jay Schieffelin, a successful manufacturer, importer, and wholesaler, trustee of Booker T. Washington's Tuskegee Institute, and later a commissioned army officer who helped to command a black regiment during the Great War. At that facility Hunt established a cordial relationship, which later would be renewed, with Schieffelin himself. He also learned a little bit about industrial chemistry, but quickly decided — much as he had rejected remaining a railroad porter like his brother-in-law — that "there was no future for me in a job like that."

He joined and soon became secretary of St. George's men's Bible class, a group whose membership included a number of the city's immigrants and poorer citizens, but also a few of its financial and political moguls. Its leader was the prominent mayor of Brooklyn, which at the time was still an autonomous political entity. Speakers such as New York's police commissioner, Theodore Roosevelt, often attended those gatherings, and Hunt came in contact with the church's senior lay warden, J. Pierpont Morgan, one of the world's wealthiest bankers. In the mostly white, lower Manhattan neighborhood where Billy Hunt lived (most likely without revealing his full racial identity), worshipped, and worked, he contended that he crossed paths with the notorious radical Leon Trotsky. But Trotsky did not, in fact, reside in the city until a number of years later.

St. George's solicitous Reverend Nelson believed that Hunt was honest, hardworking, and ambitious. He therefore helped get him another, very different job as a messenger with a Wall Street brokerage firm, where, Hunt boasted, he "became a more or less familiar fixture among the Bulls, Bears, and Lambs frequenting Mssrs. Price, McCormick's 'ticker room.'" Price and McCormick, Hunt recalled, "in addition to their strictly stock-brokerage business, also were large cotton brokers." One day he had to deliver a packet of cotton samples to the offices of the Greek consul. "It was the first time," he wrote decades later, "I had ever heard tell of a Consul or a Consular Office" — a dubious assertion for someone who claimed to have spent months residing in the official quarters of the American minister to Siam. Hunt also had graduated from the same preparatory school as one Negro consul, John Thompson, and in Boston he came to know another, Archibald Grimké. Yet at that point, he dramatically added, "I naively whispered sotto voce that I would like to be a Consul myself, in fact, decided I would become one. But how?"

Hunt must have been aware that throughout the country black people's circumstances were drastically worsening in the wake of the Supreme Court's devastating 1896 *Plessy v. Ferguson* decision that sanctioned state-sponsored racial segregation. And although he had acquired an education superior to that of most whites and resided in "progressive" New York City, as a "colored" man in his mid-thirties, he really was just spinning his wheels with little chance for advancement as a Wall Street underling. Many white Americans perceived and treated all Negroes as little more than cogs in an undifferentiated, perpetually inferior caste, despite obvious variants in their circumstances and abilities. So Hunt faced a profound dilemma. His ambitions notwithstanding, he hesitated to reinvent himself and permanently pass over into the white world, a chancy move that would force him to disavow a major portion of his identity. It might uncouple him from his sisters, as well as useful, admired friends such as the Gibbses. He was becoming increasingly impatient, however, and eager for more tangible success than hard work and destiny thus far had allotted him. But at that juncture, fate (with an undeniably sharp nudge) intervened.

Several months after William McKinley's 1897 inauguration, Billy Hunt claimed many years hence, "when the time arrived . . . for passing out the spoils of office to faithful henchmen, the President appointed Judge Mifflin W.

Gibbs of Arkansas to be Consul of the United States to Madagascar." "When I learned of his appointment," he added, "it was jokingly suggested that [Ida Gibbs] approach her father with reference to the possibility of taking me along as his . . . clerk." M. W. Gibbs received numerous "applications for the post [but] his daughter's intervention outweighed all others, and the new Consul's choice fell on me."

Billy never conceded the connection, but Ida's appeal to her father must have gained credence by emphasizing the international odyssey that he probably had first formulated in 1889 to impress her with his worldliness. Otherwise, what in his background as an apprentice groom and jockey, saloon flunky, Pullman car porter, bellman, grocer's assistant, and Wall Street messenger qualified him even for a minor consular position? Billy acknowledged that he "had no previous experience to fit me for such a career," but would have highlighted his Massachusetts education, including a year at Williams College, and of course his Republican Party affiliations and loyalty.

Mifflin Wistar Gibbs knew little about William Henry Hunt, and much of that may have been fabricated. Gibbs also probably asked him few questions as they prepared to depart. But through his correspondence with the judge's daughter and a scrupulous perusal of newspapers, Hunt had learned far more about his new patron and mentor. He had saved a bit of money, but not enough to take him halfway around the world (a trip that was not yet authorized and never would be reimbursed by the State Department), so he negotiated a loan from his employer, which he used to buy a ticket as a steerage passenger bound, ultimately, for Madagascar. "Thus," Hunt wrote, "all barriers were swept aside and everything was all set for the long journey."

At that point, a bizarre stroke of luck may have spared both Billy Hunt and Judge Gibbs. They first tried, but failed, to book passage on the overcrowded SS *La Bourgogne,* which, Hunt wrote, "met disaster in mid-ocean." That vessel collided with another in the Atlantic, resulting in the loss of fifty lives. Instead, they soon departed on *La Champagne,* its sister ship, "of the same line," wrote Billy, "being firm in the belief that lightning never strikes twice in the same spot."

The distance and differences between a life as lived and that life as remembered and later reported can be vast. Many people whom he encountered over the years most likely heard about Hunt's earlier globe-circling journey, a trip that probably began as a wishful fantasy but soon evolved into a useful, even an imperative account. And though he represented himself as a man in his late twenties, he really was thirty-five. At any moment, an errant wave could have swept away his wondrous and elaborate sand castles, yet somehow they survived. In time, his fantastic tales — an audacious "colored" man's risky instruments of sustenance and enhancement — may have become his own reality. As V. I. Lenin famously asserted: "A lie told often enough becomes truth."

Hunt thus embarked on the first leg of a splendid adventure that in time made him, like Ida and Hattie Gibbs, a verifiable world traveler. Starting on that seminal ocean voyage with M. W. Gibbs, and then during his long career with the Department of State, William Henry Hunt ultimately visited and came to know many of the destinations that, in his early years, he had so graphically envisioned and longed to see.

Lightly bronzed yet otherwise not unlike Horatio Alger's fictional boys, Billy Hunt was born a slave and raised in ignorance and poverty, but gradually he shaped the life he dreamed of and aspired to preserve for posterity in his memoir, "From Cabin to Consulate," which reveals, also blurs and shrouds, yet often ennobles and glorifies his youth. Some segments seem fully based in fact, others most likely are fiction. In its entirety, however, though frustrating for the historian in hopeless pursuit of unembellished truth and accuracy, Hunt's autobiography paints such fascinating and exceptional pictures that its distortions become forgivable and almost endearing.

By the time Hunt headed away to what would be his first of five far-flung consular posts, he had, in Alger's words, "risen from the ranks." "I have made a good beginning," said Harry Walton, one of Alger's fictive heroes, much as Billy made his own favorable start. Billy Hunt, the fatherless son of a white slave owner, had acquired an influential new black "father" in M. W. Gibbs. As the two men set off together on January 1, 1898, an alleluia chorus of celebratory church bells pealed out just after midnight that icy New Year's morning as the old city of Brooklyn officially became a borough of greater New York. Sailing through the inky harbor, past France's recent, iconic gift to the people of the United States — the rapidly oxidizing colossus that portrayed a toga-draped woman holding aloft a torch and welcoming (most) strangers from around the globe — Billy realized that he had progressed well beyond his inauspicious origins. He had effectively shrugged off his first skins and seamlessly morphed into William Henry Hunt, a name infused with the bountiful gravitas of male Anglo-Saxon privilege, as he dexterously began positioning himself to become an urbane and increasingly successful citizen of the world.

Richard Mentor Johnson, Martin Van Buren's vice president and the father of several mixed-race daughters, probably including Maria Ann Alexander. (National Portrait Gallery, Smithsonian Institution / Art Resource, N.Y.)

Maria Ann Alexander (Gibbs), most likely the daughter of R. M. Johnson and his slave Lucy Chinn (Alexander). Maria became the wife of Mifflin Wistar Gibbs and the mother of six children, including Ida Gibbs (Hunt) and Hattie Gibbs (Marshall). (Moorland Spingarn Research Center, Howard University, *Negro History Bulletin*)

Mifflin Wistar Gibbs. Entrepreneur, first elected African American judge, and U.S. consul to Madagascar. He was the husband of Maria Alexander and father of Ida, Hattie, and four other children. (Hunt Papers, Moorland Spingarn Research Center, Howard University)

Donald Gibbs, one of Maria and Mifflin's sons. He too attended Oberlin College, but his sisters always outshone him. (Hunt Papers, Moorland Spingarn Research Center, Howard University)

Donald and Ida's sister, Harriet (Hattie) Gibbs Marshall, noted musician and educator, about 1907. (Moorland Spingarn Research Center, Howard University)

Oberlin College graduating class of 1884. Third row from bottom, second from right, Mary (Mollie) Eliza Church; second row from top, far right, Anna Julia Cooper; third row from top, third from right (in hat), Ida Alexander Gibbs. (Oberlin College Archives)

The abolitionist and orator Frederick Douglass was Mifflin Gibbs's mentor and then a U.S. consul in Haiti. Ida Gibbs visited him the day before his death in 1895. (Moorland Spingarn Research Center, Howard University)

John Mercer Langston, lawyer, U.S. consul, and congressman. The Alexanders purchased his former home in Oberlin, where they and later the Gibbses lived for many years. (Moorland Spingarn Research Center, Howard University)

Williams College class of 1898, as freshmen (1894 or 1895). William Henry Hunt (circled, far right, in cap) attended Williams for only one year. (Williams College Archives)

The Reverend Alexander Crummell, an early pan-Africanist, worked for years in Liberia. Ida Gibbs and Anna Julia Cooper lived for a while with Crummell's family, and he was one of the first ministers of St. Mary's Episcopal, Consul Hunt's church in Washington. (Moorland Spingarn Research Center, Howard University)

Archibald Grimké, lawyer, activist, and U.S. consul in Haiti, with his daughter
Angelina, a poet and Dunbar High School teacher. Both of them attended Ida Gibbs
and William Hunt's 1904 wedding. (Moorland Spingarn Research Center, Howard
University)

Mary (Mollie) Church Terrell, in the photo she gave her friend when Ida Gibbs Hunt married and went to Madagascar. (Hunt Papers, Moorland Spingarn Research Center, Howard University)

Mollie's husband, Robert H. Terrell, onetime principal of Dunbar High School, then a federal judge. He and William Henry Hunt both graduated from Lawrence Academy. (Moorland Spingarn Research Center, Howard University)

Mollie Church Terrell and her daughter Phyllis, born while Ida lived with her parents. Phyllis was a flower girl in Ida and William's wedding. (Moorland Spingarn Research Center, Howard University)

Poet Paul Laurence Dunbar. He and his wife Alice lived next door to the Terrells and Ida Gibbs in the early 1900s. Washington's "colored" high school was later renamed in his honor. (Moorland Spingarn Research Center, Howard University)

The crusading journalist and political activist Ida B. Wells (later Barnett) used the pen name "Iola," probably inspiring Ida Gibbs Hunt to sometimes call herself "Iola Gibson." (Moorland Spingarn Research Center, Howard University)

Tamatave, Madagascar, circa 1902, when William Henry Hunt was consul there. (Hunt Papers, Moorland Spingarn Research Center, Howard University)

(Above) A street in Tamatave, on a card sent to Consul Hunt shortly after his departure from Madagascar. (Hunt Papers, Moorland Spingarn Research Center, Howard University)

(Left) The Cosmopolitan Correspondence Club seal on a card sent to Consul Hunt. Hunt joined this Milwaukee-based writers' exchange group in 1900. (Hunt Papers, Moorland Spingarn Research Center, Howard University)

Ida Gibbs Hunt in a jinrikisha in Tamatave, 1905. (Moorland Spingarn Research Center, Howard University, *Negro History Bulletin*)

Madagascar's Queen Ranavalona III, the island's last monarch, exiled in 1897 by Governor General Joseph Simon Gallieni. She was much admired by William Henry Hunt, who sojourned with Gallieni at her onetime palace. (Hunt Papers, Moorland Spingarn Research Center, Howard University)

General Gallieni, who became Consul Hunt's friend and mentor in Madagascar, on a postcard commemorating his career. (Hunt Papers, Moorland Spingarn Research Center, Howard University)

Booker T. Washington was the most powerful African American of his era and an old friend of Mifflin Wistar Gibbs, but he nonetheless schemed to scuttle Consul Hunt's career. (Moorland Spingarn Research Center, Howard University)

Writer, musician, and U.S. consul James Weldon Johnson yearned to replace Consul Hunt in France. He later became executive secretary of the NAACP. (Moorland Spingarn Research Center, Howard University)

In 1907 Ida Gibbs Hunt wrote that St.-Étienne's surroundings (seen here) were "beautiful." (Hunt Papers, Moorland Spingarn Research Center, Howard University)

Main Street of St.-Étienne, near the American consulate, during Hunt's tenure, circa 1913. (Hunt Papers, Moorland Spingarn Research Center, Howard University)

Two unidentified friends of Consul Hunt, accompanied by their local guides, in Algeria, which Hunt visited in 1922. (Hunt Papers, Moorland Spingarn Research Center, Howard University)

Scholar Carter G. Woodson founded the Association for the Study of Negro Life and History in 1916, published Ida Gibbs Hunt's work, and wrote about the Gibbs family. (Moorland Spingarn Research Center, Howard University)

Susan McKinney Steward was the third African American woman to become
a licensed physician. In 1909 she and her husband toured France with the
Gibbs-Hunts. (Moorland Spingarn Research Center, Howard University)

Captain Napoleon Bonaparte Marshall, Hattie Gibbs's husband, was an officer with the 369th Regiment and was seriously wounded in France during World War I. He later became a U.S. military attaché in Haiti. (Emmett Scott, *Official History of the Negro in the World War*, Special Collections, University of Virginia Library)

Lieutenant James Reese Europe, also from the 369th Regiment, was the renowned band leader who took American jazz to France. (Moorland Spingarn Research Center, Howard University)

Consul Hunt (in foreground left) with French officials during World War I. (Caroline Bond Day Papers, Peabody Museum, Harvard University)

Postcard saved by the Gibbs-Hunts spoofing the American military, circa 1917. (Hunt Papers, Moorland Spingarn Research Center, Howard University)

W. E. B. Du Bois and Ida Gibbs Hunt were friends dating from 1897, probably around the time this photograph was taken. He immortalized her in his novel, *The Quest of the Silver Fleece,* and they worked together in the post–World War I Pan-African Congresses. Du Bois remained the most important intellectual and political influence in Gibbs Hunt's life. (Moorland Spingarn Research Center, Howard University)

Haiti's Dantès Bellegarde was his country's minister in France and later in the United States. A friend of the Gibbs-Hunts and the Gibbs-Marshalls, he participated in several of Du Bois's Pan-African Congresses. Pictured here with Du Bois, circa 1940. (Moorland Spingarn Research Center, Howard University)

Jessie Fauset, an acclaimed writer and onetime teacher at Dunbar High School, became an editor of *Crisis* and chronicled Du Bois's 1921 and 1923 Pan-African Congresses. (Moorland Spingarn Research Center, Howard University)

Educator and 1930 Spingarn medalist Henry Alexander Hunt met the Gibbs-Hunts at the 1921 Pan-African Congress in Paris, and again in the 1930s when he joined President Franklin Roosevelt's "Black Cabinet." (Moorland Spingarn Research Center, Howard University, *Crisis*)

362 Guadeloupe — Ilet en rade de Pointe-à-Pitre

Harbor at Point-à-Pître, Guadeloupe, where Hunt served as consul, circa 1927. (Hunt Papers, Moorland Spingarn Research Center, Howard University)

Porto Delgado, San Miguel, Portugese Azores, 1930, during Consul Hunt's tenure there. (Hunt Papers, Moorland Spingarn Research Center, Howard University)

Envoy Extraordinary and Minister Plenipotentiary Charles Mitchell and his wife Elizabeth in Monrovia, Liberia, 1931. (Hunt Papers, Moorland Spingarn Research Center, Howard University)

Scholar and editor Charles Spurgeon Johnson visited Liberia and wrote a 1930 report on corruption there that angered many people. He later became a member of Roosevelt's "Black Cabinet" and then served as president of Fisk University. (Moorland Spingarn Research Center, Howard University)

William Yerby, another early African American consul whose career closely paralleled that of William Henry Hunt. (Moorland Spingarn Research Center, Howard University)

Caroline Bond Day, an anthropologist who chronicled mixed-race families, corresponded with Consul Hunt in the Azores. (Collection of the author)

Wenonah Bond, Caroline's younger sister, with Ida Gibbs Hunt in the Bonds' back-yard, 1922. Ida wanted Wenonah, a Dunbar High School student, to return with her to St.-Étienne. (Collection of the author)

(Left to right) Anna Julia Cooper, Ida Gibbs Hunt, and Mary (Mollie) Church Terrell graduated from Oberlin in 1884, and remained friends for seventy years. The painting in the background is of Cooper's Le Droit Park (Washington) home where this 1952 "reunion" took place. (© 1952, *The Washington Post*)

Anna Julia Cooper around the time when she defended her PhD dissertation at the Sorbonne in Paris. Gibbs Hunt, who lived in France, probably attended the defense. (Moorland Spingarn Research Center, Howard University)

Dunbar High School teacher Mary Burrill (left) and Howard University's Dean Lucy Slowe were a longtime Washington couple. They introduced the Gibbs-Hunts to David Leer, the orphaned teenager who became their foster son. Burrill's brother had been Consul Hunt's aide in St.-Étienne. (Moorland Spingarn Research Center, Howard University)

Renowned composer Andy Razaf (born Andreamentaria Razafinkeriefo). His father was a Malagasy prince and his mother was a daughter of the early African American consul John Lewis Waller. Clifford Alexander, the author's husband, and Razaf were close friends, possibly relatives, who called each other "cousin." (Moorland Spingarn Research Center, Howard University)

1115 New Hampshire Ave.

My dear Wenonah,

Thanks for your card announcing the birth of your little daughter. Our hearty congratulations! May she grow up to be as sweet and good as her mother.

I saw your mother yesterday at a tea and she showed me that picture of you and the baby. She looks bright and lively. Hope to see her when I do get to New York.

Mr. Hunt joins me in love and congratulations

Affectionately "Uzzer Muzzer"

Feb 27. '38

Best regards from husband.

Note from Ida Gibbs Hunt to Wenonah Bond Logan, signed "Uzzer Muzzer" (Other Mother), February 1938. (Collection of the author)

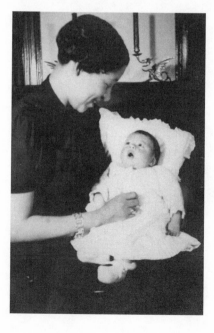

1115 New Hamp. Ave.
Washington D.C.

WASHINGTON D.C.
FEB 28
5:30 PM
1938

BUY U.S.
BON
ASK YOUR POSTMASTER

3 CENTS

Mrs Wenonah B. Logan,
264 Lenox Ave.,
New York, N.Y.

Baby Adele Hunt Logan (Alexander), the author, with her mother, Wenonah Bond Logan. Wenonah's mother, Georgia Bond, showed this photograph to Ida Gibbs Hunt early in 1938. (Collection of the author)

PART II | WORLDS APART

The Madagascar Portfolio, 1898–1907

Colonials on the Great Red Island

Consul-designate Mifflin Wistar Gibbs and his pro-tégé William Henry Hunt sailed from New York City on the French liner *La Champagne,* with the financially strapped Hunt agonizing below deck in steerage. Once their ship docked in Le Havre on January 9, 1898, they boarded the chilly, overcrowded boat train bound for Paris, where they registered at the modest but reputable Hôtel de Binda. "Despite the rain, fog, and muddy streets," Hunt reported, they gaped at the City of Lights' storied landmarks as they strolled its tree-lined boulevards.

Hunt wrote Robert Terrell that he found the French bitterly divided that winter over the ugly Dreyfus affair, which sprang from charges of military espionage and then became tarnished by virulent anti-Semitism. But, Hunt added (clearly with a knowing wink), he and Gibbs reveled in the "Bohemian side of Paris at the Folies Bergeres, which interested the Judge immensely." The pair even caroused with an unnamed white countryman, who laid "aside his exception to the dark-skinned brother and really enjoy[ed] himself." Duty prevailed, however, and Gibbs made his obligatory appointment to confer with the American ambassador, Horace Porter, concerning bestowal of the exequatur, the host country's formal authorization of his consular status and official permission to act. The French, Madagascar's recent colonizers, would draw up and issue that requisite document.

The population [of Madagascar], which was ever changing, was mixed in nationality, shades, color, caste and race, baffling all ethnological or anthropological study. There was, however, no color line; and all other social and moral qualities being equal, all the elements blended harmoniously. . . . [Yet] Madagascar has ever been like the big red hot iron, and everyone that touched it got his fingers burnt.
—William Henry Hunt, "From Cabin to Consulate," circa 1949

Gibbs claimed in his memoir that he first learned about what became known as "*l'affaire* Waller" at that session in Paris with Ambassador Porter. Consul John Lewis Waller's story, one of the most bizarre, intriguing, yet unsettling episodes concerning an American diplomat at any time or place, has since been extensively researched, analyzed, and retold.

Waller was born into slavery in Missouri about 1850. During Reconstruction, the ambitious young man did all that he could to elevate his status. He acquired some education and, like many other former slaves, moved west to Kansas, where he qualified to practice law, published a newspaper, and plunged into Republican politics. Judge Gibbs, whom party officials sent to that state on an investigatory mission in the 1880s, never admitted knowing Waller, but the two men must at least have crossed paths, because they shared friends and interests, and served concurrently as delegates to several Republican presidential conventions.

When Benjamin Harrison assumed the presidency in 1889, John Waller received only a negligible patronage job in reward for his efforts and began lobbying for a consular position. A few black men with such aspirations were dispatched to Liberia or Haiti, where Waller and Gibbs both hoped to go, and Vancouver, Gibbs's longtime place of residence, appealed to Waller as well. But two years later, the president selected Waller to serve as the first African American consul in Madagascar. That appointment generated ample criticism. Several "white" newspapers asserted that "it was a mistake to send a Negro to that country; the natives, though dark themselves, feel that the white man is their superior, and think that a white man should be sent to represent a nation which they believe to be a nation of whites." Officials at the consular service had long held that all such appointments should take into account presumed prejudices in the host countries, which served as their excuse for granting very limited opportunities to Jews, Negroes, recent immigrants, and members of the lower classes — and none at all to women.

Waller arrived at the post with orders from his government to maintain alliances with Ranavalona III, the Malagasy queen, though France had already asserted its right to handle Madagascar's external affairs. At first, as per his unequivocal instructions, Waller dealt mostly with the indigenous leaders, but that angered French authorities to the extent that their foreign minister dispatched a letter of protest to the U.S. Department of State. The consul's behavior, he insisted, might well be read as a belligerent act against France. The secretary of state backtracked, chided Waller, and, contrary to his own department's prior directives, ordered him to interact only with the colonial officials. Waller complied with that mandate to an extent, but also continued to fraternize with the island's monarchy, and alienated the French by criticizing their plans to indenture legions of Malagasies, then ship them off to labor in other distant colonies. In that respect, he acted with undeniable provocation.

Late in 1893, under Grover Cleveland, the new Democratic president, Georgia's Edward Telfair Wetter, whose father (like Billy Hunt's) had been a slaveholder in the Old South, arrived in Madagascar as Waller's replacement. Wetter's presence foretold trouble for his predecessor, but Waller rashly remained on the island to lobby the queen and her advisers about his scheme to attract investment and settlement by black Americans. Those leaders finally yielded to Waller's appeals and granted him use of a vast tract, deep in the island's interior, which he proposed to name Wallerland and where he envisioned a utopian Negro American colony. His efforts resembled those of several bold black men, including M. W. Gibbs, who sought overseas homelands for aspiring members of their race, but Waller also harbored avaricious ambitions not unlike those of his white capitalist contemporaries, including a few mercenary members of the consular service.

Except for the ruling families, Waller cared little about the Malagasies and excluded others from his new venture, which called for unremunerated acquisitions or land leases and a cheap, involuntary labor force to be brought in from the nearby British-ruled island of Mauritius. Madagascar's underdeveloped terrain, natural resources, and indigenous people were mere fodder for his mercenary designs. Despite protests from the French, Waller distributed promotional materials touting rent-free acreage and detailing his proposals to form towns, cultivate rubber trees, and build processing facilities and timber mills. Then he sealed his ill-fated contract with the royal family through the marriage of his own fifteen-year-old daughter to Queen Ranavalona's nephew. One anticipated investor (soon to become Waller's lawyer) was the ailing former consul to Haiti John Mercer Langston, the Alexanders' and Gibbses' onetime neighbor in Oberlin.

What they saw as Waller's brash efforts to usurp their authority outraged the French, who claimed that the United States had imperialistic aims in respect to Madagascar, and that Waller sought illegal profits from the burgeoning export trade. To settle an unrelated financial dispute, E. T. Wetter convened a consular court, for which he served as prosecutor, judge, and jury member. With little debate or delay, that stacked tribunal found Waller guilty of mishandling the estate, entrusted to him as consul-executor, of a recently deceased American merchant who had lived on the island.

Instead of leaving Madagascar while he had the chance, Waller holed up in the port of Tamatave, monitored by both Wetter and France's colonial forces, who soon besieged his residence and arrested him. The French charged Waller with treason because he had allegedly endangered two of their undercover agents and supplied arms — a pair of pistols — to a Malagasy cohort. He had also sent his wife, Susan, a letter, which the vigilant French intercepted, detailing atrocities committed by soldiers in the colonial army. Waller's second trial, conducted in French (which he neither spoke nor understood), was a sordid, biased farce during which Consul Wetter all but refused to secure legal counsel for his predecessor. The predetermined guilty verdict resulted in a sentence of twenty years, to be served in a prison in France, where Waller was transported in chains. That excruciating ocean journey to Europe evoked dismal images of his ancestors' travails during the Middle Passage to the New World. If, in Billy Hunt's words, Madagascar was a "red hot iron," ex-consul John Waller got more than just his "fingers burnt."

The French wanted to leverage the incident to deter any future imperialist initiatives vis-à-vis Madagascar on the part of the United States, and at first only a muted official American response acknowledged Waller's plaints about the legal proceedings' gross injustices and his subsequent imprisonment. Susan Waller's vigorous lobbying, however, began energizing and reshaping opinion in the black and even the mainstream press. Several newspapers charged the Cleveland administration with abandoning an American citizen and accused the secretary of state of racial discrimination. One article asserted, "The action of the French is undoubtedly founded on their observations that a government which permits lynching and burning alive of its Afro-American citizens at home would not exert itself to protect them so far away from home."

Despite Queen Ranavalona's lament that "I would rather die in my palace than yield," the struggles with France for control of her vast domain ended in 1896 with the predestined victory of the powerful colonial army, which lost only twenty men in battle but at least six thousand more to malaria and dysentery — the dreaded "bloody flux." By contrast, legions of the queen's soldiers, including John and Susan Waller's high-born son-in-law (their daughter had returned with her mother to the United States, where she gave birth to her Malagasy-American son, Andreamentaria Razafinkeriefo, later known as Andy Razaf), perished during those clashes. For years thereafter, the Malagasies retold legends about the predatory crocodiles that lurked across the gore-soaked battlefields to pinion corpses and the mortally wounded in vise-like jaws, then lug them off to feed on in secluded riverine lairs. That autumn, the French legislature ratified the annexation of its country's newest colony. But for a few exceptions — such as the long-independent Republic of Liberia, founded, sponsored, and thereafter dominated by American interests, and Italy's ongoing struggles with the resilient Abyssinian empire — France's subordination of Madagascar completed the late nineteenth-century European conquest, division, and colonial remapping of Africa.

Public outcries about the United States' abandonment of Waller began to sway President Cleveland, who had eked out only a narrow victory in 1892 and hoped to make inroads among black Republican voters four years later. His administration negotiated the ex-consul's release, yet had to appease France's intransigence, so both nations finally compromised to avoid further escalation of the dispute. The agreement set aside Waller's claims to Malagasy lands and his threatened suits against the French for slander, false arrest, and imprisonment. The Department of State acknowledged France's rule and full economic control over Madagascar, denied any American territorial ambitions, and conceded that Waller had made "a deliberate attempt to give information to the enemy, to the prejudice of the military situation of France." Rubbing salt in Waller's psychic wounds, State Department officials also confirmed the legitimacy of Consul Wetter's charges. Only after Waller had spent six months in prison did the French grant his freedom.

With the exception of Waller's wife and his attorney, J. Mercer Langston, who died soon afterward, everyone involved had behaved badly. Waller extolled his noble aims, but he was motivated primarily by greed exacerbated by hubris. Wetter pursued his own petty accusations, then scarcely lifted a finger to extricate a fellow American consul from a dire fix (albeit one largely of his own making). The Malagasy royal family used Waller to challenge France's hated new hegemony by granting him a dubious covenant for land in a part of the island where they maintained no authority, and the French, hell-bent on consolidating their colonial power in Madagascar, arrogantly overreacted. For months, the U.S. Department of State and the president had hedged and vacillated, forcing Waller to cool his heels in bleak confinement. Those officials must have assumed that an obscure black American, even one who had been hauled off to a French dungeon, would not become an international cause célèbre. But he did!

That sordid drama played out scarcely a year before Gibbs and Hunt prepared to leave France for Madagascar, by which time John Waller had rejoined his family in the United States, where he often received accolades as a speaker in African American forums. But new investment potential and prospects of Negro resettlement abroad beckoned him again. Waller became captain to a company of black soldiers (possible future colonists, he thought) when he served in Cuba during the brief, imperialistic Spanish-American War.

Hunt's analysis of the Waller incident reveals his lockstep approval and blind advocacy of his country's dubious conduct. "The evidence, and particularly the contents of [Waller's] own letters produced at the court martial," he later wrote, "prove that he was unquestionably guilty of the offense charged against him, which justified the sentence." "[Only] the energetic intervention of the American Government," Hunt insisted, "spared Waller the humiliation of serving out the full prison sentence." Despite Hunt's unqualified praise for his government's actions and contempt for what he called Waller's "crass stupidity," the sight of two new African American officials en route to Madagascar evoked vivid memories of the former consul's recent, disastrous "back to Africa" venture. So hostile silence and cold stares greeted Gibbs and Hunt as they set out from Marseille. One fellow passenger, a white Frenchman, expressed an "annoying suspicion lest there should be a repetition of the case of John L. Waller." But Hunt claimed that he and Gibbs "sailed from France with a firm resolve to dispel any doubts in the minds of the French officials as to our attitude regarding the Franco-Malagasy imbroglio." Together they would prove, Billy Hunt glibly wrote his pal Robert Terrell back in Washington, "that all Coons are not alike."

Consul Gibbs and his aide had taken the train south from Paris via the Rhône River valley, then they crossed the Mediterranean on the steamer *Pei Ho*. Their ship eased through the Suez Canal (an engineering colossus of the century that France had recently ceded to Britain in exchange for that country's withdrawal from Madagascar), sailed the Red Sea to Djibouti, made brief calls in Aden, Zanzibar, and the Seychelles, followed by several penultimate stops along Madagascar's extended, tortuous shoreline, before arriving at their final destination that March.

As Billy Hunt later wrote in his memoir, "Tamatave might best be described as 'sui generis,' and no idea can be conveyed by saying it was like such and such a town, for it was like no other place in the world." At dawn, he gazed from the ship across the *pangalanes,* the palm-fringed necklace of lagoons and canals girdled with sand dunes heaped up by the Indian Ocean's trade winds, which stretched hundreds of miles along the island's east coast.

The French had recently dredged out that chain of waterways to facilitate the transport of local produce by barge. And there, Hunt later wrote, he first caught sight of the shabby but distinctive port that became his home for the next nine years.

Overhead, storm-clouds hovered, through which the morning sun was trying desperately to penetrate. Conspicuous in the foreground were four lofty palm trees, like sentinels standing guard over the sleeping town.... Widespreading mango trees, high church spires and minarets added beauty to the sky-line, while the attractive bungalows built along the semi-circular waterfront floated before the eyes like bright windows.... We had not gone more than a hundred yards from the steamer when the sun was suddenly dimmed, ... as the rain commenced to pour down in torrents, it seemed like the very heavens had opened up.... [Then] like a bolt out of the blue sky, the sun brush[ed] aside the dark clouds and reappeared in all its glory.

Gibbs and Hunt were greeted by Consul Edward Wetter, who, Hunt wrote to Terrell, "on arrival of his successor, conduct[ed] him first to the cemetery of the town and point[ed] out the graves of many former American consuls [including] the first, who had been a victim of Malagasy fever" — and also, perhaps, that of Consul Victor Stanwood, who was murdered in 1888. Wetter, Hunt learned, had circulated rumors that "the Judge had Waller coming out as his clerk, which among these Frenchmen is like shaking a red-sheet in the face of a mad-bull!" Owing to his "unimaginable temper [and] pompousness, [Wetter] has not one single friend in Tamatave." He had become an opportune target for lewd jokes when he sent his Anglo-American wife back home to Georgia so that he could set up housekeeping with a young Creole Malagasy concubine whose wrathful mother was threatening "to write Mrs. Wetter." The wily and obstructive Mr. Wetter, Hunt added, also kept Gibbs's exequatur hidden away from Joseph Simon Gallieni, Madagascar's new French governor general, for several weeks. Hunt, who cautioned Terrell that "all this gossip is confidential, *sub rosa*," conceded that although the ex-consul's behavior would be perceived as "obnoxious" even in "Cracker Society," Wetter was nonetheless one of the "most methodical and thorough office men I ever knew." And on March 20, the supposedly efficient Edward Telfair Wetter swore in William Henry Hunt as Mifflin Wistar Gibbs's consular clerk, "thus," Hunt later would write, "officially placing my name on the government pay-roll."

Madagascar, the world's fourth largest island at nearly a thousand miles in longitude and three hundred across, has unique origins. Mervyn Brown, its authoritative Anglophone historian, maintains that the local people are mostly of Malay origin. Nearly two thousand years ago, he contends, waves of migrants launched outrigger canoes and began leaving the South Pacific archipelago that is now Indonesia. Over several centuries, they and their successors navigated a northwesterly route by way of the Indian subcontinent, altered course, skirted the Arabian peninsula, rounded the Horn of Africa, and went south down that coast to what later became known as the Straits of Mozambique, which they traversed to the uninhabited island that Marco Polo (who had heard about it but never reached it himself) first called Madagascar. Those settlers' descendants often referred to their homeland as "the country that lies in the midst of the sea," while the vivid colors of its laterite escarpments led outsiders to label it the Great Red Island. That ecological "eighth continent," the last populated of the world's major habitable land masses, received the Africanized Malays who were its earliest permanent residents shortly before, or at the start of, the second millennium A.D. By the 1600s Europeans began venturing there as fortune seekers, traders, and missionaries, and pirates hid out along its craggy shores. But the original people's physiognomy, languages, and culture — Malay, enriched by Indian, Arab, and coastal East African influences — remained dominant.

During the next century, Madagascar became a pawn in the international slave trade, with black, mainland East Africans pressed into involuntary servitude there, while merchants shipped thousands of copper-skinned Malagasies, destined for bondage throughout the Americas, around the Cape of Good Hope and across the Atlantic. More than a few African Americans (including the Harlem Renaissance writer Claude McKay, and Ida Gibbs's friend Mollie Church Terrell, whose coral and silver necklace, similar to others of Malagasy origin, was passed down from a forebear who kept it safe through the Middle Passage and during many decades of enslavement in the United States) heard various stories about their "Mologlaskan" ancestry. Madagascar's involvement in the transoceanic slave trade was supposed to have ended by 1820, but it illicitly slogged on. And as in many other parts of the world, slavery flourished on the island through most of that century.

Hunt described Tamatave's climate as "unsalubrious," inundated by "constant rains," and seasonally ravaged by fierce cyclones that twisted up out of the Indian Ocean. But he acknowledged that much of the island was arable and bounteous, with staples such as breadfruit, yams, taro, and rice (all traceable to its majority residents' South Pacific origins) cultivated in abundance. It also was home to mammoth baobab trees, an array of palms, cacti, and giant ferns, and more species of the Orchidaceae family than any other place on earth. By the late nineteenth century, Madagascan silks, hardwoods, and spices came to be valued and traded internationally.

According to Governor General Gallieni, a career military man who had cut his teeth in the French Antilles, Senegal, and *l'Indo-Chine,* Queen Rana- valona III, the last of the island's indigenous sovereign monarchs, found it "difficult to forget her former grandeur" even after the rout of her army, so in 1897 Gallieni exiled her to France's nearby Réunion Island. His government soon granted her a pension, then dispatched her to faraway colonial Algeria, where, with rare interruptions, such as a ceremonial trip to Paris several years later, she passed her remaining years. Once Gallieni had "liberated" the Mala- gasies from their long-preeminent, homegrown feudal rulers, he designated French as the island's official language (along with, but superior to, its own dominant Merina and Malagasy tongues) and began transforming his new colony into an integral, productive component of *la France orientale.*

Gallieni did not eradicate the slaves' inferior status, but he ended tradi- tional bondage per se, much as France had terminated slavery in its older Caribbean colonies in 1848. In its stead, he imposed levies, called *corvées* or *prestations,* on the Malagasy men, which could be satisfied by performing fifty days of hard labor every year to expedite his ambitious public works projects. On one occasion Billy Hunt described the "indigenous population [as] beasts of burden for these Frenchmen, [and] in a state of semi-slavery." "If there is any reliance to be placed in the passage about the meek inheriting the Earth," he added, "they will certainly deserve their own some day."

To facilitate his administration, Gallieni imposed a form of indirect rule called *la politique des races* that geographically divided Madagascar into nine ethnic groups. Local chiefs retained some degree of autonomy, but French companies and individual *colons* received generous land concessions, and all Europeans and Americans fell under a legal system separate from the *justice indigène,* which reinforced the natives' inferior status as French subjects, but not citizens. Between 1896 and 1906, the decade sometimes called Madagas- car's Golden Age, Gallieni laid the foundations for a huge, unified colonial state as he supplemented his mostly white administration with "colored" civil servants and soldiers from France's other colonies in Asia, continental Africa, and the Antilles. He prodded French planters to grow vanilla, cloves, and coffee for export; set in motion a number of sanitation and health initiatives;

began the construction of canals, roads, and railways; attempted to westernize education; and founded the Académie Malgache, an institute that even now remains dedicated to preserving the island's culture. In whole, such efforts were referred to as *la mission civilisatrice,* and ultimately, of course, the success of any and all such "civilizing" colonization depended on strictly maintaining odious myths of racial supremacy. A few critics protested Gallieni's rigorous enforcement methods, but Hunt staunchly defended the governor's tactics. "[W]ith the Malagasy," he stated, "experiences have shown that in dealing with children, the stern iron hand of command must be felt before these people can be made to understand what is good for them."

A couple of years after he and Consul Gibbs arrived in Madagascar, Hunt joined a little known but far-flung new organization, the Cosmopolitan Correspondence Club. Postcards began streaming in from a number of American cities and from foreign venues including Canada and Mexico; France, Italy, Portugal, Germany, and Yugoslavia; Zanzibar, New Zealand, and Japan. A typical message read, "Je serais hereux d'échanger des cartes postales vue avec vous" (I'll be happy to exchange picture postcards with you), and its sender printed the letters "CCC" accompanied by a three- or four-digit identification number on one corner of each piece of illustrated mail.

The CCC was an association chartered in Milwaukee, Wisconsin, and dedicated to slaking its participants' thirst for information about and images of the world. In some ways it resembled a century-old World Wide Web (WWW). On its yellow and black seal the organization's name adorns a buckled belt that encircles two griffins whose claws cradle a globe held above a banner marked: "RESPONDEZ S'IL VOUS PLAIT." And like the modern WWW, that once widespread CCC could also make race invisible. But despite his racially ambiguous appearance, lest any of his fellow members have reservations about corresponding with a person whom they even suspected of being a Negro, Hunt declined to send a snapshot to the CCC's headquarters for publication in its journal, writing Ida Gibbs in 1903, "[I]t is unnecessary to say then, I do not . . . intend sending my photograph." Over the next three decades, many CCC correspondents, who with few exceptions never laid eyes on him, remained among Hunt's frequent pen pals.

In part through those epistolary associates, Hunt set out to educate himself further. One *carte postale* promised him "a catalogue of Books and Pamphlets about Madagascar." The cards also introduced him to Europe's cities, towns, and landmarks as his halting prep school French grew ever more fluent. Thus began the deliberate Europeanization of William Henry Hunt. In that remote Indian Ocean locale, he became, in the Malagasies' terminology, almost a *lahifotsy* (white man). His tawny-skinned American "blackness" seemed to fade like a sun-bleached sepia photo as he secured his honorary membership in Madagascar's "white" upper class, which included merchants from Europe and the Asian-Pacific rim, members of the Western Christian clergy, ranking French colonial military and civilian officials, a small community of select private citizens, and the ministerial delegations from Great Britain, Germany, and Italy.

To Vice Consul Hunt, all that was French increasingly seemed superior and "civilized," while he considered the generic Malagasy "a child of spontaneity," in whom he saw elements that were part "savage," part amiable and meritorious. Once, Hunt maligned the *indigènes'* "national character" as "a simious intelligence by which they rapidly acquire a superficial knowledge of things," but in a more magnanimous instance, he lauded the Malagasies as "an intelligent race," typified by fine "physical, mental and material endowments."

He praised several sub-Saharan Africans whom he met on the island, foremost among them "the outstanding Colored Frenchman" from Senegal Blaise Diagne, a civilian employee with the French-Malagasy customs service who, Hunt added, later became "High Commissioner for the French Colored Colonial Troops during the World War, Under Secretary for the Colonies," and even, for a while, a tactical pan-Africanist. Another such man with whom Hunt would cross paths in later years was the black Guadeloupean Sosthène H. C. Mortenol, at that juncture an up-and-coming military officer on the Great Red Island. Hunt welcomed the opportunity to serve in a French colony where, he wrote, "a man is judged by his ability and character, and not so much stress is placed upon one's racial origin." He argued that the French in Madagascar bore the metaphorical "white man's burden" to bring Europe's and Christianity's blessings, their own peerless culture, an effective, modern infrastructure, and a solid work ethic to the undermotivated local people.

Hunt and Gibbs also personified that supposed "white man's burden," with their stamina, perseverance, and dedication to duty, although lapses in communications and balky equipment frustrated their efforts. When their American-made typewriter broke down, for instance, they never received the funds needed to repair or replace it.

One unanticipated task assigned to Gibbs's ill-equipped consulate proved to be vexing, but memorable as well. In April of 1899, he reported in his autobiography, "I was in receipt of a cablegram advising me that the flagship 'Chicago,' [commanded by] Admiral [Henry L.] Howison, would . . . stop at

Tamatave, and instructing me to obtain what wild animals I could, indigenous to Madagascar, and have them ready to ship thereby for the Smithsonian Institute at Washington, D.C.," which at the time was assiduously developing the ambitious new National Zoological Park. "In compliance with this instruction," Hunt later wrote in his own memoir, he and Gibbs set to work, "and with the invaluable assistance of a large number of natives . . . transformed the Consular premises into a miniature zoo, to the great annoyance of our neighbors, whose nightly slumbers were disturbed by the . . . cries of our noisy charges." That project offered Hunt the perfect excuse he needed to study the island's rare fauna. "None of the larger animals and few of the smaller animals that roam over the plains and in the forests of South Africa," he added, "are anywhere to be found in Madagascar." The most prevalent were "the lemur, . . . including the 'ring-tailed,' the 'broad-nosed,' the 'brown mouse,' the 'dwarf,' and the 'fosa' [usually spelled fossa, and not in fact a lemur but a lithe, predatory catlike mammal] and 'aye-aye.'" His memoir includes vivid descriptions of the nocturnal or diurnal habits and varied diets of the creatures that he and Gibbs graciously hosted on the consular grounds.

In addition to the lemurs — the most primitive of all primates with their saucer eyes, bony fingers, and prehensile tails — Madagascar was home to reptiles, from chameleons resembling tiny pea shoots up to snarling crocodiles and ancient sea turtles as large as swine. It teemed with venomous insects, birds galore (though the gigantic *Aepyornis,* or elephant bird, widely thought to be Sinbad's roc, had recently become extinct), rodents of all sorts, "river pigs," and herds of humpbacked zebu cattle, which were prized as determinants of wealth and figured prominently in Malagasy rituals.

After six weeks during which Gibbs and Hunt assembled those fractious animals, on May 22 the venerable USS *Chicago* hove into Tamatave's harbor. But Admiral Howison, whom Hunt termed a "cranky and grouchy old sealord," cited Madagascar's pervasive unhealthiness (he "saw Bubonic Plague, Yellow Fever and Cholera germs literally floating about in the air") as an excuse for refusing to transport the consulate's raucous living assemblage back to Washington as ordered. Whether the irascible admiral considered the Smithsonian project truly perilous, beneath his dignity, or too formidable or frivolous to carry out, or whether, with an attitude that reflected the U.S. Navy's burgeoning racism, he simply chose not to cooperate with a Negro American consul, can only be guessed, but after the cargoless *Chicago* set sail, Consul Gibbs's problem concerning exactly what to do with his rejected feral tenants loomed large.

He therefore titled his follow-up cable "Procuration of Live Animals, as per Order of the Department, and Declination of the Admiral to Receive Them on Board." Cutting to the crux of his beastly dilemma, Gibbs wrote, "It was then, Mr. Secretary, that I sadly realized that I was confronted by a condition. Over seventy years of age, 10,000 miles from home, a beggarly salary, with a menagerie on my hands, while bankruptcy and a humbled flag threatened to stare me in the face." He saw only three options: sell, liberate, or keep the animals on at his makeshift consular compound "at [U.S.] Government expense."

When, with his nonexistent Merina or Malagasy and meager French, Gibbs asked the locals — who chose not to understand him — about selling the animals, they replied, "I get you more like him, I can." Colonial authorities also warned the consul that he could release the creatures only "at my peril." "Having been a member of the bar, and retaining much veneration for the quixotic capers of the judicial twelve," the former judge explained, "I 'polled' them . . . on their desire to leave . . . and found a hung jury, swinging by their tails; eleven indicated 'aye,' but the twelfth, with his double affirmative cry of 'Aye, Aye' [Gibbs's pun on the name of one of the island's lemurs], being equal to a negative, hung them up." "Meanwhile," he added,

> they bid fair to be a permanent exhibit. . . . Regarding the item of food, . . . I anticipate a monthly increase of cost, as the animals' appetites seem to improve in captivity. I conclude, Mr. Secretary, with but a single solace. They may possibly eat their heads off, but their tails give abundant promise of remaining in evidence. Patiently awaiting instructions as [to] the future disposition of these wild and wayward wards of the government, I have the honor to be, Your obedient servant, M. W. Gibbs

The memo's recipients in Washington may have smiled privately, but a dour State Department official cabled back directing that "the animals be returned to their habitat," a decision Hunt called "very gratifying to our neighbors." The vice consul, however, bemoaned the loss of such a "rare collection of Madagascan Fauna," and derided the entire affair as "a waste of tax payers' money."

By early 1901 M. W. Gibbs, who was healthy overall but nonetheless seventy-eight, needed a long, restorative leave. "The Doctor tells me that his bladder trouble does not get better," Billy Hunt wrote Ida, adding that she should "persuade [her father] to come home on a year's vacation." Perhaps Consul Gibbs, who kept a diary and had already begun mapping out a comprehensive autobiography, had resolved to remain in the United States even before leaving Madagascar, or he may have made his decision final only after reuniting with family and friends and recuperating in comfort back at home, with access to more reliable medical care.

Hunt praised his mentor as a "brave, capable and intelligent Consular Officer," but Gibbs himself harbored deep concerns about colonialism. Long before he went to Tamatave, he had lived for a decade under a somewhat similar system in Vancouver. "The French in Madagascar, the English in Africa, and the Americans in the Antilles," Gibbs lamented in 1902. "'O! Civilization'; what crimes are committed in thy name?" These views portended his upcoming rejection of Republican Party policies and practices. In the wake of the Spanish-American War and gunboat diplomacy, his country's harsh, largely new imperialism appalled him. Gibbs called the Filipinos a "heroic people . . . struggling to attain [freedom] from the Spanish yoke." But the United States "became their hostile enemies and destroyed that identity and an independent entity for which they fought." No such doubts, however, gnawed at William Henry Hunt.

Shortly before Gibbs departed, Hunt received a letter from a man named William Libbey requesting Madagascan postage stamps for his daughter's collection. Hunt, who had thoroughly familiarized himself with even the more arcane departmental regulations, concluded that a request from any American deserved a prompt response. So he assembled a set of stamps and sent them off to Libbey. That singular act initiated many warm exchanges with the man who Hunt learned was an explorer, rifleman, distinguished instructor of earth sciences, and dean at Princeton University, where he was a colleague of Professor Woodrow Wilson, who soon would be selected to head up that elite institution. Professor Libbey solicited his new epistolary acquaintance to write a series of articles about Madagascar for the journal of his professional organization, the esteemed American Geographical Society. Between 1901 and late 1904, Hunt submitted four such treatises for publication, the handwritten (a result of the consulate's often inoperative typewriter) manuscripts of which remain archived in the society's New York City headquarters.

In "The Population of Madagascar," Hunt detailed the colony's human diversity. Of its roughly 2,500,000 residents, he wrote, only 28,000 were Europeans, almost all of them French, including an occupying army of nearly 24,000. He also revealed an impressive knowledge of the island's ethnic and tribal divisions, and both its precolonial and more recent history. Hunt's second article, "The Inauguration of a Railway in Madagascar," opens with his observation that the "eyes of the civilized world . . . turn towards the great underdeveloped continent of the East, and the neighboring large islands, as one nation after another gains a foothold in them. Now it is the gold fields of South Africa, again it is the navigation of the Congo River, . . . [or] the progress of France in the Great African Island." Another one lauds the advances in sanitation, health care, and education under Gallieni's colonial regime. Despite his lavish praise for the French, however, Hunt asserted that when it came to industrial advancement, his own famously entrepreneurial countrymen had "a better chance of succeeding in an enterprise of this kind than . . . foreign elements who are thus far on the scene."

Those essays speak clearly to Hunt's patriotism and intelligence, his observational, research, and reportorial skills, and his interest in and knack for natural and political history, anthropology, and geography, yet they also reveal an apparent disdain for Madagascar's indigenous people and culture. Prompted by Professor Libbey, one of its prominent officers, the American Geographical Society published a couple of articles by Hunt, then rewarded and elated him by making him an honorary member.

Once Gibbs resolved to remain in the United States, he promised to plead Hunt's case to succeed him as consul with his contacts in Washington, but also warned him, Hunt recalled, that "I had no more chance . . . than a cat in hell without claws." That prediction, however, proved to be unduly pessimistic. In September 1901, when Hunt received the welcome though unexpected news announcing his promotion, he wanted to know "how and with what influence the Judge had so cleverly worked the oracles in my behalf." Gibbs had, in fact, sent the State Department a photograph of Hunt, so that "they might see what sort of a 'son of a gun' I was commending," and the paternalistic older man added, "[S]ometime I will write you more fully of how I brought about your appointment [and] elevation to representation of one of the greatest governments in the world." But the new Consul Hunt soon learned that William Libbey had dashed off a spate of laudatory letters about him to some well-situated cronies. "One of the Professor's friends," Hunt confirmed, "had taken up the matter of my promotion" with ranking State Department officials. Gibbs no doubt assisted Hunt as best he could, but a white friend in court surely carried more weight than a comparably worthy black one. For his part, Hunt expressed "deep gratitude" to both his sponsors. At least numerically, the U.S. Consular Service was marching steadily uphill in those years. Its nearly eleven hundred employees at three hundred consulates around the world contrasted with fewer than one hundred men who worked directly for or at the State Department itself.

At about the same time, a curious case of muddled identity may have occurred back in Washington. Following the 1898 Spanish-American War, the United States had acquired the Caribbean island of Puerto Rico. Three years later, seeking a new governor for the territory, President McKinley decided that he wanted William Henry Hunt to fill the position. He may have heard about Consul Hunt from the State Department, and learned that he had graduated from a respected preparatory school and matriculated at Williams College. And Billy Hunt also claimed to have met Theodore Roosevelt, McKinley's successor, in Groton, Massachusetts, and later at St. George's Church in New York City. On one occasion, President Roosevelt reportedly suggested that Hunt was a man who would "blend in" with Puerto Rico's tan-skinned Creole population. But the William Henry Hunt who received the presidential appointment and served as governor from 1901 to 1904 already held a less high-profile post there with the recently imposed American territorial forces, and was the son of an eminent former secretary of the navy and ambassador to Russia. That William Henry Hunt was a white southerner close to Billy Hunt's age who also had attended several New England academies. There may have been more than one occasion in their careers when those two public servants with somewhat similar credentials, carrying the same, seemingly prestigious, Anglo-Saxon name, were confused with one another.

Far more than Gibbs had done, Consul Hunt courted a relationship with Governor General Gallieni, in which, he added, such "barriers as differences in age, language, race and rank were cast aside." On the very day that Hunt learned of his promotion, Gallieni solicited the new consul to accompany him to Tananarive (present-day Antananarivo), Madagascar's inland capital, "an honor," Hunt boasted, "which had never hitherto been shown a Foreign Consular Officer in Madagascar." Gallieni's invitation reflected his affection for Hunt, but can also be read as a tacit gesture of apology for his country's maltreatment of Waller, the former American consul. It symbolically resecured the ties between France and the United States — two old and vital allies.

Their trek, however, proved to be daunting. It was the first attempt ever made to reach Tananarive's inland plateau, a mile above sea level, by automobile. Gallieni's new Panhard-Levassor touring cars took the group, including, in the governor's words, "les quatre plus grosses legumes de la Colonie" (the colony's four fattest beans), southwest, via a tangle of rutted, muddy tracks, across two hundred miles of mountains, jungles, swamps, and rivers. Hunt recalled the entourage of military chauffeurs, French mechanics, and *gendarmes* that guarded them from "dissident natives, or 'Fahavalos.'" "An imposing escort of husky Malagasy boys . . . called upon to give us a push up the steep inclines," also accompanied their party. Those local "boys" transported the "Europeans" over the most rugged stretches on shoulder-borne palanquins, though Hunt said that he looked forward to the time in Madagascar when "men as beasts of burden . . . will gradually disappear." Those particular travelers may have been moderately respectful, but some porters complained that their passengers urinated or even defecated on the men who carried them aloft.

They left the humid coast behind, stopped by the colony's leper hospital, then motored on to the "Asylum for the Feeble-Minded." For Hunt, the most exhilarating part of the adventure unfolded as they ferried across the treacherous Betsiboka River. That torrent teemed "with enormous crocodiles," he later wrote, "and we saw their gruesome heads bobbing up . . . in all directions." Grabbing a "carabine," Hunt took aim, gleefully fired, and "hit several snouts which disappeared immediately." Other members of the entourage joined in that chaotic blood sport until the turbid river ran red. Such machismo exploits reflected the spirit of the times and would be popularized a few years hence by ex-president Teddy Roosevelt's renowned African safaris.

The whole trip, Hunt raved, epitomized Gallieni's "far sighted vision of the decisive role the motor car was destined to play in the life of generations to come." He vividly described the scene as they drove by the verdant, terraced rice paddies and neared their final destination, the deposed queen's sprawling and ornate palace aerie, which Gallieni had appropriated just a few years before: "Several thousand natives, dressed in their snow white lambas [Malagasy togas], literally covered the many hills hedged about the city. The dense throng, outlined against the eternal hills like a blanket of snow, stood impassive until the first automobiles they had ever seen passed down the road before them, then suddenly the white clad multitude rose up in unison, cheered, and welcomed their Governor General back to his capital." Once they arrived in Tananarive, Gallieni "telegraphed to Paris" word of their "historic" feat, but for the jubilant new consul, the exquisite pleasures of his host's hospitality had only begun.

Gallieni "ordered one of his saddle horses placed at my disposal," wrote Hunt, and every morning he and the governor general together enjoyed a brisk "horseback ride before breakfast." But Hunt had ambivalent feelings about the tan-skinned, regally attired, somewhat Europeanized, and recently exiled Queen Ranavalona III. (Madagascar's former royals were widely traveled, and they had converted to Christianity in the 1860s, although most of the islanders practiced indigenous religions, while others were Muslims.) Hunt wrote about and saved pictures of the queen, and a later biographical article about him even maintained that he taught her to ride. Hunt may not have made that allegation himself, but he did not quash or correct it, although Gallieni had, in fact, banished Ranavalona a full year before Gibbs and Hunt even arrived in Madagascar. Hunt nonetheless basked in the lavish opulence of the deposed queen's royal abode, and the unchallenged assertion that he had served as her equestrian instructor could have reflected his sense of identity with and romantic nostalgia for her bygone glory, as well as his own occasional proclivity for self-aggrandizement. He established a solid relationship with Governor General Gallieni, yet at the same time he may have rued France's imperious expulsion of the big island's once aristocratic "colored" monarchs.

During that memorable sojourn, Gallieni seated Hunt "at his right hand at the table in the spacious Salle à Manger." Every meal featured at least one course ("Langouste a l'Américaine," "Croquettes a la Maison Blanche," or "Gateau Lafayette") celebrating Gallieni's honored guest and their countries' historic bonds. Hunt's blissful month in Tananarive, he later wrote, seemed like a "continual round of banquets, dances, dinners, luncheons, receptions and weddings," and only after prolonged, heartfelt *au revoirs* did he finally return by auto and rail to Tamatave.

Once there, Billy Hunt's consular life resumed its usual rhythm. He had suffered a bout of "Malagasy fever" (a local form of malaria) soon after he arrived, which lent him a degree of immunity from further attacks, so he remained healthy thereafter. He also, however, followed a sage American traveler's counsel to "keep your head cool, feet warm, and your bowels open," to which he added his personal credo about the unceasing need for impeccable personal hygiene in the tropics: "keep yourself clean," a prudent directive that firmly positioned cleanliness next to godliness. In those years many Europeans and Euro-Americans believed that frequent and vigorous soapy scrubbing would prevent any abhorrent transference of African blackness.

Hunt had difficulties retaining a vice consul, recruiting in turn a hot-headed French *colon,* an Indian who soon forsook Madagascar, a tippling Italian, and a capricious Englishman. But he enjoyed an active social life, especially with his band of international chums who dubbed themselves the "Gastronomes." He and those gentlemen enjoyed "tennis parties every afternoon," followed by "the classic whisky and soda," then stag dinners that included "carefully chosen . . . wines and liquors . . . served by our Native Boys." Their repasts featured roasted suckling pigs, congratulatory toasts, discourses on current events, "off the record" oratory by the host, and concluded with further imbibing and group renditions of "English College Glee Songs." Even such informal activities reinforced the image and reality of the foreign service as an all-male, all-"white" enclave.

Two years after Hunt received his promotion, he again crossed paths with former consul Edward Wetter, and their encounters quickly took on other, convoluted dimensions. After shipping his white wife of many years back home to the American South in 1897, Wetter had stayed on in Madagascar. For a while he and a local woman, whom Hunt described as a "washed-out creole" (probably someone whom the French and locals designated a *métisse*, or of mixed race), shacked up in, of all places, the Anglican bishop's rectory, which the pair had boldly appropriated in the bishop's absence. On his return, the irate cleric dislodged the wayward couple, who then, wrote Hunt, scuttled off "into the interior with a band of native boys to exploit a mining concession." In 1903, however, Wetter resurfaced in Tamatave. "I was humiliated and shocked to learn that a former United States Consular Officer had forgotten his self-respect to such an extent," Hunt fastidiously added, but European and Asian men who lived on the island, where their otherwise inhibiting social fabric might easily fray, often pursued just such ill-advised endeavors. They indulged in excessive drinking, took up with indigenous women, and sometimes even entered into formal contracts with Malagasy families to purchase their pubescent daughters' sexual favors. In this instance, Wetter's illicit affair also may have evoked for Consul Hunt all-too-familiar memories of American white men who had forced themselves on their female slaves.

Hunt called on Wetter, whom he described as "emaciated, [with a] bushy beard that lent him the air of a cave-man." But the ex-consul assumed a "pompous and threatening manner," and Hunt eyed his host "continually fumbling" with a metal object he soon ascertained to be a "38 Automatic Colt Revolver *loaded*." Hunt characterized Wetter as a

Georgia backwoodsman [who] liked a man of color in his place, which was, in his estimation, in the corn fields. Like a flash of lightning I recalled the classic trick, "it went off accidentally," and just as Wetter was trying to get his anemic finger on the trigger and probably "bump me off" ... with his concubine as sole witness, [I] got up out of my seat, calmly shoved the revolver out of his reach, ... and continued our conversation as if nothing had happened. ... For once in my life, my wits worked with lightning rapidity.

Hastening back to his office, Hunt looked into the rates and schedules for passage on ships headed back to the United States, then cabled the State Department detailing Wetter's ignoble downfall and requesting five hundred dollars "to repatriate the former Consul." When the department approved that amount, Hunt notified Wetter, who refused to "express a word of thanks for the Government's generosity." Rather, he craftily tried to finagle his return by way of Réunion Island, where Governor General Gallieni had first exiled Queen Ranavalona, and where, Hunt suspected, Wetter planned to set up housekeeping again with his Malagasy lady friend. Hunt vetoed that transparent ruse, but attended to his new ward's medical needs, writing Ida Gibbs that "I have at last brought 'Uncle Samuel' to terms with regard to Wetter's repatriation. . . . I am paying . . . his Hospital [bills], 75 dollars out of pocket. None of which he deserves." Like a stern, reproachful parent, Hunt then "accompanied him on board the steamer" as the petulant Wetter departed from Tamatave by himself, bound home to Dixie at last.

Billy Hunt behaved more honorably in his dealings with Wetter than Wetter ever did with former consul Waller. His obsession with Wetter, however, an amalgam of anxiety, generosity, sympathy, and contempt, suggests that Hunt (subconsciously perhaps) perceived the rendezvous as an overdue confrontation with his own truant white father, culminating in both the salvation of and mastery over him. At the same time, Hunt boldly "rescued" a woman of color — not unlike his mother — from the clutches of a sexual predator. Though grounded in truth, this Oedipal episode also may have been romanticized in its retelling to make Consul Hunt appear, once more, as a swashbuckling yet magnanimous hero in the artfully crafted saga of his own life.

Hunt also submitted several memoranda to the State Department detailing trade possibilities with Madagascar. One, titled "Spider Spun Silk," he noted, was "quoted and commented on in American newspapers," while the New York *Butcher's Advocate* reprinted in full another such report. In that jocular account, Hunt wrote, a newcomer to Madagascar might be welcomed by "natives hauling into his garden . . . an infuriated ox, . . . to the immense acclamations of the crowds and considerable detriment to the flower beds." Concerning the centrality of zebu cattle to Malagasy life and culture, he added that "the Malagasy with his ox is like the Irishman with his whisky, when he is glad he drinks for joy and when he is sad he drinks to drown his sorrow. . . . If your wife presents you with a baby, kill oxen, when the baby is circumcised, more oxen; . . . if you offer up a prayer against famine, kill and eat an ox." (The opportunistic French profited from those rituals by imposing a tax on each such beast that the local people slaughtered.) Though clearly perceptive, Hunt's reports at times seem patronizing.

It is hard to reconcile differences between the description of his and Ida Gibbs's courtship in his memoir and the picture that emerges from their correspondence. In "From Cabin to Consulate" he wrote of a "desultory" relationship, in contrast to his true role as Ida's pursuer. But why would he want to make their marriage appear almost inadvertent, rather than the result of his own manly quest? In a patriarchal world that prized male dominance, did Ida's greater education and sophistication, and her family's affluence and influence, make Billy feel a bit inferior and thus inadvertently defensive? In contrast to several letters in which he beseeched her to accept his proposal, he later insisted that there had been "no serious thought or suggestion of courtship between us." "Having known Miss Gibbs — on the fly — as it were, for some years," he continued, "there seemed to be a certain element of safeness about it." After a fifteen-year, largely long-distance friendship, marriage must have seemed a very safe, much overdue, welcome, and expedient step forward. Whatever explains these disparities, Billy negotiated a home leave, he and Ida wed at last, and after a honeymoon in New York and Paris, followed by a tedious delay due to a longshoremen's strike in Marseille, in June 1904 they arrived in Tamatave on the ancient steamer *Irrawaddy*.

Billy reveled in nature's majesty and embraced its affinity with his new conjugal life in the balconied consular quarters on Tamatave's palm-lined but unpaved rue de l'Amiral Pierre. "Among the cherished memories of those days, was the ... panorama overlooking the harbor of Tamatave and the boundless expanse of the Indian Ocean from the windows of our bedroom," he wrote. "What a thrill," he added, "to lie in bed at night and watch with eager eyes the moon rise. . . . A tiny speck appeared on the horizon, which gradually [grew] larger and larger, assuming the form of an immense plate, then suddenly it appeared to have leapt out of the ocean and [floated] into space like a soul astray." "Sunrise ... offered a similar spectacle," he recalled. "[I]t dawned upon me why the Malagasy call it in their language, 'Maso-Andro,' the eye of the day."

Ida Gibbs Hunt had already reached Tamatave that August when her indomitable slave-born mother, Maria Alexander Gibbs, died at the age of seventy-eight, but because of the sluggish mails, she and Billy did not learn of that grievous loss for more than a month. If his estranged wife's death distressed M. W. Gibbs, however, he rallied in fine fettle. The following March, according to Mollie Church Terrell, "Nobody took a livelier interest in the [Roosevelt inaugural] festivities than did Judge Mifflin W. Gibbs of Little

Rock, Ark., who stands erect under the weight of four score years and apparently enters into the enjoyment of social pleasure with the freshness and zest of youth."

On the far side of the globe, once Ida had fully settled into Billy's consular quarters, he became more content and productive, and at last — possibly with her editorial assistance — completed the series of articles on Madagascar long promised to the American Geographical Society. Ida meanwhile wrote her sister Hattie that "BH improves with age. . . . He's been especially kind lately, though he's an awful tease." Her husband was very solicitous indeed, perhaps overly so. "BH stays with me always at night," the once independent Ida confessed, "and comes up a dozen times a day to see what I am doing." Sometimes they squabbled, but "soon made it up." "I am quite happy here and enjoy my home," she added, but missed old friends and favorite avocations. She fretted about her hair becoming brittle, and her beige skin freckling in the fierce tropical sun, and asked Hattie to send balms, hairdressing supplies, and sheet music. As a French-speaking American woman, Ida thrived among her new social set in Tamatave, mostly made up of European colonials. Governor General and Madame Joseph Simon Gallieni welcomed the new Mrs. William Henry Hunt to their island, and Ida began attending an array of social functions, even holding her own "At-Homes" each second and fourth Wednesday. In almost every way, she became the American consul's model spouse, hostess, and helpmate. Billy was overjoyed, and Ida bragged to Hattie that her ebullient husband said, "I'm 'hot stuff.'"

But problems of protocol sometimes arose. Billy Hunt found himself honor bound to decline an invitation from the British consul in which Ida was not included because she had not yet called on that official's wife. And Ida was more judgmental than Billy about Madagascar's racial and social inequities. She described her husband's friends, a couple named Bannerjee, as "high class Indians and well-to-do," but added, "Of course the French wouldn't quite accept them as equals." Yet much like Billy, Ida also spoke with a degree of condescension about some of the "natives" whom she met.

Like many of the island's privileged women, she played the piano, dabbled in her rose garden, and attended services and musicales at the Western churches. She outlined but never finished a novel about the colony, and dressed in pale linens, though she purchased silk saris and admired the indigenous women's hairstyles and their gowns, which were "loose and flowing and more graceful than our stiff fashions." "One reads of heathen adornment," she wrote, "but it is only necessary to look about the stores and streets to conclude that human nature is the same the world over." Ida acquired a decent vocabulary in several of the local languages and, shaded by her parasol, rode in the island's two-wheeled jinrikishas pulled by Asian coolies, or was carried about (like "all women of the upper classes," she explained) in a *filanzana,* one of Madagascar's wood and leather sedan chairs, borne on the shoulders of four runners. The ubiquity of such primitive modes of transport reflected the subordination of many impoverished or laboring-class Malagasies, yet also spoke to their passengers' dependency. A diplomatic incident might have ensued had one of those bearers injured or abandoned Ida, or any such "European" woman, in a remote quarter of Tamatave.

Billy wrote that life in Tamatave "suited Ida's temperament perfectly," and believed that his wife basked idly in the comfort of their abode, where three in-help, including a French chef, did her bidding. "I am not overburdened," Ida confessed. They sent out the laundry daily, and a "manservant" hand-polished their floors with his coconut brushes. Yet she kept abreast of social issues back home, and sometimes retreated to a separate sphere about which "BH" probably knew little. Ida's interests at the time focused on race, gender, and social inequities in the United States, and she had not fully formulated her broader global visions. Soon after she arrived, Ida drafted an outraged response to Thomas Nelson Page, who was a leading spokesman for the antebellum slaveholding South's faded (presumed) glories, pursuant to his rancorous essays on "the Negro problem" that *McClure's Magazine* ran in spring 1904.

Page's assertions, Gibbs Hunt wrote, were "not only unjust, but largely untrue." Only a generation after slavery's demise, she argued, that institution's legacy bore primary responsibility for her community's interminable hardships. "You say that the immorality of the Negro race has . . . increased since slavery," she fumed, then demanded, "How do you know that?" She seemed especially incensed that even in the new century nothing protected a "young colored girl . . . from the seductions of some white 'gentleman.'" Concerning Page's charges of rampant crime among African Americans, she responded, "Colored people are arrested for so many trivial offenses which are overlooked . . . in [the] case of white people," and she condemned "cruel penal servitude [and] the evils of the convict lease system." He had ranted on at length about lurid tales of sexual assaults by black men, but she accurately retorted by saying "how often lynchings occur . . . on suspicion [of rape] only. . . . Over 100 in the South every year."

As to Page's complaints about public expenditures on education for blacks, Gibbs Hunt corrected him, stating that the money earmarked for African

American youngsters amounted to only "about 1/5" of what was spent on whites. Their schooling, she added, was available only "2 or 3 months a year" in the South, where they had to "walk miles" to wretched, segregated facilities that often fell victim to arson attacks, or even "Ku Klux raids." And she rued the tragic reality that so many members of her race still lived in "abject poverty, . . . keeping them always in debt to their employers." They faced "prejudice increasing in the trades" as well, and had "no opportunities for apprenticeships." But despite such grievous liabilities, she continued, the Negro laborer "does not strike, is not an anarchist, [and he] works for lower wages."

Gibbs Hunt also attacked the nefarious writings of William Hannibal Thomas, a shrewd avatar of black self-hatred, whom Page had cited as the primary authority for his harangues. Her advocacy of women's rights and loyalty to her father and husband probably stoked her wrath at the misogynous Will Thomas, who, like them, had sought for a while to pursue a consular career, and she brushed aside as "base libel" his demeaning assessments of other Negroes' unsavory conduct.

Ida Gibbs Hunt provided no facile solutions and sadly concluded that "the Negro question will settle itself as the God of nations deemeth best." *McClure's*, which provided a popular print venue for a variety of white journalists, ran another response to Thomas Nelson Page's articles iterating the horrors of lynching (Mollie Church Terrell's refutation of him appeared in a different journal) but did not publish Gibbs Hunt's sizzling rebuttal — or she may never have mailed it off. But that was just as well, because for eagle-eyed observers at the Department of State, it would have been an incendiary piece to have attributed to any up-and-coming envoy's wife.

Ida accompanied her husband on all his overseas assignments, where she usually lived in colonial comfort like a number of affluent white women of her day, but their first of many extended separations began in mid-1905 when she returned to Washington. They would not see each other for two years. Thanks to her father, Ida had a sufficient financial nest egg to underwrite the expense, because the diplomatic service, while arguably prestigious, paid poorly. It did not yet reimburse its appointees for their spouses' travel, and remained the almost exclusive realm of elite white "gentlemen" who worked more for the aristocratic lifestyle and the honor of serving their country (and sometimes enriching themselves through shady ventures) than for the meager salary. Ida may have missed her independent life back home, and Billy's doting surveillance and blanket approval of colonialism could have made her uneasy as well. As a Gibbs woman, Ida took to heart her father's critiques of imperialism with its associated abuses of power. Billy Hunt also insisted that his wife should not remain in such a debilitating climate for more than a few months at a time, a well-intended, chivalrous limitation in which he included all American and European women. Though disease was rampant and some Americans called Madagascar "the white man's grave," Ida did not fall seriously ill there. But sanitation facilities were poor, and in addition to "Malagasy fever" and other endemic malarial strains, dysentery, leprosy, and cholera were omnipresent, while intermittent outbreaks of bubonic plague further ravaged the island. "Life in the tropics, however alluring," her husband warned, "after a certain time begins to show its effect on the most robust constitution, . . . and one needs a rest and change of environment and climate."

Just as Ida arrived back in the United States after joining her sister Hattie in Paris, the mutiny called the *Menelamba,* or Rising of the Red Shawls, broke out in Madagascar. It would be the Malagasies' last significant armed resistance to French rule for another four decades. The fighting was limited to the inland south, far from Tamatave, but its ramifications resonated at the consulate as well. Like every consul, Hunt was responsible for the welfare of all Americans in his domain, and he corresponded with State Department officials about the death of one such person at the hands of lawless *fahavalos* (guerrillas) during the rebellion. He assured his superiors that the prison sentence of only five years handed down by a "native" court under the colonial *justice indigène* was appropriate, because the white man had not died as a direct result of his wounds, but rather from peritonitis that set in when he failed to receive timely medical care.

Soon after Ida Gibbs Hunt got home, she became a sponsor of Washington, D.C.'s new "colored" Young Women's Christian Association (YWCA). She also read, heeded, and saved an informational broadside titled "What is the Niagara Movement?" Her friend W. E. B. Du Bois had convened the first Niagara Conference on the Canadian side (a symbolic protest against his own country's entrenched racism) of the international falls during the summer of 1905, a month before she returned to the United States, which was just as well, since that gathering, largely composed of Du Bois's Talented Tenth, only included men. It was thus far, however, African Americans' most significant organizational effort to demand their full citizenship rights. Several Niagara-ites also belonged to the Bethel Literary Society, Gibbs Hunt's old quasi-political circle in Washington, and the "Declaration of Principles" that emerged from the initial conference addressed the same racial injustices — concerning education, labor, and legal and voting rights — about which she had recently challenged Thomas Nelson Page.

Du Bois tried to recruit a number of established and influential as well as up-and-coming Negro men for his group, including a young attorney, musician, and soon-to-be United States consul named James Weldon Johnson. But like several others, Johnson declined because he did not want to pick the wrong horse in the bitter, escalating tussles between W. E. B. Du Bois and Booker T. Washington. Despite many obstacles, the Niagara Movement soon coalesced into a duly incorporated entity. Dr. Du Bois (who had earned his Harvard University PhD) thus fashioned the rudimentary core of a focused alternative to Dr. Washington (both Harvard and Yale had recently bestowed honorary doctorates on him) and his more conservative, accommodationist tactics.

The second Niagara assembly gathered in August 1906 at the iconic site of Harpers Ferry, West Virginia, where in 1859 the militant white abolitionist John Brown had stormed the federal arsenal to protest slavery. Richard Greener, a former United States consul, went that sophomore summer as Booker T. Washington's undercover spy, although as a Harvard graduate, he also felt a strong kinship with Du Bois, his fellow alumnus. The previous year's exclusion of women had been reconsidered (although the revised resolutions still spoke only of promoting "universal manhood suffrage") in favor of somewhat improved gender inclusiveness. The conference's distaff contingent did not participate in the formal sessions, but did form a Women's Committee. They dutifully raised money to support Du Bois's endeavor and were invited to the diverse ceremonial and social events. That small group included activist women of both races, several of whom, like Gibbs Hunt, soon followed Du Bois on to Niagara's ideological successor, the National Association for the Advancement of Colored People (NAACP). For its time, the Niagara Movement was progressive, though somewhat elitist and confrontational, and was seen by many critics — black and white — as alarmingly radical. It was a highly controversial affiliation for the wife of anyone serving in a diplomatic capacity.

Ida Gibbs Hunt also attended the National Association of Colored Women (NACW) convention in Detroit, where she delivered a paper detailing her observations of African women and protesting the outrages committed by Belgians in the Congo. (In one notorious case, Belgian mercenaries burned and ransacked the Congolese pygmy Ota Benga's home village, then bound and shipped him off to the United States to be exhibited at the 1904 St. Louis World's Fair. Later he was transferred, caged, and displayed to gaping crowds at the Bronx Zoo's monkey house, where he was widely advertised as the "missing link.") "Because of the subjugation to which Africans have had to submit," Gibbs Hunt exclaimed, the "cry now is 'Africa for Africans.'" NACW members exhorted her to initiate social service clubs abroad, she wrote, the intended "result to be an International Association of Colored Women."

Back in Washington, she celebrated her thirty-nine-year-old sister Hattie's marriage to the young attorney Napoleon Bonaparte Marshall, who had received his undergraduate and law degrees at Harvard, where he first got to know W. E. B. Du Bois. Their 1906 wedding, while not as large or elaborate as Ida and Billy's, nonetheless was a stylish affair for which Hattie had selected and purchased her chic, Parisian-silk bridal gown when she and Ida traveled together in France the previous summer. Both the service and reception took place at Hattie's conservatory, which was awash in music and flowers. At that point, of course, the new Mrs. Marshall, like all married women, had to resign her position with the District of Columbia's public schools. Soon thereafter Nap Marshall took leave of his bride to serve as an appeals lawyer for a beleaguered company of African American soldiers in Texas.

The controversy began that spring, when despite protests about widespread discrimination in the South, the army dispatched several Negro infantry units from the Midwest to a fort near Brownsville, Texas. That region's Anglo-Americans heartily embraced Jim Crow, and thus they both spurned and demeaned the newly arrived troops. Tensions escalated when a group of residents assaulted some black enlisted men. Their white officers accepted the ugly reality that the Brownsville citizenry's abuse of "colored" people was simply part and parcel of the well-established order of southern life. The sores festered, but exactly what happened one fateful day that summer was never fully clarified. Whites claimed that a cadre of uniformed Negroes stormed their town and fired wildly into a store. One local man died and others were injured. Military police rounded up and interrogated a small contingent of soldiers, who refused to implicate their colleagues. No hard evidence justified any courts-martial, but the army's inspector general maintained that the blacks had entered into a conspiracy of silence to protect an unidentified band of criminals among them.

President Theodore Roosevelt rubber-stamped the army's recommendations posthaste and, by executive fiat, declared guilty and dishonorably discharged almost every man (167 altogether) in those units — even though five of them had previously been awarded prestigious Congressional Medals of Honor. Subsequent investigations correctly found that such retribution should never have been imposed without due process of law, and raised the possibility that the sole conspiracy may have been a scheme concocted by whites in Brownsville who hoped to rid their town of the unwelcome Negro troops. As a counsel for the accused, who unsuccessfully appealed their mass dismissals all the way up to the Supreme Court, Nap Marshall became disillusioned with both Roosevelt and the whole Republican Party.

Another event reflecting the temper of the times targeted Ida Gibbs Hunt's Oberlin classmate and former teaching colleague Anna Julia Cooper, who for several years had served as the principal of Washington's M Street High School. At first, Cooper was lauded, but her insistence on providing students with a rigorous classical education soon put her at odds with many whites, including members of the District's board of education, who believed that even the most cerebral Negro youngsters should receive only industrial or vocational training. Cooper, however, saw to it that the school stayed fully accredited. She demanded the highest standards of academic achievement and negotiated scholarships for her best pupils at her own alma mater, in the Ivy League, and at other first-rate "white" northern colleges. Cooper's stance distanced her from Booker T. Washington and loosely aligned her with progressives such as W. E. B. Du Bois.

That debate's origins can be traced, in part, to a lecture that Du Bois had delivered in the nation's capital in 1902 (a significant event that Anna Julia Cooper, Ida Gibbs, and their former Oberlin classmate Mollie Church Terrell almost certainly had attended), when he excoriated recent attempts around the country to limit the academic curricula offered to black youths. But in the *Plessy v. Ferguson* case of 1896 the Supreme Court had sanctioned state-sponsored segregation, and then three years later, in *Cumming v. Richmond County, Georgia, Board of Education,* the justices determined that educational policy decisions should reflect local standards and practices. That ruling authorized (actually encouraged) many jurisdictions to curtail, or even eliminate, their Negro high schools.

Cooper's reputation suffered a critical blow when investigators uncovered some isolated instances of in-school smoking and drinking. She had loyal supporters, but critics scavenged her closets for skeletons and, finding none, created a whopper. They spread what her biographer, Louise Hutchinson, calls "a distasteful rumor with moral overtones" and hinted at a love affair with her foster son, who also taught there. The board of education grudgingly retained

Cooper for a while, but condemned the "loose methods" its members said had occurred under her administration. The next spring they voted not to renew her appointment as principal. Hardest for Cooper to swallow was the failure of both Mollie Church Terrell (her old friend and a former board member) and Mollie's husband, Robert (he preceded Cooper as principal and was then appointed a federal judge thanks to Booker T. Washington's endorsement), to speak out on her behalf. Angered, hurt, and mortified by her unjust dismissal, Cooper left Washington for Missouri and would not return for five years. Although she and Mollie Church Terrell later cooperated in such efforts as the "colored" women's club and settlement house movements, that rift never fully closed. Ida Gibbs Hunt had returned to the District only temporarily, and must have been relieved that she really did not have to choose sides in that ugly and tragic internecine dispute.

And as the controversy over Cooper raged, the poet Paul Laurence Dunbar, their brilliant but troubled Le Droit Park neighbor, died from tuberculosis, probably exacerbated by his alcoholism and gonorrhea. A decade later the acclaimed M Street High School, where both of the Church-Terrells, the two Gibbs siblings, and Cooper all had taught or administered, would be named in his honor.

Ida meanwhile fostered her husband's advancement. Before leaving Tamatave she wrote her sister, "If you hear from Pa or read in the papers of Mr. Hunt's being transferred anywhere, wire us at once," adding that "the State Dept. wrote . . . that his application for a transfer would be considered in due course." A noncommittal assistant secretary of state had responded to M. W. Gibbs that his prior request to have Hunt reassigned "to some other post not so remote . . . will receive very careful consideration when a suitable opportunity arises." Though Hunt had no white sponsor, friend, or relative in the State Department to further his progress, it's quite possible that William Libbey again spoke out on his behalf. (And might some addled department official have confused Billy with the white William Henry Hunt?) As a result of his grace, perseverance, increasing diplomatic skills, and mastery of French, Billy Hunt enhanced his own prospects, but his wife adroitly boosted his career as well. In 1906 Secretary of State Elihu Root reorganized and professionalized the consular service, and that November, while Ida was at home in Washington, a ranking department official first imparted the welcome news to her: "I am glad to be able to tell you that your husband is to be transferred to St. Etienne, France, which is a consulate of the same grade as the one he now occupies. This will gratify Mr. Hunt's wish for a change and will doubtless prove an agreeable post.... I suppose he will be able to leave Tamatave for Europe in about a month."

Hunt had done everything his superiors demanded, and more, and they rewarded him with an assignment in what he regarded as the world's second most wonderful country. His dispatches detailed Madagascar's resources that might be developed to the advantage of his own nation, his solid *amitié* with Governor General Gallieni helped to repair the United States' slightly tattered relationship with France, and he kept his nose scrupulously clean. Unlike his predecessors, John Waller and Edward Wetter, William Henry Hunt never sullied the office of consul, never embarrassed his country or himself. He avoided being seared by the "red hot iron" that became his metaphor for Madagascar. He recalled his halcyon "red letter days" with Gallieni; Madagascar's looming mesas made it widely known as the Great Red Island; red had been the Malagasy royal family's signature color; and the 1905 anti-colonial revolt often was called the Rising of the Red Shawls.

When his successor, James Graneth Carter, a Tuskegee Institute alumnus, letter carrier, tailor, and newspaperman who would remain in Madagascar for much of the next thirty-six years, replaced him at the end of 1906, Hunt prepared to leave after almost a decade. Like many of the French *colons* living on the island, Hunt disliked the pompous bureaucrat who had arrived from the *métropole* the previous autumn to relieve Governor General Gallieni — a brilliant, charismatic administrator, as well as Hunt's old friend and patron whom he sorely missed. Hunt had expressed his concerns that with Gallieni's inevitable departure "the wheaten loaf might soon become unleavened bread," and the consul prevailed on Professor Libbey to extend the vibrant French general an invitation to lecture in the United States.

Sorting through his memories and memorabilia, Hunt recalled a panoply of world events that had transpired during his nine years on the Indian Ocean island, including the United States' "annexation of Porto Rico, purchase of the Philippines, and the Cuban Independence," France's simmering Dreyfus affair, Queen Victoria's death, and the Russo-Japanese War. But he did not mention outrages such as the mutilation and murders of rubber workers by white Belgians in the Congo, Germany's slaughter of eighty thousand "natives" in its Southwest Africa (today's Namibia), the recent outbreaks of violence targeting black people in American cities, Jim Crow's inexorable ascendancy, and the end of any Negro representation in the U.S. Congress for decades to come.

Early in James Carter's long tenure (seeking the State Department's approval to acquire a new typewriter for the consulate became his first administrative task), a shrewd visitor observed, "There is an idea generally prevalent in Madagascar that all Americans are Negroes." And why ever not? American travelers scarcely went there at all, and merchants or exporters from the United States seldom attempted to set up commercial enterprises in that faraway, French colonial locale. The unsuccessful mining venture of Edward Telfair Wetter, a white man, was a rare anomaly in Madagascar. His predecessor, Consul John Lewis Waller, who had worked, schemed, fallen from grace, and been shanghaied, tried, and hastily convicted, of course, was black. Since Judge Gibbs and his deputy reached there early in 1898, all of their country's official representatives had been "colored." For decades, with few exceptions, those were the only Americans the Malagasies ever encountered.

As the sole governmental representative from the United States in Madagascar, with no larger legation, mission, or embassy anywhere on that enormous island, Consul William Henry Hunt had maintained almost total control over his own destiny as well as his country's diplomatic dealings there, both with the white French colonizers and with their brown-skinned subjects. Such would hardly be the case once he and Ida Gibbs Hunt reached continental France.

6

France, 1907–1918
La Ville Noire and la Guerre Mondiale

William Henry Hunt and Ida Gibbs Hunt both got to France in 1907, she that summer from Washington by way of New York, he earlier in the year, straight from Madagascar. The consul later recalled how the "empty champagne bottles standing on the tables in the smoking room vouched for the splendid send off I received from my Tamatave friends." The rattletrap freighter that should have carried him all the way to Europe crossed the equator, labored farther up Africa's east coast, entered the Gulf of Aden and the Red Sea, and wheezed through the strategic Suez Canal to Port Saïd. Then, almost predictably, it broke down altogether. So Hunt debarked and boarded a cross-desert train bound to Cairo. Once there, he savored the comforts of the legendary Shepherd's Hotel, where he claimed to have stayed years before with the storied but anonymous benefactor of his youth, then set off again, northwestward from the ancient city of Alexandria, sculpted more than two millennia before from the Nile Delta's antediluvian muck.

After a turbulent crossing, Hunt arrived in Marseille, continental France's southernmost and notably Africanized port, which teemed with a broad spectrum of "colored" transients and sailors from around the globe. He lamented leaving behind the "blue Mediterranean shores and warm sunshine, [and] purchased a railroad ticket for what would be my home for the next twenty years." Reversing another leg of the journey that he and Judge Gibbs had taken in 1898, he hunkered down into his reserved seat on the coach bound north via the Rhône River valley to Lyon, then transferred onto a secondary line that doubled back forty miles southwest to gritty, industrial St.-Étienne, near the eastern edge of France's rugged Massif Central. Hunt noticed that the city where he would be stationed was situated at "a higher altitude than Lyons. . . . We seemed to be going up-grade all the time." "The train felt like an ice-box," he later grumbled, adding, "I had not suffered so much from the cold since leaving New York in December 1897." As the frigid *chemin de fer* carrying him toward his final destination chugged and belched through the grimy Terre-Noire tunnel on the last day of January, he observed that the "whole region was disfigured with unsightly coal mining shafts . . . and iron and steel rolling mills which seemed to cast an air of desolation and gloom."

His genial second-in-command, Hastings Burroughs, who, Hunt would write, "had been connected with the consulate some twenty odd years," greeted him at the depot. Burroughs also served as an Irish Protestant evangelical minister, having taken on a self-assumed but thankless "mission to spread the Gospel [and] convert Catholics to Protestantism" in heavily Roman Catholic France. Decades before, he had married a Stephanoise (as St.-Étienne's residents are known) and remained from then on in his wife's hometown. Burroughs soon retired and would be replaced, in turn, by five Americans, all of whom became the Hunts' protégés and friends. The first of them, a Howard University–educated pharmacist named Edmond Autex Burrill, whom the State Department transferred to France from his former post in Venezuela, immediately succeeded Vice Consul Burroughs. Hilary Brunot, Hunt's predecessor as consul, had already departed from St.-Étienne for an assignment in Spain. He had turned over the consulate to Burroughs, who on February 7 reassigned it to Hunt's authority.

State Department officials offered little encouragement and virtually no promotions to the very few Negroes in their employ, and almost never granted them favored posts in Europe, partly on the assumption that Europeans shared many white Americans' racial biases. So with Jim Crow in the ascendancy in the United States, almost the only such men to serve abroad went to Africa, though the department sent a few to South America, where race was more loosely defined and profoundly shaped by class. A rare exception was George H. Jackson, a graduate of Yale's medical college who had worked for a while as a missionary in the Belgian Congo. He received his first consular assignment in 1899, then became one of W. E. B. Du Bois's Niagara-ites. Dr.

Jackson served for nine years in La Rochelle, a French port on the Bay of Biscay, where he married a Frenchwoman. The next such appointee, William Yerby, another physician, went first to the English colony of Sierra Leone, on to Senegal, then to La Rochelle (following Jackson), Portugal's Oporto, and back once again to France. Soon after Hunt's arrival in St.-Étienne, George Jackson was reassigned to Cognac, where he stayed another year. That brief interlude, however, remained deeply etched in his memory, and two decades later he authored a hefty tome titled *The Medicinal Value of French Brandy* (1928).

Nor would the State Department's near exclusion of "colored" men from Europe change in the foreseeable future. Its decision makers did not offer an additional foreign service assignment on that continent to any African American until the late 1920s, when they sent just one. But they nonetheless recognized William Henry Hunt as an able consular officer, and apparently yielded to the exhortations of his wife and influential father-in-law, and perhaps even his prior booster Princeton's William Libbey. And certainly he was a known commodity. As an official in Washington commented at the time about one of the few other Negro consuls who was familiar to him, he at least was preferable to "some new coon."

His government's mind-set back in the United States, however, did not stifle the convivial Billy Hunt, who expediently began cultivating contacts among the region's "outstanding families." One leading Stephanois, he recalled, introduced him to "everyone worthwhile, and recommended me to his Tailor, Bootmaker and Haberdasher, who served me faithfully for twenty years." The same fellow, he added, saw to it that "I was admitted to membership in the 'Grand Cercle,' being Saint Etienne's leading commercial and social organization." Hunt often thanked his lucky stars, but also would have known that due to embedded racism, such affiliations and privileges never would have been made available to a Negro American at home. "I had been the pampered child of fortune," he wrote. His new French associates treated him as the valued representative of an esteemed and increasingly powerful nation — hardly a "colored" man at all.

Few Negroes from the United States dispersed to provincial hubs such as St.-Étienne in that period, but some did go to Paris, as tourists or to study, create, or entertain. Most Parisians embraced those sojourners, who included the lyricist James Weldon Johnson (his works ran the spectrum from "Under the Bamboo Tree" and "Congo Love Song" to "Lift Ev'ry Voice and Sing")

and the expatriate painter Henry Ossawa Tanner, whose art was more esteemed in Europe than in his country of birth. Tanner had left the United
States after encountering bigotry when he married a white woman. In many
Frenchmen's eyes, those "colored" Americans, like Consul Hunt, had little in
common with their own colonial African subjects. The capital's vast Musée
d'Ethnologie-Trocadéro featured dioramas and artifacts of "primitive" peoples
and their cultures, and became a prime destination for both American visitors
and local residents, while *les Français* still venerated the enduring scientific
racism of Dr. Georges Cuvier, who had publicly displayed the genitals of an
African woman named Saartjie Baartman, whom he redesignated the Hot-
tentot Venus. Some of Europe's newer cartoons and advertising art depicted
doudous, fictive colonial women, often mulattoes, characterized by massive
buttocks, limited intelligence, amoral accessibility, and unbridled sexuality,
as well as goggle-eyed "Sambos," lecherous *chocolats,* servile hirelings, priapic
spear-shaking Ubangis, or man-eating cannibals. But most Europeans whom
the Gibbs-Hunts encountered during their residency in France saw and
treated them as influential, sophisticated, and refined Americans who bore
little resemblance to any such demeaning stereotypical categorizations.

Hunt wrote about his early months there in characteristically disarming
fashion — "My appointment as Consul and assignment to a European Consulate, both achieved in the short space of ten years, was enough to muddle the
head of an untutored chap like me" — but he also contended that his "transfer
was interpreted as a mark of the State Department's confidence in my ability
to measure up to the situation." He vowed to equal or exceed his employers'
expectations as he worked diligently and closely with the Stephanoises, other
Frenchmen, and a variety of his own compatriots, yet one early episode reminded him that the nearly autonomous authority he previously wielded on
behalf of his country in Tamatave would never be matched in St.-Étienne.

A few weeks after his arrival Hunt received a surprise visit from a man
who was charged, in a new departmental function, "with the biennial inspection of Consular Offices in all parts of the world." That unidentified State
Department inspector had to wait awhile in the anteroom because another
appointment occupied the consul. By the time Hunt broke free and tried to
deal with the man's queries, he recollected, "[M]y visitor rose up in all of his
five feet and some inches of dignity and unmasked his identity in a voice more
in keeping with a mule driver than a Consular Officer [saying] something as
follows: 'I am Inspector W——, I shall be back soon and I am going to inspect

you,' and stormed out of the office." "I was sure he would ... hang and quarter me when he returned," Hunt added. "It may be that he was disgusted to find the Consular Office in such a cubbyhole, and if so, I do not blame him."

The probing appraisal went on for three days, Hunt recalled, and when the department's overseer prepared to leave, the two men set out together for a promenade and farewell meal. "The city of St. Etienne is practically all run out of one street, which is about seven miles long and bisects the town," Hunt explained. As they strolled along the promenade, "all persons we met ... would raise their hats to us. Every person I had met since my arrival in the city happened to be on the street that morning." The once huffy inspector, impressed by the ubiquitous respect shown Consul Hunt, submitted a favorable report and recommended an upgrade in the shabby consulate. "I was afterwards fortunate to lease ... the second floor in a building centrally located in City Hall Square," Billy Hunt reported, "where the combined offices and residence remained." He called his spacious new facilities that faced the main plaza and adjoined the grandiose *hôtel de ville* (city hall) the Ville Noire. Perhaps he conceived that appellation as a Gallic inversion of his own country's White House *(Maison Blanche),* or relished the irony of a lone Negro American consul reigning over a circumscribed "black city" within the otherwise all-white St.-Étienne.

Consul Hunt also reestablished contact with Joseph Simon Gallieni, Madagascar's former governor general, who had returned the previous year to his home in Lyon. During Hunt's first months in France a letter in response to one of the consul's own arrived from Gallieni, who wrote: "I am very satisfied to learn that we are neighbors. St. Etienne is not far from Lyon and I think that I will see you again before long time." And see him he did. Scores of the region's luminaries assembled for the banquet that Hunt arranged and hosted for Gallieni at St.-Étienne's most elegant hotel. That ceremonial tribute and reunion featured fine food and wines, and laudatory toasts interspersed with warm remembrances of the two men's collegiality and cooperation during the near decade they had worked together on France's great colonial island.

But Hunt's official consular business always prevailed. His first report from St.-Étienne to the Department of State in May 1907 addressed the thorny issue of "lunacy in France." He collected, quantified, and analyzed data about the country's mental asylums and their inmates (insane women, he observed, greatly outnumbered men), and his dossier on madness included a meticulous accounting of French "lunatics ... epileptics ... hysterical children ... and idiots."

Ida Gibbs Hunt meanwhile lingered back in the United States. Billy urged her to "prolong her stay," but by July he had equipped and furnished his up-graded quarters "at considerable expense." When "Mrs. Hunt arrived," he remembered, "she had only to walk in and hang her hat." As one stateside Negro journal reported, she was "royally received [at] her husband's post in the land of the Napoleons. . . . The city was profusely decorated in her honor, and public officials and foreign consuls paid their respects . . . at the American consulate."

Not long after Ida rejoined her husband she wrote a friend back home that "St. E. is not a pretty town but the surroundings are beautiful." The city itself, located in France's industrial heartland between the broad Loire and Rhône river valleys, sits two-thirds of the way southeast from Paris en route to the Mediterranean. But the Burgundy wine region peters out north of St.-Étienne, and Languedoc lies to its south. Aveyron, home to a panoply of sumptuous dairy products, is fifty miles southwest. Dating back at least to the eleventh century, St.-Étienne is old but hardly quaint or picturesque; close to much, but celebrated for little, that is most cherished about France. Rather than cheese, truffles, fruit, wine, flowers, perfume, or foie gras, its most sig-nificant indigenous commodities were iron ore, coal, and asbestos — essential but toxic extractions from the local mines. The diligent Stephanoises also made firearms of all sorts, *bicyclettes, tramways électriques,* fabrics, and satin ribbons, and that unsightly mining and manufacturing district was blessed with the unadulterated spring water essential for dyeing silk. "The weaver of St. Etienne is by nature an artist in his line," Consul Hunt maintained, and his country became the French ribbon industry's most important customer.

And an array of letters and *cartes postales* arrived at "Le Consulat des Etats Unis, 5 Place de l'Hôtel de Ville, St. Etienne (Loire)," much as they had in Tamatave, keeping the Gibbs-Hunts in touch with the world. They came from the consul's superiors at the State Department, as well as from relatives and friends around the United States, former colleagues in Madagascar, voy-agers at sea, and from locales as far flung as Brazil and Argentina; *las Islas Canarias* and Spain, Belgium, Russia, Austria, and Greece; Morocco and Dji-bouti; Australia, Japan, and *l'Indochine française.* Billy's Cosmopolitan Cor-respondence Club pen pals, identified, as usual, by both name and member-ship number, dispatched many of them, while new professional associates and Stephanoises in town or traveling elsewhere sent others. Birthday greetings, invitations, fond thank-yous, and blessings for a *Joyeux Noël* or Happy New Year poured in. During the summer of 1908 Billy received and saved a snapshot from the tenth reunion of his long-abandoned Williams College class, which shows twenty-eight upstanding white gentlemen admiring their first-born "class son." A photographic paean from one of Billy's vice consuls bears the message: "This is a picture of my . . . fiancée. Is she not a dandy?" English was sometimes the language of choice, as in "Bring 1 Pt. Rye Whiskey!" decreed by an American drinking buddy, and a few correspondents wrote both in English ("I do not know if my English style is well") and in French, then increasingly in French alone, often with salutations to "oncle" or "tante." One card addressed to "Bien cher papa" ends with "Affectueuses baisers [kisses] de votre petite." Race did not seem a liability, but neither was it entirely disregarded. One neighborly *mademoiselle* opened her note to Billy and Ida Hunt with a sweet and saucy, "Et, mes chocolats!" and signed it "votre fille [your daughter] Yasmine."

Despite his warm welcome in St.-Étienne, in short order Hunt became the innocent target of a scheme designed to discredit him with the State Department and result in his removal from that gratifying consular post. Surprisingly perhaps, a cabal of his fellow Negro Americans rather than white men in Washington hatched and attempted to implement that treacherous plot.

The incident involved another up-and-coming Negro foreign service officer, James Weldon Johnson. Johnson, an attorney and songwriter, had first visited France in 1905, and later recorded his euphoria when he found himself there to be "free from the conflicts within the Man-Negro dualism . . . free to be merely a man." Soon thereafter, he took and passed his country's recently instituted foreign service examination (Hunt, like others who had already embarked on consular careers, was grandfathered out of that requirement). The State Department then sent Johnson, who spoke and read Spanish and French, to take over its consulate in Puerto Caballo, Venezuela, where Edmond Burrill, later reassigned to St.-Étienne, briefly served as his second-in-command. In the 1890s Judge M. W. Gibbs himself had unsuccessfully sought an assignment in Venezuela, and only in 1904 did the department dispatch Jerome Peterson as its initial African American envoy there. Johnson had little to do and ample time to write over the next few years, especially *The Autobiography of an Ex-Colored Man,* his controversial novel about racial identity and passing, first (and prudently) published anonymously in 1912. But soon he became restless and peevish in South America.

Late in 1907 Consul Johnson expressed his dissatisfaction with Venezuela and his desire for a European assignment in a letter to his sponsor, Charles W. Anderson, a black Republican ward politician in New York City and one of

Booker T. Washington's trusted northern cronies. Anderson and Washington both had been incensed by the criticism of President Theodore Roosevelt voiced by Ida Gibbs Hunt's brother-in-law, attorney Napoleon Bonaparte Marshall, after Roosevelt issued blanket dishonorable discharges to the company of black soldiers Marshall had represented. And in his 1902 autobiography and at recent public events, M. W. Gibbs had made clear his own escalating discontent with the Republican Party's heavy-handed imperialism. With obvious pique, Anderson wrote Washington that he found "the name of Judge Gibbs . . . among the speakers at the Taft [soon to be the Republican presidential candidate] protest meeting." In a supposed case of guilt by association, those men used statements by Billy Hunt's candid in-laws to argue that Hunt himself should be banished from his enviable post and replaced by their candidate, the Grand Old Party (GOP) loyalist James Weldon Johnson, who already was familiar to Roosevelt as one of the virtuosos who had composed the catchy campaign song "You're All Right, Teddy."

Charles Anderson's letters to Booker T. Washington generated follow-ups from the Tuskegeean to white power brokers in the nation's capital asking "if some of our friends cannot be placed in that consular position in France, now occupied by [Hunt] the son-in-law of Judge Gibbs, [since Gibbs and Marshall] spend their time in heaping abuse upon the administration." Judge Gibbs was a major sponsor of Washington's National Negro Business League, and the invitation to Ida and Billy's wedding exemplified the men's warm, mutually supportive relationship. B. T. Washington, often called the Wizard of Tuskegee, had even contributed a glowing introduction to Gibbs's autobiography. He may (at least should) have felt ashamed about plotting to derail Hunt's career — about undermining any such able and aspiring African American. But the judge's wealth and past party activism made him, and thus (by association) Hunt, highly visible targets. As Anderson sniped, "Gibbs would probably recover his senses if his son-in-law were transferred and another colored man (Johnson) given St. Etienne." "This is the only remedy for these evils," he concluded. Nothing confirms that Judge Gibbs ever knew for sure about Washington's scheme to discredit his daughter's husband, but the absence of any further correspondence between the two older titans suggests that their friendship deteriorated, or at least cooled a lot, following Anderson and Washington's connivance on behalf of James Weldon Johnson. Such political innuendo, intimidation, and blatant abuse of power, however, were in keeping with many of Washington's endeavors, and his ways of squelching all presumed opposition and ensuring that anyone whom he deemed significant in the African American community remained fully loyal and beholden to him, and to the GOP.

Johnson had made the initial complaint to Charles Anderson, clearly anticipating some sort of relief. But he may not have known that Anderson unleashed Booker T. Washington's political wrath on his behalf, and neither his autobiography nor Hunt's memoir mentions the conspiracy. But the ambitious Consul Johnson did admit that he was frustrated and disappointed by his futile attempts to obtain an appointment in Geneva, Seville, or Nice, a plummy position on the French Riviera, which he thought he deserved and would get. One of Anderson's letters to B. T. Washington acknowledged, however, that with George Jackson and Hunt already in place, "it would be impossible to send another colored man to France." In part, the State Department considered fashionable Nice a choice assignment (and therefore appropriately reserved for a white man), and having a pair of Negro consuls already stationed in that country would surely have been seen as more than enough. Why the Johnson-Anderson-Washington plot fizzled out never will be fully explained, but Consul Hunt remained securely ensconced at his post in St.-Étienne for a long time to come.

The consuls had no residual bad blood between them, however, because three years later, in response to some unspecified prior incident or communication, Hunt wrote Johnson in Corinto, Nicaragua, where the department transferred him late in 1908 from the Venezuelan post he so disliked: "Many thanks for your thoughtfulness of me. Accept my wishes true and greetings kind for 1911." Although that is the only known correspondence between them, as two of the country's few Negro foreign service officers in that era, they likely established a degree of kinship and empathy with one another.

Johnson, meanwhile, longed to rejoin his wife, who had recently returned to New York, and realized that no one of his race would progress very far with the State Department. He therefore opted not to remain much longer in its employ, and shortly after Woodrow Wilson's 1912 election, he resigned rather than accept a new assignment in the Portuguese Azores. Soon thereafter, the savvy James Weldon Johnson became an editor at the *New York Age* (where he worked with Jerome Peterson, whom he had succeeded as consul in Venezuela), at that time the country's African American newspaper with the largest circulation and one that was covertly financed by Tuskegee's "Wizard." Johnson thus remained firmly entrenched under Washington's aegis until the older man died a few years later.

Charles Anderson himself was nothing if not the adaptable chameleon.

In 1914, no doubt realizing that Hunt was secure in his post and a respected, though currently absent, Negro New Yorker, he bestowed (as reported in the *Washington Bee*) the "handsome silver trophy donated by William Henry Hunt, United States Consul at St. Etienne, France," on the winners of an annual tournament that he organized for black basketball teams. But Anderson also continued as one of Washington's key political enforcers, from time to time even threatening the governmental appointments of the husbands of irrepressible African American women such as Chicago's Ida B. Wells-Barnett and Ida Gibbs Hunt's lifelong friend Mollie Church Terrell.

At around the same time, Ida's father fell on rocky and unsettling times back in Arkansas. When M. W. Gibbs returned from Madagascar to Little Rock in 1901 he regained his health, reactivated his law practice, civic involvements, and real estate ventures, and despite his incipient misgivings about the GOP, organized a "Fred Douglass Club" to involve Arkansas's African Americans in politics and better their chances of acquiring a fair share of federal patronage. The next year he funded and became president of an ambitious enterprise called the Capital City Savings Bank. It was only the second black owned-and-operated financial institution in the state. His enterprise opened to widespread jubilation, and for some time it seemed destined to continue successfully. The directors included Judge Gibbs himself, his earnest but lackluster son Horace, and several leaders of Little Rock's Negro business community, and those men hired a handful of eager though inexperienced employees. Few knew, and no one divulged, that right from its inception the operation was ineptly managed.

Its problems surfaced in June 1908 on the heels of the previous year's panic that had undercut scads of small banks nationwide, when only the timely intervention of the powerful banker J. Pierpont Morgan had prevented the country from slipping into an abysmal depression. A number of depositors, responding to well-founded rumors of insufficient reserves, stormed Judge Gibbs's establishment demanding their money. The deficiency was undeniable, but a result of the unsettled economic climate, underfinancing, ill-kept records, and winked-at overdrafts rather than embezzlement or fraud. Since M. W. Gibbs and B. T. Washington's relationship had eroded, it seems, no prominent black businessmen rallied to support the judge; and when Little Rock's white bankers declined to come to Capital City's assistance (as they might well have done for an enterprise operated or financed by one of their own), a state court declared it insolvent and placed it in receivership.

A grand jury handed down criminal indictments against Judge Gibbs and his cohorts. Little Rock's lawmen arrested the otherwise irreproachable eighty-five-year-old patriarch, and the court sequestered his personal estate — valued at more than a hundred thousand dollars. He managed to get released on bail, but the charges were not set aside until a year later when Gibbs, who ultimately arranged to shield most of his private assets from seizure, accepted full responsibility and negotiated a compromise financial settlement. Nonetheless, it was a truly galling defeat, since his reputation theretofore had been impeccable and his achievements legendary. No black Arkansan of his generation matched M. W. Gibbs's fame, wealth, and accomplishments, and for decades he had been recognized and extolled as a magnanimous philanthropist, canny politician, and exemplary attorney, as well as a noteworthy national leader of black capitalism.

Along with the bank crisis, after years of allegiance to and service with the Republicans (most African Americans remained faithful to what they called the Party of Lincoln), Gibbs did more than just gripe about the increasingly racist GOP. To the dismay of Booker T. Washington, among others, in mid-1908 Gibbs endorsed the Democrats' candidate for president instead of William Howard Taft, the ultimately victorious Republican. Former President Roosevelt, Taft's predecessor, had first forfeited some of his Negro supporters as the result of his harsh denigration of a company of "colored" troops in Cuba after the Spanish-American War, though he recouped much of his earlier popularity when, amid a storm of protests from white Americans, he invited Washington to dine at the White House. He further antagonized blacks in 1906 by his mass discharge of the Negro soldiers in Texas for whom Napoleon Bonaparte Marshall had served as an attorney. The roots of Gibbs's doubts about and frustrations with the party to which he had pledged his loyalty for many decades, however, can be traced back as far as his final exchange of letters with Frederick Douglass early in 1895, when the older man had warned Gibbs against blind or exclusive loyalty to the GOP.

Gibbs's growing disillusionment with and ultimate abandonment of the Republican Party also exacerbated a feud with W. Calvin Chase, editor and publisher of the *Washington Bee,* one of the country's most influential "colored" newspapers. Booker T. Washington was the *Bee*'s silent backer, and that itself may have engendered much of the ensuing brouhaha. But as early as 1904, Chase's journal, in stark contrast to the *Colored American* and even the "white" *Washington Post* and *Evening Star,* did not even mention Ida Gibbs and Billy Hunt's elegant wedding — perhaps because the editor had not received an invitation from the Gibbses and deemed that an unforgivable slap in the face. Four years later Chase ridiculed Napoleon Marshall, Hattie's husband, as "he of Texas melodramatic fame," then demeaned him as a "Negro Democrat out of a job." But nothing could have prepared M. W. Gibbs for the downright vulgarity of Chase's editorial attack during the Arkansas bank scandal when he vindictively defamed the revered and affluent tycoon, former judge, and consul as "the longest government tit-sucker . . . in the world."

Such reckless journalistic ugliness in the United States had little impact on Ida and Billy Hunt. At the same juncture the *Colored American Magazine* reported, "As a representative of the race sent to represent his government at a foreign post, [Hunt] reflects the highest credit on the race. . . . An honor rarely bestowed on a foreigner was shown him recently by the French Government in conferring on him the honorary degree of 'Official d'Academie,' given in recognition of his long and meritorious work in Madagascar."

In his memoir Consul Hunt described a unique assignment that in 1909 took him from St.-Étienne south to "the green hills and fine pastures of . . . Aveyron." Charges had recently surfaced back in Washington that a rogue cheese maker in that nearby *département* had tarnished the previously unsullied name of its most renowned dairy product. The Department of Agriculture, under whose auspices the United States annually imported half a million dollars' worth of tangy sheep's milk blue cheese, enlisted Hunt to look into the complaints. "The investigation required delicate handling," Hunt explained, because it "involved an accusation . . . against a colleague alleging that the accused manufacturer's product was made with the addition of cow's milk," an adulteration, he added, that would have resulted in *(quelle horreur!)* "an imitation Roquefort." (This is another of Hunt's delicious tales, but as retold in his memoir it seems a tad suspicious, since "genuine" Roquefort cheese comes from a locale about a hundred miles west of Aveyron.)

Hunt called on and confronted the source of the libelous charges, who "grew crimson in the face as he raised his arms in indignant protest against such an accusation, and assured me that no . . . manufacturer in Roquefort ever used cow's milk in making cheese." Hunt then triumphantly whipped out his documentary evidence, charging that "according to this letter from the Department of Agriculture, Washington, it is your firm which has made this accusation against the firm of Messr. X." "It was perfectly obvious that I had run up against an affair of commercial jealousy and rivalry," he smugly concluded. The exposed and shamefaced French prevaricator promptly confessed and repented his deceit. Hunt deemed his mission successfully accomplished, although he soon dispatched his vice consul, Edmond Burrill, to conduct a follow-up evaluation, and Burrill subsequently summarized to Consul Hunt his observations of "the blue manufacture." The American press, Hunt maintained, lauded and reprinted his own final report to the Agriculture Department, which he proudly touted as the first of its kind.

Early in 1910 Ida returned to the United States for a full year, during which period Billy met up with her only during a brief home leave. She visited her sister in New York, but spent much more time in Washington, D.C., and in Arkansas with their uncharacteristically subdued father. Ida then joined the NAACP, a new organization that had evolved out of the Niagara Movement and dedicated itself to battling all forms of racial injustice. Several of her acquaintances also became members, including the YWCA's Addie Waites Hunton and Mollie Church Terrell — though her allies warned Mollie that such an affiliation "would alienate Dr. Washington" and lead to her husband's "political ruin." Booker T. Washington, in fact, made undermining the NAACP one of Charles Anderson's foremost priorities, and at the *Washington Bee,* W. Calvin Chase similarly disparaged its African American constituents (early supporters included both Negroes and Caucasians) as the tools or dupes of manipulative white men. The NAACP appointed W. E. B. Du Bois as editor of its increasingly respected new magazine, *The Crisis: A Record of the Darker Races,* and then director of all publications and research. He moved from Atlanta to New York City, and perhaps because he was such a notoriously inept money manager, solicited M. W. Gibbs's counsel about and participation in a proposed real estate venture in the Northeast. Gibbs agreed to advise and assist his daughter's friend, but wryly cautioned Du Bois "that my experience, lo these many years, with my people in enterprises of various kinds, has not invested me with much faith in their fidelity or business capacity."

The next June, Ida Gibbs Hunt wound her way back to St.-Étienne. She may have stopped off in London, where early that month Du Bois served as a leader of the Universal Races Congress, which in some ways was an ideological successor to the 1900 Pan-African Conference and a predecessor of the Pan-African Congresses that he initiated eight years later. Nothing confirms Gibbs Hunt's presence there, but several of her acquaintances did attend that interracial gathering of progressive internationalists. The featured speakers whom she knew well included Dr. Susan McKinney Steward, only the third African American woman to become a licensed physician in her country. The conference convened just before the publication of Du Bois's first novel, *The Quest of the Silver Fleece,* featuring (as Du Bois's biographer David Levering

Lewis aptly describes her) a "cynical, delicious" protagonist, Caroline Wynn, almost certainly modeled on Ida Gibbs Hunt herself. Ida, in fact, may even have been the mystery woman, "One Whose Name May Not Be Written," to whom the crafty Du Bois dedicated *The Quest*.

In later years Du Bois admitted that he had enjoyed a number of close female friends, vibrant women with "great brains," although, he insisted, "sex indulgence was never the cause or aim of these friendships." He maintained enduring associations with some of them but asserted, "I avoided women about whom anybody gossiped." Gibbs Hunt's "brains," and her impeccable personal and professional reputation, epitomized this characterization.

The dates of the Universal Races Congress, the appearance of Du Bois's book, and the temporal congruity of Gibbs Hunt's return to France combine to suggest that she lingered for a while in London, hoping to see Du Bois, and the gathering certainly dealt with issues that deeply engaged her then, as they would even more in the future. During the ensuing years she became ever more intellectually vigorous, stayed slim, and dressed meticulously. Her hair scarcely grayed, but as she approached fifty, she needed her spectacles and was already becoming a bit stiffened by arthritis. If she hoped to kindle any sort of fires in Du Bois, however, she would have been disappointed, because he was preoccupied with other alluring and considerably younger women of color. His long-suffering wife, Nina, as usual remained back in the United States, tending to hearth, home, and child.

Just before Ida rejoined Billy that summer of 1911, he and his fellow consuls in France (by that time the burgeoning consular service included almost six hundred posts worldwide) convened in Paris for a Treasury Department conference on textiles and tariffs. Not long thereafter, as an inveterate booster of French-American trade, Hunt reported to the Department of State that "1912 was [a year] of exceptional activity in the metallurgical, coal-mining, & gun-making industries of St. Etienne." His city of residence, he explained, also offered a promising market for American-manufactured carpet sweepers, typewriters, fountain pens, and ice-cream freezers.

St.-Étienne's residents increasingly flocked to embrace their dashing American consul, recruiting him to accept the presidency of the Racing Club Stephanois, a group of athletic young men and their patrons dedicated to horse and auto racing, football (soccer in the United States), and rugby. Other involvements included his affiliation with groups that promoted well-attended boxing matches, and even advocated temperance — though neither of the Gibbs-Hunts were teetotalers. He also worked on behalf of the Club

Franco-Étrangére (Overseas France), the Croix Rouge (Red Cross), Rotary Club, and Society for the Prevention of Cruelty to Animals. All told, he participated in at least thirty French civic, social, and sporting organizations, and he dined monthly with a cadre of patrician gentlemen who called themselves the "Bons-Vivants" and quite resembled the "Gastronomes," his former epicurean cohorts in Madagascar. "Our motto," Hunt maintained, "should have been, 'We live to eat,' inasmuch as our leader was always on the alert for some new Auberge, Hotel, or restaurant . . . where some new or special gourmandise could be obtained." "I touched the French at odd and widely scattered angles," he proudly concluded.

At "a grand military dinner" held in Hunt's honor during his early years in St.-Étienne, he met many of the army officers stationed nearby. The colonel who commanded the local cavalry, the consul boasted, "plac[ed] at my disposition one of the horses of his regiment [and] includ[ed] an orderly to look after my mount, which enabled me to enjoy a daily horseback ride." That, he wrote, was a rare "privilege to be granted even to a French civilian, not to mention a foreigner," but Billy Hunt had become a skilled rider in his youth, and he remained an enthusiastic equestrian who even acquired two mares (as well as two fox terriers, Paddy Hunt and Nosi Be, the latter named after an island off Madagascar's coast) while he lived in France. Every fall, he added, one of his sporting clubs organized for "us gentleman jockeys . . . promenades on horse back . . . covering some fifteen or twenty miles over hill, down dale and across water courses, which wound up with a dinner and dance at the country estate of some member."

A similarly thrilling escapade during those halcyon years was "a balloon ascension under the auspices of the Aero-Club du Rhone" that, Hunt asserted, enhanced his "legendary reputation among my boys as an 'all round sportsman.'" That "first flight into the upper air," he rhapsodized, "remains one of the most memorable experiences of my life," and, like many others in that era, he surmised that Germany's new dirigibles (Zeppelins) represented the future of air travel. On a crisp, cloudless afternoon his small hot-air balloon, he claimed, ascended to an altitude of eight thousand feet and soared for hours above the bucolic countryside, and even a reckless, jolting touchdown in an apple orchard did nothing to diminish the glorious adventure that culminated in a "gay dinner party" nearby.

Hunt delivered commencement addresses at nearby schools, spoke throughout the region about Madagascar and the "economic situation in the United States," and accepted requests that "threw me right in the lime light, and gave rise to many occasions for me to speak in public, [although] regulations of the Consular Service discouraged such speech making by its officers" — a further reminder of how the Department of State tried to circumscribe the activities of its employees. "A number of my speeches and reports," Hunt later wrote, "were published by the Department and frequently reprinted and commented upon in the American Press." "I was a stranger and they took me in," he concluded about the warmhearted Stephanoises, adding, "the American Consul was in the estimation of the people, a 'big noise' in the community."

With their lives rolling along parallel tracks, much of Billy Hunt's official travel did not include his wife, as much of hers excluded him. But a Swiss holiday in 1912 took them together to a charming hotel "located on a wooded hill overlooking Zurich." They continued on to Bern, the capital city, where they unexpectedly met the "German Emperor William [Wilhelm] II." Although the monarch was there for an official state visit with Switzerland's president, he, like the Gibbs-Hunts, was idly sightseeing that afternoon at Bern's renowned "bear pits."

That same fall, Vice Consul Burrill, who had become the Gibbs-Hunts' close friend (his sister Mary taught English, theater, and elocution at Washington, D.C.'s "colored" high school and thus moved in Ida's academic circles), resigned from his post. Billy rather cryptically wrote that "he realized that he was not temperamentally fitted to follow a Consular career." Edmond Burrill returned to the District to live with his siblings and work as a pharmacist.

Early the next year Billy Hunt received a letter from the Reverend Frank Nelson, the associate pastor at St. George's Episcopal Church in New York City who had been so supportive when Hunt first arrived in the great American metropolis "friendless and out of work in 1895," as the consul later wrote. The two men corresponded regularly but had not seen one another for almost two decades. Nelson had taken on a short-term administrative assignment at Rome's American Church, so Hunt booked reservations for a springtime reunion with him in Italy.

The reverend greeted Hunt at the rectory, where he mapped out their itinerary for Holy Week. They visited St. Peter's, the Vatican, Capitoline Museum, Catacombs, Appian Way, and other landmarks. Nelson informed Hunt that the multimillionaire banker J. Pierpont Morgan also had arrived recently in the Eternal City. Morgan was renowned in New York for "passing the collection plate on Sunday mornings," Hunt recalled, as the senior lay warden at St. George's. That March, after touring the Middle East and North Africa, Morgan was sightseeing in Europe with his niece. Surprisingly, however, during this trip the money magnate's intriguing art curator and most frequent travel companion, the strategically renamed and newly "white" Belle da Costa Greene (the daughter of Richard T. Greener, the African American onetime consular officer who served from time to time as Booker T. Washington's undercover spy), had remained back in the United States.

On Easter morning Billy Hunt and Reverend Nelson celebrated the Resurrection at the American Church, but Morgan, who also attended that joyous observance, failed to acknowledge their presence as he feebly shuffled past their pew. Hunt noticed with concern that Morgan "did not seem to be as active and alert as in days gone by, and . . . lean[ed] on the arm of his [niece] as they left the church before the services were ended," and he shared those somber observations with Nelson. Bidding his old colleague a fond farewell later that afternoon, Hunt returned to St.-Étienne by way of Florence and Pisa — and a few days later he was saddened but not surprised to read that Morgan had "passed away peacefully in Rome to his Eternal Reward."

Unlike Rome, St.-Étienne hardly was a Mecca for American tourists of any race or class, but in contrast to the situation during Billy Hunt's near decade in distant Madagascar, some such travelers did come to his new hometown as they traversed the continent. The Hunts enjoyed several visits by and maintained a long friendship with Paul Heydel, a noted white watercolorist. The archbishop of New Orleans, and later "Senator and Mrs. Willard Saulsbury of Delaware," also stopped by. "Though the genial Senator and his charming wife were aware of the fact that I was a member of the colored race," Hunt recalled, "they could not have been more cordial and sympathetic to me."

An array of upper-class African Americans, including Hattie Gibbs Marshall, Anna Julia Cooper, Mollie Church Terrell, and Jessie Fauset, who taught at Washington's M Street (Paul Laurence Dunbar after 1916) High School, also made their ways to the region. Fauset even situated some of her fiction in provincial French *villes* that resembled St.-Étienne, and during the summer of 1909 Dr. Susan McKinney Steward and her husband joined the Hunts for an auto jaunt through the Loire River valley. Like Gibbs Hunt — and Gibbs Marshall, Church Terrell, Cooper, and Fauset — the aging McKinney Steward advocated granting women the vote, while French *féministes* recruited Gibbs Hunt to attend sessions of their own Union Française pour le Suffrage des Femmes when they convened nearby. The ultimate success of woman suffrage in France, however, long postdated its approval in the United States, where the issue galvanized but also polarized the country as it swept ever more Americans into heated debates. Du Bois became a booster too, and his 1912 and 1915 symposia in *Crisis* offered his own, as well as Church Terrell's and a number of other women's (and men's) views on that contentious subject.

Mollie's and Ida's college mate Anna Julia Cooper had left Washington in 1906, soon after her unjust expulsion from the M Street School's principal-ship, but as a tenured teacher she technically spent the next five years on an extended leave while living and working in Missouri. Then, however, she ne-gotiated her reappointment to a position with the prestigious "colored" school system back in the nation's capital. She often went to France as well. Cooper wrote about how she passed "the vacation months of July and August 1911, 1912, 1913 [at] La Guilde Internationale [in Paris], pursuing courses in French literature [and] history," and the following year she entered Columbia Uni-versity's PhD program. She soon transferred her credits to the University of Paris, the Sorbonne, not only because her topic of inquiry was French per-spectives on slavery in the colonial New World but also because its residency requirements for the degree were much more flexible than Columbia's. Ida and Anna kept in touch during the two decades when Ida resided in France. Although nothing definitively proves that they reunited in person during Cooper's summers of study in that country, thinking otherwise is almost beyond imagining, since their common interests included Oberlin College, woman suffrage, teaching, their cultural club, Le Cercle Français, and many close acquaintances.

Early in 1913 the ninety-year-old Judge Gibbs wrote his older daughter that "my days are very frail and uncertain," but he remained alert and politically engaged enough to ask her whether the recent presidential inauguration of New Jersey's former governor, the Democrat Woodrow Wilson, whom he, like a few other black apostates such as Napoleon Marshall and W. E. B. Du Bois, had backed, would have a negative impact on Billy's consular career. "I voted for *Marse Wilson* and perhaps I have some 'fluence' if it is needed," Gibbs added. Any "'fluence" would have been welcome, because "Marse Wil-son's" administration made it a mission to further segregate the federal gov-ernment by weeding out many long-established Negro civil servants and presi-dential appointees. Although Robert Terrell kept his almost singular minor federal judgeship, those hostile political purges cost the Democratic Party a number of its tenuous new Negro supporters. Wilson even replaced the black representative in Port-au-Prince, Haiti, with a white man, but he retained the "colored" consuls serving in Madagascar, Liberia, Sierra Leone, and the Danish Virgin Islands, as well as — for a while — the two gentlemen of color (Hunt and William Yerby) posted in Europe. But Judge Gibbs probably was unaware that Wilson's Princeton was the only Ivy League college that, with its erstwhile leader's endorsement, still denied entry to any African Americans at all, and he may not have recalled that William Libbey, the president's former colleague there, had been his son-in-law's staunch booster during Hunt's long interlude in Madagascar.

In 1915 Libbey, a crack marksman (he won a medal with the 1912 U.S. Olympic rifle team), reserve army officer, and advocate of civil preparedness, became president of the quasi-governmental National Rifle Association. When he went to Washington for the organization he sometimes met with Wilson, and advocated on behalf of several white candidates for appointments in the federal government. Hunt's name does not appear in Libbey's very sparse known NRA correspondence, but given his previous support, Libbey may again have verbally endorsed his onetime protégé. Certainly, for some time after Booker T. Washington and Charles Anderson's unsuccessful conspiracy, nothing seems to have further jeopardized Hunt's position as the only Negro envoy in Europe.

Judge Mifflin Wistar Gibbs reached the age of ninety-two in 1915, and visitors that spring found him increasingly decrepit. In a letter to her friend Mollie, Ida fretted, "I haven't heard from . . . Pa for some time," and in July he died at his home in Little Rock. Although the judge never matched Booker T. Washington's singular acclaim, his achievements were arguably as meaningful as, and perhaps even more diverse than, the famous Alabaman's, and for many years Washington was Gibbs's supporter and solid ally. But Gibbs became a staunch anti-imperialist, while Washington supported even his country's recent military occupation in Haiti, because, he argued, the island's black populace needed the "civilizing" influences that the United States promised to introduce. The indomitable Wizard of Tuskegee himself passed away only four months after Gibbs.

M. W. Gibbs, truly a self-made man, lived nearly a century and became an expatriate, attorney, entrepreneur, politician, judge, consul, philanthropist, and memoirist. He sponsored and advised many contemporaries and younger Negroes and interacted with Frederick Douglass, Booker T. Washington, and W. E. B. Du Bois — all giants of the African American community. Gibbs first joined Douglass, his mentor in the abolitionist movement and consular adviser, in 1849, and they corresponded until only weeks before Douglass's death almost half a century later. From the 1880s onward, he worked on and off with Washington, who prefaced Gibbs's autobiography and lauded his efforts on behalf of black entrepreneurship, though the sly connivance targeting Billy

Hunt undercut the trust those two men once enjoyed. Gibbs foresaw, and in some ways his life exemplified, the nascent pan-Africanism on which Du Bois, with Ida Gibbs Hunt's able support, would soon expand, and Judge Gibbs counseled the financially inept Du Bois about investments. Not unexpectedly, Du Bois published a laudatory obituary accompanied by a photo of Gibbs in *Crisis* magazine. And like those better known leaders, Gibbs grasped the import of education for African Americans, and of further engaging them in the political process. As an independent leader his life spanned those of that renowned trio who so profoundly influenced one another.

Two of his sons had predeceased M. W. Gibbs, but his surviving offspring, Donald, Ida, Horace, and Hattie, struggled to come to grips with his death. Despite their maturity — Hattie, the youngest, was already forty-eight — they all grieved deeply, but given the emotionally fraught intensities of father-daughter love, and the judge's closeness to and obvious preference for his adored "girls," the loss may have been most wrenching for them. Ida and her siblings convened in Little Rock to settle the estate. Almost predictably, that convoluted process would both unite and divide them for many years, but in addition to money and property, Judge Gibbs bequeathed them a legacy that extolled race pride, a sweeping world vision, social justice, and gender equity.

As usual, however, Ida spent much of her time in the States in Washington, where she surely attended a performance of Du Bois's pageant *The Star of Ethiopia,* a depiction of the African diaspora that celebrated racial unity and illuminated Negroes' proud but painful history. The production had premiered in New York City in 1913, and Mollie Church Terrell played a cameo role as Harriet Beecher Stowe in the revival in the nation's capital two years later. Ida also visited Hattie and Nap Marshall in New York's newly African American neighborhood called Harlem. Avaricious realtors had moved whites out and replaced them with Negroes who could not find housing elsewhere. The neighborhood attracted many black rural southerners who joined the surging Great Migration northward, members of the struggling working classes (including Maggie and Dallas Hughes, Billy Hunt's sister and brother-in-law, who lived near his other sister, Fannie Hunt Murray, and her children), and ultimately an array of creative "colored" people from around the nation and the world. Ida would not return to St.-Étienne until late the following chaotic year, at about the same time that an ambitious but still obscure Jamaican named Marcus Mosiah Garvey first arrived in the big city. Garvey soon became combatively embroiled in ideological and personal wrangling over the nature, content, and import of black identity with Du Bois and others of

Gibbs Hunt's associates, and his incendiary, separatist "back to Africa" message galvanized much of Harlem and beyond.

The year 1915 also was known for and stained by the production and release of *Birth of a Nation,* a groundbreaking motion picture that played to impressionable millions throughout the United States and the world. That film features hideous caricatures of Negroes — many of them white actors in grotesque black-face makeup — as rapists, jezebels, and simple-minded or corrupt ninnies, and it romanticizes the rampaging Ku Klux Klan as the epitome of chivalry and the savior of white supremacy. Incensed white mobs lynched black people near several locations where it ran. Through *Crisis,* Du Bois editorialized and organized boycotts on behalf of the NAACP, but to no avail. The purportedly visionary Virginia-born President Wilson, who facilitated, even increased, segregation in the capital city and was known to delight in "darky" jokes, showcased *Birth of a Nation* at the White House (the first film to be so honored) and endorsed it as history written in lightning. More Americans saw it than had read any current book or watched any stage play.

Despite a few deep personal losses, such as the long-anticipated death of Judge Gibbs, the Gibbs-Hunts' first seven years in Europe had been successful and quiet. After his decade as a consul in Madagascar, Billy Hunt arguably had emerged as a bona fide, bilingual citizen of the world. With his abundant charm and gracious *bonhomie,* civic endeavors, equestrian expertise, intercontinental travels, appreciation of fine food and spirits, and meticulous though relatively nontaxing consular duties, he honorably, and with increasing facility, represented his country, epitomizing the Anglo-Saxon prototype of the aristocratic, well-mannered, exquisitely groomed and attired diplomat.

Ida also lived well. She journeyed widely, attended the opera, vacationed at nearby spas, tackled and mastered a few basics of French cuisine, read and wrote a lot (after receiving her essay titled "The Fate of the 'Darker Races,'" one correspondent responded to "I. G. Hunt, Esq.," addressing her as "Dear Sir"), gave of her money, time, and talents, taught English literature to young people in St.-Étienne, and tended to her official obligations with little strain, some satisfactions, yet minimal challenges. "I don't have to do anything unless I want to," she admitted to Mollie, although United States consuls, metaphorically carrying the Stars and Stripes and personifying their country overseas, were evaluated, in part, by their wives' social skills, decorum, and discretion. But Ida may have become frustrated and even a trifle bored as she fulfilled her prosaic commitments in St.-Étienne as the respected American consul's wife. At the least, she was not truly engaged, challenged, or living up to her potential.

Even before M. W. Gibbs's death and the release of *Birth of a Nation,* however, Europe's foundations had shuddered and its skies blackened with the sudden onslaught of *la Guerre mondiale.* A political assassination in the unstable Balkan states struck the match in mid-1914, and within weeks a conflagration engulfed the continent. Under the rapacious leadership of the once benign Kaiser Wilhelm II (whom the Gibbs-Hunts had encountered two years before as a fellow traveler in Switzerland), German forces rampaged through shell-shocked Belgium into northern France.

As Ida wrote at the time, the "fratricidal war in the Balkans and the increase of armaments all over Europe . . . indicate that the forces of war prevail." Looking back on that era, Billy Hunt admitted that "France was totally unprepared to meet the situation created when Wilhelm 'rattled his sabre.' . . . The immediate outlook [in] those early days was dark indeed." However, his second country required two years of compulsory service in uniform, so "every able bodied man capable of bearing arms [was] subject to military training." Billy added that "no one who was an eyewitness could ever forget the scenes of chaos in the streets of St. Etienne." Ida's report to Mollie was even more pained: "We have about 2000 refugees here now from Belgium . . . and nearly 1000 wounded." A friend's family, including three children, "were taken to Germany as prisoners and for five months suffered all kinds of privations." "Those quick-firing guns, too, that shoot . . . six hundred times a minute, how they mow men down. It's terrible," she grieved, "the Allies will win, I'm sure, but it's going to be hard, and perhaps long."

During the war's initial weeks, Consul Hunt wrote, "news reached us that the first Infantry Regiment on leaving St. Etienne for the . . . Front, had descended from their train under a terrific bombardment of German Artillery, and a number were killed and wounded before even engaging in battle with the enemy." Thankfully, no fighting took place in his city's immediate environs, but its residents, like all the French, felt the debilitating impact of the conflict's convulsions.

For security reasons, Raymond Poincaré, France's president, relocated most of his government west to Bordeaux, while on the economic front, Hunt explained, "the Bank of France . . . stored all its gold reserves, stocks and bonds, in the vaults of the branch in St. Etienne." That sector retooled and geared up its manufacturing capabilities to meet the skyrocketing wartime demands.

St.-Étienne's creaky old factories began turning out turbines, tanks, supply locomotives, larger-bore ammunition, and rifles and cannons of all sorts and sizes to aid their country's military efforts.

From the first encounters onward, Consul Hunt often left St.-Étienne to conduct official business elsewhere, later writing, "During the war I made frequent . . . visits to Paris." He did not fully explain the reasons for those missions, though he did say that one of his closest *amis* became a ranking administrator with the capital city's *préfet de police*. Hunt may have seen General Gallieni during those trips as well, and certainly he conferred early and often with the American ambassador, Myron T. Herrick, an Oberlin contemporary of Ida's sister Hattie. Ambassador Herrick, Billy Hunt later disclosed, directed him to "visit, inspect, and report on the condition of the concentration and prison camps located in the Consular district of St. Etienne."

"Within a few weeks, there was little doubt but that the bombardment of . . . Paris was a matter of hours [away]," Hunt wrote, and "the thunder of German guns could be distinctly heard." The enemy's Zeppelins made more than fifty air raids as far west as England, and their Gothas (faster but smaller bomber planes) besieged Paris every night. Just before such attacks, "warning cannons awakened the city, and the ear-splitting shriek of sirens filled the air, the firemen would motor through the darkness sounding an additional note of warning, [and] refuge seekers would dive into their cellars or the nearest Subway station." But Hunt grew increasingly blasé. One time in his hotel after repeatedly dodging down into the *métro,* he "got fed up . . . and decided to tempt fate . . . theorizing that I had only one time to die, and might as well die in bed." Another evening found him "sitting in front of a well known café sipping Vermouth . . . when suddenly something like an ear-splitting clap of thunder out of a clear sky, dazed and deafened me." "This," he admitted, "was my introduction to the 'Big Bertha,'" Germany's deadliest cannon. The French also began calling the enemy's huge (phallic) mortar shells "Jack Johnsons," for the explosive black American heavyweight pugilist who, after kayoing his own country's "Great White Hope," and worse, bedding a series of (sometimes underage) white women, fled as an exile to Paris for several years. Despite Billy Hunt's Gallic nonchalance in shunning underground shelter, he was heartbreakingly aware, he added, that one bomb "fell into a church on Good Friday during the services, killing and wounding more than a hundred persons, mostly children."

As the hostilities escalated, Consul Hunt's duties increased and diversified. At that time, and then after the United States joined the fray, Hunt wrote that he was "authorized to extend protection to all aliens belonging to the Central Powers interned in my district." Foreigners in or near St.-Étienne were tracked down, rounded up, registered, and sometimes exiled, and "persons who were natives of the enemy countries immediately confined in Concentration Camps." Protecting American citizens was one of a consul's primary responsibilities, so Hunt was directed to contact and arrange to evacuate any of his countrymen in the region. One such person was Fayette Avery McKenzie, a onetime guest at the consulate and dean at Ohio State University, who soon became president of Nashville's "colored" Fisk University. A decade later, Du Bois, a Fisk (his first college) alumnus himself, bolstered student-led protests to force the resignation of McKenzie, a white man, because he reportedly impugned some of the school's young women, thwarted its Negro faculty's efforts to advance, and acceded to his major donors' most paternalistic demands.

Three years before the war began, in a magnanimous but pragmatic gesture, General Joseph Simon Gallieni had acknowledged his advancing age and uncertain health when he deferred to General Joseph-Jacques Joffre and declined to command the French army, but in this new time of crisis, he unhesitatingly emerged from retirement to serve his nation as the military governor of Paris. Several accounts contend that the panache and cachet that surrounded the bold and charismatic yet astute Gallieni, France's sentimental favorite, often gnawed at Joffre.

General Gallieni pulled into France's service the finest men he could find, origin and race notwithstanding. Among them was Senegal's Blaise Diagne, that era's first black representative in the country's parliament (a "colored" Guadeloupean had served briefly in the mid-nineteenth century), whom both Gallieni and Hunt had known and admired in Madagascar twenty years before. Diagne became France's key recruiter for its colonial African soldiers. Gallieni also brought to Paris Commandant Sosthène H. C. Mortenol, a Guadeloupean and the acclaimed École Polytechnique's first Negro graduate, who had served with the French army on the Great Red Island during General Gallieni's regime. Gallieni entrusted him with the antiaircraft defense of France's greatest city, and before the war ended, Mortenol would command a number of white military aviators from the United States.

Conditions in France deteriorated quickly during the Great War's first autumn, but, asked Hunt, "Who could have imagined that the . . . decisive blow [forestalling Germany's momentum] came from Gallieni's 'taxi-cab army?'" With his strategic daring (in contrast to Joffre's puzzling hesitancy), Hunt's old friend brought to fruition a scheme that caused an "initial jolt to German military hegemony." In September 1914 Gallieni conscripted the drivers of six hundred Paris taxicabs, which he dispatched, in the dark of night with all the headlamps extinguished, to facilitate the mobilization and clandestine transfer of four thousand army reserves, some of them France's dark-skinned colonial subjects. Thirty miles northeast of Paris, Gallieni's improvised motor battalion intercepted the advance of the dumbfounded German forces and temporarily halted the Teutonic war machine in its tracks. That clash, Hunt maintained, and others have concurred, marked "the beginning of a titanic struggle which caused to be sacrificed on the battle field the flower of the youth of the Allied Nations."

As a reward — or punishment — for that singular early French military success, Gallieni was named his country's war minister. Unfortunately, Billy Hunt, Blaise Diagne, Commandant Mortenol, and virtually all sentient Frenchmen were plunged into deep mourning when the ailing Gallieni died in May 1916. In those dire times, within a single, momentous year, Billy lost his two most significant mentors: the African American Judge M. W. Gibbs and the legendary French officer General Joseph Simon Gallieni.

Billy Hunt saved a memorial *carte postale* featuring a portrait of Gallieni, lean and militarily erect in his full dress uniform bedecked with a chestful of medals, his signature pince-nez underscoring his authority. The card is imprinted with a concise, capsule biography ("Né le 24 avril 1849 / Entré á St. Cyr en 1868 / . . . Tonkin, Madagascar, Sénégal / . . . Gouverneur de Paris / Ministre de la Guerre 1915") and extols the general's role in the pivotal "taxi-cab" encounter with the Germans. Additional picture postcards among those the Gibbs-Hunts preserved show Croix Rouge nurses, mutilated vehicles in *la forêt de l'Argonne,* and stark images of the gruesome "vandalisme allemande," while others feature dashing uniformed Frenchmen bidding their sad-eyed *chéries adieu,* or evoke homespun American military humor. "Sergeant [to a lieutenant about a hapless recruit]: 'I've taught him all I know, Sir; but he still knows nothing!'"

Ida Gibbs Hunt had her own perspective. "Europe is suffering now from too much civilization and science," she wrote Mollie Church Terrell, "it has all been turned in the wrong direction, chiefly devising and manufacturing things to kill one another." "I hope they'll get their fill of it," she added, "and turn to wiser methods, hereafter, disarmament, arbitration, and a federated Europe." And every night she prayed that "President Wilson . . . might do a little more protesting against outrages."

During his wife's extended absences in the United States, Consul Hunt and W. E. B. Du Bois began their own correspondence. Du Bois had requested, and Hunt provided, a photograph that he sent to *Crisis,* "with a few notes about my life, which you can work together yourself." "This war has slightly upset my plans," Hunt offhandedly confessed, adding, "I always recall with pleasure your kindly interest in me when you were at Harvard long ago." In the magazine's May 1916 issue, Du Bois included that likeness of Hunt with a paragraph about his praiseworthy work in wartime France.

Hunt's consular role further expanded during the war. When a soldier from St.-Étienne ("a member of one of the first families of the region," according to Hunt) was reported missing in action, his parents implored the consul to look into their son's whereabouts. Hunt did so, and soon learned through the International Red Cross that the young man "was safe and interned in a prison camp." The youth's father "spread the news far and wide, and before realizing the consequences of my friendly gesture," Hunt recalled, "my office was literally swamped with . . . requests of a similar nature." In response to a similar inquiry by a French officer, Consul Hunt elicited pertinent information from Ambassador James Gerard, the top United States diplomat in Germany, who remained at his post as long as the irresolute country he represented maintained its officially neutral status.

La Guerre mondiale was an event of grave consequences both for indigenous Africans and for their European colonial masters, and one way in which it increasingly became a global conflict was through the involvement of nonwhite troops. In 1916 Deputy Blaise Diagne negotiated a hard-won agreement that, over time, promised his Senegalese compatriots expanding roles in their own governance and the rights of French citizens. Then he returned for a while to his native West Africa to enlist new recruits, who previously had often balked, fled across borders to non-French territories, or mutilated themselves rather than be conscripted into the army. Many people of color in France's African and Antillean colonies lauded Diagne, but others rebuked him for reportedly receiving a financial bounty for each soldier he enrolled in the military, and some voices of protest further charged that France's vigorous recruitment methods edged perilously close to slave trading.

Nonetheless, among the black Africans who served on the front lines were thousands of *tirailleurs,* or sharpshooters, garbed in scarlet fezzes and royal blue jackets and armed with bantam machetes called *coute-coutes.* The French valued those men because, in contrast to "civilized" white soldiers, they supposedly felt neither pain nor fear. Senior officers such as Commandant

Mortenol, and many young Senegalese recruits like the soon-to-be-famous Louis M'barick Fall, numbered among them. Altogether the French army had 2 Negro generals, 4 Negro colonels, 155 Negro captains, and even more Negro lieutenants. All told, the "colored" Antilleans, sub-Saharan and North Africans, and the Indo-Chinese made up more than 10 percent of France's men in uniform. Most served France, "their" country, in menial but often dangerous support roles. In the end, those soldiers fought and died in higher percentages than did white men — in Europe, in the Near and Far East, on land and at sea, and all over Africa. Years later (in May 1931) *Opportunity: A Journal of Negro Life,* the monthly magazine of the National Urban League, observed that "since the Great War, France has been mindful of the role which her black subjects played in the defense of Paris. . . . Without the man power which her African colonies can muster, the position of France from a military standpoint is precarious."

Ida, meanwhile, became increasingly attuned to the intermeshed global issues of race and class, colonial abuses and imperialism. The war, she wrote Mollie, "must change things for the darker races. [France] must recognize and recompense . . . those who have fought with and for them." "I can't help but notice [the European nations'] inconsistency in protesting against the overrunning and annexing of weaker countries, when that is what they have been doing in Africa . . . for nearly a century," Ida fumed. "They don't want to take their own medicine. . . . Even poor Belgium is reaping what [King] Leopold sowed." Comparing grisly past events to accounts of Germany's recent outrages in Europe, she asked, "How many Congo natives had their hands cut off too?" She could hardly have been unaware of or unmoved by the recent suicide of the Congolese pygmy Ota Benga, who never overcame his morbid despondency after being kidnapped from his homeland and exhibited for years in the United States like an animal or sideshow freak. W. E. B. Du Bois also insisted that Africans had suffered more under the white colonial Belgian regime than the Belgians did during Germany's grim wartime occupation.

The war's most widely reported battles took place in Belgium and France, but the conflict spilled out from western Europe to overwhelm countries bordering the Mediterranean and the German-, French-, and British-controlled Middle East. Germany's ally Turkey made genocidal assaults on the Armenians, chronicled, among others, by the prolific writer George Horton, who was a longtime United States consul in the region. In Africa, Europe's colonial powers assigned white officers (often carried aloft on the bent, aching shoulders of Negro soldiers) to command their "native" units. German East and Southwest Africa, the Belgian Congo, British Rhodesia, and the French Cameroons suffered four years of warfare that generated countless black, brown, and white casualties, while Europe's navies faced off in the Atlantic, Pacific, and Indian oceans. Japan joined the Entente and declared war on the German-dominated Central Powers, but also invaded China, its own habitual antagonist. As the European colonizers tried to secure, maintain, and even expand their empires, those encounters beyond their own continent's confines both portended and stimulated bitter postwar wrangling over the future of Germany's colonies.

While Ida Gibbs Hunt stayed on in the United States through the first half of 1916, and her country still technically remained neutral, a new Harvard PhD named Carter G. Woodson pulled together a group of dedicated black intellectuals to form the Association for the Study of Negro Life and History; then he kicked off the *Journal of Negro History* to research, examine, and analyze pertinent local, national, Caribbean, and African issues. Gibbs Hunt became one of the organization's original lifetime members. An early issue of the journal featured her equivocal review of a turgid new novel about transnational escapades, interracial marriage, and racial passing titled *The American Cavalryman: A Liberian Romance.* The book, a fictionalized account of Charles Denton Young's exploits as a United States military attaché in Liberia, was written by Henry Francis Downing, a late nineteenth-century consul in Angola and an early pan-Africanist who, decades before, had abandoned the United States, his country of birth, to become a London-based expatriate and self-styled commentator on international issues. On the one hand, Gibbs Hunt acknowledged Downing's designated race (Negro) and his familiarity with Liberia, but she also hotly protested that the book "is written from a white man's point of view and shows a tendency to regard the white man's civilization . . . as the only true standard."

When Ida returned to St.-Étienne in mid-1916, she worked with the French Croix Rouge on behalf of the war-torn nation where she had lived for nearly a decade, and shared with her friend Mollie her experiences "knitting and crocheting, and visiting the wounded." She offered warm conversation and hot meals to hospitalized soldiers, helped them write and read letters, and translated as needed. However, even after the United States entered the struggle, the American Red Cross refused to send well-trained, much needed Negro nurses to Europe — although they had served admirably during the Spanish-American War — supposedly because it could not provide the "necessary" segregated quarters in which to house such women.

Billy Hunt gradually came to believe, in accordance with, he claimed, "the 'Consular Regulations,'" that American consuls were "officers both of the State which appoints them and the State which receives them." He recognized the potential conflicts of serving two masters, yet had "no fear of contradiction that this instruction was interpreted in both letter and spirit during my residence in Saint Etienne." At no time in his life would this quandary become more critical, and St.-Étienne's public officials and private citizens, and reports in French journals, lauded his unorthodox efforts. Consul Hunt responded to the entreaties of a number of Stephanoises who sought an "outstanding neutral party or prominent person who would be willing to vouch for the charitable and humanitarian purposes of the proposed work," in other words, someone who would serve as a liaison to gather and provide information about their missing loved ones. "Without consulting me," Hunt added, several of his associates "submitted my name to the Germans as sponsor," but before France's shrewd adversaries would accede to any such arrangement, they insisted that every such request "must be accompanied by a circular printed in both French and German bearing my signature and [the] Consular seal."

Therein lay the rub. Using that seal, Consul Hunt realized, "could not be done officially without authority from the State Department, which I knew would be firmly refused." At that point, he dramatically declared, "I cut the 'Gordian knot.'" In keeping with his belief that he must serve both his own and his host country, he acted in response to what he recognized as France's far more dire circumstances. As a self-described "outstanding neutral party," Hunt decided not to solicit the department's permission, as he knew he should, but rather he "agreed to affix on each request for information an impression in ink of the letter seal of the office," a crafty ruse that Germany's military authorities somehow found acceptable. Thus, Hunt concluded, "my name was familiar in all the German prison camps where French soldiers were interned."

The French press applauded this additional evidence of Hunt's dedication to France, even in sub-rosa defiance of the State Department. One newspaper editorialized that "the distinguished American Consul . . . has greatly facilitated our task by . . . contributing his great influence to the success of our efforts to obtain . . . information for the families so greatly disturbed as to the fate of their dear ones." Another article insisted that he "won the gratitude of the whole region by his efforts to trace French soldiers who were held captive in German prisons." "[Hunt] rendered inestimable services to the victims of the great conflict," it continued, asking, "How many prisoners of war, especially, owe to his intervention amelioration in their condition?" His assertive and contentious wartime acts on behalf of France made Consul Hunt an even more revered, beloved personage in his adopted homeland.

As at other points in Billy Hunt's life, questions arose at this juncture as to who in France may have known that his own country, in keeping with its laws and ingrained prejudices, designated the slightly tan-skinned Hunt a Negro. An anonymous poem that he saved referencing his wartime activities includes a telling metaphorical phrase, "Comme le loup blanc il est connu" (He is known as the white wolf), while a biographical sketch in a St.-Étienne journal speculated that Hunt might be a "peau rouge" — a noble Native American "redskin." To the French, the distinguished United States consul was their treasured friend and intrepid ally, not in any respect a member of the "inferior" race. Both to his hosts and to himself, Hunt seemed thousands of miles and many generations removed from France's own "primitive" colonial Antillean and especially African subjects, whom most white Frenchmen considered intriguing or forgettable, dirty or erotic, comic or devious, sometimes useful, frequently troublesome, in need of Europe's unending support and guidance, but paradoxically, perhaps, often a source of pride and honor.

Though President Wilson had sent troops to Mexico, Haiti, and the Dominican Republic, he won reelection in 1916 by pledging to stay out of what many Americans considered Europe's war alone. On behalf of the United States, he made financial advances and supplied weapons and equipment to France and England, yet still he sent no combatants. The reluctant country formally joined the conflict only in April 1917 in response to Germany's escalating truculence, especially its *Unterseeboote* (U-boat) attacks on neutral ships, and rumors of its covert approaches to and complicity with Mexico.

Despite that late entry into the war, even reservists such as Hunt's epistolary friend and Wilson's venerable former colleague, the NRA's president Professor William Libbey, demanded to be activated, and with the rank of major, he taught marksmanship at military bases around the country. As Consul Hunt later wrote, "Our Government's patience ceased to be a virtue and [we] entered the conflict to make the world safe for democracy." That phrase roused and inspired the nation, and like their white compatriots, most African Americans rallied to the cause — though many of them would have preferred first to make the southern states "safe for democracy." In *Crisis,* Du Bois urged Negroes to lay aside any grievances with their often racist country, at least for the time being, and to "close ranks" with the white American majority and the European Entente against the German-Austro-Hungarian-Turkish Central Powers.

More than a year before United States forces entered the war, Ida's forty-year-old brother-in-law, Napoleon Marshall, had volunteered and become a member of Harlem's 15th New York State Army Reserve Regiment. Another Negro who joined that unit was James Reese Europe, already one of the country's most acclaimed jazz composers and band conductors. The regiment's leaders included white liberals such as the future congressman Hamilton Fish, a Harvard athlete and graduate, like Marshall, and the wealthy William Jay Schieffelin, who twenty years before had been Billy Hunt's employer in New York City.

Marshall became one of the first new "colored" officers, but federal authorities balked at providing training even for such fit, mature, highly educated men who sought and merited commissions. Military leaders, like most of their white countrymen, believed that blacks were incapable of command, and that granting them any such prestige and influence contradicted the "proper" racial hierarchy. Yet they were needed to lead what ultimately became four hundred thousand African American soldiers during the war, nearly half of whom would serve overseas.

The issue of Negro leadership in the military soon emerged as a searing hot potato, with both blacks and whites affiliated with organizations such as the NAACP pressuring the government, especially in cases like that of Lieutenant Colonel Charles D. Young, a West Point graduate who was the nation's highest ranking black officer. Like Ida's mother, Charles Young was born in May's Lick, Kentucky. He lived near Oberlin and had inspired Henry Downing's novel *The American Cavalryman*. Young had served in the Philippines, Haiti, Liberia, and Mexico, and proudly carried his country's flag and buttressed its imperial bearing everywhere he went. But early in 1917 the army placed him on reserve status, allegedly for reasons of failing health, so it did not have to give him a well-warranted promotion to full colonel, which would put him on track to become the nation's first general of his race — who in time of war might be called on to command white men. To protest his forced "retirement," confirm his stamina, and dramatize his cause, Young rode on horseback from his home in Ohio to Washington, D.C., but to no avail. The army only reactivated him as the war ended. Officer training finally was provided for a limited number of Negro men, but only under segregated and notably inferior conditions. During the next year and a half, however, the reluctant military granted commissions to more than twelve hundred of them, mostly as second lieutenants.

Although he was approaching fifty, Du Bois, Young's pal and frequent booster, was offered a captaincy, perhaps as a sop to the increasingly vociferous NAACP. As Du Bois pondered the offer, Gibbs Hunt, who once again had returned to Washington and New York City, where she met with her friend during the winter of 1918, wrote him: "Tho The Crisis can ill afford to lose you, I bid you God speed if you choose something else for the time being, believing that your heart is true to the cause." But after due consideration and sundry advice, Du Bois resolved to stay at *Crisis* magazine and not become an officer. That spring he also delivered a eulogy for the Hunts' old traveling companion Susan McKinney Steward.

Marshall, however, had signed on as a first lieutenant. He started as a military judge advocate but was soon promoted to infantry captain. In preparation for their assignment in France, he and his 15th Regiment comrades trained in the Deep South, but that interlude was a nightmare, with fights erupting between soldiers of different races and ugly insults hurled by white civilians, one of whom called Marshall a "dirty nigger" and heaved him off a streetcar. But he had volunteered to serve, so he stepped back and swallowed his pride to fulfill a commitment to his country and his men. Since a decade before, when he had unsuccessfully defended the beleaguered military contingent in Texas, Marshall had felt an enormous responsibility for and empathy with his nation's black soldiers.

In December 1917 Captain Marshall's all-volunteer unit set sail from New York as part of the American Expeditionary Forces (AEF) sent to rev up the Entente's exhausted and dispirited troops. Once nationalized in the regular army, New York's 15th became the United States' 369th. Its members referred to themselves as Men of Bronze, white Americans designated them Harlem's Own, the French named them *les enfants perdus* (lost children) because their mother country seemed to abandon them, and their dumbfounded German adversaries would call them Hell Fighters. Those men arrived just before the New Year in Brest, France, where they were assigned to guard prisoners of war and dig railroad beds — though they had been trained for combat duty and the war-weary French had been promised fresh American soldiers, known as doughboys, to reinforce them on the front lines.

Soon, however, the United States military reconsidered that initial misassignment, and during the ensuing weeks dispersed Marshall and many of his men to other all-black American units. Much of the 369th then was transferred to a division of the French army. The Harlemites marched, slept, and sometimes died beside "colored" colonials from tropical zones forced to acclimatize to northern Europe's frigid weather. And like those shivering "native" soldiers, the dark-skinned Americans consumed French food and wine, wore French helmets, carried and fired French weapons — including what were known, from their place of manufacture, Marshall reported, as "St. Etienne machine guns." They also became the only United States troops who fought directly under France's flag, the hallowed *tricolore*.

Although the French treated Negroes such as Captain Marshall, whom they perceived as more American than black, better than their own "colored" colonial forces, the hidebound U.S. Army brass sharply enjoined *les Français*, especially *les mesdemoiselles*, to avoid any personal contact with those "over-sexed beasts" whom, they insisted, many Americans justifiably considered and treated as inferiors. Much of America's white majority feared that if those soldiers enjoyed intimate social or sexual relationships with European women, they would acquire insolent new expectations that they would bring back with them when they returned to the United States.

Napoleon Marshall was gassed, wounded, and hospitalized early in 1918. He spent several recuperative weeks with the Gibbs-Hunts, using the time to enhance his vestigial classroom French, as a number of officers with the AEF did. "[As] the first American officer to visit St. Etienne," he wrote, "I was the object of much observation on the streets." His skin color (darker than either Billy's or Ida's) underlined his visibility and uniqueness, and Marshall both personified and reinforced the Stephanoises' gratitude for the key roles that black American troops played in their salvation. On July 4, one young neighbor, striving to become bilingual herself, saluted the Gibbs-Hunts, their country, and its soldiers when she wrote: "Your little friend and la mother vous addressant of good kisses, bien affecteuses pour célebrer l'anniversaire de l'Independence Americaine."

In time, Marshall returned to the war zone, where he encountered more daunting ordeals with yet another all-Negro unit that battled under onerous conditions, without adequate arms or equipment. His letter to an African American journal during one of the Great War's penultimate clashes reported that "the cannonading was . . . convulsing." "The pen recoils from a description of the indescribable . . . I do not know yet what toll it has taken of the lives of our brave men, for the action which lulled this morning is soon to resume." He concluded, "May God be with us."

With the historian Carter G. Woodson's guidance, Emmett J. Scott wrote *The Official History of the American Negro in the World War* (1920). Scott previously had been Booker T. Washington's top aide at Tuskegee Institute, and as special assistant to Secretary of War Newton Baker, he became that era's highest ranking black government official. When Marshall returned to the front, Scott wrote, "he was wounded from shell fire on October 21, in a night raid south of Metz in an effort to capture a machine gun position." As a result of his disabilities, Scott explained, Marshall "must wear a brace during the remainder of his life." In *Crisis* Du Bois reported: "Three times he was confined to the hospital — first for a dislocated shoulder; then he was gassed; and finally he was wounded by shell fire and shrapnel . . . when he went over the top in 'No Man's Land.'" Marshall was sent to the same hospital in Bordeaux where Gibbs Hunt was tending other injured soldiers, but she learned only later that her brother-in-law was being treated there and had no chance to see him. "Is not that one of the strange coincidences of life," she wrote Du Bois, "[like] 'ships that pass in the night.'" Even with his steel corset, Captain Marshall thereafter lived with pain and never fully regained his former energy, verve, or robust health.

All told, the World War took nearly two hundred thousand "colored" AEF soldiers to Europe. Despite rampant discrimination, inferior training, inadequate equipment, unrealistic expectations, and egregious castigation from the United States military, in most instances they performed well and often sacrificed their blood. Far more than did white Americans, the French acknowledged that dedication, bravery, and success. They lauded, and their government decorated, many Negro soldiers, especially those, like Captain Marshall and others from Harlem's 369th (which spent more time on the front lines than any other American unit), who fought right beside their own. The grateful French government bestowed its Croix de Guerre on Marshall's entire regiment.

Colonial Antilleans, Africans, and a few "colored" Americans had always found their way to the continent, but the French felt deeply indebted to and grew especially fond of the African American soldiers who came over to bail them out in 1918. Those men reciprocated in a nation that, though hardly color-blind, usually savored instead of scorned *les différences* in the Negro doughboys. They contrasted the warmth of France's citizenry with the hostility they often faced in the United States, and their experiences and exposure to diverse non-American people of color broadened their horizons. It also raised new aspirations for equality at home and generated increasing self-confidence. If many of the French treasured America's black men in uniform, they may have embraced even more the jazz they brought with them, and several of the army's topnotch combos, especially Jim Europe's 369th infantry band, performed all around France. They called themselves "the best military band in Europe," and wherever they played, jubilant crowds agreed.

Thousands of African American women served as well, but almost exclusively on the home front. As the journalist Alice Dunbar-Nelson, Paul Laurence Dunbar's newly remarried widow, wrote in Emmett Jay Scott's opus on the Great War: "Into this maelstrom of war activity the women of the Negro race hurled themselves joyously." Nonetheless, she added, "Colored women since the inception of the war had felt keenly their exclusion from overseas service. The need for them was acute; their willingness to go was complete; the only thing . . . wanted was authoritative sanction."

Helen Curtis, wife of James L. Curtis, the recently deceased consul general who had died just after leaving his post as head of the United States' legation in Liberia, was one of the few Negro women who did go to France at the behest of her government, the Red Cross, and the YW and YMCAs. Curtis worked near St.-Étienne for almost two years, but white American army officers resented and criticized her vociferous protests concerning their maltreatment of the Negro doughboys. Another widow, Addie Waites Hunton, a fifty-three-year-old social worker and NAACP member (as was Helen Curtis), soon joined her. In keeping with entrenched policies back in the United States, the military- and government-affiliated entities usually ignored or neglected even the very minimal, segregated programs and facilities for the thousands of African Americans soldiers serving in Europe, but finally acknowledged that some such services must be provided for them. Gearing up, organizing, and supporting those belated but vital operations became Curtis's and Waites Hunton's primary responsibilities.

Henry Ossawa Tanner, the "colored" American artist who remained in self-imposed exile near Paris and had virtually become a Frenchman who never returned to live in the nation of his birth, nonetheless volunteered to serve his country, because in wartime he felt the strong tug of his citizenship and heritage. Most white American officers in France did not know that the light-skinned Tanner was "black," so with the ambassador's covert patronage, he negotiated a special lieutenant's commission for himself and persuaded the Red Cross's Farm and Garden Section to let him supervise a modest agricultural project. He also photographed, painted, and preserved for history images of desolate Negro soldiers standing outside, wistfully peering into a hospitality tent where American Red Cross volunteers provided aid and comfort only to white men. Waites Hunton and Curtis sought to ameliorate such inequities as best they could, and spent some of their precious free time with Gibbs Hunt. Soon they would become even closer associates.

The Entente at last emerged battered but victorious. The world welcomed the November 11, 1918, cease-fire, though the final battles and ultimate German surrender took place more than a month later in Africa's distant British Rhodesia. The armistice set the stage for the Versailles Conference, where delegates — almost all of them white men — from around the globe would convene near Paris to debate and negotiate the terms of peace, and create new international alliances to maintain a lasting accord, mediate the participants' debts, determine the reallocation of Germany's colonial empire, and hash out other global matters. That winter's victory parades in Paris included performances by America's uniformed jazz bands, especially that of Harlem's 369th Regiment. But the United States military banned all other Negro American soldiers from any participation in those celebrations, though France's and England's own underappreciated but essential colonial troops played highly visible roles, since an estimated thirty thousand "colored" French soldiers remained in Europe. As an outraged black eyewitness railed in *Crisis* that December: "England had Canadians, Australians, Scotch, Londoners, Indians and Africans in the line. France had Frenchmen, Soudanese, Senegalese, Madagascans, Moroccans, and every other race that fought under her flag in line. Every nation had all the races that fought in the war, except the United States. Although there were over a thousand Negro troops here [in Paris], the United States was represented only by white men."

People of African ancestry around the world harbored concerns about the future of the darker races — especially Europe's colonial subjects. Except for the largely symbolic 1911 Universal Races Congress and Booker T. Washington's 1912 International Conference on the Negro, which attracted white missionaries and a few elite indigenous Africans, for the first time since the 1900 Pan-African Conference, interests in transnational initiatives coalesced in the Negro community as white delegates from around the world streamed to Versailles. Several Negro Americans, including Du Bois, Ida B. Wells-Barnett, and the entrepreneur and philanthropist Madam C. J. Walker petitioned to be accredited as observers, but the State Department denied all of them the needed credentials.

Du Bois had made known his concerns about self-determination and colonial exploitation at the NAACP's September 1918 board meeting and received his organization's backing to address them publicly, both at home and in Europe. In November (Gibbs Hunt's letter expressing her full faith in him appeared in that month's *Crisis* magazine, the readership of which was approaching a hundred thousand), he provided the board with a "Memorandum on the Future of Africa." Meanwhile, on behalf of his own emergent organization, the Universal Negro Improvement Association, the Jamaican Marcus Garvey, who touted a black separatist identity in the United States, the West Indies, and Africa, organized a vociferous Armistice Day rally in New York City that attracted some five thousand Negroes.

Early the next month, the very week that President Wilson and his entourage departed for France to attend the global peace conference, Du Bois set sail for the same country with his own ambitious agenda. First, as a scholar and journalist, he proposed to investigate, compile, and write up accounts of the achievements and maltreatment of black soldiers for a major book about the darker races' central roles in the Great War, and he still hoped to shoulder the well-nigh impossible responsibility of overseeing the interests of oppressed people of color at the official gathering in Versailles. Du Bois also thought that even the war's partially compromised idealism would offer new opportunities for them to rise on what he optimistically perceived as the new tides of democracy, anti-imperialism, and anticolonialism. Lastly, he expressed his sentimental yet humanitarian concerns for the millions of exploited colonial subjects living in the continent south of Europe that he considered his historic, cultural, and spiritual homeland. Those intertwined motivations converged to shape and spur on his revitalized pan-Africanism.

With the NAACP's blessings and financial support, Du Bois recruited a core group comprising both Negroes and a few empathetic white people to assemble alternative sessions that would coincide with the meetings in Versailles. He proposed to monitor, debate, and focus attention on a plethora of international racial, social, political, and economic issues, and to do so he enlisted the participation of several NAACP members, Ida Gibbs Hunt among them. Du Bois knew that she was intelligent, financially independent but underoccupied, and informed and outspoken about global issues, abuses of power, and racial injustices. And she lived in central France. The war's recent conclusion, she wrote him at the time, raised "questions which you and I have so near at heart." Referring to his own previous designation of Europe's ongoing and apparently insatiable imperial expansionism as "the African roots of war," she warned that "the colonial side [of these matters] which, as you've said, had so much to do with causing this war, ought to be settled in the interest of the natives, as well as of Europe, or it will cause future trouble." Though Du Bois was no stranger to France, having traveled there on three previous occasions, he spoke, understood, and wrote limited French, whereas Gibbs Hunt was fully bilingual, well connected ("Mr. H. could be of great assistance," she insisted), efficient, gracious, and above all, loyal to him. Apparently disregarding any possible repercussions for her husband with his hidebound, often manipulative superiors at the State Department, Gibbs Hunt dashed off to work for several months in Paris with Du Bois, to help him organize and bring to fruition his (now their) ambitious and controversial undertaking.

As those efforts lurched along, Ida Gibbs Hunt composed a heartfelt if awkward poem, "To France," about her adopted country's bravery, *égalité,* and *fraternité* (contrasted with the United States' bigotry) and catastrophic losses: two million Frenchmen were wounded and one and a half million more died, many of whom lost their lives during the worldwide influenza pandemic. The poem reads in part:

Beacon of Liberty,
You alone was [*sic*] brave,
Brave in that highest courage,
All men's rights to save.
All men were your brothers,
Black and white and brown;
You scorned to bow to others
Who'd crush a fellow down.

Though less than artistically adroit, the poem and its message endeared her to French people of diverse origins with whom she would interact and work over the ensuing years in St.-Étienne and in Paris, especially through her resolute efforts on behalf of several exhilarating but arduous Pan-African Congresses.

7

France, 1918–1927

Pan-Africanism and Postwar Consular Life

Although Ida Gibbs Hunt knew Paris well from her extensive earlier travels and the eleven years she had lived in central France, heading there in the aftermath of the Great War to work with W. E. B. Du Bois on his Pan-African Congress must have been thrilling. From their separate points of origin, they both arrived in the brooding, postwar City of Lights in December 1918 and booked rooms at a modest hotel on the rue Richelieu. Du Bois saved copious receipts and chits detailing their incessant mutual activities throughout the winter.

With Gibbs Hunt's indispensable collaboration, Du Bois briskly set about his business. That month's report to his associates back at the NAACP argued that "what Europe ... wants in Africa is not a field for ... civilization, but exploitation." He also believed that he, she, and other well-educated, progressive American Negroes had vital roles to play in "civilizing" Africa — efforts that would help to empower the indigenous people and counteract the demeaning and exploitative acts and words of so many whites. And not only Africans cried out to him, but all of the "darker races." "Amelioration of the lot of Africa tends to ameliorate the condition of colored peoples throughout the world," Du Bois insisted, and Gibbs Hunt concurred. He had first contended that "the problem of the twentieth century is the problem of the color line" at the turn-of-the-century Pan-African Conference in London, and that color line, he often reiterated, "belts the world." Those prescient concepts and phrases took on a new resonance in the context of African Americans' expanding international exposure and awareness, and foretold the intensifying postwar global paroxysms of black cultural, social, and political initiatives.

Almost as much as their mission, Paris itself intoxicated Gibbs Hunt and Du Bois. "The purple facade of the Opera, the crowd on the Boulevard des Italiens and the great swing of the Champs-Elysées" enthralled him, while being so near and vital to her idol must have exhilarated her as they worked and schemed together pursuing the cause, far from their country's racism and beyond the restrictive shackles of any domestic alliances. Du Bois was an avid Francophile, though hardly a facile Francophone, yet despite his insufficiency in the language and reliance on Gibbs Hunt's practiced fluency, he exhorted "the American Negro [to] speak French," the mother tongue, he somewhat naively said, of a sophisticated country that discriminated on the grounds of education, class, and culture, but not race.

But Du Bois's projected congress nonetheless remained in critical straits. After a month in France, he still had no official sanction for it, and he also believed, probably with good reason, that the U.S. Secret Service was tracking his every move. One of his wary correspondents advised him that he was being "watched as if you were a German spy," while a representative of France's government warned Robert Lansing, the already dubious American secretary of state, when he arrived for the Versailles Conference that Du Bois planned to promote self-determination in the African colonies, though many skittish Europeans rigorously opposed such debates.

At that unpromising juncture, however, the outlook brightened in the person, and with the blessings, of Blaise Diagne, who still was one of only seven "colored" members of France's Chamber of Deputies. (In contrast, the United States had *no* Negro congressmen or senators at the time.) Born just off Senegal's coast on Gorée Island, one of the transatlantic slave trade's most infamous points of embarkation, Diagne was educated both there and in France, and the Gibbs-Hunts had known him years before in Madagascar when he served with the French customs service. France was deeply indebted to him because he recruited and enlisted thousands of African soldiers during the war, and its government rewarded him with the post of deputy commissioner for colonial affairs. So the enterprising Diagne, with political capital to spare and in search of a public forum through which to promote his views, persuaded Premier Georges Clemenceau that Du Bois would not try to foment any separatist, revolutionary, or Bolshevist initiatives among France's colonial peoples, as some Americans in Paris direly predicted. And Clemenceau concluded that as long as the maverick congress provided a bully pulpit for Diagne and did not impugn France's vaunted colonial *mission civilisatrice,* the erudite Dr. Du Bois could go right ahead and hold it that February, even over the United States' and England's blustering protests.

But Du Bois had other items on his agenda as well. He had also come to Europe to interview Negro American soldiers, thousands of whom remained there. Those men shared with him the egregious circumstances under which they had to function in their own country's military. To facilitate those undertakings, Du Bois enlisted the help of the quasi-governmental wartime envoy Addie Waites Hunton, whom he also exhorted to attend his congress.

During Du Bois's intermittent excursions away from Paris that winter, Gibbs Hunt staffed their organization's new offices herself, handled its correspondence, contacted and cajoled potential supporters, confirmed participants and facilities, and otherwise kept the reins of control in her own capable hands. Her feet must have skimmed the sidewalks as she bustled around the city. In St.-Étienne she was Mrs. William Henry Hunt, gracious wife of the esteemed American consul, and a pale moon who basked in the reflective light of his solar radiance. In Paris, by contrast, she could emerge as Ida Gibbs Hunt, a respected pan-Africanist in her own right and the eminent Dr. W. E. B. Du Bois's principal American partner.

One task that challenged the upcoming congress was how to define and agree on what pan-Africanism meant to the diverse participants — and to black people everywhere. In its most rudimentary but also visionary form, it aspired to offer a "homeland" in which to assemble and unify the peoples of Africa and the African diaspora. There they could cast off the shackles imposed by whites, become empowered, embrace commonalities in their heritage, and be both equals and received as such, a concept not unlike the 1940s Law of Return, which purportedly welcomed all Jews to the new state of Israel. Several noted French Zionists, in fact, endorsed and supported Du Bois's early pan-African efforts. In reality, however, at different times and places, and among different groups and individuals, that basic ideology had taken on notably dissimilar incarnations.

After the Great War, Ida Gibbs Hunt's anticolonial, pan-Africanist interests and visions began dominating her public life, but her search for black empowerment and unity was not new. She had spent her early years in a British colony on the northwest Canadian frontier in an enclave of activist African

American expatriates where, for a decade, her father served as an influential leader, amassed a small fortune, raised and molded his family. Judge M. W. Gibbs later served for more than three years as the United States consul in French colonial Africa, where he represented his country but also increasingly challenged its escalating imperialist initiatives.

Ida Gibbs's challenging liberal education, equaled in the late 1800s by few women, fewer Negroes, and almost no Negro women, had aroused and shaped her inclusive world vision. In her youth, and during and after her college years, she traveled widely. In her early forties, as the newly married Ida Gibbs Hunt, she too lived in Madagascar, an experience that shifted her thinking about race onto a larger global stage. Cohorts such as Anna Julia Cooper, who even before the 1900 Pan-African Conference in London examined intersections between problems faced by Negro Americans and people of African ancestry elsewhere, and Mollie Church Terrell, who spoke as a rare voice on behalf of women of color at international gatherings, further influenced their friend. Self-confidence, and her well-nurtured sense of justice and racial pride, led Gibbs Hunt to maintain her concerns about the intermeshed social, political, and economic plights of the world's nonwhite majority, while her probing intellect and a few outspoken colleagues coalesced to nourish her emergent black internationalist perspective. More than any other person, however, Du Bois stimulated, contoured, and elevated her keen, committed, and nuanced postwar pan-Africanism.

Its ideologies had been inspired by and intertwined in, but often clashed with, the beliefs of past giants in the African American community such as Frederick Douglass. Douglass, her father's sponsor and friend, had urged Negro Americans to get to know the world and its diverse people and cultures, but always to return home, join hands with whites and other blacks, and strive to become full-fledged citizens of the United States as they worked to uplift the race and honor their nation. The sage and usually optimistic Douglass believed that, in time, they would reap democracy's and capitalism's rewards — but never at the expense of their own racial identities. Not that pan-Africanism necessarily stood in opposition to integration (in recent years Du Bois had struggled to reconcile the apparent contradictions between that movement's implied overarching separatism and his own and the NAACP's efforts for desegregation, inclusiveness, and parity with their country's white majority), but it sought alternative solutions that might liberate, unite, and empower the manifold peoples of Africa and the worldwide African diaspora.

One representative of an earlier generation who had espoused such an Afrocentric vision was Anna Julia Cooper's mentor Alexander Crummell, who became Du Bois's exemplar as well. To reinvigorate his African roots, Crummell had lived, preached, and taught in Liberia in the mid-1800s. Another African American partisan, Martin Delany, first opposed emigration, but later touted Negroes' voluntary departure from what he saw as an incurably hostile white country, and he himself joined Crummell in West Africa. Though many of them later dejectedly returned home, for generations, legions of "colored" Americans (men and women) had sailed "back" to Liberia, to settle, govern, heal, educate, or proselytize for Jesus. Those Americo-Liberians became part of and mercilessly governed a Negro republic where, not unlike Europe's white colonialists throughout Africa, they too maintained a repressive hegemony over the indigenous majority. And in his somewhat ill-considered designs to create discreet, self-sustaining communities of expatriate African Americans first in Madagascar and then Haiti in the 1890s, Consul John Lewis Waller also had promoted his own variant, acquisitive manifestations of a capitalistic and political pan-Africanism. Their dreams and plans of unifying and empowering members of the darker races helped those black American transnationalists, and many others, move beyond the bitter legacies of slavery, Jim Crow, and colonialism and prompted them to acknowledge, explore, and embrace an African-based identity and culture — and wove common threads into their otherwise often inharmonious beliefs.

Yet even as Du Bois was fashioning his own newly refocused pan-Africanism, Marcus Mosiah Garvey touted notably different manifestations of a related ideology. Just before the war began, Garvey had founded the Universal Negro Improvement Association (UNIA) — his advocates claimed that its initials stood for "United, Nothing can Impede our Aspirations" — which appealed mainly to legions of poor migrants from the South who were streaming into northern cities. Their leader emphasized race pride, self-determination, even self-segregation, and espoused a sovereign black nation in West Africa — with himself as its self-proclaimed ruler. As quixotic as it sometimes seemed, his militant nationalism, or Black Zionism, struck fear and loathing into the hearts of many white (and quite a few Negro) Americans and among Europe's colonial overlords. Garvey, often called the Black Moses, was, after all, a British Jamaican.

In 1920 Garvey's International Convention of the Darker Peoples of the World attracted tens of thousands to New York's Madison Square Garden. Several of his emissaries visited Liberia that year, hoping to solidify his aspirations, and he unsuccessfully petitioned the League of Nations for a land grant in West Africa. Spouting grandiose claims, though unfortunately using somewhat deceitful means, he raked in his disciples' nickels, dimes, and dollars to create the Black Star Steamship Line (renaming its rust-bucket vessels the *Frederick Douglass* and the *Booker T. Washington*) with the intent of generating new international commerce to reflect, but totally reconfigure, the old transatlantic slave trade's legacy so as to benefit, not whites, but the peoples of the black diaspora. Garvey proposed to transport boatloads of his followers "back to Africa" on those ships. Yet for all his charisma and utopian philosophy and dreams, he remained an intemperate separatist who excoriated lighter skinned Negroes as white wannabes and (metaphorically) climbed into bed with white ideologues who also touted racial "purity" — but in their case to further segregation and white supremacy in the United States, which they considered to be a country established, under God's command, by, of, and for Caucasians.

Although Garvey and Du Bois, whom the former maligned as a mealy-mouthed mulatto, were really only promoting variant pan-African visions, they became wary adversaries. As their vitriol intensified, neither man seemed willing to move beyond personal animosity, bluster, and egotism to find grounds for any accommodation that could lead toward a constructive detente. As UNIA branches sprang up around the United States, in the Caribbean, and in West Africa, Garvey's followers increased into the millions. The movement adopted a red, green, and black "African" flag; published a journal; reveled in pageantry, parades, and bombastic rhetoric; and established a uniformed women's auxiliary. Ida and Hattie's brother Horace Gibbs supported the UNIA and exhorted his sisters to do the same, but both women, especially Ida, remained committed to Du Bois's more elitist but minimally less provocative pan-Africanism. Garvey's excesses led to an investigation into criminal charges of mail fraud and resulted in the Justice Department, especially its tenacious new lawyer John Edgar Hoover, targeting him as a seditious alien.

The most pivotal brouhahas over Garvey still lay a bit in the future, however, as early in 1919 Du Bois unsuccessfully sought the credentials he needed to observe the Versailles Peace Conference, where he hoped to monitor the darker races' interests. He also solicited a range of participants, including a few supportive whites, for his own embryonic congress.

Du Bois's proposed agenda focused on analyzing the current international situation vis-à-vis colonialism and imperialism. He formulated a slate of demands that sought full recognition of the world's handful of autonomous black nations; addressed issues of labor, education, politics, and economics throughout the world's impoverished "colored" belt; and assessed the Caribbean and African colonies' status and projected their progress toward eventual self-rule and independence. He urged potential attendees to join him in Paris to develop and extol a new sense of purpose and self-awareness — a symbiotic global black identity — that superseded their diverse origins, nationalities, ideologies, or affiliations. Such plans, however, generated ample criticism in both Europe and the United States among white conservatives and imperialists who argued that the congress's leaders might opt to conspire with the dreaded forces of international Bolshevism.

Despite daunting obstacles, the Pan-African Congress opened on February 19 with an address by Blaise Diagne, who claimed that his paradigm for racial unity should inspire all people of African ancestry. Fifty-seven delegates joined in, from fifteen countries and colonies. Sixteen United States representatives included several whites from the NAACP, as well as Addie Waites Hunton and George H. Jackson, Du Bois's Niagara Movement chum and a former consul in France who had served in the 1890s as a physician for Belgium in the Congo and was thus one of the few Americans who had even been in sub-Saharan Africa. Seven people purportedly represented France, among them Captain Matthieu Boutté, a Louisiana Creole who had not yet returned home after the war. In deference to her husband's career, Gibbs Hunt, who unlike the others bore no title except "wife of," also claimed France, not the United States, as her formal affiliation. She and Waites Hunton, who shared her internationalist and feminist leanings, were the only female delegates. Ethiopia sent a spokesman, thirteen came from the Antilles, including seven Haitians and two Martinicans. Gratien Candace and Achille-René Boisneuf, new Negro members of the French Chamber of Deputies; the war hero Sosthène Mortenol; and Henry Bérenger, a white civil servant, all hailed from Guadeloupe. Three Liberians were emissaries, notably the country's soon-to-be president Charles Dunbar Burgess King, who shuttled between Versailles and Paris. The remainder came from India, the Philippines, several Portuguese-controlled African territories, Spain, Belgium, England, and international black interest groups. The "colored" ex-mayor of London's borough of Battersea took part, but the British let no one living in their West Indian colonies attend.

Diagne chaired the formal sessions. Liberia's C. D. B. King sought international advocacy for his financially reeling country and offered it as a sanctuary for Negroes from any place in the world. George Jackson condemned the

United States' internal racist policies and practices, as did some of the French Antilleans, while several Europeans defended their own countries' supposedly benevolent imperialism. Out of respect for France's willingness to host the congress, many delegates heeded those appeals and, in what became almost a paean to colonialism's purportedly enlightening, elevating, and civilizing attributes, retreated from the demands for self-government articulated at London's Pan-African Conference of 1900. Attired in a modest but chic lace-collared black wool frock (a French dressmaker fashioned many of her clothes, some of which she kept for decades thereafter), *chapeau*, and pearls, Ida Gibbs Hunt did not appear on the program but provided a critical running translation from her central perch right next to Du Bois. Addie Waites Hunton, however, addressed the entire assembly about women's expanding roles in a changing world.

At the final gathering, the delegates recommended meeting biannually thereafter and proposed publishing a quarterly, trilingual (English, French, and Portuguese) journal of issues for debate. Although they could point to few tangible accomplishments, they believed that their congress signaled a stellar spiritual and intellectual renewal. The participants hoped to make the global leaders assembled in Versailles aware of their concerns, but their voices were scarcely heard at that venue. Speaking on behalf of his well-educated and informed American colleagues, Du Bois maintained that he knew what was best for the race and thus bore a responsibility to steer the world's underdeveloped masses in the proper direction.

Under Diagne's patronage, with Gibbs Hunt's invaluable partnership, and despite the obstacles he faced, Du Bois did all that he could with the Pan-African Congress, and he received ample, mostly positive press attention in Europe and the United States. The congress also helped to solidify a international consciousness among many diverse black people around the world. Superficially, the collaboration between Diagne and Du Bois was successful, but inherent dissonances and complexities in such a transnational alliance, combined with both partners' egos and autocratic bearing, portended future conflicts. As the sessions drew to a close, Du Bois established a four-person Pan-African Association to map out the next gathering. Diagne served as its president with Du Bois as secretary. The other two officers were the African Progress Union's Edmund Fitzgerald Fredericks, originally from British Guiana but now a resident of England, and Ida Gibbs Hunt.

Soon after the congress concluded, Du Bois met with several members of the American delegation in Versailles, where he circulated his resolutions and (he claimed) first suggested a mandates commission that the larger conference could institute to realign and chart the future of defeated Germany's colonies. Would they fall under the new League of Nations' aegis, or be annexed as spoils distributed among the victorious European countries? That spring of 1919, opportunistic Britain and France commandeered control over most of the German territories in Africa, thus expanding their own already ample colonial empires. Financially hobbled Liberia, which had lost nearly 40 percent of its sovereign domain to those two powers' incursions over the past seven decades, remained independent, but securely pinioned under the United States' heavy thumb.

The same week that the congress met in Paris, Captain Napoleon Marshall's unit, soon again to be New York's 15th Army Reserve Regiment, started homeward. Though hospitalized for many months and partially disabled, Marshall retained his commission for years afterward. The regiment's musicians, led by Lieutenant James Reese Europe, had won Frenchmen's hearts when they performed their bracing marches and rags during the war, and that spring they became equally celebrated back in the United States. To honor the unit's heroes, the novice Malagasy-American songwriter Andy Razaf, grandson of the former consul John Waller, titled one of his first published musical endeavors "The Fifteenth Infantry." The 15th's returnees took New York City by storm as they strode up Fifth Avenue and through Harlem in a boisterous welcome-home parade, then prepared to spread their scintillating music around the country.

Early that May, Massachusetts's governor invited them to play for the public in front of the state house before their sold-out performance at a nearby concert hall. Everyone in Boston seemed thrilled about the evening event except one of Lieutenant Europe's drummers, and during the intermission that disgruntled, intoxicated musician fatally stabbed the man known as the "King of Jazz." In contrast to the recent jubilation, mourners lined the streets of New York and Washington (James Europe had grown up in the nation's capital, where his sister Mary taught at Dunbar High School) to honor and memorialize him. Both blacks and whites grieved over the tragic demise of the man who had personified the very best of American music and disseminated it around the world.

Two months earlier, Du Bois had set off from France home to New York City. "We are both sorry to learn that you cannot come to St. Etienne," Ida Gibbs Hunt wrote him at the time. "I hope you are still solvent. Ha! ha!" she merrily teased in reference to the exorbitant costs of living during their long sojourn together in Paris, then signed herself: "Yours for the cause." Weeks later, back at the NAACP, Du Bois replied, "I am full of regret that I did not get to St. Etienne," adding that he had chatted on the telephone with his old Harvard buddy Captain Marshall, Gibbs Hunt's ailing brother-in-law.

Mollie Church Terrell attended neither Du Bois's congress nor the Versailles Peace Conference, but she did go to Zurich for a concurrent gathering convened by the Women's International League for Peace and Freedom (WILPF). Church Terrell was delighted to be there, but astonished to find that "I was the only one present at that meeting who had a drop of African blood in her veins." However, she proudly continued, "[T]he only delegate who represented the dark races of the world had a chance to speak in their behalf." "You may talk about permanent peace till doomsday, but the world will never have it till the dark races are given a square deal," she exhorted her white colleagues that week, incorporating language and sentiments from a letter she had recently received from Gibbs Hunt. Church Terrell also engaged in a series of spats with the WILPF over its genteel but thinly veiled racialist initiatives. Not long thereafter, she threatened to resign from its board when the organization excoriated the alleged rapes of European women by France's "colored" colonial soldiers still stationed in Germany, yet failed to condemn the killings and other assaults on vulnerable black people in Haiti by members of the United States' all-white army of occupation.

Church Terrell later wrote that in March 1919 she left Zurich planning "to visit my classmate, Mrs. Ida Gibbs Hunt, whose husband, the Honorable William H. Hunt, was United States Consul at St. Etienne." "I bought my ticket to Paris," she continued, "with the understanding that . . . I could leave the train, buy a ticket to St. Etienne, . . . return to that station, and then resume my journey," but the conductor informed her "firmly, not to say roughly," that she could not detrain at all to transfer for that side trip. "I was bitterly disappointed to learn that after coming so many thousand miles I could not go to see my friend who was just around the corner, so to speak." At that impasse a French soldier who had overheard the dispute leaped to her defense: "When he saw how unhappy I was because the conductor had forbidden me to go to St. Etienne, [he] became indignant and used language which would not look well in print." "It was an outrage!" he cried. "Even if I wanted to stay on the train and go straight through to Paris," Mollie Church Terrell went on, her new cavalier "would not let me do it." "When we reached the station at which

I would have to change cars for St. Etienne, [he] snatched up my two suitcases and put me off, explaining... what I would have to do and what time my train would leave."

Mollie finally arrived in St.-Étienne at two in the morning. No transportation was available to any public accommodation, so all alone she lugged her bags through the dark, empty streets. Finding a hotel at last, she roused an indignant porter who insisted that every room was occupied. She told him that she was a dear friend of the American consul but could hardly awaken him at that hour. When the concierge learned of her prestigious destination, Hunt's Ville Noir, he grudgingly provided her with a stuffy attic cubicle for the night. "The next morning I surprised my classmate and her distinguished husband," she concluded. "The short visit with the [Gibbs-Hunts] was enjoyed all the more because of the difficulties experienced in making it possible."

Leaving St.-Étienne to pause in Paris on her way home, Mollie Church Terrell met with Blaise Diagne, recently returned from the Pan-African Congress. He was "tall, very dark (almost black), straight as an arrow, self-possessed, dignified, and full of reserve power," she recalled, and Diagne arranged for her to visit the Chamber of Deputies, though U.S. Army officers had curtly excluded her from the tour of France's battlefields that they had arranged for white WILPF delegates. Instead, with the formidable Captain Matthieu Boutté, also fresh from Du Bois's congress, as her able guide, Terrell gained an opportunity to see "the terrible destruction of the villages and towns, . . . and the beautiful age-old structures which had been shot to pieces."

Back in the United States, the ensuing months saw considerable destruction during the so-called Red Summer, a designation that symbolized not just the presumably disruptive impact of international Bolshevism but the blood spilled around the country as whites lynched scores of blacks. President Wilson refused to support legislation that would enable the federal government to combat such heinous vigilantism. Many major American cities, the nation's capital among them, where explosives were detonated and the historian Carter G. Woodson, for one, narrowly escaped being pummeled by white thugs, suffered through violent confrontations that resulted in massive property damage, many injuries, and deaths. Ida sought Mollie's interpretation of those events, writing her that the international edition of the *Herald Tribune*, the most widely read American journal in Europe, gave the cause of the Washington disorders "as [black men's] attacks on white women." "Is that true?" she incredulously asked, adding, "I doubt it."

The riots, in fact, could be blamed in part on the *Washington Post*'s incendiary charges to that effect, but Mollie told her that, more than anything, white "marines who didn't like to see colored men wearing the uniforms of soldiers so cockily about the streets and who wanted to teach them to keep their place" had ignited them. "Anyway," Ida replied, African Americans' newly militant responses "showed that [the] general slaughter of Negroes . . . won't be suffered any longer. . . . Washington has awakened, and I'm glad of it!" Largely as a result of the war, the city's "colored" residents did indeed awaken. Ongoing racial oppression rendered them increasingly impatient and angry as they girded themselves to fight back. These events overwhelmed the city's police force, but hundreds of active-duty soldiers, their mission ultimately facilitated by torrential, street-clearing summer rains, at last brought the convulsions to an end. As to the current world situation, Ida continued in confidence to her friend, "[Y]ou are about right, the white man is a hopeless case when it comes to doing anything for the Darker Races besides exploiting them for his own interests, but . . . the worm will turn yet."

Soon after Du Bois arrived back in the United States, the NAACP bestowed its prestigious Spingarn medal (endowed by its wealthy benefactors, Joel and Arthur Spingarn) on Archibald Grimké, one of the organization's founders, a towering intellectual, lawyer, activist, and his nation's onetime minister in Santo Domingo, but an avowed opponent of Du Bois's pan-African initiatives. He was the brother of Ida's longtime pastor, the Reverend Francis Grimké, and father of the teacher, poet, and playwright Angelina Weld Grimké — all of whom had attended Ida Gibbs and Billy Hunt's wedding. Ida dashed off a warm note from St.-Étienne congratulating Archibald Grimké on that "well-merited recognition of your long struggle for freedom and justice irrespective of race." The next year's Spingarn prize would go to Du Bois alone for his highly lauded leadership of the 1919 Pan-African Congress.

That summer, with memories of the wartime contributions of African American soldiers still fresh in his memory, Achille-René Boisneuf, a Guadeloupean pan-Africanist and novice member of the Chamber of Deputies, rose to protest the decrees issued to France by the American army's "brass," which were intended to ensure that his countrymen emulated and enforced the United States' discriminatory practices. Boisneuf denounced those ugly affronts to the Negro doughboys, and recommended that his government officially apologize to any black Americans who had been ill-used in France during or after the war. A white deputy, however, supported the United States military's ultimatums because, he protested, any intimacy or assertions of racial equality between the races might diminish Europeans in the eyes of their colonial subjects. But the chamber rejected the position put forth by that white member and endorsed Boisneuf's proposal condemning all racial and religious prejudices and asserting its determination to respect human rights.

Meanwhile, New York City's Harlem was becoming the primary home of the nascent Negro Renaissance, as well as a major terminus for rural black southerners' Great Migration northward. That accelerating urbanization and population shift realigned much of the United States' demographic focus, but provided little relief from its ongoing racism. In many ways, however, increased international travel and even voluntary exile offered alternate opportunities, as first a trickle and then a steadier stream of black Americans headed to Europe. If New York and Washington became hubs of the stateside Black Renaissance, a similarly creative heart of darkness pulsed in and around Paris, as more people of color from the United States, the Caribbean, and Africa began gathering there to simmer and stir up a diverse new political, intellectual, and creative stew.

The passage of constitutional amendments that imposed prohibition and guaranteed woman's suffrage reflected the United States' volatile postwar climate in a time of major social revolution. This was the Jazz Age, which brought syncopated music, speakeasies for illicit imbibing, and a new sexual freedom typified by cast-off bras and corsets, short skirts and shorter hair sported by sassy flappers who shimmied, drank, smoked, voted, and called themselves New Women. The era also heralded the appearance of the New Negro, younger black people who were better educated than their parents, more militant, and poised to stretch their wings. Among them were Angelina Weld Grimké, Mary Burrill (the sister of Billy Hunt's former vice consul; years before, she and Angelina may have had a gay romance), and the poet Georgia Douglas Johnson. All three were New Negroes, New Women, and Dunbar High School teachers, and they all wrote plays linking the traumas of war with issues of sex and race.

Soon after the armistice, many of the "colored" men in uniform returned to the United States from Europe, but a number of Francophone students, travelers, and workers from the Caribbean, Africa, and Southeast Asia arrived anew or remained in France, as did more than a few Negro American soldiers and other black Yankees who were seeking a sympathetic venue in which to study, perform, debate, frolic, and otherwise express themselves. Although some bigoted or envious white American tourists deplored their ubiquity and unfettered presence, Paris became one of the world's most hospitable cosmopolitan cauldrons and played a nurturing role in the development of an emerging transnational, neo-African culture. The recuperating postwar city was more conducive to that black diasporic discourse, dialogue, and creativity than much of the woefully segregated United States, or than France's own poor, distant, and dependent "colored" colonies.

The year 1921 was a difficult one for both of the Gibbs-Hunts. In Washington, Mollie Church Terrell's husband, Robert, suffered an ultimately fatal stroke, and Billy's brother-in-law, Dallas Hughes, died in New York. On a professional level, the critical consular role that Billy had played during the war receded to its former pedestrian level. But he at least was among the group of distinguished African Americans whom Du Bois solicited to attend his Second Pan-African Congress. Ida, however, who had done wonders to ensure the previous gathering's success and served on the permanent Pan-African Association secretariat, was not included in her husband's invitation.

Ida Gibbs Hunt felt hurt, angry, and baffled, yet was determined to remain involved. So she blithely wrote Du Bois asking, "[H]ow is the Pan-African Congress coming on? I know very little about it." Nonetheless, she added, "I am saving any clippings for you that I come across on colonial questions, mandates, etc." "I want to go to the P.A. meeting in Paris, and *may* be able to get to London," she entreated her fickle colleague. She also shared her concerns that the League of Nations, lacking the United States' membership (despite President Wilson's exhortations, the American Congress, acting on its most isolationist impulses, had refused to cede even a modicum of the country's autonomy in order to join the League, a bitter defeat that may have triggered the stroke that disabled him for the remainder of his second term), could not ameliorate, deflect, or unravel the world's conflicts.

Perhaps Du Bois thought he could manage without Gibbs Hunt because he had acquired two new aides: Lieutenant Rayford Logan and Jessie Fauset. Logan, a 1917 graduate of Williams College (where Billy Hunt had spent his brief, unhappy college career), would remain in France long after the war and made a good living there trading in international currencies. He met, enjoyed, and even played baseball with members of the expanding Negro American community in Paris. Logan signed on to the pan-African enterprise at the behest of Fauset, who had been his French teacher and mentor at Dunbar High School. Fauset left her academic post in Washington when Du Bois, whom she had devotedly assisted without pay for many years, secured a salaried editorship for her at his *Crisis* magazine in New York.

Gibbs Hunt finally received a brief response from Du Bois informing her that Logan was expediting his mission in Paris, and that her sister and brother-in-law, the Gibbs-Marshalls, planned to attend the congress — which she already knew. But he also wrote: "I am counting on your presence and strongly hope that after the conference I can come to St. Etienne." Brushing aside his prior snub, Gibbs Hunt mentioned a recent meeting she had convened, "of which Mr. Logan will probably tell you." And casting light on the increasing friction between Du Bois and Blaise Diagne, who had spearheaded the 1919 gathering, she warned, "All seemed to feel that you have disregarded your aide too much; and Diagne is quite indignant." She and her cohorts, she added, "should like to consult together and know what you are going to do, beforehand, if possible."

The difficulties, however, persisted. The troublesome logistics included determining the many delegates, confirming locations for the upcoming sessions, and garnering financial support. Tensions also increased between Du Bois and Isaac Béton, an Antillean professor and the congress's incoming president, who threw up his hands and suggested canceling the conference altogether. Du Bois's testy response to Gibbs Hunt began: "I hope you will agree with me that it would be unwise to give up the work . . . and fail to hold a congress this year, . . . I am therefore, calling the congress in my capacity as ranking member of the Executive Committee." "I hope I can count upon your cooperation," he added, cajoling, twisting his longtime ally's arm, and pulling rank to ensure her compliance: "Despite all personal feeling we must rally to this great cause."

Gibbs Hunt, in fact, rallied with alacrity, and within a few weeks she negotiated a fragile truce among the congress's quarrelsome alpha males. Language difficulties nevertheless aggravated their conflicts. Du Bois's limited French, and the Antilleans' and Africans' imperfect English, lost much of their original nuance even in Gibbs Hunt's, Logan's, and Fauset's precise translations. The partially mollified Béton wrote Gibbs Hunt: "I read with great interest and attention the good council [sic] which you gave me. Be assured I will follow it." "After you left you were covered with praise," he added, deeming her diplomacy far preferable to Du Bois's egotistical posturing. He urged that in the future she should play a "mois effacé, plus actif" (less concealed, more active) role. Gibbs Hunt responded that she remained deeply devoted to their common cause and was especially gratified "that I succeeded in my efforts to bring about an understanding." She closed with a modest demurral to Béton's exhortations, insisting, "I don't wish any place 'more active.'"

After persevering in the face of Du Bois's aloofness and helping to organize the Paris and Brussels sessions, Ida was disappointed that she could not attend the London meetings, "tho I had made all preparations to come," she wrote. If the otherwise genial Billy Hunt became aware of Du Bois's epistolary rudeness toward his wife, he may have nixed those plans himself, though his more than two-hundred-page memoir never once mentions her pivotal pan-African activities.

Even with the locales agreed upon, who would attend remained up in the air. Ultimately, the expanded international contingent included people from Belgium and the Congo, France's sub-Saharan, Antillean, and Far East colonies, Portugal and Portuguese Africa, Abyssinia (Ethiopia), Haiti, India, Spain, and Denmark. Helen Curtis, the widow of a former United States consul in Liberia, chose to affiliate herself with that nation, where she had recently returned to live, rather than her own.

But unlike the previous congress, a few British West Indian delegates attended, as did several budding militants — among them, David Levering Lewis speculates, a young nationalist from *l'Indochine* who later assumed the name Ho Chi Minh. Europe's wary imperialists, however, forbade any representation from their North African colonies. An interracial group from the NAACP came over, and the Gibbs-Marshalls arrived in Paris with Consul Hunt. Among the other American Negro delegates were U.S. Army Colonel Charles D. Young, the expatriate painter Henry Ossawa Tanner, the former consul George H. Jackson, and Henry Alexander Hunt, one of Du Bois's astute comrades who was principal of the Fort Valley (Georgia) Institute. One can imagine that Henry Alexander Hunt and William Henry Hunt, two similarly southern-born, tall, light-skinned African Americans, near the same age, may even have speculated as to whether they might be related to one another.

During the Paris and Brussels meetings, Jessie Fauset further usurped Ida Gibbs Hunt's former role. She translated, delivered a speech, became Du Bois's scribe — and his paramour. The near exclusion of Gibbs Hunt's name (though she may have read a paper titled "Imperialism and the Darker Races" in French and English) from Fauset's accounts of the activities that appeared in *Crisis* in the next months could reflect the younger woman's discomfort with someone who preceded her in Du Bois's snarled personal life. The two women's backgrounds were much alike. Both had been born into the Negro gentry, had graduated from first-rate "white" colleges, wrote and spoke French fluently, and had taught at the M Street (recently renamed Paul Laurence Dunbar) High School. Both had strong feminist and internationalist leanings, their poetry lauding wartime France was markedly similar, and both of them almost deified Du Bois. He enjoyed many relationships with comparably gifted women for his professional benefit as well as, in some cases, his personal diversion and indulgence.

Fauset's subsequent articles in *Crisis* cite the congress's very few female delegates only in passing, and fail to mention at all the small contingent of "colored" Francophone women who were residing in or passing through Paris at the time. Flanked by a white Frenchman and Commandant Mortenol, Diagne again presided, while Du Bois, Gibbs Hunt, and an Ethiopian delegate shared center stage. Though scarcely acknowledging Gibbs Hunt's presence, Fauset almost seemed to swoon as she reported, "On that platform was, I suppose, the intellectual efflorescence of the Negro race." Among those, she added, "Dr. Du Bois loomed first."

The Negro American attendees probably tired of the kudos that many colonials heaped on France, Belgium, and Portugal, but they clung to Du Bois's vision. He had been enthroned as the United States' foremost black theorist and intellectual. If his followers knew in their hearts that his efforts were largely symbolic, they longed to commit themselves to a mission that transported them past American provincialism. As pan-Africanists they embraced universal issues, found a higher purpose, and tapped into a collective racial identity. They examined global questions beyond the boundaries of critical but narrower domestic matters, and their involvement, cogent debates, and analyses refute the prevalent though simplistic assumption that African Americans of their era were neither concerned with nor well informed and sophisticated about world affairs.

Even after the congress began, underlying tensions between the delegates continued. Rayford Logan recalled the escalating disaffection of Senegal's Blaise Diagne, who declared, "I am a Frenchman first and a Negro African second," while a compatriot added, "We don't want to think of ourselves primarily as Negroes; we are French." Those men sought closer ties to France, not independence. The uneasiness generated by Garvey's exhortations and other charges that linked pan-Africanism to Bolshevism disturbed Diagne as well, especially since V. I. Lenin had recently called for self-determination throughout the colonial world.

The Second Pan-African Congress's final manifesto mollified the Europeans concerning their tutelary roles in respect to their "colored" empires. The document gently reproved France's *mission civilisatrice* and Portugal's "native code," arguing that such policies should be mended, not ended, and insisting that "as experience and knowledge grow," the colonies' progress toward self-rule would advance as well. And when the Negro Americans compared colonialism to the horrors of home-grown segregation, they may have found the European alternatives in some ways preferable. Portending his future socialist sympathies and affiliation, Du Bois also argued that the wealthier nations should be obligated to "correct maladjustment in the distribution of wealth." The congress concluded that either Africa's colonized millions would have to be uplifted and assimilated by France, Belgium, England, Portugal, and Italy on a basis of full equality, or white Europeans could anticipate the emergence of one or more independent Negro superstates. Du Bois and his associates also claimed that the Second Pan-African Congress had planted the seeds that might transform political and economic power relationships throughout the world. To further those goals, he expanded the interim Pan-African Association to include Logan and Béton, while Ida Gibbs Hunt's new favorite, Commandant Sosthène Mortenol, who had started his military career in Madagascar while Consul Hunt was living there, briefly served as its treasurer.

After the meetings adjourned, the Gibbs-Marshalls and perhaps Rayford Logan returned with the Gibbs-Hunts to the Ville Noire in St.-Étienne, but Du Bois did not join them, as he had insisted he expected and wanted to do. Rather, he and Dantès Bellegarde, Haiti's new minister to France, who had joined his country's contingent at that year's congress, boarded a train bound for Geneva to present the League of Nations' Mandates Commission with a report concerning the ongoing abuses of colonial laborers in Africa recently drawn up by the congress. Du Bois then took a few days off to unwind and enjoy Switzerland with his new lover, Jessie Fauset.

As the year drew to a close, another highly publicized milestone reflected Ida Gibbs Hunt's deepest interests. The Prix Goncourt, France's premier literary award, went to René Maran, an Antillean-born civil servant and writer, for his controversial book *Batouala: A True Black Novel*. *Batouala* exposes the debilitating impact of French colonialism. One of its most devastating statements is "Civilization, civilization, pride of the Europeans, and charnel house of innocents . . . you build your kingdom on corpses." Many outraged Frenchmen protested that the novel was designed, even destined, to foment indigenous rebellions in Africa, and further carped that the prize would never have gone to Maran had he been white. Du Bois honored Maran by portraying him on the cover of the May 1922 issue of *Crisis*.

If pan-Africanism and other manifestations of a transnational black political and cultural identity shaped much of Ida Gibbs Hunt's life, her husband inhabited a somewhat different world, although as an inveterate extrovert, and out of deep affection for his wife and her family and his admiration of Du Bois, he did attend (but most likely without informing his superiors at the State Department) much of the 1921 Pan-African Congress. Soon thereafter, however, a cherished old colleague from St.-Étienne (unnamed in Hunt's memoir), who at that juncture was serving as a top government official in Algeria, extended Consul Hunt an irresistible invitation to see colonial French North Africa for himself.

From his hotel in Algiers, Hunt later wrote, he "looked out upon one of the populous public squares and the entrances to the principal Mohammedan Mosque." The spindly minarets, haunting calls to prayer, tinkling bells and cymbals, silent veiled women, scrawny animals, and the scents of incense, cumin, turmeric, and roasting meats all entranced him, while the city itself evoked memories of Madagascar's deposed and exiled queen, Ranavalona III. The aging queen had recently died right there in French Algeria.

After rounds of diplomatic handshaking and backslapping, Hunt and his friend boarded a train to "Biskra, a fertile oasis on the edge of the Desert of Sahara." In addition to sightseeing at the verdant, storied Garden of Allah, Hunt observed the filming of a motion picture based on Voltaire's novel *Candide* (probably the Italian-made movie titled *L'Ingenuo*), "a unique sensation," he mused, "especially when I saw the picture thrown on the screen in France some months later."

On their return to Algiers, his host surprised him with an unexpected dividend for the next few days. Hunt recalled his "first aeroplane flight . . . in charge of an experienced aviator." He and the jaunty pilot they had engaged landed at Oran to visit "the Headquarters of the famous French Foreign Legion," then took off south across the Sahara, where the sky's cobalt dome plunged into boundless tan dunes laced with faint tracings of green. For many centuries, caravans of Arab traders had crisscrossed those sands from oasis to oasis, transporting precious salt, spices, gold, ivory, Islam, and captive sub-Saharan slaves. Consul Hunt and his *bon ami* also probed the Casbah's labyrinthine alleyways and visited the secluded estates of some wealthy Muslims, where, he wrote, "one never meets the women folk, and they are never seen or referred to in any way." In those patriarchal domiciles they partook of multicourse banquets that included "Cousse-Cousse" and baby lamb "roasted to Allah's taste" and intended, he learned, to be eaten only with the fingers. Blissfully sated, Hunt recrossed the Mediterranean as "the wind howled, the ship rolled, and pitched, and bounced, and grated, [and] the waves seemed like huge mountains," and then traveled north by rail from Marseille home to St.-Étienne.

Throughout those early postwar years the peripatetic, popular, and very capable Billy Hunt was the only African American consul serving in Europe, and one of the few men of his race who had survived the United States' decade-long purges of black government personnel. Rayford Logan even told colleagues that he believed one likely explanation for Hunt's extended term in France was that for some time State Department officials simply did not know for sure that he was a Negro.

Starting in 1919, the department agreed to cover the expenses of immediate family members who traveled on official business with its consuls between posts, or to and from the United States. So in 1922 Consul Hunt and his wife took a two-month leave, during which they went to see their sisters in New York — where Ida also purchased a ten-apartment residential building.

Soon thereafter, Hattie and Captain Napoleon Marshall left for Haiti, where President Warren Harding had appointed him as military attaché, a post Marshall may have learned about from a fellow pan-Africanist, the recently deceased Colonel Charles D. Young, who had once held that position himself. In 1920 ex-consul James Weldon Johnson, by then a Du Boisian and a critic of American foreign policy, had also visited Haiti. His subsequent report charged that under the United States occupation many Haitians lived and died much as the Belgian Congo's hapless people had during King Leopold's old reign of terror. Most of the marines who policed Haiti and instituted Jim Crow mandates at places of public accommodation were southern, and all of them were white.

Ida Gibbs Hunt, who turned sixty that autumn of 1922, also visited Washington, D.C., where, as the *Washington Bee* reported, she delivered a lecture at Dunbar High School titled "The Women of France," in which she maintained that "the status of women [has] widened since the war." "Men," she added, "have learned to recognize woman as an important factor in the world's work," and assured her young audience that "the menace to marriage and the family, which so many saw in this new independence of women . . . has not been borne out by the facts."

Her speech focused on the political activities of *les Françaises,* who, unlike their American sisters, had not yet been granted suffrage. "By the ratification of the Susan B. Anthony Amendment," she wrote, women in the United States obtained "the right to vote and hold office throughout this country," but she failed to mention total disfranchisement in Washington, or the ongoing attacks on black southern voters. As for French women, "[W]hatever may be feared from their participation [in government], they cannot bring the world to a more upset condition than it is today under men's control." Throughout the world, Gibbs Hunt insisted, women were hardly "indifferent to the vote," but she also acknowledged that many of them failed to make the most of the limited opportunities they already had. "The [French] National Woman's Suffrage Union," some of whose conferences she attended, "has nearly a hundred groups throughout [the country]." She named several "well known 'feminists,' as they are called in France," and argued that after the courage the "weaker sex" had shown during the war, "a grateful nation now seems more disposed to listen to their demands, [though] men in the French Republic are not disposed to give women the ballot without a struggle." Gibbs Hunt was overly optimistic, because France's women did not gain full suffrage for two more decades, following another bitter war. In closing, she claimed that the world "has seen woman's sphere gradually widen until it is now quite generally conceded that her sphere is any place that she can fill."

After that appearance, Ida Gibbs Hunt, who had no children but "adopted" a series of French girls, invited a Dunbar High School student named Wenonah Bond (her mother, Georgia Bond, was a Book Lovers' Club member who had joined the WILPF in response to the entreaties of her friends Mollie and Ida) to return with her to St.-Étienne. Wenonah, who had studied with Dunbar's dedicated teachers, including Anna Julia Cooper, Angelina Weld Grimké, Mary Europe, and Mary Burrill, already harbored a nascent feminism and envisioned herself a citizen of the world. She longed to go to France, and thereafter cherished the snapshot that she identified as "Mrs. Hunt & I," taken that week under her family's backyard grape arbor. But Georgia quickly declined Ida's invitation on her daughter's behalf, sparking a testy intergenerational feud when she decided that she could not, or would not, let her intrepid fifteen-year-old leave the country. But Ida's influence would remain strong. A decade later Wenonah toured Europe, debating and analyzing global issues while on study fellowships in Denmark and England. In a letter reprinted by a black New York newspaper in 1932, she would write:

[I]f every human personality is sacred and contains . . . some spark of goodness, we cannot hold it in slavery; we cannot segregate it; . . . we cannot impose unsympathetic white governments on Africans, and Indians, and Haitians; we cannot allow it to be crushed in a heartless economic system, or killed by murder, or capital punishment, or warfare. . . . We are unworthy of our heritage of civilization if all we have learned to do is to build better guns and powerful machines. . . . Unemployment! Race prejudice! War! All the same disease in a slightly different form. What a holy mess we have made of things.

Gibbs Hunt soon revised her Dunbar lecture to spotlight the United States. In this essay, retitled "The New Sphere of Women," she wrote, "In no respect is the revolution wrought by the recent war more evident than in the changed status of woman." "During the great struggle she worked as faithfully as did the men for the final triumph of democracy. . . . Do you suppose that these are the same women, with the same views, the same narrow tastes [after those] years of intensive labor?" Answering her own rhetorical question, she said, "Far from it." "Employers wish to pay them less, [but] this must cease. . . . Equal pay for equal work is the growing demand. . . . She is taking on a new dignity with her new freedom and independence, and men are learning to respect her, and to work along beside her, forgetful of sex at the moment." While in the past, she concluded, a few women

> have labored, spoken and written on these subjects, . . . they have been the exception and not the rule. . . . For some time the growing independence of woman has been looked upon by many as a menace, but recent years have demonstrated that it is only necessary to allow her to put her talents to some useful end and to employ them for the well-being of society. . . . She is no longer satisfied to be treated as a child and told that men will give her what is best. . . . She wishes to have a voice and a vote in settling public matters.

Nothing indicates whether this feminist deposition was ever delivered or appeared in print, but it is the first known occasion on which she signed any of her work "Iola Gibson," accompanied by the parenthetical addendum: "A pen name sometimes used by Ida Gibbs Hunt."

Before laying out that provocative piece, Gibbs Hunt may not have felt the need to create and adopt an alias, but the practice was not uncommon for African American (or many other) women. As far back as the 1830s, the black Quaker Sarah Mapps Douglass had held forth under the pen name Zillah in the *Liberator,* an abolitionist journal, and in 1868 South Carolina's Frances Rollin strategically re-sexed herself as Frank A. Rollin to author a biography of the pan-Africanist pioneer Martin Delany. Ida's friend Mollie Church Terrell — the recent widow of an appointed and therefore politically vulnerable federal judge — sometimes had used the flowery name Euphemia Kirk.

Those women, who wanted to challenge traditional boundaries and cast light on the complexities and double burdens of being both black and female, had employed such pseudonyms to move their writings into the public domain, sidestep controversy, and especially, perhaps, to protect loved ones from possible negative repercussions. But Ida Gibbs Hunt's use of the literary alias Iola Gibson raises further questions as to its more specific origins.

The briefer Iola was a pen name adopted by the feisty journalist Ida B. Wells, whose antilynching crusade, ferocity at the 1893 Chicago Exposition, and work in the "colored" women's club movement had motivated Gibbs Hunt. And *Iola Leroy* was the title of that same year's novel by Frances Ellen Watkins Harper, an early suffragist and abolitionist colleague of Ida's father in Philadelphia. Gibbs Hunt must have identified with and been inspired for decades by Watkins Harper's mixed-race but black-identified upper-class protagonist. In the novel Watkins Harper calls the locale where the slaves held their subversive prayer meetings "Gibson's woods," so Gibbs Hunt's adoption of that surname further suggests her radical intent. In addition, if with a little sleight of hand the "o" and "l" in Iola are compressed into one another, they visually become a "d," as in Ida, then folding in a touch of auditory elision, GibbsHunt sounds a lot like Gibson.

And so, it seems, Ida Gibbs Hunt, speaking covertly as Iola Gibson, empowered by the combined influences of the World War, woman suffrage in the United States, and her work with the Pan-African Congresses, gained maturity, independence, and a more authoritative voice. But she must have guessed that her protests that men treated women like children (might she have been thinking of her husband or Du Bois?), quasi-socialistic calls for "world peace" and "equal pay for equal work," and demands for French women's full suffrage would not sit well with Consul Hunt's State Department superiors. She did not date this essay, which she probably shared with her sister or with colleagues like Mollie Church Terrell and Addie Waites Hunton, who worked in the 1920s with a new organization called the International Council of Women of the Darker Races (ICWDR).

Although the National Association of Colored Women's members had exhorted her as early as 1906 to initiate women's social service clubs abroad, the "result to be an International Association of Colored Women," Gibbs Hunt wrote, that was not to be. Perhaps because she brooded about the impact that such involvement might have on her husband's career (while he was a consul in Nicaragua, James Weldon Johnson wisely first published his provocative novel *Autobiography of an Ex-Colored Man* anonymously), she did not join the new

ICWDR, but kept abreast of its activities and probably offered its members food for thought. This revised treatise, along with Gibbs Hunt's other miscellanea found among the papers of Antoinette Mitchell's family, combine to suggest her ties to the enclave of Negro expatriates living in France in the 1920s. With her husband Louis, a jazz musician, soul food chef, and booster of amateur baseball, Antoinette Mitchell had relocated to Paris shortly before the war. The couple became charter members of a small but burgeoning African American community in Europe, and they enjoyed the company of some of Ida Gibbs Hunt's close colleagues such as Rayford Logan.

That same year, 1922, a brutal boxing match transfixed the European continent. The dark-skinned Louis M'barick Fall, a former Senegalese *tirailleur* known in the ring as Battling Siki, kayoed the white French idol and titleholder to become Europe's new middleweight champion. For at least a decade Consul Hunt had involved himself in boxing promotion in St.-Étienne, but this brutal contest roused myriad Frenchmen's latent malaise about colonialism and "black power," though Siki equally embraced both Senegal and France. Much like the heavyweight fighter Jack Johnson before the Great War, Siki too flaunted his fame and fortune, reveled in his notoriety, challenged old racial protocols, and defiantly married a white woman. He even boldly promenaded around Paris with his pet lion cub on a leash.

Having returned to the French capital, Ida Gibbs Hunt continued her work with the Pan-African Association, charged with maintaining interest in the cause between the biennial congresses. But the tensions between W. E. B. Du Bois and Isaac Béton did not abate. As the 1923 gathering neared, she reported to Du Bois that the French Antillean "doesn't understand your brief and American business-like way of writing him," adding: "I shall do what I can to try to unite the factions for I see that there is much bad feeling and misunderstanding, and the officers are ready to drop it all. . . . It would be too bad to let all of *our hard work* in the past go to naught." Béton, she pleaded, "has no funds whatever, [and] the Association is already heavily in debt to him for the initiatives he has taken at his own expense." She also told Du Bois that she had "talked further with M. Béton, Logan & others, and think that I have persuaded them all to join hands," and she planned to confer soon again with Guadeloupe's representative, Gratien Candace. In this instance, Rayford Logan, usually Du Bois's unwavering supporter, demurred a bit to endorse Gibbs Hunt's more tactful approach.

She also scolded Du Bois. "If I am to be ignored, misunderstood, and mistreated as I was last time it's hardly worthwhile, and simply because I criticised some details in lack of organization, taking it for granted that we were all united on fundamentals. . . ." — then strategically retreating, she added, "But let that pass now. We are all probably to some extent to blame." After caucusing with her cranky team, however, their frustrations with Du Bois resurfaced, and she entreated him, "We tried to come to a decision on holding a Congress this year in Lisbon since you wish to do so . . . but we know so little about the affairs in Lisbon or with you." "You have no more right to call a Congress in your name alone than M. Béton had to postpone one," she pointedly went on, lauding Béton's stewardship and out-of-pocket generosity. "I shall contribute something to the Ass'n and Congress, but half of what I give I want to have put to M. Béton's credit." Concurrently, she reassured Béton that he indeed would be "reimbursed one of these days."

"What other delegates besides yourself [will come] from America?" her fusillade at Du Bois continued. "Is the Ligua Africana [Liga Africana, the federation of Europeanized "colored" Portuguese] cooperating? Are Americans furnishing the funds? You tell me nothing but that you are calling the Congress in London & Lisbon." "It is not only *reasonable* curiosity but my right to know the details." However, she continued, "I do not blame you for taking the initiative and calling the Congress, since you are the founder of the Association." "You will come to France, I suppose, and I should like to meet you and talk over matters with you," but then she deliberately goaded him: "if you consider a woman's ideas worth anything."

Many of their letters are gone (Gibbs Hunt later asked Du Bois to keep one note "strictly private . . . then destroy it," and in contrast to her other copious souvenirs, she saved nothing from him), but despite his arrogance, Du Bois's surviving correspondence does not disparage her views based on gender. Rather, he considered *any* variant approaches inferior to his own. "We must not seem to the public to have a split in our organization," Gibbs Hunt concluded. "I am anxious to be cooperative with you and all of the others," but her prickly postscript persisted: "Please tell M. Béton that I paid my dues to you. . . . Remember I gave you 200 F[rancs]?"

Du Bois's wrathful, self-serving response represented the nadir of their decades-long relationship. Vitriol curled from each line of his six-page typewritten letter. He blamed the "obdurate" Béton and Gibbs Hunt in full for the continuing impasse over arrangements for that autumn's congress, but maintained that as the committee's "ranking member," he could do whatever he wanted — though he still had no funds for the upcoming "P.A.C." and relied on his aides in France to take care of that irksome necessity. He wrote that he "tried repeatedly to disabuse [Béton's] mind" of the idea that he (Du Bois) could raise money for the congress, since doing so would create a conflict, since he also served as an employee of the NAACP.

"There is some mistake with regard to the 200 Francs which you contributed," his retort to Gibbs Hunt continued, though that amount, he scoffed, only "amounted to approximately $10." He presumed that it was intended to pay for her membership dues, and refused even for "a moment [to] assent to the statement that I . . . withheld funds from the Pan-African Association." Her claim to that effect, he railed, maligned his integrity and "has already given rise to . . . difficulties." But after his discussion with Gibbs Hunt, Béton had written Du Bois: "You gave Mrs. Hunt a receipt signed by yourself on a scrap of paper and promised her a regular receipt from Miss Fauset. This receipt has never reached her. I am sure . . . that you will not deny these facts, and having confidence in your probity, I am convinced that you will hasten to forward to their real destination, that is to say to our office, the two hundred francs that were entrusted to you." Du Bois petulantly directed Gibbs Hunt that she must "make it clear to the committee that . . . I cannot be responsible for any contributions." "With regard to the Crisis in the American Library at Paris," he had turned over her contribution to the NAACP. If she had any quarrel with that, she should take it up directly with the association's secretary, not with him! Early in October, assuming an implausibly placid façade, Ida Gibbs Hunt replied that "your long and frank letter pleased me so much. . . . You know that I would make no reflection on your honesty and have perfect confidence in it."

With little doubt, Du Bois used, abused, and misused both Gibbs Hunt and — although with no larcenous intent — her money, as he did with other supporters such as Jessie Fauset and Isaac Béton, and would later with Haiti's esteemed Dantès Bellegarde. Gibbs Hunt had recently donated one hundred dollars to the NAACP through Du Bois and specifically earmarked a portion of that gift to provide a multiyear subscription to *Crisis* for the American embassy's library in Paris, yet that reallocation obviously never came to pass. Nonetheless, she bit the bullet and facilitated his appeals for a donation from the National Association of Colored Women, which granted the upcoming congress a modest sum. Even with their rancorous exchanges still fresh in her mind, Gibbs Hunt consented to cochair the upcoming London session and supplemented Du Bois's and Logan's frantic, last-minute fund-raising endeavors (to which she contributed even more of her own money) among supportive Parisians as well as black American expatriates or sojourners.

The Third Pan-African Congress assembled in London in November 1923 with Du Bois, Logan, and Gibbs Hunt serving as its executive triumvirate, but new spats popped up almost daily. Béton and his cohorts Diagne and Candace refused to attend, their absence reinforced by the sensitivity of France's negotiations over repayment of its war debts to the United States, while other expected participants withdrew after clashing with Du Bois about shaky financial support for the congress — which the NAACP ultimately agreed to back yet one more time. Several white British socialists joined the assembly, but with three of its French trailblazers absent, overall participation declined from two years before. Some of the Americans, Logan and Gibbs Hunt among them, maintained lasting friendships with the black Gallic pan-Africanists, but no such gathering would ever again convene on French soil.

Undaunted, Du Bois opened that year's first session with "The History of the Pan-African Movement," and the second with his talk "The Black World at Present," which Ida Gibbs Hunt followed with her lecture titled "The Coloured Races and the League of Nations." To some extent, Du Bois may have rued his own previous irascibility, because he asked her to address that major forum. Unfortunately, no full text of her speech survives. Despite Gibbs Hunt's deepening disillusionment with the League of Nations, she still regarded that body as the most, really the only, effective instrument for preserving world peace, while women's moral powers, she insisted, must be tapped "to prevent another holocaust" — a prophetic concept, and a word rarely used in that way, at that time.

Remaining publicly optimistic, Du Bois pronounced his gathering a success, but this Pan-African Congress attracted less press attention than had its predecessors. A French journalist wrongly (but perhaps intentionally so) claimed that Du Bois was operating in cahoots with Marcus Garvey. Du Bois hotly denied that assertion, but many Negro colonials latched on to it as an added though specious excuse to distance themselves from a movement spearheaded by someone who purportedly worked in concert with the contentious Black Moses. Though Garvey had attracted the intermittent support of several influential American black women, including the journalist-reformer Ida Wells-Barnett and the recently deceased entrepreneur and philanthropist Madam C. J. Walker, he rejected Europe's supposed tutelary role in the colonies and espoused a position that Rayford Logan bluntly described as "back to Africa and kick the white man out."

Much as the nasty earlier conflict between Booker T. Washington and W. E. B. Du Bois divided African Americans, so did this feud in the 1920s between Du Bois and Garvey, with its bitter squabbles over color and class, cleave the community. Garvey denounced what he saw as the hypocrisies of integration and touted his Black Zionism, primarily on behalf of dark-skinned, less well-to-do Negroes in the United States and the West Indies. He scoffed that Du Bois spoke only for the supposedly assimilationist, often mulatto Talented Tenth. But the editor foresaw and argued to his *Crisis* readers that Garvey's empire would crash and burn, and its leader go down in flames. When the Justice Department's bulldog investigator J. Edgar Hoover (who had no love for Du Bois either) prevailed in the crusade against him, Garvey was arrested, indicted, tried, and convicted on charges of mail fraud, and late in 1923 — still defiant — he was imprisoned in a federal penitentiary.

The Third Pan-African Congress largely echoed the initiatives from two years before, but its new propositions espoused subject peoples' right to armed self-defense, called for an end to Africa's residual pockets of slavery or peonage, and demanded a "colored" representative on the League of Nation's Mandates Commission. The movement's fault lines also emerged more clearly. Most Negro American delegates believed that the world's subject peoples should move boldly toward self-governance by disengaging themselves from the European powers, but the depleted French contingent preferred to identify with and advance within the extant colonial system. This was Consul Hunt's position as well.

After the first sessions adjourned, Du Bois went to St.-Étienne for his long-promised visit with Ida and Billy Hunt, before heading off to the congress's follow-up meetings in Portugal. He and Gibbs Hunt seem to have at least superficially cobbled over their recent spats, and on his return to the United States Du Bois recalled that brief sojourn with obvious pleasure — at least his time with the urbane Consul Hunt. In an article that appeared in the January 1924 *Crisis* magazine he wrote, "I came to Lisbon by [way of] St. Etienne, where America has its one colored European Consul." And the next month he needled his country's white officialdom when he wrote that "the most popular man in town — head of the French and Foreign Clubs, chief sportsman, guest of a hundred hosts, and [most] welcomed of all business men, is one of us — Hunt, the only American Consul of Negro descent in Europe. The State Department is worried over Hunt. He deserves a promotion and they dare not promote him."

Following the gathering in Lisbon, Du Bois proceeded on to Liberia, where he served as the United States envoy to the second inaugural of President C. D. B. King. Setting foot for the first time on African soil transported him into a frenzy of emotional and journalistic excess. He gushed in *Crisis*, "Africa is at once the most romantic and the most tragic of continents." He spoke with the American diplomatic delegation, including its chief of mission, Consul General Solomon Porter Hood, a minister and devoted NAACP member, and met a new consular clerk named Lillie Mae Hubbard, the first Negro woman to do any such work for the State Department. Du Bois conferred at length with King, whose country was in dire financial straits and in danger of losing its sovereignty as a result of the huge debts it owed to both European nations and the United States. Those discussions also hammered the final nails into the coffin of the recently imprisoned Marcus Garvey's scheme to establish new settlements of the UNIA's Western Hemisphere supporters in the singular African republic. Soon thereafter, President King issued an ultimatum declaring that the Garveyites would no longer be welcome in Liberia.

But with all the profligate pageantry surrounding King's inaugural, and in the face of the Americo-Liberians' economic, governmental, and personal exploitation of the indigenous people, Du Bois foolishly suspended his otherwise acute and rational powers of observation. He clung to a romantic notion that Liberia remained a lone polestar guiding his idealized pan-African visions of black political independence, and his self-assumed blinders enabled the extravagant rhetoric that distorted his reports written for *Crisis*. Those accolades surely informed Ida Gibbs Hunt and William Henry Hunt as they tried to further shape their own impressions of the country.

Soon afterward, a tense internecine squabble resurfaced in France. *Les Continents*, a new journal published by Negroes from that country's colonies led by the brash novelist René Maran, accused Deputy Blaise Diagne, the revered pan-Africanist, of wartime treason to his Senegalese motherland. The article claimed that Diagne had mastered "the art of selling his brothers, . . . gave his race the kiss of Judas," and enriched himself at the expense of black men whom he had enlisted and who, despite France's promises, still had not received their citizenship rights after the war. The unsigned essay, probably written by Maran himself, charged that Diagne had received a "commission for each soldier [he] recruited." Diagne, in turn, excoriated *Les Continents'* editors as Bolshevists and sued them for libel. During the trial the deputy had to face the public humiliation of hearing one of his countrymen, a former army *tirailleur*, testify that he (Diagne) "was paid well enough not to need twenty sous for each recruit." Nonetheless, Diagne prevailed. The court-awarded damages were so substantial that the magazine folded in December 1924, although it then merged with the comparably anticolonial Madagascan

Tribune du Peuple Malgache. Logan and Gibbs Hunt defended their old Gallic friends, but Du Bois, still fuming at the French defections from his recent Pan-African Congress, sneered that "Diagne is a Frenchman who is accidentally black."

Such quarrels hardly represented the totality of blacks' endeavors in postwar France. A Negro Renaissance — more than just a circumscribed Harlem Renaissance — welled up in the United States, but some of the stimuli for that creative era lay in emergent French influences on African Americans at home and abroad during and after the war.

In Paris, young people such as Martinique's Nardal sisters, Paulette and Jane, the first colonial Negro women to matriculate at the Sorbonne, convened similar gatherings. They advanced what they began calling *l'internationalisme noir* — black internationalism. Paulette Nardal had received a degree in English literature (her thesis critiqued Harriet Beecher Stowe's abolitionist yet condescending *Uncle Tom's Cabin*) in the early 1920s, while Jane studied classics. Jane also informed a visiting American that her life story was more than just a revised configuration of "The Autobiography of a Re-Colored Woman," a cheeky reference to James Weldon Johnson's *Autobiography of an Ex-Colored Man.* Most of Paris's few "colored" Francophone students were men, but the Nardals shimmered among them. They flirted with the Western world's emerging feminism, observed and exalted America's New Negroes, put black culture in a transnational framework, and became emissaries between French intellectuals and the Harlem Renaissance as they corresponded with, cultivated, saluted, and promoted talented people of color around and across the Atlantic. During her European travels Jessie Fauset sometimes met with Jane and Paulette Nardal, as did Anna Julia Cooper. While Fauset's editorship at *Crisis* reflected her lasting devotion to Du Bois and his pan-African efforts, she cast her own writings, and those by others of the world's manifold black and brown people, within an evolving global context shaped by race, class, and gender.

The Pan-African Congress's proposed quarterly never got off the ground, but in addition to *Les Continents,* which appeared then disappeared in 1924, and the *Tribune du Peuple Malgache,* Paris's Negro Francophones created and circulated other postwar journals. *L'Action Coloniale* had jump-started those initiatives in 1918. *La Race Nègre* (which sometimes translated and published Marcus Garvey's writings) succeeded the short-lived *Voix des Nègres,* and more soon followed. The Nardals and Maran wrote and translated for several such publications, while the Guadeloupeans Maurice Satineau and Stéphane

Rosso contributed to others. Much like their American counterparts — the NAACP's *Crisis* under Du Bois's editorship, the National Urban League's *Opportunity,* even the UNIA's *Negro World* — those chronicles generated by "colored" Frenchmen dealt with global culture in the context of geopolitics, colonial exploitation and oppression, and America's domestic racism. They suggested that all people of the African diaspora had many kindred concerns. The United States–based periodicals garnered and addressed a new international readership, while those that originated in France sought and found an equally receptive Negro American audience.

One literary contributor and younger luminary of the Harlem Renaissance was Langston Hughes (a nephew of the Langstons from Oberlin, old friends of Ida Gibbs Hunt's family), who spent several years abroad. Another was Claude McKay, a Caribbean-born Negro American of maternal Malagasy descent who intermittently lived and circulated among the rising clique of "colored" writers in Paris. But McKay preferred southern and central France, and spent much more of his time traversing, working, and residing in that part of the country. His references to and familiarity with American consular activities there, and the fictional mulatto protagonist whom he called Etienne St. Dominique in his manuscript "Romance in Marseilles," suggest that he was influenced by a visit with Consul Hunt (a rare individual who was fully conversant with his mother's ancestral homeland) in St.-Étienne. And that other rising son of Madagascar, Andy Razaf, now residing in or near New York City, continued writing snappy lyrics for many of the songs that accompanied the Harlem Renaissance.

Those intertwined circles of Negro Americans, Antilleans, and Africans evolved and became ever more complex in the 1920s and later. Living in St.-Étienne, working with Du Bois and others on behalf of that decade's Pan-African Congresses, and spending time with a group of acquaintances in and around Paris such as Rayford Logan, Henry Ossawa Tanner, and Antoinette and Louis Mitchell, Ida Gibbs Hunt inhaled the essence of their intoxicating creative, political, and intellectual worlds. And like Jane and Paulette Nardal, she embodied a robust *internationalisme noir.* But while Ida and Billy Hunt both may have patronized the Mitchells' trendy new club and eatery in Montmartre for *le jazz hot,* as well as the fried chicken, *pieds de cochon,* or other nostalgic tastes of black America, for the consul, Paris really meant one thing above all others: the United States embassy, overseen by the omnipotent State Department.

Except for short-term appointments in Haiti and Liberia, the growing department brought in no new African Americans to serve abroad between 1906 and 1924, but in the latter year it hired Clifton R. Wharton as a legal clerk in Washington. In part, that may have come about by accident, since Wharton, like Hunt, was not readily identifiable as a Negro from the photo accompanying his application. The recent passage of the Rogers Act consolidated the diplomatic and consular branches and helped to standardize recruitment, examination, and conditions of employment. But when Wharton aced the department's qualifying exam and came to the nation's capital, his designated race became apparent, and he did not get to attend the prestigious foreign service school as did most able white men. Instead he was sent to Monrovia, Liberia, as he fully expected, since Jim Crow still reigned supreme.

So Wharton joined Hunt, William Yerby, and James G. Carter as the United States' earliest Negro career foreign service officers. But little altered the service's overall patrician, masculine (only two white women had been deemed fit to join the exclusive "club"), Anglo-Saxon composition. The assemblage of private American citizens living in or visiting Europe, however, presented a more realistically diverse picture of their country.

In March 1925 Anna Julia Cooper — who would herself have made a splendid government emissary — was finally ready to defend her PhD dissertation, "L'attitude de la France a l'égard de l'esclavage pendant la Révolution" (France's views concerning slavery during the Revolution) at the Sorbonne, and the school prepared its grandiose *salle du doctorat* for the oral examination. Cooper donned her black academic robes featuring Oberlin's crimson and gold master's hood (Ida Gibbs Hunt, with her own advanced Oberlin degree, had received an equivalent one), and the chancellor gaveled open the session. "After three solid hours of grilling questions and grueling fear," Cooper later wrote, "the mentor . . . rapped a third time for the sentence to be pronounced." "Bien satisfait," her exacting questioners announced, "vous êtes Docteur." "I could not realize that all was over till people . . . I had not seen before, took me by the hand," she continued. One was Jane Nardal, another was a white American with whom Nardal claimed she exchanged a few testy words, and a third was likely Gibbs Hunt. The next December, France's ambassador to the United States delivered Cooper's diploma, which Washington's white-male-appointed city commissioners bestowed on her during a solemn ceremony at Howard University. She was sixty-five that winter when her degree brought to four the number of female PhD's teaching at Dunbar High School — but few other careers were open to any such brilliant, ambitious, highly accredited "colored" women.

At much the same time, in what became, perhaps, the decade's most no-torious legal case, Leonard Rhinelander, heir to one of New York's hefty real estate fortunes, had secretly wed a pretty brunette named Alice Jones, whom everyone agreed hailed from the metaphorical wrong side of the tracks. Such class-hopping occurred often, even in the hidebound Rhinelander family, but Leonard's father bullied his son into trying to annul the marriage on the grounds that the beige-skinned Alice was a Negro who had deceived Leonard by concealing that purportedly shameful fact before the secret nuptials. The couple's marital contract, the Rhinelanders' team of attorneys argued, was based on fraud and deceit, and thus should be voided.

As the legal melodrama unfolded in posh Westchester County, interest in the case skyrocketed, and so did the voyeuristic press coverage. Group-ies assailed the participants every time they entered or exited the dreary courthouse, and the erotic snapshots of and letters from Leonard and Alice's steamy premarital liaisons titillated everyone who followed the proceedings. The trial climaxed with the sobbing "Dusky Alice," as the tabloids called her, stripping naked to the waist in the judge's chambers for the counsels and jury (all of them white men) and members of the press to examine her. They ascertained that, though she wore gloves and long sleeves in court and covered her face and neck with powder to lighten her complexion, if she and Leon-ard had been sexually intimate before they wed, as they undoubtedly had, he never could have mistaken her racial identity. That mortifying display evoked ghastly images of unclothed slave women being eyeballed and groped at pub-lic auctions or whippings, but despite the racist and manipulative pleas by the Rhinelanders' attorneys, the jury heeded the judge's charges and decided in the defendant's favor. While it might be foolhardy for a wealthy white boy to marry such a low-class wench, and Alice probably seduced him, they found that she did not fraudulently mislead him. The Rhinelander case dramati-cally thrust the hot-button but usually whispered issue of miscegenation into the public dialogue — though the American majority chiefly deplored the possibility of Negro men having sex with white women, not the other way around.

Members of the black press applauded the 1925 judgment but expressed mixed feelings about Alice herself, who they believed was ashamed of and wanted to disown her complex racial identity. Du Bois editorialized about the case in *Crisis,* arguing that, legal or not, such interracial liaisons occurred frequently and, over time, had generated his country's variously brown- or tan-skinned Negro population. The *New York Herald Tribune's* Paris edition, a principal link to home for thousands of Americans in France, challenged the decision, however, and rued the fading viability of the United States' antimiscegenation laws. Gibbs Hunt wrote to Du Bois, enclosing clippings of her response to the *Tribune*'s commentary, signed not with her own name but with her pen name, Iola Gibson. As published, her letter to the editor of the newspaper says in part:

> It is absurd to call any one a negro as fair as Alice Jones Rhinelander. . . . If there are other reasons why the marriage should be set aside, well and good, but the one drop of African blood is not sufficient reason. There have been many such inter-racial marriages in America. . . . When will people learn that marriage is a personal matter, and that human nature will assert itself? Who can assert that it will be a century or so "before any colored person will be recognised as having every social right of a Caucasian in America"[?]

Gibbs Hunt's closing question quotes the *Tribune* itself, and it was fortunate that she used her pseudonym, because even any such tacit acceptance of interracial unions jabbed a sharp stick into a hornet's nest. Only two days later "An American Citizen" responded to "Iola Gibson's" letter, saying that her countrywomen "do not approve of intermarriage." That anonymous tirade — one of several printed in the newspaper — concludes: "Nothing could be more disgusting than to see in Europe . . . a white girl on the arm of a negro. . . . [T]he vast majority of American citizens look upon her with the utmost contempt."

Gibbs Hunt debated miscegenation and viewed France's emergent feminist movement in the context of sexual inequities, racism, and colonialism. With those issues so tightly interwoven, many white Americans and some of their French counterparts placed all females and members of the darker races into similarly demeaning categories. Women like Ida and her spiritual "sisters" used their variant visions, nurtured at soirées in Washington, New York, and Paris, to challenge such assumptions, and to explore and express their transatlantic identities. They created and continued to refine an emerging international black feminism as they sought to overcome or supplant the prevalent and degrading stereotypes of "colored" women.

In a kindred vein, Caroline Dudley Regan, the wife of a commercial attaché (a position much like that of consul) at the American embassy in Paris, facilitated an upsurge in the visibility and marketability of Negro women. In 1925 she brought to France from the United States a dazzling young "colored" dancer and comedian named Josephine Baker to perform in a new extravaganza called *La Revue Nègre*. Because Regan was a wealthy, socially prominent white woman, her high-profile entrepreneurial project apparently did not discredit her diplomat husband as Ida's feminist pronouncements and unconcealed leadership with the Pan-African Congresses may have harmed Consul Hunt's career.

Josephine Baker became an object of curiosity, adoration, and imitation in France. She seemed to link New Negroes — supposedly epitomizing both modernity and "savagery" — with New Women, and she embodied America's Roaring Twenties as well as a magnetic, "primitive" blackness. Laughing with her audiences and at herself, *La Baker* poked fun at and flaunted traditional notions of female sexuality. She combined the racy new American Charleston with seductive old Antillean *beguines,* and Parisians went berserk when Baker, much like the French Senegalese Battling Siki, titillated the city by sashaying along its boulevards accompanied by a sleek, "tame" leopard. Baker danced on at the Folies Bergère (where in 1898 Consul M. W. Gibbs and Billy Hunt first encountered risqué French music-hall entertainment), bare-breasted, with a tutu of bananas half-concealing her exquisite rump, and on other occasions, strategically situated ostrich plumes quivering between her thighs.

In the United States (and in Paris), Negro women often straightened their hair, tried (like Alice Jones Rhinelander) to lighten their complexions, and emulated "white" speech, in part to assimilate themselves into the majority community. Some Frenchwomen, by contrast, began copying Baker's lacquered coif, bronzing their pale skins with makeup or by sunbathing. They also adopted "colored" jargon to become, or seem, "black." Baker was an exotic symbol, but also their new reality of "colored" women. As Jane Nardal wrote, "[T]he vogue for Negroes these last few years has led to their being considered as a folk destined to serve as amusement, to see to the pleasure, artistic or sensual, of whites." Legions of enraptured Europeans, as well as many Americans, considered Baker and the erotic freedom she purportedly epitomized an antidote to the woes of the world. Unlike their stateside counterparts, the Parisians had no Prohibition, so they quaffed champagne, cognac, or Pernod as they danced, romanced, and partied away their postwar blues.

Those overheated images of "colored" womanhood simultaneously attracted and repelled "well-bred" people like Ida and Billy Hunt. But France's lust for Africans and African Americans, often called *négrophilie,* revealed the ways that they and their vaunted creativity were admired and emulated for the same "primitive" qualities from which sophisticated folks like the Hunts skittishly sought to distance themselves. Many privileged, educated Negroes enjoyed or at least tolerated, yet also felt a need to explain away, the dissonances of modernism and "savagery" that most whites interpreted as black peoples' presumably seductive essence.

Billy's memoir reveals very little about his and Ida's private lives, while her writings from this period provide a good deal of information about her activities and commitments but little about her marriage. A rare exception appears in a letter from Ida to her brother Horace in the mid-1920s. It focuses on the siblings' ongoing maneuverings over the disposition of property ("It's the Gibbs fate . . . to be always buying real estate, or the Gibbs mania perhaps," she wrote) willed to them by their father a decade before. However, she continued, "B [Billy] has gone to Paris for three days and I am a widow. . . . He didn't . . . want me to go with him and I didn't insist." A well-meaning white American friend, she added, maintained that "I ought to have gone; . . . says she wouldn't trust her husband in Paris alone, ha! ha!" "But being an Alexander," she concluded, "I do not worry."

What did she mean when she penned those words? Might she have thought, but was not concerned, that her vigorous sixty-two-year-old spouse, who claimed to be only fifty-six, could be patronizing Josephine Baker's extravaganzas at the Folies Bergère or otherwise carousing in Paris? Partly in defiance of slave-era and ongoing Jim Crow traditions that gave white males unrestricted sexual access to Negro women, a number of African American men did just that after the Great War, and some of them entered into steamy affairs with *les femmes Françaises*. That practice infuriated many white American visitors, who deemed sex between a Negro man and any white woman to be a mortal sin, but since the war had decimated the ranks of able-bodied European youths, a number of Frenchwomen openly consorted with "colored" men at trendy Paris *boîtes* such as Louis and Antoinette Mitchell's bailiwick of "soul" cuisine, American jazz, and free-flowing booze. But Ida shrugged off her friend's obvious suggestion of possible indiscretions on her husband's part. She may have found the implications absurd ("ha! ha!") and trusted Billy without reserve. Yet this ready evocation of her maternal Alexander heritage clearly confirms that she attributed much of her own perspective, grit, and *savoir-faire* to the fortitude and self-confidence amply provided by her long-deceased mother and grandmother.

In and around St.-Étienne, the energetic Billy Hunt meanwhile continued to engage in *la vie sportive*. A "Rallye Passe Partout" ("the snow was deep, the north [wind] violent and the atmosphere sharp") in which he participated challenged the contestants' equestrian expertise to track and capture an elusive quarry. The cavalcade of boisterous horsemen galloped across the frozen countryside chasing a "small hot air balloon which had been previously sent up in the air," but that particular day one bold jockey alone snared the elusive "prey," and a local newspaper exuberantly applauded the victor: "Our felicitations . . . to Mr. Hunt, the very popular American Consul."

Hunt relished speed, sport, and competition of all sorts, including motor car rallies and the Tour de France, which annually cycled through his drab, industrial city. In 1925, like everyone in the country, he would have read about the Croisière Noire (Black Crossing), a widely reported safari of sorts. France's Citröen company sponsored the caravan of autos and *camions* that crossed Africa from Morocco thousands of miles southeast. The party sailed the Straits of Mozambique then traversed Madagascar to Tamatave, Consul Hunt's previous post. That sprint across the Great Red Island, in fact, quite resembled the overland trek that Hunt had taken with Governor General Joseph Simon Gallieni in 1901. Popular magazines featured, and the next year's Paris International Exposition exhibited, the excursion's photos and the resultant paintings that adapted the lush art deco style to evoke exquisite but stereotypical and primeval images of the "Dark Continent." The official cinematographer became so enamored of Madagascar's people, animals, and landscapes that he returned there to shoot a feature motion picture. But many Europeans differentiated little between Africa's wildlife and its human denizens, and the whole extravaganza reinforced orthodox impressions of the French empire's abiding power and glory. Both the exhibits and accompanying press coverage depicted virile white men as dashing, ultracivilized conquering heroes, who continued to maintain their appropriate dominion over the darkly magnetic, benign, grateful, often scantily clad, and reputedly aboriginal subjects.

Such visions of "primitive" people held a visceral appeal for lots of white Americans and Europeans, but anticolonialism, with its indelible "pink" tinge, generated minimal enthusiasm. (Ida Gibbs Hunt often read socialist literature, yet insisted to Addie Waites Hunton, "I am not a Bolshevik. I love peace, but I don't like to be a dupe.") After 1923, and in the wake of the black Frenchmen's refusals to continue supporting his efforts, W. E. B. Du Bois's hobbled Pan-African Association attracted neither the money nor the interest to convene another biennial congress. But in 1926 he once again exhorted a group of African American women, including his own wife, Nina, Jessie Fauset, Addie Waites Hunton, and the ever loyal Ida Gibbs Hunt, to start raising the funds he would need to hold a session in New York the following year.

But by then the Gibbs-Hunts' time in France was careening toward a dead end. During Christmas week of 1926, State Department officials informed the consul that they would shut down his post altogether the next spring. Ida advised the Du Boises that she would not be in Europe the upcoming summer to welcome and host their daughter, Yolande. Billy arranged to "ship the archives and furniture to Lyons" and relocated his deputy to the consulate in Marseille, and the death of his sister Maggie Hunt Hughes in Harlem further saddened him. "My new assignment would be announced in a subsequent despatch," he mourned. "I proceeded to blot out twenty years' existence in the short period of three months."

An admiring French sportswriter would look back and applaud: "Vive America, Valhalla of the God of Sports! Mr. William H. Hunt . . . was born in the country which gave us the Babe Ruths, . . . the Metcalfes [Ralph Metcalfe, a budding Negro sprinter who later triumphed at the Olympics], and Lindberghs [Charles Lindbergh embarked on his epic transatlantic flight in the spring of 1927]." The reporter continued his paean by reconfirming Hunt's altered year of birth and bruiting his youthful athleticism, when "he won . . . flat races, pole vaults, high and broad jumps" — exaggerated, but not altogether groundless assertions. "But the ruling passion of the young collegian," that cursory biography continued, "was riding, and he . . . blossomed out as a fairly good jockey." "On all the Hippodromes, Velodromes, Autodromes, and Footballodromes," the accolade ended, "is seen the tall silhouette of the American Consul."

Hunt's supporters would not let him set off to his new assignment without challenging the American government's seemingly irrational decision to close the consulate, but those efforts predictably failed. The consul was reluctantly leaving stalwart allies in St.-Étienne and his beloved Ville Noire for the small, predominantly black-populated island of Guadeloupe, a remote French Caribbean colonial outpost that was not considered in any way desirable or prestigious.

Downcast members of the rugby club that Billy Hunt had sponsored for many years ("I would accompany 'my boys' on their expeditions of conquest or defeat," he later wrote. "Their ardour was truly wonderful.") gave the consul an imposing, inscribed bronze trophy. Other comrades presented him with a handsome portrait of himself in full equestrian regalia astride his jaunty white mare, lovingly signed by every member of the riding club. One of the many events celebrating his successful tenure and ruing his imminent departure included sentimental toasts all around, including Hunt's own heartfelt salute, which, he declared, found "several of my *hardest boiled* friends sitting around with tears in their eyes."

Gentlemen, it is more than twenty years since you welcomed me so warmly to your very active and industrious city. I came, as you recall, from your great Colony of Madagascar. Your compatriots out there understood France all the more through their close union with the Native races [and] I have also learned to know and love better France.... [S]he has become my second fatherland. Tomorrow, between us, will hollow out the unfathomable depths of an ocean. But, it is said, the seas draw men closer together rather than they separate them. From afar as well as near, I will be beside you in whatever may happen.

Consul William Henry Hunt thus said good-bye to beloved colleagues in what had been his home for two full decades. That was longer than he ever had, or ever would, live in any other given place.

"Finally," Hunt later reminisced, "the curtain was rung down on a seemingly interminable round of farewell banquets, dinners, luncheons and vin d'honneurs." On a brisk spring morning in 1927, he reported, he and Ida "found an unusually large crowd of friends assembled at the station to bid us bon voyage." "Mrs. Hunt was loaded with flowers and gifts," he continued, and when a horde of sports-loving youngsters erupted in their "club yell, ... I thought the roof of the station had been lifted off by the reverberation as the train pulled out."

They took the *chemin de fer* west to the Atlantic, arriving that night in Bordeaux, where, Billy wrote, "the sidewalks in front of the cafes were alive with uniformed French colonials ... awaiting the outgoing steamers for France's West African or West Indian possessions," and they must have caught sight of the city's most famous landmark, a one-eighth scale model of the Statue of Liberty — France's legendary gift to the Gibbs-Hunts' home country. But like many others in that seaport, they were headed off to one of the *vieilles* (old) colonies. For Ida, with her unyielding anti-imperial bent, the scene must have evoked the dismal conclusion drawn by René Maran in his polemic novel *Batouala:* "[I]f one could know on what continuous evil the great colonial life is based, it would be spoken of less — indeed, it would be spoken of no more." Ida, however, had her perspective, while Billy had his. Twenty years after arriving in France from subject Madagascar, they once again were going to what Consul Hunt, using the very same phrase, but with fervent approval and concurrence, also chose to call "the great colonial life."

Snapshots from Guadeloupe, 1927–1929

For a while, rancor and disappointment nearly paralyzed Ida and Billy Hunt. After two decades in France, Billy resented being sent into "exile," although in the early 1900s Virginia's G. Jarvis Bowens, a Negro American, but not a career consul, had served in Guadeloupe for five years with few regrets, despite several civil disturbances that reflected the islanders' contempt for colonial injustices. Nor did Ida like being relegated to what she saw as the French West Indies' murky backwaters, far from the United States', Antilles', and Africa's "colored" Francophones who congregated in and around Paris and generated the exciting postwar *internationalisme noir.*

Although she was frustrated and exhausted from her unappreciated efforts on behalf of three past Pan-African Congresses, and still scarred from the barbs that W. E. B. Du Bois hurled at her in conjunction with those gatherings, Ida nonetheless helped raise funds to replace the final withdrawal of the NAACP's backing. She did not, however, attend the sessions in New York's Harlem that August, which attracted more than two hundred delegates and nearly five thousand observers.

Ida wrote her friend Addie Waites Hunton wishing the congress infinite success, but wistfully protested, "I've worked hard . . . without receiving much thanks . . . tho I'm not working for thanks but for the good of the cause." "I've often tho't that the

She saw the drifting mists gathered in the west—that cloud field of the sky—arm themselves with thunders and march forth against the world. Louder and higher and lower and wider the sound and motion spread, mounting, sinking, darking, . . . the monstropolous beast had left his bed. The two hundred miles an hour wind had loosed his chains. . . . The sea was walking the earth with a heavy heel.
—Zora Neale Hurston, *Their Eyes Were Watching God,* 1937

P.A.C. works too openly, and that simply served to cause the colonial powers to give us a few of the reforms asked for as a little sop, while throwing a cordon of armed force around us," she added, and proposed that the organization might be renamed the "Human Rights Ass'n, or True Government Association, or League of Oppressed or Subjugated People." She also insisted that she scarcely could fathom the "helplessness of 12,000,000 C[olored] people in the U.S.... They need only summon & use their force. We need to establish another underground railroad, larger and better organized than the old antebellum one."

The 1927 Pan-African Congress focused largely on the United States' occupation of Haiti, calling for the removal of American troops and restoration of self-government there. Before adjourning, the organizers announced plans to hold a fifth session, for the first time on African soil, two years hence in Tunisia. But the French, incensed that previous gatherings had forecast the inevitability of an autonomous superstate comprising their former North African colonies, vetoed any such undertaking. Triggered by the 1929 stock market crash, the Great Depression would begin imposing economic dampers on many similar ventures, so other such structured pan-African efforts emerged — revitalized and further politicized — only after World War II. The 1920s congresses stimulated robust transnational dialogues between generations of diverse black thinkers and doers, yet their formal incarnations and achievements were ephemeral. For the foreseeable future, Du Bois's and Gibbs Hunt's global visions virtually fizzled out.

As for Consul William Henry Hunt, though his official vita said that he had been born in 1869, he was sixty-three when he left France, and with three decades of experience under his belt, he ranked as his country's seniormost African American foreign service officer. No serious blemishes marred his record, yet he found himself sentenced to what he and many others saw as a third-class consulate in an ostensibly irrelevant locale in the French Caribbean. Guadeloupe was not France proper. Rather, it was a peripheral outpost designated, like a number of others, *France d'outre-mer* (overseas France). As a first assignment, colonial Madagascar, a far larger, more populous island, seemed to offer a novice such as Hunt ample prospects for advancement, but for a seasoned professional, Guadeloupe was a different story altogether and a possible career dead end, though he again could operate almost autonomously, much as he had in Tamatave.

That May, Du Bois championed Consul Hunt, railing in *Crisis* that he deserved a promotion instead of a transfer, and sharply questioned why the State Department had dispatched him to Guadeloupe. Although Hunt later filled his memoir with felicitous citations about himself from a panoply of white French and American publications, he never mentioned any black journals or journalists at all, not even Du Bois, except in the singular context of his having been a solicitous Boston acquaintance in the 1890s. Nonetheless, the editor — ever ready to leap into the fray to identify and challenge racial injustices — wrote, "What a curious way for the United States to reward a faithful public servant," adding: "The treatment which the United States is meting out to the colored men in the diplomatic and consular service is beneath contempt. . . . Hunt . . . with [a] long and honorable record, . . . rated by every test as [a] consul of unusual ability, [has] been practically demoted and turned aside instead of being given [his] rightful chance to rise. Hunt has been sent from one of the most important manufacturing districts of central France to the little island of Guadeloupe."

Du Bois also wrote that the State Department ordered James G. Carter, who in 1907 had replaced Hunt as consul in Madagascar, "to take his wife and young child to West Africa." After twenty years in the tropics, Carter refused the post in Liberia and, Du Bois added, "finally has been allowed to go to Calais." The department, he carped, "is using every device to get rid of some of its best servants, simply because they are men of Negro descent."

A few months later, a fractious debate over diplomatic representation in the eastern Horn of Africa reconfirmed the narrow limitations of black Americans' opportunities in the foreign service. Early in 1928 Abyssinia (Ethiopia) received its new American ambassador, a white man, precipitating a tumult in the black press as to why the State Department would not, at the least, send a Negro to represent the United States in that unique, sovereign "colored" monarchy. But the mainstream *Time* magazine offered a threefold explanation — or excuse. First, the incoming ambassador knew the country well because he had served there as the American consul for many years. Second, Abyssinians "do not consider themselves racially homogeneous with aboriginal Africa"— as if most "colored" Americans did. Third, the kingdom's feudal rulers, it was argued, wanted a diplomat sent to them who was a member of the United States' dominant racial majority, not its categorically demeaned, darker-skinned minority. What remained unsaid was that State Department officials really did not deem any black person worthy enough or "qualified" to fill a prestigious ambassadorship anywhere, even in Africa.

In respect to Hunt's situation, it seems likely that, at least in part, officials at the State Department made their distaste for, even alarm over, Ida Gibbs Hunt's high profile with the Pan-African Congresses (and perhaps her unrepentant feminism too) an unstated reason to retaliate against her husband by sending him to a locale they deemed more appropriate than St.-Étienne for a French-speaking Negro consular officer. Consul Hunt's association, by proxy through his wife, with such a patently "black" cause also removed any lingering confusion over his designated racial identity. But the department's bureaucrats would have wanted to make their determination pertaining to a minor matter such as that discreetly, so as to generate minimal attention. It might have caused a flap to replace the experienced, tactful, and well-liked Consul Hunt with a white man, or to have drummed him out of the consular service altogether, but shutting down the consulate, then shipping Hunt off to a remote, "colored" Francophone venue, hardly could be faulted, and exposed department officials to little potential mainstream criticism as to their possibly racist bent. That reassignment, however, also conveyed the message, and the reality, that its ranking members were master puppeteers who maintained full control over Hunt and all other — especially perhaps the very few African American — foreign service employees.

Notwithstanding such speculations about and explanations for his transfer, Billy and Ida Hunt's scarcely noticed voyage from Bordeaux across the Atlantic on the SS *Le Flandre* in the spring of 1927 was uneventful. (Coincidentally, that same month the dashing white aviator Charles Lindbergh was taking off in the opposite direction, his monoplane barely skimming the ocean's spume, on his inaugural nonstop solo flight from New York to Paris in an unheard-of thirty-three hours.) Two days out to sea, in the hazy distance, the Gibbs-Hunts caught sight of the craggy but beguiling Portuguese Azores, and that would be their last glimpse of land for more than a week. As they neared Guadeloupe, they first spied the nearby key known as La Désirade, where Christopher Columbus purportedly waded ashore in 1493, and which, they learned, housed the local leper asylum. That may have seemed a sinister portent.

Vistas of the main island, nonetheless, could delight new arrivals. The "sun-kissed sea," as Billy Hunt called the Caribbean, was a turquoise more sublime than that of the Mediterranean off *le Midi* of France. A portentous thunderstorm, crackling with electricity, drenched the couple as they approached the port, but the sky rarely showed the steely tints it did in St.-Étienne. No growling locomotives or mines and factories belching soot and noise intruded on the scene. Pelicans wheeled, then dive-bombed in the harbor for meals. Fishing craft, donkey carts, rusty *bicyclettes,* and rattletrap jitneys outnumbered the few Citroëns or Renaults. Many of the diligent islanders (shopkeepers, artisans and civil servants, watermen and farmers) smiled, nodded, and beckoned their welcomes. The women wore multitiered skirts in brilliant hues and madras patterns, and wrapped their heads in intricately knotted turbans. In their leisure time, young and old stomped and whirled to *beguines, merengues, bamboulas,* and *bombés.* They sang, whistled, or hummed, tapped out sophisticated African-derived cadences with bones and drums, clicked cymbals, thrummed guitars, and rattled gourd maracas. Coconut and banana palms swayed to a more languorous rhythm than that of France's biting *mistral,* and whiffs of vanilla, cocoa, coffee, and spicy *rôti* mingled with the ocean's briny scent. Mangoes and papayas, guavas and passion fruit grew in riotous abundance, while hibiscus, bougainvillea, and jacaranda perfumed the air. Could Ida and Billy Hunt have been mistaken? Might this Arcadian isle be their Paradise Lost?

Guadeloupe, in fact, is not a single island, but an irregular cluster. Its main land masses, resembling on the map a butterfly at rest, are Basse-Terre, the mountainous west "wing," where the unpretentious administrative capital is situated, and low-lying Grand-Terre to the northeast. Basse-Terre, Grand-Terre, the nearby keys of La Désirade and Marie Galante, and a chain of seven or more even smaller ones, altogether constitute an area of slightly less than seven hundred square miles, but the loss of Saint-Domingue (renamed Haiti in 1804) during the revolutionary 1790s had made greater Guadeloupe the largest of France's remaining Caribbean conquests.

Once ashore, harsh realities jolted the Gibbs-Hunts out of any illusions. His vice consul, Billy Hunt learned, was "laid up with a fever," due, he contended, to the man's negligent ingestion of contaminated water and the island's "deplorable sanitary conditions." And the bleak Hôtel des Antilles where Ida and Billy first were housed, he wrote, "gave me an acute attack of the heebie jeebies." Though far better than the flimsy cabins inhabited by many of the local residents, Billy described as "repulsive" the facilities assigned to him in Grande-Terre's Pointe-à-Pître, the commercial center and chief seaport. With a population of twenty-six thousand, it was Guadeloupe's largest *ville.* Visitors sometimes claimed that its wrought-iron balconies, fountains, slapdash traffic *étoiles,* and cobbled streets, many of them named for French military heroes, gave that Caribbean city the atmosphere of a tropical Paris, but the conditions appalled Billy: "My first impressions of Pointe a Pitre are lasting because I could never persuade myself to like the dreadful place during two years residence there. . . . Liberia [where the department sent him later] and Madagascar were gardens of Eden in comparison." With a more resigned tone, Ida drily commented in a note to Du Bois: "We may learn to like Guadeloupe better, but up to now we are not enchanted."

The situation spiraled downward when the Gibbs-Hunts moved into their official residence. A crew of "clumsy natives" unpacked their crates, and they found much of their furniture damaged beyond repair owing to slipshod packing in France. Little china or glassware, Billy later recalled, withstood the "rough handling on board ship." "No insurance," he protested, "could re-place those accumulations of twenty years and more in a backward country like Guadeloupe."

The doorways were so low that he "was obliged to bend almost double to enter" each room. His quarters lacked gas or electricity, "bathroom, running water, or sewage system," and the courtyard was "one of the filthiest mosquito breeding mudholes imaginable, infested with some of the largest rats to be found outside the sewers of Paris." When an American pesticide manufac-turer shipped him a generous supply of rat bane, "one of my favorite diversions at night," Billy crowed, "was to spread the poison on slices of bread . . . and watch its effect!" As to other vermin, "the bite of a mosquito," he (mistakenly) continued, "is said to be responsible for the many cases of *elephantiasis.*" Care also had to be taken to avoid *"Filaria,* a small, eel-like worm very prevalent in Guadeloupe, which enters the body through drinking water [or when] bath-ing in the rivers." That parasite could cause blindness in people who impru-dently partook of the local waters, so the Gibbs-Hunts washed their faces, hands, and bodies guardedly, and drank only "rather expensive" bottled *eau minérale* shipped from Europe.

Within a short time, Consul Hunt discerned an "acute animosity" toward his country because many of the "darker people of the island" thought that France was planning to transfer Guadeloupe to the United States in partial payment of its World War I debts. "[It] would have seemed laughable," Hunt wrote, "had it not been so obviously preposterous." Those folks "had been so completely hoodwinked by . . . unscrupulous politicians, both white and na-tive, that they were constantly in a mortal funk" lest they be deprived of their affiliations with France — and though many Caucasians considered them sub-ordinates, they were, in fact, French citizens. But since Guadeloupe's wealthi-est sugar baron had long been scheming with a stateside cohort to negotiate just such a transfer, the islanders' fears of appropriation were hardly groundless. Only a decade before, purportedly to reinforce its hemispheric security, the United States had demanded and purchased from Denmark the nearby Virgin Islands, and its draconian military occupations on the island of Hispaniola (Haiti and the Dominican Republic) reinforced the Guadeloupeans' trepidations — as did, Hunt heard, grisly reports of "burnings, lynchings, and racial prejudice" in the American South. Those facts and fears combined to shape the island's Negro majority's perspectives, though Hunt argued that the manipulative white French governor was circulating his own baleful rumors of a pending American takeover.

The governor, Louis Gerbinis, was "named by the Minister of Colonies, with the consent of our . . . Representatives in France," Filogenes Maillard, a Guadeloupean scholar, wrote in *Crisis*. By indirect vote, however, Guadeloupe's and nearby Martinique's male citizens chose Henry Bérenger — a white attendee at prior Pan-African Congresses and delegate to the France–United States deliberations over war reparations — to represent them in *le Sénat*. "By direct popular suffrage," Maillard added, voters "elect two deputies who sit in the *Chambre des Députés;* the present ones are [Gratien] Candace and [Achille-René] Boisneuf, both black." Deputy Candace, a middle-of-the-road politician and author, had held that post for a decade, and Ida Gibbs Hunt had worked with both him and Boisneuf at two previous congresses. Candace was one of the first Antillean leaders cautiously to challenge France's supremacy, but he also spent much of his time in Paris, where he fraternized with white Frenchmen and other members of the colonial "colored" elite from the Caribbean and Africa, some of whom thought of themselves as significant players in the republic's political and intellectual life. By 1927, however, Boisneuf, a moderate socialist and the sometime mayor of Pointe-à-Pître, had returned for good to his ancestral island home.

Men such as Gerbinis and Bérenger, Candace and Boisneuf officially used standard European French, which also was written and supposedly prevailed in the island's schools, but a creole version was the everyday tongue for anyone locally born or raised, race notwithstanding. For most young people, it was "the language of their parents, of their beliefs and traditions, of their oral literature, both spoken and sung, . . . handed on from generation to generation." That New World *patois,* though difficult at first to comprehend by French-speaking newcomers such as the Gibbs-Hunts, fused classic French with vocabulary, structure, metaphors, and intonations borrowed from indigenous West African languages reconfigured over time by Guadeloupe's diverse residents.

Roman Catholicism, similarly incorporated and tempered by robust African influences, prevailed as the dominant faith. As the Guadeloupean poet and teacher Emmanuel Flavia-Leopold soon would contend in Nancy Cunard's epic *Negro: An Anthology* (1934), "[T]he white mythology as taught by the priest is contradicted at various points by the local mythology." According to Flavia-Leopold, that syncretic religion combined "fatalism, catholicism and endless superstitions." Even in the simplest homes, he added, "on a lowly bracket beside the cup where oil burns in her honour, stands . . . a poor little statue of the Virgin, queen of heaven."

But the island's Caribbean locale did not circumscribe its residents' sense of national identity. An apocryphal anecdote retold in *Crisis* claimed that a French lawyer had recently groused that the Antillean outposts "cost us money every year." "Except as a possible source of prestige," he added, "they represent an almost total liability to the mother country." Overhearing those grievances, a listener from Guadeloupe echoed the sentiments expressed by islanders who had participated in the Pan-African Congresses when he interrupted the grumpy *avocat* to say: "That is perhaps true, *Monsieur,* but we are French and love France." "The . . . Guadeloupean feels an attachment for France that is little short of phenomenal," the article concluded. They certainly were French insofar as that affiliation benefited the mother country. Some eleven thousand Guadeloupean troops proved their allegiance when they fought, and fifteen hundred died, in the Great War. And during the war, General Joseph Gallieni, of course, had entrusted the black island-born Commandant Sosthène H. C. Mortenol with the antiaircraft defense of Paris itself.

In some ways the Guadeloupeans had been French for generations, but four hundred years before, the indigenous Caribs reigned supreme. They were the ones whom Columbus first encountered when he disembarked at a remote spot in the "West Indies" that he designated Notre Dame de Guadalupe d'Estremadura because his ship had been spared in a tropical tempest. For more than a century its specific European affiliation remained in dispute, with the Caribs repulsing Spain's attempts to pacify them, until France (which also seized Saint-Domingue, Martinique, and several other smaller nearby islands) coopted its colonial rivals and imposed a treaty on the beleaguered local residents in 1635. The French began ambitious colonization efforts and introduced a plantation system based on slave labor and dominated by the arduous but lucrative cultivation of sugarcane.

Most of the Caribs had died out or fled, so slave traders brought in and auctioned off continuing waves of black workers from Africa. Legions perished, but they far outnumbered the "Indians" and the white island French. They retained what they could of their traditions and populated the *habitations,* as the larger plantations became known. For three centuries those enslaved Africans cultivated and processed the cane, built up the colony, and enriched their masters. Despite the formation of several isolated, seditious maroon communes, and thwarted rebellions that would be dwarfed in their intensity by the upheavals in Saint-Domingue, Guadeloupe flourished for many years as the region's most prosperous island, and the Netherlands, Spain, and England (which briefly seized control twice during the eighteenth century) continued to challenge France's authority.

The juridical *Code Noir* of 1685 defined slavery's parameters, tried to reduce Negroes to objects of exchange and exploitation, and specified the administration of draconian punishments. Black people were not even allowed by law to read or write. In 1794 revolutionaries in Paris declared the abolition of slavery on the island, but it was almost immediately reinstated, after which it survived until general, permanent emancipation in 1848. As in much of the rest of the region, after the critical labor reorganization that resulted from the final termination of bondage, the ruling class insisted that without coercion the former slaves would not work. So they shipped in hordes of indentured colonial East Indian laborers. Their arrival and continued residency further scrambled Guadeloupe's social, cultural, economic, and political mix, as well as its demographic gene pool.

Sugarcane remained the dominant crop well into the 1900s, but overproduction combined with an upsurge in cheaper beet sugar elsewhere sent the profitability of most of the Caribbean's cane into a tailspin. Nonetheless, its chief by-products, molasses and rum (Billy Hunt quoted a glib French pundit who maintained that rum "is the life blood that runs through the veins of the Guadeloupean"), continued as pillars of the island's agriculturally based economy.

The sometimes patronizing Consul Hunt contended that little overall progress had been made there during three centuries of French dominion because "the native prefers to live at the expense of Mother Nature as much as possible." "It is not altogether his fault that he has a tendency to indolence," Hunt added. Rather, it should be attributed "partly to the sentimental leanings of his forefathers," and partly to environmental benevolence. "Nature," he argued, "has generously lavished her gifts on these improvident children."

Those convictions closely paralleled and reflected the views of a majority of Europe's colonialists.

As to the prevailing customs and practices, Maryse Condé, Guadeloupe's revered senior scholar and writer, recalls that in her childhood many islanders displayed treasured family photographs "to show where they come from and their social ascendancy." "Practically all social functions, except official receptions," stated one of the Gibbs-Hunts' American Negro contemporaries, "are closed to one race; . . . but no legal discrimination exists, and prejudice seldom comes out into the open." Ida Gibbs Hunt found most of the people whom she encountered to be gracious enough, though a bit aloof, yet also wrote W. E. B. Du Bois about her distaste for the societal inequities she observed, which she attributed to the legacies of slavery and French colonialism. She confessed that she was "surprised to find so much racial prejudice here . . . between white? and colored creoles." That oddly positioned question mark in her letter suggests that she believed some "white" Guadeloupeans might well be considered Negroes if judged by stateside standards.

Yet not many of Guadeloupe's residents, in fact, were designated white. Those few were either *métros* from continental France (*l'Hexagone*) or *békés*, as the island-born Europeans are known. Far more were *mulâtres* (mulattoes) or *métis* ("half castes"), who displayed admixtures of black and white and even infusions of indigenous or Asian "blood," though a majority were descended from Africans alone. And most local people agreed that *la noirceur de la peau* (the skin's blackness) and other physical attributes of *négritude,* including hair texture, nose breadth, and fullness of the lips, often contributed to determining one's social and economic standing.

But according to Condé, in her early years those African-imprinted features confirmed a "unique brotherhood with people of the same color," since many Negroes saw Caucasians as "the enemy." "Affiliation with mulattoes was not tolerated," Condé insists about her own dignified, brown-skinned family's convictions, "because they were the bastards of whites." In the Antilles, she observes, racial divisions differed from those in the United States, where "toute personne qui est soupçonée d'avoir une goutte de sang noire est classée nègre" (everyone suspected of having even a drop of black blood is classified a Negro). That anomalous social and legal construct was well understood and seen as the norm by North American mainlanders such as Ida and William Hunt because it did so much to define their prescribed nonwhite identity in their own country, where law and practice combined to determine that everyone who was believed to have any Negro "blood" at all (like the recently exposed

Alice Jones Rhinelander) was considered black, and therefore genetically, so-cially, and legally inferior. In Guadeloupe, however, many mulattoes — the mixed-race Creoles who made up much of the petite bourgeoisie — thought they had little in common with their darker brethren. One might hear "sale nègre!" ("dirty black man," but more tellingly, the French Caribbean equiva-lent of "nigger") hissed out in Pointe-à-Pître's *rues* and byways. Those diverse "colored" islanders, on the other hand, often acknowledged their common political and economic interests, and colluded in their critiques of and (usu-ally perfunctory) challenges to the white European hegemony.

Ida Gibbs Hunt's new consular home was not really the cultural waste-land she first feared. The erudite Antillean Jane Nardal arrived there from Paris early in 1928 to teach Latin at Guadeloupe's Basse-Terre Lycée. A limited number of "colored" youths received a classical education at Pointe-à-Pître's selective Lycée Carnot, and *la crème de la crème* might then be sent on to study at universities in France. The island nonetheless had too few schools, libraries, or highly literate citizens. Even empathetic observers such as Filogenes Mail-lard haughtily contended that "the child, whose traditional modes of thought no amount of schooling can ever Europeanise, stands at the threshold of west-ern civilisation [yet] knows nothing of its complexity."

Recent Guadeloupean literary achievements included works by the white, island-born poet Saint-John Perse, who was educated in France and then served with his country's elite foreign service. The "colored" islanders' output must have intrigued Gibbs Hunt even more, because those writers reflected concerns similar to ones that emerged from the Negro Renaissance's cultural explosion in her own country. Oruno Lara's *Histoire de la Guadeloupe* (1921) was the first colonial history written in French by a nonwhite author, and it assessed a proud yet painful Negro past. Lara also wrote a biography of Com-mandant Mortenol, the island's military hero who had so impressed Gibbs Hunt in their common pursuit of pan-Africanism. In 1923 Lara completed his first novel, *Question de couleurs (Blanches et Noires),* and Suzanne Lacas-cade's tragic romance, *Claire-Solange, âme africaine,* appeared the next year. Those efforts were published in France, but were read and discussed through-out the French Caribbean, as were Gratien Candace's naval studies, Maurice Satineau's journal, *La Dépêche Africaine,* and Stéphane Rosso's radical con-tributions to *La Race Nègre,* while Gibbs Hunt herself devoured essays that analyzed international Bolshevism in the militant *Revue des Deux Mondes.*

In the realm of popular culture, France was abuzz about Josephine Baker's first motion picture, *La sirène des tropiques* (1927), in which a visiting white adventurer woos an exquisite Antillean *mulâtresse,* portrayed by Baker, on her home island. Scantily dressed and encircled by "natives," she performs "jungle" dances and a spirited Charleston, then follows her debonair *amour* to Paris, where she becomes a continental sophisticate, though the racial chasm between them supposedly precludes any possibility of marriage. *La sirène* exemplifies the persistence and prevalence of inane stereotypes of colonial "colored" women (*doudous*), but no known reports reveal whether the film ever played in Guadeloupe. Baker realized that the formulaic movie diminished her, so she developed and produced her own extravagant, yet comparably clichéd stage show "about the French colonies, which included . . . tom-toms from Madagascar, cha-chas from Guadeloupe . . . and finally my appearance as the Empress of Jazz."

Despite her discontent with many aspects of their lives at Consul Hunt's new post, for Ida, an advantage of having relocated to Guadeloupe was that her sister Hattie and brother-in-law Napoleon Bonaparte Marshall were still in Port-au-Prince, Haiti, only a day's boat trip and several hundred miles away. In 1922 President Harding had appointed Captain Marshall, who retained his army reserve commission after the war, as a military attaché at the legation in Haiti. Marshall served there during a substantial portion of the extended occupation — launched by President Wilson in 1915, it dragged on for almost twenty years — of the island republic under the United States' self-assumed hemispheric authority imposed a century before by the Monroe Doctrine. President Theodore Roosevelt's early twentieth-century corollary had beefed up the original doctrine and laid out his country's sacred "mission" to maintain, by whatever means deemed necessary, civic order and fiscal stability in the Caribbean and throughout Latin America.

The occupation, however, fell under attack from both within and without, as the insult to their sovereignty outraged many Haitians and generated intermittent armed protests. The NAACP's James Weldon Johnson had gone to Haiti in 1920 and issued a searing report about the corruption, sexual assaults, and other brutality he observed at the hands of U.S. Marines. Criticism soon followed from other organizations, including the Women's International League for Peace and Freedom (WILPF), to which Ida Gibbs Hunt, Mollie Church Terrell, Addie Waites Hunton, and Helen Curtis belonged. *Occupied Haiti* (1926), the WILPF's account that Waites Hunton and Curtis enhanced with their contributions, states that "today a foreign power enforces order in Haiti and puts down all lawlessness but its own . . . these [things] do not spell order, they spell despotism." Those ongoing critiques condemned the

Americans' gross misconduct and exorbitant expenses funded out of woefully meager Haitian treasury funds. The three-thousand-man force had also indefinitely suspended the national constitution, dismissed the legislature, and imposed press censorship and widespread racial segregation. Many men among the all-white army of occupation denigrated the local people as "niggers" or "cockroaches."

As a suspect African American reserve army officer and lawyer, Captain Marshall constantly had to watch his back. Even the civilian clerks at the restructured legation — where white appointees had replaced the former Negro chiefs of mission — tried to sabotage Marshall, but the bilingual "colored" war hero maintained his credibility in that largely black Francophone country, where most of the white military men from the United States spoke little French or Haitian Creole. Marshall went to Haiti hoping to join in a constructive stabilization process, but he also aspired to have his peripheral military position upgraded to diplomatic status. During her trips back to Washington, his wife twisted political arms and lobbied fruitlessly toward that end in the halls of Congress. Captain Marshall's bitterness toward his government's heavy hand intensified, along with his deep anxieties about security issues on the chaotic, impoverished island as his Caucasian compatriots grew increasingly unwelcome there. The Haitian diplomat Dantès Bellegarde, an old friend of the Gibbs-Marshalls, Gibbs-Hunts, and Du Bois, had been the keynote speaker at the most recent Pan-African Congress (though he never really considered himself a pan-Africanist), where he scathingly declared that his countrymen "fear the American because he carries in his belt a deadly Browning, but have ceased to consider him a man of lofty intelligence and ideals. The American action in Haiti is in bankruptcy."

Hattie Gibbs Marshall meanwhile immersed herself in efforts to advance education and women's opportunities in Haiti by raising the funds that she needed to purchase land and build, furnish, and maintain a girls' vocational training school there. She also assembled, studied, and analyzed research materials, and conducted myriad interviews that resulted in the publication of her comprehensive textbook, *The Story of Haiti, from the Discovery of the Island by Christopher Columbus to the Present Day* (1930), especially intended for high school and college students in the United States and dedicated to her late father, Mifflin Wistar Gibbs.

In all, Billy and Ida's first year in the French Caribbean slipped by with few unforeseen or dire developments. Even after a quarter century of marriage, however, they still viewed their new island home from contradictory perspectives. The wretched legacies and widespread manifestations of colonialism continued to dismay Ida. Billy, on the other hand, expressed his professional and personal regrets that France's vaunted *mission civilisatrice* had resulted in little advancement — which he defined as Europeanization. The local people, he sadly contended, "had not made much progress during [three] centuries of French colonization."

Billy fulfilled his consular responsibilities, though he remained somewhat dispirited and missed colleagues and activities associated with *la vie sportive* in and around St.-Étienne. There would be no road rallies or hot air balloon or airplane ventures on the island, even when Germany's *Graf Zeppelin* circled the world in twenty-one days (easily outdoing Jules Verne's fictive nineteenth-century circumnavigation). And he would have been sorry to learn that in September 1927 Professor William Libbey, his epistolary friend and former booster with the State Department, died in Princeton. Soon thereafter, Henry F. Downing, the black onetime consul whose novel Ida had reviewed in 1917, died too. But Billy and Ida got to know Guadeloupe quite well and continued to conduct their usual transnational correspondence, although they welcomed few visiting dignitaries or even personal friends. As in Madagascar many years before, the Gibbs-Hunts, with two intervening decades in *l'Hexagone* behind them, were treated by local officials and other islanders much like upper-class Europeans — though always American, and therefore somewhat suspect, Europeans.

In June 1928 Ida Gibbs Hunt engaged in another minor but testy exchange with Du Bois. She sent him a check with a note requesting a signed copy of his new novel, *Dark Princess: A Romance* (a utopian fantasy about evolving geopolitical alliances among the darker races set, in part, during a hauntingly reconfigured 1923 Pan African Congress) for her husband's birthday. But Ida had read in *Crisis* and heard from friends that the Du Boises' only daughter, Yolande, had married the rising Harlem Renaissance poet Countee Cullen, whose poem "Heritage" ("What is Africa to me:/Copper sun or scarlet sea...") had made him a new exemplar of cultural pan-Africanism. The Hunts had not been invited to that event, which many Negro New Yorkers extolled as the season's premier social occasion. The guest list (some fifteen hundred attended a gala reception at the Upper Manhattan mansion of A'Lelia Walker, only child of the recently deceased hair products entrepreneur and sometime Garveyite Madam C. J. Walker) was said to include every "colored" person of note. Ida Gibbs Hunt bristled at the slight and must have been especially peeved, since, only a year before, W. E. B. and Nina Du Bois had entreated her to hostess Yolande in France. She also had good reason to believe that she had served as the bride's role model. David Lewis, Du Bois's biographer, argues convincingly that Yolande had been raised to emulate the "cosmopolitanism" of her father's savvy protagonist Caroline Wynn, patterned on Ida Gibbs, in his earlier *The Quest of the Silver Fleece.* Ida's letter was courteous if cool, and a touch sarcastic. "Just a word of congratulations on your daughter's marriage," she wrote, "even if you did forget us." Du Bois promptly mailed off the auto-graphed novel for Ida to give Billy and contritely responded: "I am so sorry you were among the forgotten in the wedding invitations. It is inexplicable how successful I was in forgetting some of my very good friends."

But soon the Gibbs-Hunts' soporific ennui as well as the sting of any such petty snubs vanished in a flash during the cataclysmic episode that henceforth defined their Caribbean sojourn. Both of them wrote detailed accounts of the event that for decades thereafter French Antilleans called *le cyclone du siècle,* the hurricane of the century.

Writing the following winter in *Crisis* magazine, Ida explained that she "had rented a pretty and solidly built summer house or villa in the mountains at Trois-Rivières," a village that lay in the shadow of La Soufrière, a smol-dering, mile-high volcano near the south shore of Guadeloupe's Basse-Terre island. "The scenery is wild and beautiful all around," she exclaimed in a let-ter to Addie Waites Hunton, and the verdant rainforest served as a favorite destination for local hikers and picnickers. Ida's *petite maison de campagne* (country cottage) was situated only a few miles but many long hours away from her husband, who continued his humdrum daily regimen at the consul-ate in Pointe-à-Pître on the northeasterly island. She vacationed throughout the summer in the cooler, mountainous hinterlands, where Billy joined her most weekends.

On Wednesday morning, September 12, Ida reported, the breeze stiffened without prior warning, "a terrible wind arose . . . and by ten o'clock it was blowing a perfect gale accompanied by driving storms." Compared to modern forecasting methodology, as imprecise as it remains, in the 1920s most people outside the United States still estimated the potential power and course of hurricanes only when they spied leaden clouds massing on the horizon, raised a moistened finger to test the winds, pondered the foreboding silence that fol-lowed a crescendo in the droning chirps of tree frogs and insects, or heeded traditional omens such as blossoms that abruptly furled their petals or ani-mals that trembled, then bolted off seeking the security of higher ground. The Associated Press wire service cabled out a terse dispatch, which appeared in a number of stateside newspapers, reporting that a "tropical storm of considerable intensity" was churning apace through the mid-Atlantic. As the angry tempest rolled in toward Guadeloupe, Ida and her "*bonne*" (housemaid) observed its escalating fury from their hillside veranda.

Many potential hurricanes die aborning in Africa's Sahara desert, but often in late summer airborne eddies migrate westward out of the Gulf of Guinea, gather strength, then feast on the ideal combination of nutrients that they need to survive and flourish, including elevated temperatures, moisture slurped up from the warm sea, and complementary trade winds. As any such embryonic storm starts rumbling across the ocean, humid heat stokes it like a furnace. The mightiest of these take their generic name from, and coalesce over, Portugal's cluster of volcanic Atlantic peaks called the Cape Verde Islands. From there, no intervening land masses impede their progress until they reach the Caribbean's easternmost Lesser Antilles. Those isles' diminutive size in the boundless surrounding waters makes them elusive targets, but also leaves their vulnerable residents with no opportunity, means, or place to flee as danger nears. The word hurricane itself, connoting both a big wind and an evil spirit, is one of the very few in English that derives from an indigenous Caribbean language.

The 1928 Cape Verde hurricane made its initial landfall on French Martinique, where the white United States consul cabled his superiors in Washington that hundreds of homes were being washed into the sea. But, he blithely reassured them, "those were negro huts of no particular value." A radio message from Martinique soon alerted a manager of the West India and Panama Telegraph Company stationed in Pointe-à-Pître that a monstrous storm was barreling in on them. The overgrown infant already measured much more than a hundred miles across, its intensity increasing by the hour. The diabolic storm steered a beeline course dead on toward Guadeloupe as its cyclonic winds wheeled counterclockwise around a well-defined but quiet eye.

One of Ida's Trois-Rivières *amies* strolled into town at dawn and started back home a few hours later. By then she scarcely could walk upright. Leaning into the stiffening gale, she slipped, tumbled, and became the first patient whom Ida assisted as the cyclone's force accelerated. As the storm "grew more and more furious every minute," Ida wrote, other "neighbors came in for refuge, . . . crying and praying and calling on all of the Saints." She recalled how she "retired to the north bed-room and lay down to still my beating heart." People caught in hurricanes frequently succumb to such episodes of irresistible lassitude resulting from mental, emotional, and physical exhaustion, sometimes even falling asleep while strapped to makeshift rafts or harnessed in the crooks of trees, as gales howl and water laps around them.

Soon the hurricane sighed and paused. The silvery sun blinked through a moist, hazy scrim as the evil eye sidled across Guadeloupe. That eerie lacuna, the tranquil hub around which every such storm circles, seduces its marks into thinking the worst is over, but the fiercest winds stampede in with the subsequent wall of clouds. The heaviest onslaughts lay ahead.

"The rain poured in torrents, the wind whistled, roofs blew off, trees and branches fell on and around the house, and the air was full of sounds of destruction," Ida's account continued. Throughout the day more and more acquaintances sought the sanctuary of her cottage. They had to shout to be heard above the shrieking gusts as windows shattered and doors were "blown off their hinges." The house flooded, quaked, and lost its roof, yet seemed sturdier than most of the local people's bungalows, many of which were destroyed. Ida, her servants, and neighbors, however, survived relatively unscathed. Compared to many others, she wrote, "we felt blessed after all."

One thought consoled her throughout: "I've long had the impression or presentiment, that I was not due to die by violent means." Ida also believed that her husband was in less danger than she, because "Pointe-à-Pitre, situated on a sort of bay or channel, was more protected than here." She could not foresee how even more horrendous damage would be wreaked on that low-lying terrain.

Ida nonetheless remained deeply distressed because she had no way to contact Billy, since "all wires were down and all means of communication cut off." As the hurricane began to abate in their locale, then gallop off northward, the awesome losses left in its wake emerged more clearly, with "reports of terrible destruction by wind and sea, of houses felled and numerous persons drowned." But after a couple of anxious days, a youth "living near the consulate came in to say that Mr. Hunt was all right." Even after receiving that welcome news, Ida still yearned to rejoin her husband, so she and several of her cohorts screwed up their courage and set off toward "the Pointe" on Grande-Terre.

A clamorous crowd gathered at the seething and engorged Rivière Salée — the usually serene, mangrove-fringed saltwater sound that divides Guadeloupe's two main land masses. Frenzied voyagers, Ida recalled, "solicit[ed] boats to be ferried across to Pointe-à-Pitre, for the bridge had been blown away." With their pleas reinforced by timely promises of a few francs, she and her party secured the use of a skiff, with the services of a woefully inexperienced local man to navigate it. When they first caught sight of the stricken main port, "what scenes of devastation met our eyes! My pen is powerless to describe them." She and Billy had a bittersweet reunion, because many of their belongings had been saturated or swept away. As she soon informed W. E. B. Du Bois, "Nearly all of our pictures that you saw and so many mementoes ... are ruined." However, she added, "we could only be too thankful that our lives were spared and feel that more than many others we have been blessed in every way."

Consul Hunt directed his wife to return immediately to Trois Rivières because the conditions in Pointe-à-Pître, where he was obliged to remain, seemed far worse. And yet, Ida reported, his mandate "nearly cost me my life, for, on [re-]crossing the Rivière Salée with my friends, we came near being drowned." As they started back, she wrote, "we were borne by the current too near a rope which had been placed across the channel, and our not too skillful oarsman could not avoid it so it caught us and nearly overturned the boat." Waves hurled the hapless pilot into the torrent, while roiling floods tumbled Ida and the others cowering with her in the wayward dinghy headlong toward a concrete breakwater that would have smashed it to tinder. Yet with good fortune, aided by swift but favorable tides, they avoided a fatal collision and "were soon hoisted up onto the masonry" — safe once more on solid land.

Ida had a strong constitution and did not get sick as a result of her ordeals and exposure to the elements, but within the week she returned to Pointe-à-Pître to care for Billy, who, she reported, had fallen "ill with grippe and fever." As so often is the case with firsthand accounts, Billy's and Ida's perceptions, descriptions, and memories of circumstances surrounding that traumatic event diverge from one another, and in his memoir he gave his spouse no credit for nursing him when he succumbed to both flu and malaria. Rather, he insisted, "I was looked after by a neighbor, thanks to whose devoted and skillful care, I finally pulled through."

Ida further explained that their problems were exacerbated because "isolated as we are and with all means of communication cut off, the outside world was ignorant of our fate for days and days." "Terrible electrical storms with the loudest peals of thunder I've ever heard, and a cry of fire in the night with the tocsin sounding the alarm" rattled Guadeloupe for weeks thereafter. "When the wind rises and the earth trembles," she concluded her compelling saga, paraphrasing the Old Testament's Fifty-fifth Psalm, "one longs for the 'wings of a dove to fly far, far away' from this *pays d'epouvante* [frightful country]."

In his own account, Consul Hunt recalled that their "first intimation of a hurricane was on Tuesday afternoon September 11th through an official message posted at the Cable office." Pointe-à-Pître's mayor mobilized "the Town Crier [who] called the people together with his drum and warned them to take every precaution," but fierce winds ripped down the few telephone and telegraph lines that might have disseminated lifesaving information. "Warnings were sent out, but never reached the out-lying districts," he added. The islanders' ignorance of the impending threats and a total lack of preparations may have been the most effective killers of all.

Violent gusts drove in from the east, swerved around to the south, then reinforced the impact of downpours and undersea tremors to generate an isolated tsunami — the treacherous saltwater surge that can sweep in hours before the storm's main frontal assault. "A Tidal Wave drove the [ocean] ... into the town," wrote Hunt, "bringing with it boats and barges, one of which was found high and dry in the Public Square." "A small verdant island situated in the harbor," he continued, "was submerged by 10 or 12 feet of water. It was estimated that more than sixty persons, men, women, and children, perished on that island the night of the hurricane."

It soon became so blustery, Billy wrote, that "the doors of my office began to yield to the force of the wind, [then] there was a slight lull. The gales quieted somewhat, the rain decreased a bit, and the sun almost pierced through the cirrus clouds." After the eye eased by, however, a more ferocious assault roared in. "Rain began to fall heavily and the wind seemed to carry everything in its wake ... with increased violence" throughout the day. "I had to risk my life to cross the open patio," added the intrepid consul. "[D]ebris [flew] in all directions and on all sides" as previously benign palm fronds mutated into slashing scythes. "I heard a terrifying noise," he said, and "as I looked towards the grey sky, I saw the roof of our house raised by the wind and carried swiftly toward the harbor and out into the ocean."

As Billy Hunt reported in his memoir, he "sat through that unforgettable night of terror" barricaded in the tempest-besieged United States consulate. The barometric pressure dropped so precipitously that his eardrums throbbed: "The noise was horrifying as if we were traveling on a subway express train passing through a tunnel ... winds howled, the rain fell in torrents. ... [It] continued with hurricane force ... reaching a velocity of over 175 miles an hour." His estimate, in fact, was not far off. Official reports confirm that the winds blasted at their peak sustained intensity for a full day around Guadeloupe, at times exceeding 155 miles per hour, making that storm, in modern terminology, a category 5, or "catastrophic" event, as indeed it was.

Billy Hunt called it "the most thrilling experience of my life." Thrilling, tragic, or both, this hurricane was exceptionally fierce, bringing death and destruction not only to the islands near Guadeloupe but through much of the northern Caribbean and the southern United States as well. Except for the apocalyptic Gulf of Mexico storm that had inundated Galveston, Texas, in 1900 and claimed perhaps eight thousand lives, this was the deadliest natural disaster in United States history. In 1928 the West Indies proportionally suffered more fatalities than did the North American mainland, and wherever the tempest struck, injuries and loss of life were far greater among poorer black and brown people than among more affluent whites — as is almost always the case.

Flies swarmed and maggots feasted in Guadeloupe, and the foul gases that within a few days bloated the decaying bodies nauseated survivors. "Many people were killed in and around Pointe a Pitre," Consul Hunt wrote, "too many in fact, to think of burying them separately, so as a sanitary precaution, the health authorities built a funeral pyre and burned all the bodies of the victims." Acrid smoke poisoned the air as impromptu disposal crews sprinkled the cadavers with lime, then cremated them. The sight and stench of charred flesh, and howls from the sick and injured, assaulted the senses. Hunt reported to his State Department superiors that at least nine hundred persons lost their lives during the storm, while disparate records calculate that from six hundred to two thousand Guadeloupeans died as a result of the hurricane. Others were never accounted for at all. Before the demoralized local citizenry could make accurate tabulations, they threw up their hands, turned their backs, and simply refused to continue counting the corpses. Throughout the region, decomposed or mutilated human remains washed up or were unearthed for years thereafter.

Leaving Guadeloupe in shambles, the storm swept on to Montserrat, Antigua, Nevis, the Virgin Islands, and Puerto Rico, where it dumped two feet of rain and became known as the San Felipe (it struck on that saint's holy feast day) *huracán*. It skirted Hispaniola's north shore, strafed the Turks and Caicos, and roared past the Bahamas before mauling the mainland, flooding the Florida Everglades and leaving death, destruction, and misery in its wake. Zora Neale Hurston, a rising star of the Harlem Renaissance, was a Floridian. She collected black survivors' grim remembrances of that legendary hurricane, then immortalized its heartless swath through her home state in the epic novel *Their Eyes Were Watching God*. Such storms, however, lose their menace and intensity as they travel inland and become deprived of the atmospheric fuel so lavishly proffered by tropical seawaters, and the wicked San Felipe hurricane sputtered out over the cooler, arid plains of the United States' upper Midwest by September 19.

The 1928 storm was not even Guadeloupe's most lethal. One in 1776 had killed an estimated six thousand. But a century and a half later, Ida and Billy Hunt both lamented, countless persons died on that island. Others drowned or became food for the sharks as fishing boats splintered, foundered, or vanished at sea. Winds, rain, and floods ravaged houses, schools, government offices, and medical facilities, where vital records, equipment, furnishings, and supplies were sodden, mildewed, and rendered useless, or altogether lost. Without regard to age, gender, race, or social standing, supplicants flocked to rural shrines and chapels and the larger towns' somber Catholic churches, but neither God, Jesus, and the blessed Virgin nor a pantheon of African deities gave them much help or solace. Pointe-à-Pître, Billy reported, became "a perfect picture of a city that had been dynamited." Only its heavily reinforced concrete police station, he added, survived unscathed.

Mosquitoes hatched in stagnant pools, then droning swarms pervaded the island, and malaria and yellow fever flourished during the ensuing weeks. Potable water became salinated or polluted with feces and sewage, which expedited the spread of cholera that claimed even more lives. Thousands of donkeys, cows, goats, pigs, and flocks of poultry perished, as did legions of the island's ubiquitous rodents. Subsistence crops were destroyed, meat and fish rotted and reeked. Mountain streams carrying rich topsoil, vegetation, and debris cascaded over their banks and rampaged down the denuded hillsides. Landslides buckled tracks of the narrow-gauge rail lines, and dirt roads, once barely adequate, became oozing, impassable troughs of red-brown mud. Sugar mills were flattened, with many of them rendered inoperable for years to come, and exports fell to a third of what they had been before the disaster. "The island's economic future has received a serious setback," Consul Hunt drily reported. Physically, structurally, and economically, the storm crushed Guadeloupe's flawed but exquisite "butterfly" beyond recognition.

With Consul Hunt's aid and encouragement, Pointe-à-Pître's Negro mayor launched an urgent appeal to the American Red Cross. That agency, already deluged by pleas for relief from the similarly storm-stricken southern United States, nonetheless prepared to cable a substantial donation to Guadeloupe. But an unattributable communiqué to the Red Cross from the State Department warned of the supposed problems inherent in doing so: "In view of the rottenness of local politics on the island it might be inadvisable to hand such a large sum as ten thousand dollars to the local political gentry who range from café au lait to café noir in complexion." Rather, the patronizing message continued, "The governor of the island, a white Frenchman from continental France, would seem to be the appropriate person to handle the money. According to the Consul's [Hunt's] latest report, he is a man of integrity and long service in the colonial career"— though that dispatch differs from Billy Hunt's later assessment of Governor Louis Gerbinis (whose name he discreetly never mentioned) as a petty gossipmonger.

"The first relief ship," Hunt recalled, "arrived at Pointe a Pitre, on October 7th with food and hospital supplies." But in an abrupt and dumbfounding about-face, island officials rejected his efforts to secure aid for Guadeloupe from his own country on the prideful pretext that "France was able to cope with the situation without outside help," although they expressed "deep appreciation" for the offer. They asked only that the U.S. Weather Bureau include the French Antilles in its future storm forecasts and alerts. Gibbs Hunt wrote Du Bois, who had become swept up in the ugly, misshapen politics of obtaining help for the underserved Negro hurricane victims in the American South: "Perhaps you know that the French Red Cross refused the $10,000 that the American Red Cross offered to place at the disposal of the sufferers here." "I cannot say," she added, "whether politics or French 'delicatesse' dictated it. It's too bad anyway!" It was "too bad" indeed, though many Guadeloupeans, her husband claimed, still harbored grave misgivings that the offer had strings attached and was part of a "dark scheme" for the United States to acquire their island. They were heedful of the harsh American military occupations elsewhere around the Caribbean, especially in Haiti, so legitimate concerns about further subjugation more than irrational paranoia led them to reject aid from the United States.

For more than a year Du Bois had urged Gibbs Hunt to write him something about Guadeloupe. She had made several abortive attempts to do so, and when Deputy Achille-René Boisneuf, her colleague in the early Pan-African Congresses, died, she had provided biographical data for Boisneuf's obituary in Crisis. But the hurricane gave her the topic, inspiration, and impetus needed to tackle a more substantive project. "We have lost so much, I would not mind making a few dollars," she conceded. "My other [submissions]," she added, "I hope to get paid for by your magazine or some other, but this one I contribute." "The article on Guadeloupe," she fretted a fortnight later, "is about finished, but needs retouching," "I could not get it copied for the last boat, so I'm sending it on hoping it will not be too late . . . I'm so upset by this catastrophy [*sic*]." Despite her recent pique at being "among the forgotten" for the acclaimed Du Bois family wedding, she warmly signed her note, "au revoir et bientot." Du Bois was delighted. "Thank you very much for the vivid article," he wrote. "I'm going to use it in an early number of THE CRISIS." A week later he confirmed that "it will be published in the JANUARY CRISIS."

Once conditions on the island improved enough that larger cargo and passenger ships could approach Pointe-à-Pître's storm-wracked harbor, which had been silted up and littered with reeking detritus and mangled boat hulls, Ida sought her metaphoric "wings of the dove," booked passage, and fled that *pays d'épouvante* for the United States, where she had missed milestones such as the release from prison and subsequent deportation of Marcus Garvey, and the recent election of President Herbert Hoover. She spent weeks with her sister Hattie, who owing to her poor health had returned from Haiti (which the hurricane had spared) to her residence in New York City's Harlem. Frustrated, disillusioned, and bitter that his assignment as a military attaché in Port-au-Prince never led to a more prestigious foreign service appointment, Captain Marshall resigned early in 1929 and rejoined his wife.

Nap and Hattie Marshall devoted much of their time, energy, and assets to supporting several informally adopted children, and to a foundation they administered called the Save Haiti League. Although Haiti had suffered from its own partially self-inflicted traumas long before the United States military occupation, more Negro Americans began to identify with the escalating plight of the troubled nation that epitomized their dreams of an independent black republic in the Western Hemisphere, while New York's burgeoning Caribbean immigrant population contributed to an increasing awareness of the problems there. The Gibbs-Marshalls raised private aid for Haiti's people, as did a handful of others such as the ambitious black West Virginia banker Charles E. Mitchell. They also supported its exiled patriots who castigated the ongoing American subjugation of their island. Those activities represented the Gibbs-Marshalls' well-meaning but thankless attempts to offset the hardships and outrages they had observed during a seven-year tenure there. Hattie had almost completed her history of Haiti. She shuttled between New York and Washington, where she still oversaw her music conservatory, but Captain Marshall's war injuries flared up again. He was in his early fifties when his kidneys began faltering as well. To qualify for a military pension he needed a 30 percent permanent disability rating, but an intransigent and miserly army medical board officially declared him only 29 percent disabled.

Although a few caring friends expressed their concerns that he might be drinking too much, in many respects Napoleon Marshall still functioned ably. He had nearly finished a memoir, *The Providential Armistice: A Volunteer's Story* (1930), about his experiences during and after the Great War. In February, Gibbs Hunt wrote Du Bois from the Gibbs-Marshalls' New York flat, both requesting additional copies of the recent issue of *Crisis* in which her essay appeared and asking the editor if he had read "Captain Marshall's article on Hunt in the Sunday 'World.'" Marshall's newspaper piece also blasted the United States' ill-conceived, poorly executed, and ruthless reclamation efforts in Haiti, and he excoriated the white American marines stationed there. Her brother-in-law, she added, "got knocked down by an automobile the other evening, but was not seriously hurt" (perhaps she feared he had been overimbibing), so she further implored Du Bois: "Drop in if you can." He, in turn, promised to visit them all very soon.

Back in Pointe-à-Pître, Billy Hunt became increasingly disheartened, frustrated, and irate because, he wrote, "with the supremacy of questionable politics . . . and the petty prejudices which kept the people divided among themselves, an American Consular Officer labored under a decided disadvantage." So as soon as the worst of the crisis had passed, Hunt asked for and received permission to take a home leave. In confirming that request, department officials ordered him to return posthaste to the nation's capital, leaving behind any personal belongings.

Shortly after he arrived back in Washington, still plagued by poor health, Hunt met with the State Department's chief of personnel to articulate his concerns about Guadeloupe. He even suggested that the department close entirely its consulate there, a recommendation that, to his surprise, his superiors authorized. Soon thereafter, Hunt was astonished to receive notice of his reassignment to head the consulate at St. Michael's (São Miguel) in the mid-Atlantic Portuguese Azores, so once again he went back to Pointe-à-Pître to pack up and ship off his few salvageable household effects. The seeming extravagance of that duplicative trip, however, aggravated the finicky U.S. General Accounting Office, which for many months afterward refused to reimburse him, prompting Billy Hunt's petulant outburst that all the associated "trouble and worry made my experiences during the hurricane seem like a thunder storm in comparison."

In less than two years, Guadeloupe had become their worst nightmare instead of a flawed Eden. On New York City's Hudson River docks that portentously cold winter of 1929, Billy and Ida boarded the Italian liner *Saturnia*. Once again they bade family and friends good-bye, initiated ambitious plans to tackle and master a new language, put behind them three separate and diverse interludes in France and her far-flung colonies, resolutely looked ahead, and headed off for a different experience altogether in the remote but fabled Azorean islands.

9

Odysseys through the Portuguese Atlantic, 1929–1931

Puz me a escrever na areía
Ao som do mar que corria,
Veío o mar, tirou-me a penna
Apagou-me o que eu fazia.

I tried to write on the sand
By the sound of the surging sea,
But the sea came and took my pen
And destroyed what I had done.

—From a Portuguese Azorean *fado*, or folk song, transcribed and translated by E. Seeman and published by M. Longworth Dames in the journal *Folklore*, 1903

In mid-February 1929, with Billy and Ida Hunt ensconced in their cabin, the SS *Saturnia* put out to sea from New York. The "luxuriously appointed" liner, as Hunt later described it, docked the next day to pick up more travelers in Massachusetts, a state known, he added, as the locale of "several large and well-to-do colonies of Azoreans and Portuguese which have been settled for many years." As the *Saturnia* pushed away from its Boston pier, replete with a "noisy contingent of passengers . . . amidst deafening shouts of 'bon voyage' which echoed from the quai and steamer," Hunt recalled, the hour was well past midnight. Thus he once again set forth east across the Atlantic, this time on a "five-day voyage to the Azores."

"The ocean was smooth as glass," and the assemblage in first class was "composed of several attractive young men and women [who] enjoy[ed] numerous parties of tennis, shuffle-board and other games on the spacious upper deck." Hunt admitted that several were young enough to have been his grandchildren, although (already in his mid-sixties and still recovering from malaria) he boasted of an unflagging vigor: "I managed to hold my own with the best of them in prowess and skill in all the games we engaged in." The consul a bit pompously continued that most of those engaging youths were "college graduates, and consequently personified that refinement and simplicity which characterizes the well bred persons of all races."

But as the liner neared the mid-Atlantic archipelago that was the Gibbs-Hunts' final destination, the carefree camaraderie and climatic serenity of the first four days on the ocean ended abruptly as the ship "began to roll and pitch." "The sea increased its violence," he wrote, and "bounc[ed] the Saturnia from one wave to another as if it were made of cork." The conditions deteriorated so precipitously that the captain contemplated not letting any passengers off at Ponta Delgada on the island of São Miguel (or St. Michael's — the Anglicized spelling was and is almost as common as the Portuguese), his next scheduled port of call, and instead heading straight through to Lisbon. At the last minute, however, he decided to risk the late-evening disembarkation.

The crew, Hunt reported, "began by dropping the trunks into the tossing lighters with the greatest difficulty." "One of the trunks belonging to our Vice Consul [Carleton Wall] missed the upward surge of the lighter and landed on top of a huge wave [but] was fortunately recovered before being dashed to bits." Once the luggage had been cast overboard, "the Captain turned his attention to discharging us, which was accomplished under perilous conditions." "Mrs. Hunt and myself," the consul added, "were literally pitched into the bouncing life boat — which I thought every moment would be dashed to splinters against the side of the Saturnia — and landed safely in the arms of the dashing boatmen." He acknowledged that the ship-to-shore dinghy "was manned by an intrepid crew of efficient and experienced seamen who proved equal to the emergency." Finally, the "lights on the quais at Ponta Delgada began to pierce the thick fog . . . through a drenching rain storm," although he and Ida "doubted whether we would ever reach those lights alive." But the sturdy little landing boat bumped and threaded its way between treacherous reefs and headed into port via somewhat calmer waters. That hair-raising escapade convinced the much relieved Consul Hunt "that after all, perhaps, my final resting place was not to be 'Davy Jones's Locker.'"

In that dramatic fashion, Hunt arrived in the Azores to replace his white predecessor. He thus became the first African American consul to serve there, though sixteen years before, the State Department had tapped James Weldon Johnson for the same position. But knowing that institutional racism would curtail his further advancement in the foreign service, Johnson had declined the offer and left the department altogether. The offer itself nonetheless demonstrated that as early as 1913, ranking department officers assumed that the Azoreans would not object to having a "colored" man represent the United States in their domain. Maintaining their country's established racial inequities obsessed many white Americans, but residents of the few foreign locales that saw Negro consuls at all usually deemed their race immaterial and properly focused instead on their qualifications and performance. So in 1929 the tan-skinned Consul Hunt became the United States' official emissary, and its prestigious and welcome face in mid-Atlantic Portugal.

The geologically unstable Azores, which the Gibbs-Hunts had spied in the distance when they sailed from France to Guadeloupe two years before, are situated nearly twenty-three hundred miles east of New York City, more than eight hundred northwest from Morocco, a little less than that and almost due west of Portugal itself, just where Europe's, Africa's, and North America's suboceanic tectonic plates converge. The Gulf Stream laps them, and they lie in the paths of occasional Atlantic hurricanes, but in the years shortly preceding the Gibbs-Hunts' arrival, they had been spared major seismic tremors or volcanic upheavals. The irregularly configured chain zigzags from southeasternmost Santa Maria hundreds of miles north and west over to tiny Corvo, which Hunt observed, is "nothing more or less . . . than a crater rising about 400 feet above the surface." Between those seagirt outposts sit São Miguel, Terceira, Pico, Faial, Graciosa, São Jorge, and Flores, and Hunt heard tell that "a tenth island was discovered by an English explorer who might have established a colony thereon if the sea had not swallowed it up before his return." In the widespread folkloric legendry about lost continents, he further reported, some Iberians claimed that the Azores were "the mythical Atlantis of Plato." Around and between the nine populated isles lurk the threatening crags of volcanic rock called *formigas,* or ants. The total land area of the archipelago is little more than nine hundred square miles, and when Hunt arrived its population hovered just under a quarter million — roughly that of St.-Étienne or Guadeloupe. Half resided on São Miguel, with half of those in Ponta Delgada itself, which at the time, Hunt declared, was the "third city in size and importance in the Portuguese Republic, only Oporto and Lisbon ranking higher."

The Azores were totally uninhabited in the mid-twelfth century when the North African navigator Sherif Mohammed al-Idrisi first recorded their existence. In the late 1300s or early 1400s Portugal's audacious seamen rediscovered al-Idrisi's islands, which, according to most accounts, they called *Açores,* for a mid-Atlantic goshawk, though others argue that the name is a usurpation of *azuis,* plural of the Portuguese word for blue and reflecting their oceanic venue.

Before anyone else in Europe (except for the Vikings' several inconclusive traversals of the North Atlantic in the late medieval era), Portugal's shipbuilders constructed seaworthy vessels, and its sailors, or *marinheiros,* mastered the skills needed to sail south around Africa's western hump, secure in the knowledge that they could negotiate the tides and winds to return home safely. Hunt admiringly wrote that Portugal often was called the "Mother of Navigators."

Portuguese clerics and slave traders soon began studding Africa's coastline with missions and fortresses to protect their expanding empire and sequester their newly captive chattel. Equally anxious to vanquish Islam, they became the first whites to try to convert black people to Catholicism, even while wrenching them from sub-Saharan domains and selling, exporting, and putting them out to labor in their islands' new cane fields. As Europeans demanded that their collective sweet tooth be assuaged, planters learned that sugarcane could be cultivated only in locales that never experienced a hard frost, and Portugal began populating the mid-Atlantic chain with a mixed bag of denizens. The embryonic agricultural settlements and work conditions on the Azores and other Iberian Atlantic and Mediterranean isles thus created early prototypes for the brutal, demeaning plantation slavery that began proliferating in the 1500s throughout the hotter regions of the more recently colonized New World. But the Azores' climate ultimately proved too temperate, its land too scant, and terrain too rocky to sustain further slave-based sugar production, and in that particular locale those endeavors quickly petered out.

The Azores' white settlers dreaded, and thus ruthlessly quashed, any slave insurrections. So by no later than 1600, the islands' European overlords shipped off most, but not all, of the remaining black people held there in bondage to Brazil, Portugal's vast tropical colony. Brazil itself soon became home to a larger, more Africanized community and culture than anyplace outside the "Dark Continent," and state-sanctioned enslavement outlasted its tenure anywhere else in the Western Hemisphere.

By the time Billy Hunt arrived, the Azores had put both slavery and sugar cultivation centuries behind them, and he contended that the most significant newer exports were members of the poor but aspiring local peasantry. The United States' recently instituted immigration laws (skewed to favor lighter skinned, preferably English-speaking northern Europeans) curtailed that exodus and restricted the number of legal arrivals from all of greater Portugal to only twenty-five hundred a year. But what Hunt somewhat patronizingly called the "peasant crop" of emigrants had been so substantial for so long that "today there are perhaps more Azoreans living under the American flag than in the archipelago."

Because of the islands' location and unique history, more than a few of the residents, some of whom who were descended in part from African slaves, free people of color, or even Moorish pirates, looked not unlike similarly mixed-race Americans such as Billy and Ida Hunt. The Azoreans considered themselves European, but in many instances their features and coloration reflected (and still do) a complex heritage and the varying traces of "black blood" seen around and across greater Iberia. A small contingent of those darker-skinned Portuguese had participated in W. E. B. Du Bois's 1923 Pan-African Congress when it convened in Lisbon.

A number of Azoreans and their diasporic compatriots from the Madeiras and Cape Verdes — the latter nearer to and therefore more influenced in every way by sub-Saharan Africa — emigrated to and settled in coastal Rhode Island and Massachusetts, often in their own discrete communities. There, Anglo-Americans and African Americans deemed them Portuguese-speaking "colored" people, their foreignness making them somewhat more palatable to the white majority than their own "homegrown" Negroes.

Despite the early removal of the islands' bondmen and the "whitening" of the remaining Azorean population, scraps of Negro lore and legacies survived. Contradictory local stories tell of malefactors being banished to Portugal's colonies in Africa as punishment for their misdeeds, and São Miguel, the Azores' patron saint, is often portrayed crushing a black Satan beneath his feet. But São Benedetto (Saint Benedict), widely known as "the Moor," who was the son of Iberian slaves, is a revered figure whose image appears throughout the islands. African-influenced Moorish architecture is ubiquitous, and a number of Azoreans hang *figas,* amulets carved in the shape of a clenched fist and intended to fend off evil, around their necks. Those charms, which are even more prevalent in Brazil, reflect indigenous West African beliefs. The Azores' population was and is over 95 percent Roman Catholic, but Africa's religious doctrines and practices shaped their Catholicism less than that in the Cape Verdes, Brazil, French Guadeloupe, or other such locales. Much as they did in continental Iberia, however, a few of the local people reluctantly admitted to a suspect and long-suppressed Jewish or Muslim heritage, and like the Gibbs-Hunts, a number of the English and North American sojourners were Protestants.

When Consul Hunt arrived, the islanders still cultivated some bananas, oranges, grapes, olives, and hothouse pineapples. Several flour mills and food- and tobacco-processing plants operated there as well, but in the previous century insects and fungi had decimated much of the local production of potatoes (as they had throughout Ireland at the same time) and fruits. The citrus also required wooden crates for shipping and export, which presented a problem because the Azores had become critically deforested. Living in the middle of the sea, many Azoreans became skilled whalers who manned the eighteenth- and nineteenth-century whaling vessels that traversed the world's oceans, especially out of northeast American ports. Thousands of those seafarers abandoned their homes and families and relocated to the United States to benefit from greater economic opportunities. But commercial whaling dwindled after the 1850s as more accessible and affordable sources of heating and lamp oil emerged elsewhere, so fishing — especially cod, a mainstay of Portuguese-Atlantic cuisines — dairying, and subsistence farming provided the islands' most prevalent employment. A few men and women also cloistered themselves or otherwise dedicated their lives to the Catholic Church. The larger towns fostered tradesmen, civil servants, and various professionals, while artisans tanned, tooled, and fashioned leather goods, made ceramics, and wove straw hats, satchels, and baskets. Some of the women took on menial jobs in the mills or cigarette factories, while others toiled over fine embroidered linens, laboring at their home industries for meager handfuls of *centavos*.

Although the Azores maintained their strongest ties to western Europe, felicitous but informal diplomatic and trade relations with Britain's New World colonies antedated the establishment of the North American republic. In 1795 John Street and Thomas Hickling became the first official United States representatives, and for some time their country maintained consulates on both São Miguel and Faial. Three generations of the Hicklings and two of the Dabneys (an affluent family prominent in the New England whaling industry) served in those Atlantic islands throughout almost the entire nineteenth century.

Some Azorean elders recalled stories they had heard about the newly emancipated American Negroes who sailed from Maryland in the 1820s, bound for the African settlement that became Liberia. Their ship moored at Saõ Miguel's Ponta Delgada, and they came ashore and strolled around the grounds of the Hicklings' consulate. A century later Consul Hunt flatly declared that "St. Michael's [was] the one post to which I was assigned where America is held in deep affection." Lured by the balmy climate and life's leisurely tempo, more than a few United States citizens moved, or returned, to the Azores, and Hunt observed that "on holidays almost as many American flags as Portuguese can be seen floating to the breeze."

He admired Portugal's dominion "over the world's greatest Colonial Empire after England and France," but local residents insisted, and rightly so, that their islands were not among the mother country's many colonies that stretched around the globe, though some people protested that they were treated as such. "The so-called 'adjacent islands,' the Azores and Madeiras," Hunt explained, "are officially included as part of Continental Portugal." Then as now, the Azores make up three Portuguese provinces, but because of their location, they usually appear on maps of Africa. By 1822 Brazil had established its full independence, and Portugal's remaining colonies included Mozambique, across from Madagascar on the East African mainland, Guinea, and vast Angola, "the size of Belgium, France, Portugal and Spain combined," Hunt reported, and the source of millions of black people who, over almost four centuries, had been enslaved and sent to Brazil. The Cape Verdes, Principe, and Sao Tomé, where indentured Liberian laborers were sometimes taken to supplement the insufficient local workforce, were the other Portuguese Atlantic island clusters. In addition, Portugal claimed the Indonesian archipelago's North Timor; Macao, abutting British Hong Kong; and Goa, Damão, and Diu on the Indian subcontinent's west coast. Like France's and England's at that time, Portugal's empire, populated by a panoply of the world's diverse, oppressed, and largely impoverished darker races, remained a colossal one, upon which the sun never set.

Starting with Consul Hunt's assignment in 1929, the Azores became one terminus of what some State Department officials disparagingly came to call the "Azores-Madagascar-Liberia circuit," approved for the intermittent assignment of some of its few "colored" employees. They viewed São Miguel as a peripheral, undemanding post that would neither enhance nor ruin a foreign service career. In Hunt's case, it also may have seemed appropriate to his gradually declining vigor in his later years. As a result of his designated race, Hunt was never institutionally encouraged and mentored, or given critical assignments, formal training, or much of a chance to develop, display, and benefit from his professional skills or personal assets. After more than three decades of effective, loyal service, the department had pretty much put him out to pasture — out of sight, out of mind.

Few government officials in Washington, it seems, cared much about the Azores, or even Portugal in its entirety. It was a reliable ally, but also widely seen as western Europe's most underdeveloped nation, and politically and diplomatically one of its least significant. When King Manuel II abruptly left his throne in 1910, the first equivocal attempts were made to set up a parliamentary democracy. But those efforts proved ineffective, and within a few years the high costs of World War I — Portugal had joined the Entente — undercut the already fragile economy.

In 1926, during the chaotic period when a cabal of right-wing military officers forcefully usurped the shaky new nonroyal regime, the African American Consul William Yerby in Oporto barely escaped with his life when a bomb blew out the window by which he was standing. Portugal's new military junta soon abolished the parliament, suspended most civil rights, and installed as its finance minister a little known economics professor named António de Oliveira Salazar. Not long before Consul Hunt got to São Miguel, Salazar seized full control of the government and instituted a virtual police state. He ruled for decades as one of Europe's most peremptory dictators, with the Presidente da República Portuguesa, António Óscar de Fragoso Carmona, serving as his right-hand man. In 1929 the new president-for-life Fragoso Carmona signed Consul Hunt's exequatur (which the Portuguese called a *carta patente*), the host country's official permission for him to act. The designated governor general who presided in Ponta Delgada at the time was the authoritarian *Açoriano* Colonel Feliciano António da Silva Leal. This was the increasingly despotic political situation when Hunt arrived to represent his country.

Both Ida and Billy, he later wrote, enjoyed the islands' "uniform and agreeable" climate, although, he added, "the surrounding ocean lends a sort of dampness to the atmosphere." Their household effects and clothes often became blanketed with a corrosive rust or downy mold. Nonetheless, the Azores largely were free of the health hazards that plagued the lives of foreign service officers in much of Africa and the Caribbean. "All kinds of flowers are in bloom all winter," Billy Hunt remembered, and the year-round mildness offered "many opportunities for outdoor activities — tennis, bathing and horseback riding and motoring."

One favorite excursion was to São Miguel's Vale das Furnas, "a retreat of the monks in bygone days," Hunt reported. It was an eerie habitat of fire and brimstone characterized by spectacular scenery and "remarkable thermal and mineral springs." That also was the epicenter of the island's *caldeirões* (cauldrons), most notably the Boca de Inferno, or Mouth of Hell, where, he explained, "the entire region is an arid waste, the white soil is streaked with sulphur, and uncomfortably hot under foot; fragments of upturned stones are too hot to handle with the naked hands. Huge waves of sulphurous vapors fill the air and the earth trembles with continuous rumblings, which provokes an uncanny feeling that all is not working smoothly in the lower regions."

"The peasants sing its praises in song and poetry," Hunt added, "the wealthy classes use it as a summer resort, scientists wonder at its curious phenomena, scholars and students are interested in its odd history, and all unite in admiring its marvelous scenery." But sulphur also was widely feared and believed to portend a demonic presence in that "abode of evil spirits and goblins." Hunt recalled that "whispered accounts relate the blood curdling story of a small girl . . . who accidentally fell into this boiling cauldron, and shortly after, only a heap of charred bones belched forth to explain her fate."

Like many of those who made up the Azores' tightly knit international community, the Gibbs-Hunts and other "leading citizens and officials, [joined] the 'Club Michaelense,' which offers its members during the season a series of popular dances." Belonging to a "white" social club such as that, of course, would have been inconceivable even for the most respected Negroes virtually anywhere in the United States. "Those occasions," Hunt blithely wrote, "gave us an opportunity to shake the dampness, mothballs and wrinkles out of our 'glad rags' and skip the light fantastic." He also considered São Miguel's "upper classes cultured and refined, the peasant classes polite and respectful," and those "peasants" never failed to "raise their hats and salute you with a friendly smile and cheery salutation, 'Viva Senhor.'" Ida Gibbs Hunt did not suffer from the multiple hardships that afflicted her brother and his wife, or her sixty-year-old younger sister and her husband. During their mostly pleasurable sojourn in São Miguel, she and Billy hosted or attended a number of diplomatic functions, socialized at the Club Michaelense, and visited the Azores' natural attractions.

Billy Hunt's chatty epistolary relationship with Du Bois also flourished. Not long after the State Department reassigned the consul from Guadeloupe to Saõ Miguel, the editor of *Crisis* magazine ran a brief though flattering item about Hunt. The out-of-date photograph accompanying it shows him, not on either of those unsung islands, but rather at the peak of his consular glory, being honored by uniformed French officials before he left St.-Étienne. Ida Gibbs Hunt's intermittently contentious correspondence with Du Bois slackened off, however, although they may have seen each other in summer 1929 when she delivered a talk titled "Harriet Beecher Stowe and the Woman Suffrage Movement" at a program memorializing the celebrated white abolitionist held at New York University.

That December Billy Hunt wrote Du Bois about his new life in Ponta Delgada, and shared with him the challenges of learning Portuguese. He and Ida, Billy noted, made use of an Azorean "professor's" tutelary services, but he admittedly acquired only a "limited knowledge of the language," though his linguistically gifted wife fared a good deal better. Much of the local upper class, as well as others who traveled widely and often, could speak English, yet Hunt's lack of fluency in the islands' primary tongue kept him from establishing the intimacy he had fostered with many of Madagascar's, St.-Étienne's, and Guadeloupe's Francophones. On his part, Du Bois hoped to negotiate a clerical position at Hunt's consulate for Lillie Mae Hubbard, the State Department's first female African American employee to serve overseas, and a frequent correspondent whom he had met in Liberia five years before. In response to Du Bois's request, Hunt said that while he would have been pleased to have Hubbard join him in the Azores, the clerk's post had already been filled by Carleton Wall, not his choice but a capable African American gentleman from New Jersey who at various times served his country in Liberia, France, and later in the Spanish Canaries.

Hunt also corresponded with a novice anthropologist named Caroline Bond Day who was working on her master's degree at Radcliffe College with the Harvard University professor Earnest Hooton — one of the few white advisers to Carter G. Woodson's *Journal of Negro History*. Bond Day, a former protégée of Du Bois at Atlanta University, was analyzing the physical manifestations and socioeconomic impact of racial admixtures. When she completed her controversial thesis in 1930, she became the first African American, female or male, to earn an advanced degree in anthropology. Because the old picture of Hunt that Bond Day's mother, Georgia, a friend of Ida's in Washington, had given her was blurred, the younger woman wanted and needed a clearer image. The replacement photograph that Consul Hunt sent her portrayed him as every inch the estimable American diplomat, with precisely parted curly silver hair and a clipped mustache, garbed in a formal gray morning suit, sporting a white wing-tip collar and checkered silk ascot pierced with a pearl stickpin. For Bond Day, William Henry Hunt physically typified a number of lighter-skinned African Americans for whom their white, almost always male, ancestry visibly exceeded their black, and his accomplishments reflected the hard-won status and unexpected achievements of a few distinguished members of their legally designated and concurrently demeaned race.

Few guests visited them in the Azores, but the Gibbs-Hunts kept up their correspondence with relatives and friends in France, Guadeloupe, and the United States, from whom they learned that Archibald Grimké, a major activist and onetime consul, and Edmond Burrill, Billy's former vice consul in St.-Étienne, had died, the latter possibly by his own hand. And at this juncture Hunt's memoir loses its precision. He provides few acute observations about his Azorean tenure, and the text becomes scarcely more than a vivid travelogue. Judging from what he wrote, however, Billy and Ida Hunt did little of real import in Saõ Miguel. And perhaps that reflected the altered reality of their public lives. Nonetheless, he was delighted to be back (technically) in Europe. The State Department allowed no other Negroes any new or improved assignments, though a year later Hunt's colleague William Yerby was reassigned from Oporto to Nantes.

Late in 1929 in New York City, W. E. B. Du Bois and his longtime cohort Napoleon Bonaparte Marshall, Ida's brother-in-law, faced a battery of radio microphones and news cameras when they testified at a contentious gathering convened by the renowned Foreign Policy Association to discuss the United States' ongoing occupation of Haiti. Marshall and Du Bois joined a small chorus of anti-imperial criticism, although the American government continued to insist that its military presence, already past its fifteenth year, remained essential to maintaining fiscal and civic order in that Caribbean nation.

Du Bois protested that dark-skinned Haitian guests of white visitors from the mainland had been denied entry to a Port-au-Prince hotel, then brusquely redirected to the servants' quarters. Far worse, U.S. Marines had gunned down scores of cane workers, armed only with *coco macaques* (literally translated as "crazy monkeys," but in fact just the farmers' walking sticks), who were protesting newly imposed taxes. Du Bois acknowledged that the American occupiers were effecting minor improvements in health care, but argued that they also had reduced the peasants to a state of peonage to reap profits for a few prosperous Haitians, and especially to benefit white American investors. Captain Marshall added that when he had served there as a military attaché from 1922 to 1929, he had witnessed flagrant, brutal abuses by his country's marines, and he also reported that the State Department had imposed a usurious, no-bid loan on Haiti from a prominent stateside banking house. Such occurrences further indebted an already bankrupt country.

Offering a longer-range perspective and a more contextual — though hardly a sunnier — picture, Hattie Gibbs Marshall's school text *The Story of Haiti* came out in 1930, greeted by ample praise from boosters such as Haiti's distinguished diplomat Dantès Bellegarde, whose government had recently transferred him from Paris to serve in Jim Crow Washington, D.C., as its top representative to the United States. Gibbs Marshall also wrote Du Bois that to promote her new opus she had traveled down to Nashville's Fisk (which Du Bois himself had attended), then "south as far as Tuskegee making talks in many schools on Haiti, and endeavored to impress my hearers with the necessity of our children knowing more of the black peoples of the world, that we might mutually inspire and aid each other." Du Bois recommended the book and advertised it for a nominal fee in *Crisis* magazine, as did Carter G. Woodson in the *Journal of Negro History* and the editors of the National Urban League's *Opportunity,* but reviews beyond those in the African American press were almost impossible to come by, few libraries or stores carried it, and the grueling job of marketing and selling remained up to Gibbs Marshall alone if she was to make any money on it to support her family or contribute to their charitable endeavors.

The Gibbs-Marshalls' situation (like that of many others) declined as the Great Depression intensified. Few people were beyond its reach, and the 1920s' brilliant Harlem Renaissance began losing its luster. The *New York Times* nonetheless yielded to demands from organizations such as the NAACP and finally called for general editorial capitalization of the word "Negro." As was typical of the times, neither Hattie nor Napoleon had work that provided them with much income. They continued trying to maintain their philanthropic efforts through the Save Haiti League, but as his health faltered, so did his law practice. Her conservatory in Washington thrived insofar as its students and reputation were concerned, though she could barely pay her teachers, much less herself.

In late summer 1930 doctors opted to hospitalize Captain Marshall for his diabetes at Walter Reed, the flagship U.S. Army hospital in the nation's capital. During the Great War he had been wounded three times and received France's Croix de Guerre, but the military continued to challenge his eligibility for subsidized medical care. He struggled in vain, Hattie wrote Ida in the Azores, "with the powers for more compensation." Marshall had become deeply disillusioned with both the Republican and Democratic parties, yet confidentially shared with Du Bois his hope to return soon to New York City and run for a judgeship on the Socialist ticket. Du Bois, who admitted that he often voted for Socialist candidates but was not (yet) a party member, answered, "I am glad to hear that you are better and planning to come back." However, he bluntly advised: "You should not for a moment think of any political campaign. It would be fatal."

Marshall told Du Bois in the fall of 1930 that he had recently asked his white New York congressional representative to submit a private bill "for my relief," and he also sent the editor a copy of his brief memoir, *The Providential Armistice.* He hoped that "wide distribution" of the publication, which laid out his wartime exploits, would help "Negroes to know whether they are to be used for cannon fodder . . . perhaps an ultra patriotic but rather ignoble use." He reluctantly admitted that although he was only in his early fifties, he had, in truth, become "permanently & totally disabled." Because Du Bois still expressed a dogged determination to complete his long-awaited history of black soldiers in the Great War, Captain Marshall shared further details about his own military experiences that he was using to petition the War Department for his delayed or denied financial aid. He dispatched similar information to Chicago's Republican Oscar De Priest, who in 1929 became the country's first Negro congressman since 1900, and the first ever from the North. "I am happy to say that my Harvard Class [of 1894] is backing me loyally," Marshall boasted to Du Bois about their common alma mater. Among his supporters in this fruitless war on the military, he counted the class chairman and "members of the Hasty Pudding Club." "So 'on with the dance,'" he buoyantly concluded, "let's go down fighting!"

Hattie meanwhile told Ida that she had stayed on in New York "trying to save this house." "Have been here 2 months away from my husband," she wrote. "I suppose Washington society is talking about it," she continued, then bluntly concluded, "tant pis!" ("tough luck!"). Her arthritis was worsening, and with "low funds I am starving myself . . . I do not weigh 100." Although her spouse was in far worse health, she added, he "still sees the rainbow between the clouds with a keg of gold at its end." A week later she reported that she "fell on an 8th Ave street car." Her legs had been weak, painful, and swollen for a decade, but now she needed crutches to get around at all, and an obliging janitor had to carry her upstairs to her third-floor apartment. "My health and problems weigh heavy," Hattie concluded, glumly adding, "you have not suffered as I."

Captain Marshall remained at Walter Reed that Christmas season, only getting out of "prison" for one day to see his wife, who had returned to Washington for the holidays. That was, she ruefully noted, "the first time he has had his clothes on for over 6 months." When the hour came later that evening for him to return to the hospital, he pleaded, "I don't want to leave here."

The situation further declined. "The receiver took over my house," Hattie informed Ida about her New York residence, and she had to move into a hotel, but she still was better off than the growing legions of jobless and homeless Americans, some of whom were reduced to living in the shantytown encampments that their sarcastic denizens began calling "Hoovervilles." Ida sent her sister several checks and turned over a share of the Arkansas property that their father had left her in his will ("merci beaucoup pour votre generosite," Hattie gratefully responded), but the real estate market had become so depressed that they had to accept a miserable offer to sell any of the family's holdings at all. But remaining ever hopeful, Hattie added, "Getting out of debt will help wonderfully, then I can commence to prepare for the future, which looms as Capt. improves."

In Chicago, with no job and little to no income, the old Garveyite Horace Gibbs, their only surviving brother who during his sisters' long absences overseas had looked after the Gibbs family properties, had serious woes of his own. Late in 1930 he agonized to his siblings, "I have never been the same mentally or physically since my accident." (I have been unable to determine when that mishap occurred or what it entailed.) Horace's wife told Hattie that he recently had squandered a pile of money gambling, went on a drunken binge, then "hid . . . and slept it off. He came home penitent and cried like a baby." Such aberrant behavior must have profoundly pained a proud and upright family like the Gibbses. Without a quick bailout, the distraught letter continued, their telephone service and "water would be cut off . . . and they had no coal" for the winter. The Chicagoans wanted to join Hattie in Washington and asked her to find them a house. She had deep concerns about that proposal, but deemed it her sisterly duty to help.

In the Azores, however, Consul Hunt once again enjoyed his tennis matches and cherished mornings on horseback. In contrast to his own vitality, Billy wrote, "the very movements of the average native are the embodiment of listless indifference. It is hard for me to conceive of these easy going people engaging in any continued or vigorous labor," although on another occasion he praised their manifest "shrewdness for business." What Billy called the islanders' "dulce far niente," which he translated as an "alluring idleness," represented for him much of the "unique pleasure of living in the Azores," but it was intertwined, he claimed, with a profound longing or nostalgia conveyed by the local people's folk songs. Much like the *pescadores'* (fishermen's) *fados,* those haunting *saudades* strummed and sung by the landless peasants conveyed a general melancholy. Most of the devout local women, constrained by confluences in their culture that exalted and imposed both a swaggering Iberian masculinity and a patriarchal Catholicism, attended and served but wielded no power in their church or in politics. They had little education, rarely participated in public events, and usually stayed home caring for the children and elders, and many of them dressed in black from head to toe, including capes, shawls, and *carapaças* (shroudlike hoods), which, for the

Gibbs-Hunts, contributed to a pervasive funereal aura. Both Ida and Billy nonetheless expressed their deep admiration and affection for the Azoreans.

Near the end of 1930, and all too soon for Consul Hunt, notice arrived from Washington that he had been "advanced to the grade of Second Secretary in the Diplomatic Service [and] assigned as Secretary of Legation in Liberia." He learned that his replacement, once again a white man, would arrive in about a month from a post on the Portuguese mainland. The orders directed Hunt to arrange for the immediate transfer of himself, his wife — an Azorean housemaid and Nosi Be, their plucky, pampered fox terrier, would accompany them — and their paraphernalia to Monrovia. "It frequently happens to Foreign Service Officers that just at a time when they are getting their bearings, beginning to learn a new language, and mingle in the social life at some new post, the Department decides to transfer them to another country," he explained. Given the United States' (most of the world's, in fact) woeful economic conditions and forecast, the Gibbs-Hunts had little choice but to head on to Liberia, but only with profound regrets expressed by Billy's rhapsodic assertion that "St. Michael's was by far the most delightful assignment during my career of more than 34 years in the Foreign Service of my country." Nonetheless, he added, after scarcely two years there, that departure did not evoke the same "heart-swelling wrench" he and Ida had experienced on leaving France after two decades.

Although much of their correspondence from this period has disappeared, on January 24, 1931, Ida Gibbs Hunt wrote W. E. B. Du Bois assuring him that "the books arrived all right. Many thanks." "Langston Hughes certainly has talent," she observed about the emerging Harlem Renaissance writer who twice had stopped in the Azores while on his recent, epic Atlantic crossings. "You probably already know that Mr. Hunt has been transferred to the diplomatic branch and sent to Liberia," she reported. "It is a promotion in grade and in salary, yet not exactly the post, or place, he would have chosen. The climate is very trying, but having been in a tropical country, we know how to take some precautions. . . . Perhaps we shall not be there long. . . . We'd just begun to feel at home here and form a few relations. The English group especially, seem to regret our departure — Mais, c'est comme ça dans la service du gouvernment." "I am enclosing something," she went on, that "I wrote the other day which you may publish if you wish. I've signed a 'nom de plume' [probably Iola Gibson] which I have used [before]." Du Bois apparently never ran that unidentified and perhaps controversial piece, but Gibbs Hunt's letter shows a continuing reluctance about revealing her identity in print, possibly embarrassing or discrediting her husband and thus jeopardizing his liveli-hood and reputation. As she so often did, she appended "kind regards to Mrs. Du Bois," with whom she had collaborated a few years before when they raised funds for the Fourth Pan-African Congress.

What should have been the Gibbs-Hunts' fairly short trip to Monrovia, Liberia, turned into a seriocomic odyssey, far more extended and convoluted than their longer (in distance) and briefly hazardous voyage to the Azores. "My first concern," wrote Billy, "was to ascertain the available steamship con-nections between the Azores and West African ports," but soon he learned that there was no direct link at all. So he booked passage on a steamer bound southeast to Funchal, on Portugal's Madeira Islands, planning to transfer there for sub-Saharan Africa. "On the day of my departure," Consul Hunt recalled, "an unusually large party of . . . friends and officials assembled to bid us bon voyage, despite our brief residence in Ponta Delgada." With Ida at his side, he jauntily saluted, "hopped into the Government Launch, which had been placed at my disposal," took it out to board the larger vessel moored farther out, and again set off to sea.

A couple of days later their ship dropped anchor in Funchal's harbor, which seemed ominously quiet, Hunt recalled, since it usually swarmed "with a crowd of noisy boatmen soliciting passengers or offering post cards or other trinkets for sale." The unexpected difficulty, he learned when the captain went ashore and finally reported back (he was gone for so long that Hunt feared he had been "kept as hostage"), was that a popular insurgency, purportedly triggered by the skyrocketing cost of bread, had paralyzed Madeira, and "neither pas-sengers nor cargo would be permitted to land." Despite the captain's fervent pleas to the "revolutionists" who obstructed their dockage that "among the passengers on board was an American Diplomatic Officer who must land at Funchal willy-nilly, to make connections for Liberia," the standoff continued. Heated bargaining and negotiations to defuse the impasse lasted for several days, but, Hunt continued, their captain "alas! was finally compelled to give up the struggle and continue the voyage to Lisbon." So they regrouped, and steamed off toward continental Europe.

Though he knew that the State Department would challenge the greater than anticipated travel expenses he ultimately submitted, Billy Hunt acknowl-edged that he always "had cherished a secret desire to see Portugal," adding that "tradition has it that Ulysses founded a colony on the banks of the Tagus [River] near Lisbon." When he and Ida reached that coastal city and debarked several days later, the United States consul greeted them, and his clerk made the necessary arrangements to accommodate them and facilitate their further travel. That entailed catching a different vessel back to Madeira, then boarding yet another one that would take them on to Liberia. But the next ship from Lisbon to Funchal would not depart for at least two more weeks. While Billy "pretended to have been deeply chagrined by the turn of events," he set out to make the most of the unexpected respite in mainland Portugal.

He and Ida ventured all around the capital of what he called "the tightest little dictatorship in Europe," delving into and reveling in its eclectic history. They visited the "University City of Coimbra," where Premier Salazar had taught economics for many years, and traveled to the north near Oporto (whence came Billy's replacement in the Azores, who had served there with Consul William Yerby), stopping by several nearby villages that over the centuries had "felt the yoke of Christian, Moor, Pagan and Roman." Then they meandered back southward to explore the Moorish architectural marvels at Tomar and Sintra. Lord Byron, Billy Hunt blissfully reported, had once characterized the latter site as "the most blessed spot on the habitable globe." They motored out from Lisbon to the ancient cathedral town of Évora, surrounded by crumbling Roman ruins and nestled amid silvery olive groves and "gorgeous rolling vineyards as far as the eye can see." In all, Billy thought that "the imposing monuments of [that county's] past greatness surpassed in beauty and architecture anything I have seen elsewhere in my travels."

After a "thrilling fortnight" spent rambling through Portugal, he and Ida again set off to sea on a ship headed back to Madeira, but not before ascertaining that Salazar's forces had quashed the minor revolt that had prevented their disembarking the previous month — although, he observed, "the real causes of the uprising, it seems, were political, and not the high price of bread, as first reported." Similar sporadic rebellions that year in unquiet outposts of Portugal's empire bedeviled its military despots. They took no chance of any recurrence of that ancillary Atlantic mutiny, wrote Hunt, having several "gun boats anchored in the harbor, armed soldiers [posted] on the quais, and sentinels on guard before the Government Buildings."

Once they docked, the Gibbs-Hunts contacted the consulate, disregarded the murmurs of unrest, and registered at a quiet hilltop *pensão* from which they could observe "the commodious harbor and beautiful panorama of Funchal." But their travel farce continued unabated when they learned that the steamer on which Billy had booked "for Liberia had sailed the day before [their] arrival, and the next outgoing" ship would not arrive for another half month. He and his fellow consul, however, shrugged, laughed it off, and agreed that "there was nothing to do but to take it easy and try to see something of Madeira while I had the opportunity." Hunt knew that many travelers considered "sun kissed" Madeira the "most fascinating and romantic" of all the Iberian-Atlantic islands, so during their unexpected sojourn, he and Ida negotiated its precipitous slopes in local ox-drawn "sleds" and savored the fine weather and the hospitality of António da Silva Leal, Salazar's interim governor general and the ranking official in the Azores during Hunt's tenure who just had been reassigned to clamp a lid on the simmering turbulence in Madeira.

Billy and Ida Hunt finally departed from Funchal on the SS *Almanzora,* an overpriced, seedy, and perilously small cargo vessel. It struck out almost due south, dropped anchor a few days later at Tenerife in the Spanish Canaries, then went on to Las Palmas, the largest town on Gran Canaria, Tenerife's sister island. There the Hunts debarked and dined with Clifton R. Wharton — the first African American hired by the State Department under the revised regulations of the 1924 Rogers Act — and his family. "I was delighted with this opportunity to have a talk with Consul Wharton, who had previously spent [five years] in Monrovia, and I obtained first hand information relative to conditions at my new post," Hunt later wrote.

"The Consul's word picture," he added about Wharton's account, "was not at all cheerful. I did not fear the climatic conditions, as I had already lived in tropical countries, but ... Liberia's woefully backward state of development ... depressed me painfully." Hunt did not mention, though Wharton must have told him, that two Negro American officials had recently died in Monrovia from virulent tropical fevers, and that renewed "native" uprisings had broken out in Liberia's interior. Far worse, in response to international reports of corruption, the government's fiscal excesses, and its collusion in forced labor, the president and vice president had been compelled to resign. The United States nearly shut down diplomatic relations with the country, while dire economic and political travails further threatened its autonomy. Wharton's blunt assessment of the African republic differed notably both in substance and in style from Du Bois's outrageously sunny appraisal in 1924. Hunt admired and respected Clifton Wharton, the astute, skilled, and handsome young consul, but could not have predicted that almost three decades later he (finally) would become the first African American to rise through the rigidly unwelcoming ranks of his country's foreign service and become an ambassador in Europe.

Wharton's clerk, Lillie Mae Hubbard, who had followed him from Liberia, escorted Billy and Ida on a shopping jaunt in Las Palmas, and the Gibbs-

Hunts stayed overnight at a pleasant hotel. Clifton Wharton's empathetic wife, Harriette, confided in her diary: "What a shame to send such old people to the tropics. . . . They are not anxious to go." At best, Consul Hunt's new assignment reflected the department's callous disregard for the infirmities of age, especially when it came to its African American employees; at worst, it was a deliberate slap in the face to a respected Negro senior foreign service officer. The following day Harriette Wharton further mused, "Can't help but think about the Hunts . . . Clif quite touched too."

With pods of whales undulating in its wake, the *Almanzora* left the Canaries and headed south around Africa's western bulge, past Portugal's Cape Verdes, where the Sahara's sand-gorged winds generate the fiercest Atlantic hurricanes. It veered east toward the mainland, and during the next week dropped anchor along the colonial coast, first in Dakar, Senegal, a port of debarkation for many black people destined for slavery in the Americas, and home, wrote Consul Hunt, of "a number of educated Senegalese." They included France's Gorée Island–born pan-Africanist Deputy Blaise Diagne, whom, Hunt boasted, "I had known intimately." Next came England's tiny Gambia, an alluvial sliver encircled by Senegal, then Conakry, French Guinea, its piers piled high with mountains of dusty peanuts awaiting export. Departing from Conakry the *Almanzora* churned on to the Gibbs-Hunts' penultimate stop at Freetown, capital of the old abolitionist British colony of Sierra Leone — which had terminated its own domestic slavery just three years before — where they left the ship and "passed some time ashore ploughing through its sandy streets." There, the relieved consul and his wife learned that the final leg of their journey to Liberia should take only another day.

But as the *Almanzora* approached Monrovia, disembarkation proved even more perilous than in the Azores. All along that treacherous coastal stretch — the worst expanse of ocean in the world for catastrophic thunderstorms — from the time of the earliest slave traders well into the twentieth century, ships often foundered, even within sight of land, with passengers and crews tragically lost at sea. Because Liberia's capital city had no deepwater harbor, the surfboats of the adept Kru tribesmen who paddled out to ferry newcomers ashore had to contend with sharks, tides, reefs and sandbars, and crashing breakers that could strand new arrivals aboard their vessels for days. The recent visitor George Schuyler, a brilliant but sardonic Negro journalist, soon would write: "Great iron canoes that could hold everybody in a big native town, come puffing into the harbor from across the waters — from distant, strange lands where the people's skins are white. A wonderful place, indeed, Monrovia!"

Voyagers first spied Monrovia's landmark Cape Mesurado (or alternately, Montserrado) lighthouse. Then, Billy Hunt later recalled, he and Ida saw "numerous villas clustered on the hillside set in a background of deep green [that] offered a picturesque scene," but those idyllic vistas conveyed a deceptive impression, and the SS *Almanzora* had to drop anchor "four or five miles out in the open sea." "While our impedimenta were being lowered into the bouncing surf boat," Hunt complained, "some adroit sneak-thief profited by the occasion to purloin both my Kodak and portable typewriter." He suspected that the *Almanzora*'s conniving captain had conspired in and duly benefited from that larceny. The landing boat, he wrote, was manned by "five [oarsmen] on the starboard side and five on the port side, a steersman who stood in the boat's bow, and a headman" ceremonially garbed in stark white robes. It mounted and breached the waves, then plummeted heavily into the troughs between, with queasy passengers clutching at the narrow gunwales for dear life — but finally the Gibbs-Hunts stepped out onto solid land. Starting with their late January departure from São Miguel, that trip, less than halfway across the Atlantic, took nearly two months. If, as Consul Hunt admiringly contended, Portugal was indeed the efficient and nurturing "Mother of Navigators," that venerable mistress of the seas had been lackadaisical, incompetent, even conspiratorially obstructive during their protracted 1931 voyage.

William Henry Hunt, nearing retirement but formally transferred at last from the consular service into the diplomatic corps, stood on the brink of becoming the first United States foreign service officer to complete the triangulated Azores-Madagascar-Liberia circuit of appointments offered as a pitiful sop to able and ambitious African American internationalists. And at that point, as Clifton Wharton, the good-natured but already sage young consul, had counseled him, "There was nothing to do but trust your luck and face the music."

10

Liberia, 1931–1932

Negative Forces, Forced Labor, Forced Out

The Yankee Consul is the man
  Who lives a life of ease;
He dwells down in the Yucatan
  Or in the Caribees;
He mingles with the mild Chinee,
  Or savage Fuzzy-Wuzz;
He even goes to gay Paree,
  And this is all he does:
...
He shivers in Siberia
  For many weary moons;
He sizzles in Liberia
  And dances with the coons;
Where camel bells go ting-a-ling
  And Afric skeeters buzz,
Why this is every blessed thing
  The Yankee Consul does.
—George Horton, "The Yankee
Consul," *Saturday Evening Post,*
April 19, 1924

Despite any lurking misgivings W. E. B. Du Bois may have had, he announced his friend Consul William Henry Hunt's 1931 transfer to Liberia with ample fanfare in *Crisis* magazine: "William Hunt, senior Negro Foreign Service Member stationed at St. Michael, has been reassigned as consul and second secretary of the American Legation at Monrovia under minister Charles E. Mitchell. Mr. Hunt . . . entered the diplomatic service nearly forty [actually, thirty-three] years ago. He has not simply been transferred to Liberia, but transferred out of the consular service into the diplomatic service at a salary of $4,000." That annual stipend was in keeping with Hunt's new assignment and appointment level, but was nonetheless an almost humiliating pittance. Mitchell, the recently arrived American chief of mission, received $10,000, and $4,000 was what the State Department had paid the first diplomatic representatives whom it sent to Liberia in the 1860s, despite nearly seven decades of continuing inflation since. Yet given his country's and the world's deteriorating economic circumstances during the Great Depression, that meager remuneration was, nonetheless, a blessing. *Opportunity,* the National Urban League's race-conscious monthly magazine, editorialized at the time: "Only in Liberia, where the physical hazards are well nigh insuperable, are American Negro citizens represented in the diplomatic service above the grade of consul. And even the consular service is now practically closed to Negro youth."

Between February 1898, when Hunt and his future father-in-law, M. W. Gibbs, took charge of the consulate in Madagascar, and March 1931, when William Henry Hunt and Ida Gibbs Hunt reached Monrovia, his career had taken him many places, but after two decades at a respected, if ancillary, post in France, it progressed in an ultimately descending arc. The State Department sent Hunt to Guadeloupe, which he considered a desolate Antillean outpost of French colonialism, and then on to the diplomatically insignificant Azores. At last it assigned him, as it did virtually all its few black employees, to troubled, disease-plagued Liberia. Since first granting the republic limited diplomatic recognition during the Civil War, the department dispatched more Negroes there than everyplace else in the world combined, and for men of any age that often reviled post almost never provided a stepping-stone for career advancement. Hunt avoided it for over thirty years, though perhaps it was preordained that at some point before his retirement he too would be sent there. When that finally happened, he was almost sixty-eight, and what a grim departure gift Liberia proved to be.

During the more than three decades that Hunt served as "the Yankee consul," an array of African Americans had represented their country in Liberia, but for most, unlike Hunt, that was the only assignment the foreign service ever offered them. In 1897 President William McKinley had appointed the African Methodist Episcopal Zion (AMEZ) Reverend Owen Lun West Smith as minister resident and consul general, and he stayed four years, a little longer than did M. W. Gibbs in Madagascar. In 1903 the department abruptly recalled Smith's successor, Missouri's Dr. John R. A. Crossland, following a battery of bizarre criminal charges made against him by the host nation, including assault, fraud, housebreaking, even "wife stealing." The Reverend Ernest Lyon, who was born in British Honduras and then settled in Maryland, fared better. In 1908 he persuaded Liberia's president to pay tribute to Booker T. Washington by ordaining him a knight of the National Order of African Redemption, a tribute that the country previously had bestowed only on white men. During Lyon's tenure in Liberia, however, his wife died from yellow fever. A number of grieving Monrovians deemed her funeral the year's most memorable event. The leaders of Liberia's government developed such excellent rapport with Reverend Lyon that since they had no other diplomatic representation in the United States, he became the African nation's official spokesperson after returning home.

During the Liberian assignments of Lyon and his successor, William Demos Crum, another physician and a political activist, who had tried to retard the post-Reconstruction assaults on civil rights in his native South Carolina, Benjamin O. Davis became the chief military attaché. Davis barely survived blackwater fever — a form of malaria so named for the patient's dark, murky urine resulting from acute kidney malfunction. Like his fellow Negro officer Charles Denton Young, who both preceded and succeeded him in Liberia, Davis had previously been assigned to the Philippines during the U.S. Army's harsh suppression of those islands' indigenous independence struggles following the Spanish-American War. In those same years Richard C. Bundy became the State Department's second in command in Monrovia, and after Lieutenant Davis, Major Young returned to serve under Crum. The post and title of military attaché there was hardly nominal, since Young, whom devoted comrades described as an officer who "swore like a trooper and drank like a gentleman," sustained a grave gunshot wound while leading an attempt by the Liberian central government's ill-equipped, ill-prepared, and abusive Frontier Force militia to suppress a disruptive inland "native" insurrection. As for Crum, his medical training notwithstanding and despite taking all reasonable preventive measures, he too fell victim to one of the region's deadly diseases and passed away not long after his late-1911 return to the United States.

The next year George Washington Buckner, yet another physician (with few Western-trained doctors of their own, most Liberians welcomed such medical expertise), succeeded Crum. Buckner's memoranda to his superiors in Washington alerted them to the Liberian administration's culpability in what he considered slave trading, and he suggested that the United States assume control of the republic for seven years to impose critical reforms. He was followed by James L. Curtis, who died in 1917 a few weeks after departing from Monrovia. At that juncture, his widow, Helen, headed off to help her country (and race) in France during the Great War. Like Ida Gibbs Hunt, she soon emerged as a Du Boisian pan-Africanist, and returned to teach in Liberia through 1927.

Richard Bundy had stepped in as the chief American minister on an interim basis in 1912–13, and then assumed that post again several years later. His anthology "Folk-Tales from Liberia" (1919), with its stories of medicine men, arrogant or crafty kings who traded their slaves for guns from Europe, and such pearls of wisdom as "You should never curse the crocodile . . . until you have crossed the river," reflects a deep immersion in his adopted homeland's indigenous culture; yet he too reiterated earlier accusations about the Liberian government's venal connivance in unfree labor. In 1919 President Woodrow Wilson sent a rare Negro Democrat, Dr. Joseph Johnson, to Monrovia, and his stay encompassed Charles D. Young's return, as a full colonel, after the army had deactivated him throughout the recent war and thus denied him the opportunity to distinguish himself as a battlefield leader. Military higher-ups thereby successfully avoided further promoting Young—which would have made him his nation's first African American general. He died in 1922 while on a ceremonial military reconnaissance tour in nearby colonial Nigeria.

The next envoy sent to Monrovia was New Jersey's Solomon Porter Hood, an African Methodist Episcopal (AME) minister, NAACP stalwart, and former missionary in Haiti. In 1924, soon after Du Bois visited the Gibbs-Hunts in St.-Étienne, Hood greeted and feted the editor, who, as the United States emissary to C. D. B. King's presidential inaugural, was granted the notably pretentious title of special representative of the president, envoy extraordinary, and minister plenipotentiary. Lillie Mae Hubbard, the Mississippi-born daughter of Baptist evangelists in Liberia who became Du Bois's correspondent, had started working at the consulate in 1922 as a clerk, while Carleton Wall, who later joined Hunt in the Azores, arrived soon after. The perceived romance of "returning" to West Africa, whence came some of his unidentifiable ancestors, quite enthralled Du Bois. He thought that the self-governing Negro republic, where his idol Alexander Crummell had lived and worked for years, virtually embodied his pan-African dreams, but also believed that its central government needed to constrain the sometimes obstreperous tribal chiefs.

Du Bois's stateside antagonist Marcus Garvey, though incarcerated in a federal penitentiary at the time, still hoped to "repatriate" thousands of his Universal Negro Improvement Association (UNIA) devotees in Liberia, but white administrators in the neighboring colonies had protested to President King that they opposed any settlement of Garveyites, who were assumed, one Englishman complained, to be "working for the overthrow of European supremacy in Africa." So King, Du Bois, and Hood (encouraged by the outspoken Helen Curtis) colluded to thwart the Garveyites' reinvigorated "back-to-Africa" ambitions.

Clifton R. Wharton arrived in 1925 and spent the next five years as consul and chargé d'affaires. The perceptive and outspoken Henry Carter also represented his country in Liberia, though alcoholism would derail his foreign service career, while C. E. Macy served as acting minister until 1927. William Treyanne Francis took charge after James G. Carter, the longtime consular officer who had replaced Hunt in Madagascar, flatly declined the appointment. Francis, a lawyer from Minnesota, repeated the increasingly familiar accusations of government collusion in exploiting unfree labor first made a decade before by Buckner and Bundy, then reiterated and reinforced by Wharton. Francis reported to the State Department: "Officials of the Liberian Government have knowledge of, are engaged in, and are making large sums of money by the exportation of forced labor which has developed into a condition analogous to slavery. . . . I do not think that this Republic will ever be a success until the United States, or some other Government equally as friendly, picks it up and shakes it into a realization of its stupidity." A young clerk named William C. George, who persevered to become a foreign service officer sixteen years later, arrived just as Consul General Francis passed away in mid-1929.

Liberia's adverse health conditions and woeful medical care took a heavy toll both on the locals and on transients, including those sent by the U.S. Department of State, who had little or no resistance to the region's diseases. Its employees or members of their families died there (at least) in 1866, 1882, 1886, 1891, 1893, 1910, 1912, 1917, 1929, and 1930.

In 1930 Samuel Reber Jr., a white man dispatched to Liberia from a post in Peru, took charge of the Monrovia legation on an interim basis, and he joined Wharton in continuing to facilitate negotiations with recently arrived representatives of the Firestone Tire and Rubber Company. Charles E. Mitchell replaced Reber early in 1931, at which time the State Department upgraded his title from minister resident and consul general to the far more exalted envoy extraordinary and minister plenipotentiary. Mitchell was a garrulous, Maryland-born accountant, banker, and college administrator who had relocated to West Virginia. His previous international experience was limited to a brief term on the United States government's advisory Virgin Islands Commission, followed by his collection and dispersal of private humanitarian and financial aid (much like the Gibbs-Marshalls' philanthropy) for suffering Haitians pursuant to the American military occupation of their country. The United States' official relations with Liberia, however, had become so fraught with tension and mistrust that the department instructed Mitchell not to present his credentials to the republic's president at all, thus undermining the new envoy's authority and effectiveness. Despite his efforts to counter the situation, Mitchell occupied an anomalous position as chief emissary to the sovereign government of an autonomous nation that his own country refused to fully recognize.

Long before there was a country called Liberia, fifteenth-century Portuguese sailors had been the first Europeans to reach the region. Then the international Atlantic slave trade flourished there for nearly four hundred years, as it did all along black Africa's coasts. In 1822 the American Colonization Society (ACS), an organization founded, funded, and overseen by affluent whites with the mission of sending Negroes "back to Africa" as a preferred alternative to emancipating them within the United States (where many slaveholders feared endemic servile insurrections such as the ones that had beset Haiti), sponsored a settlement near the southwest corner of equatorial Africa's Atlantic bulge and called it Monrovia, to honor President James Monroe. The ACS merged that territory with others, expanded it until it about equaled in size the state of Tennessee, named it Liberia, meaning land of freedom, and joined forces with United States government authorities to dispatch several politically well-connected white men to serve as the early governors. From the time of their arrival, most of those Americans, white and "colored" alike, complained about the "native problem," in large part because the "uncivilized" indigenous people understandably resisted appropriation of their land and attempts to usurp their traditional mores and livelihoods.

In 1847 Liberia became an independent republic with the recently manumitted, Virginia-born quadroon Joseph J. Roberts installed as the first president. A number of black American leaders, such as Martin Delany and Alexander Crummell, acted on their pan-African convictions and lived and worked there in the mid-1800s, while in the period following the United States' general emancipation of its slaves, thousands more aspiring freedmen headed over to the young country. English served as the official language; the flag almost replicated the Stars and Stripes, except that it featured only a single large white star on a deep blue field; and the constitution was modeled closely on that of its sponsor nation, although the Liberian document, by contrast, iterated that "none but Negroes or persons of Negro descent shall be admitted to citizenship of this Republic."

By the Civil War's end, the ACS had sent nearly twenty thousand settlers to Liberia. A few black American emigrants also ventured off to Haiti, or later Cuba, while others, like the Gibbses, had gone to Canada. But many of the new pioneers who sought social and economic mobility and an escape from their own country's pervasive racism in "mother Africa" died there or returned home ailing, disillusioned, and poorer than when they had left. Although some of the men had children with or even married indigenous Liberian women, the resituated Negro American population did not replace itself. The newcomers' mortality rate was extremely high because they had no immunity to yellow fever or malaria, which was (and until the recent AIDS epidemic, remained) the region's most prodigious killer. By 1900 they and their linear kin numbered scarcely fifteen thousand.

Conflicts simmered and then burst to the surface. The "colored" interlopers from the United States declared themselves "white," proposed to bring Christianity and "civilization" to the "natives," and callously manipulated the central government. Those African Americans, reconfigured as Americo-Liberians, and tribes such as the Bassa, G'debo, Gola, Kissi, Kpelle, Kru, Loma, and Vai, continued to confront one another. Indigenous Africans made up more than 95 percent of the republic's populace, but with unparalleled longevity, the Americo-Liberians' True Whig Party retained its hegemony from 1870 until after World War II. It segregated the majority (much as lawmakers in the southern United States enacted and imposed Jim Crow regulations), collected their taxes, appropriated their labor, conspired to reconfigure and regiment their lives, and denied the "natives" — and all women — any voting rights. Centuries of slave trading had stripped West Africa of many of its best and brightest and undermined its traditional societies, so the more recently arrived American Negroes were able to take advantage of longstanding intratribal feuds. They combined coercion and superior weapon power with meager material enticements, and resorted to methods of control that quite resembled those that the imperial European nations employed in their colonies.

In 1917, almost concurrently with and to appease the United States, Liberia's government declared war on Germany, which at that time was one of its best (and very few) trading partners. It sent a small contingent of troops to assist the Entente in Europe, and an Allied forces naval station operated along the coast for two years. In retaliation, German U-boats heavily shelled Monrovia.

While the True Whigs abused their authority to quash any political opposition, they otherwise were notably less effective and often faced bitter "native" uprisings, not unlike those that Europe's colonial forces strove to tamp down elsewhere on the continent. Liberia's administrators found themselves in the unenviable position of trying to establish and maintain a modern industrial and capitalist "Western" state with few industries, little capital, escalating public debts, and a meager, agriculturally based economy in a region where parasitic trypanosomiasis, or sleeping sickness (often fatal to the draft animals needed for clearing and cultivating the land), was endemic. Except for some peanuts, palm oil, and coffee, the nation produced nothing that other countries would buy. Public vice and fraud abounded; the administration of justice often was corrupt, incompetent, or vindictive; and grievous sanitary conditions generated wellsprings of pestilence. Liberia's colonial neighbors encroached on its sovereign territory, and the infrastructure was poor to non-existent, making communications and inland transportation and development well nigh impossible. Nonetheless, the republic had survived for almost a century.

Into this abyss galloped the Ohio-based Firestone Tire and Rubber Company and its wholly owned African subsidiary, called the Firestone Plantations Company, which kicked off its operations in 1926. Liberia's appeal for Firestone was that it lay in the world's narrow equatorial belt where rubber trees thrived, and the United States needed rubber. And unlike other such locales, Liberia fell under that country's sphere of influence and was not the colony of an imperial European nation. With the legation's representatives serving as intermediaries, Firestone's executives negotiated an agreement with the Liberian government, promising payment for the use of up to a million acres on which they (actually, their "native" laborers) would plant and cultivate rubber trees, tap them, and harvest, minimally process, and export the pallid, spongy latex. The company also consolidated much of Liberia's debilitating international debt with an interest-bearing megaloan of its own; brought in Euro-American overseers, engineers, surveyors, and agronomists; and became the nation's largest employer, vowing to improve communications and electrical services, build sewers, roads, rail lines, hospitals, and schools, and refill the national coffers. It accomplished almost none of those things, but created pristine residential enclaves — white Ohio islands of "civilization" on Firestone's plantations amid a "primitive" black African sea — for its managers and their skittish wives. Until the discovery of offshore oil in the 1970s, rubber remained the republic's most important industry. But unfortunately for Firestone and its African hosts, the worldwide Depression deflated rubber's market price, well below the costs of production.

Late in 1929, in response to contesting howls of protest from both human rights advocates and defenders of Liberia's autonomy, the League of Nations — to which, unlike the United States, Liberia belonged — prepared to dispatch a delegation to inspect, investigate, and report on allegations of governmentally sanctioned forced labor in nearby Spanish, Portuguese, and French colonies, on the Firestone plantations, and in the private domains of the republic's leading politicians. Cuthbert Christy (the League's three-man commission informally bore his name), a peevish English practitioner who specialized in tropical medicine, ostensibly headed the team. Christy pooh-

poohed the possibility of continued Liberian self-rule and argued that white men must be brought in to govern, because, he insisted, the republic was a century behind Europe in its development — then he gratuitously threw in that "U.S. Negroes were a hundred years behind whites." The second member was Arthur Barclay, Liberia's feeble onetime president, who since leaving office had become Monrovia's leading private attorney. As well as anyone, he understood his country's singular history, culture, and politics.

Choosing the third member of the commission was more difficult. The secretary of war's former special assistant Emmett Jay Scott, by then a top Howard University administrator who had visited Liberia in the early 1900s, and W. E. B. Du Bois were both suggested for the designated Negro American position. Scott declined, and federal officials nixed Du Bois. With those two out of contention, Charles Spurgeon Johnson, a former National Urban League director of research and founding editor of its journal *Opportunity*, and a sociologist at Fisk University, was nominated as the third member. With President Hoover's preapproval, the League of Nations appointed Professor Johnson to fill the slot.

Early in 1930 Johnson went first to the League's headquarters in Switzerland for a briefing before journeying on to sub-Saharan West Africa. Despite onerous personal, bureaucratic, and environmental obstacles, he traveled widely throughout Liberia and interviewed scores of the country's tribesmen, Americo-Liberians in both the public and private sectors, and members of the State Department's contingent in Monrovia, including Henry Carter, who, Johnson unhappily recalled, arrived at their sessions "half tanked," then rambled on and on about the republic's woeful deterioration. Johnson observed and documented conditions all around Liberia and began to compile his findings.

Virtually alone, Charles S. Johnson prepared and wrote the commission's final report. He emphasized the gaping cultural, economic, and power gulfs between the indigenous majority (with whom he sympathized) and the Americo-Liberian minority (with whom he did not), though a number of Negroes both in the United States and in Africa attacked him for those supposed biases and his subsequent judgments. He not only acknowledged the "natives'" implicit disempowerment but, as many whites and blacks already had, he further suggested that their vulnerability might require aggressive intervention by the League of Nations, the United States, or one or more of the European powers, to protect them from the presumably dire predations of modern life.

The Christy Commission's most disturbing conclusion was that Liberia's officials at least tolerated, and routinely benefited from, forms of involuntary labor that closely resembled slavery. The commission absolved Firestone (perhaps overgenerously so, though its offenses did not approach those of Belgian overseers who had maimed or killed myriad Congolese rubber plantation workers around the turn of the century) of any untoward practices, but it determined that in many instances the country's administrators demanded several months a year of coerced labor from the indigenous people, who often were abused, tortured, or forced to work without pay. In addition, one of the republic's, notably its Americo-Liberian leaders', few sources of income came from supplying indentured laborers for the cocoa plantations on the nearby Spanish island of Fernando Po, and in several French and Portuguese coastal colonies. Thousands of native Liberians, many of them mere boys corralled by the central government's brutal Frontier Force, toiled there under appalling conditions. Perhaps half died, others became ill or were seriously injured, and the twenty-five-dollars-a-head acquisition fees — munificent sums in the meager African economy — from that trade in human labor ended up in the pockets of leading politicians. The report that the League of Nations' investigators compiled characterized such practices as barely distinguishable from slave trafficking. Charles Johnson also recorded and put forth evidence of coerced concubinage, or sexual slavery, as well as imposition of the practice called "pawning," in which women, children, and other vulnerable individuals were placed under the aegis of powerful persons in exchange for monetary loans or forgiveness of debts.

On reviewing Johnson's account, however, Du Bois — defensive of the country's autonomy and fixated on maintaining its leaders' imperiled reputations — contended in *Crisis* that "pawning is . . . a method by which native children are adopted into civilized Liberian families for purposes of education." Very tactfully and with deference to the revered editor, Johnson replied that Du Bois confused "pawning" and "adoption." Others also protested that Johnson misinterpreted what he saw, and insisted that those were traditional, necessary, well-accepted sorts of interpersonal contractual relationships throughout West Africa, and really did amount to benevolent adoptions, in which the "pawns" in essence became family members and then worked (indefinitely) as domestic servants — purportedly in exchange for their own personal protection and betterment.

Although President C. D. B. King and Vice President Allen Yancy maintained their own ignorance and innocence, and professed shock at the commission's findings, the new scandals, combined with long-term fiscal mismanagement or malfeasance, soon brought about their forced resignations, thus deflecting the legislature's threats of impeachment. Everyone knew that the King-Yancy regime had ruled with an iron hand. It rigged elections, censored mail, and tolerated little free press or free speech. Waste and graft abounded, government employees routinely plundered the "uncivilized" majority to enrich themselves, and the friable infrastructure was crumbling. At that juncture Edwin Barclay — Liberia's secretary of state and the very embodiment of nepotism, since he was a favorite nephew of the former president, who was himself a member of the Christy Commission — stepped in as the new leader. The second president Barclay started by restructuring his administration to emulate even further the means and methods that European powers had used for decades in governing their African colonies and controlling their "native" populations. His tenure began auspiciously, with promises of sweeping reforms and the swift excision of public corruption. But year after year (he assumed the presidency by fiat in 1930, was elected two years later, and remained in office through 1944) Edwin Barclay arrogated more and more power unto himself, and quickly became as omnipotent a ruler as his patently corrupt predecessors.

Intermittently, though for nearly two decades, Department of State representatives in Liberia had informed their superiors in Washington about the republic's endemic civil wrongs. But the issuance of the commission's report and the escalating improprieties it exposed generated a greater outpouring of diverse opinion and protest from African Americans than any prior international development. Some even protested that the findings advanced Firestone's interests because exporting workers to nearby European colonies depleted the company's indigenous labor supply and provided the Americo-Liberian administration with a stabilizing source of income. That, it was tortuously argued, served to mitigate the white American rubber czars' clout.

Black American clergymen (especially Baptists, AMEs, and AMEZs) had founded most of Liberia's churches and schools and played major roles there in religion and education. Determined to maintain their power bases and maximize their influence, they too leaped into the heated debate. The churchmen claimed that they alone had the wherewithal and moral authority needed to teach, "civilize," and shepherd the region's pagan majority into the arms of Jesus. They bombarded the United States government with criticism and judgments similar to those of State Department representatives, but opposed any League of Nations involvement that might undercut their own authority and appear to sell out Liberia to alien contingents. Some Negro Americans, Du Bois prominent among them, however, advocated the separation of church and state; mistrusted the clergy, parochial schooling, and all religion; and characterized the "missionary enterprise as the hand-maiden of capitalistic and imperialistic designs."

Du Bois and others who shared his emerging socialist convictions also claimed, as did Negro Americans of various political stripes, that Liberia must be viewed within a global context of the Western powers' colonial histories and racist practices. A few years before the Liberian scandal erupted, his own Pan-African Congresses had excoriated all residual forms of quasi-slavery or peonage, but Du Bois contended that this new flap over forced labor downplayed, forgave, or ignored similar practices rampant elsewhere. To develop and maintain their African colonies' infrastructures, for many decades the French had, in fact, shuttled innumerable black workers around to distant locales and imposed harsh annual work requirements (*prestations* or *corvées*) on the "natives" — as, for example, to, from, and within colonial Madagascar before, during, and after Hunt's tenure there. In the March 1931 issue of *Crisis,* which came out as Ida and Billy Hunt arrived in Liberia, Du Bois wrote: "[S]lavery in Liberia, slavery in the Belgian Congo, slavery in the British, French and Spanish Colonies of Africa, slavery in British Burma and in Latin America, are all detestable institutions which must be abolished. Liberia is no more guilty than England." He was right, of course, and the southern United States' peonage and convict-leasing initiatives were quite similar and equally as heinous, but there was no reasonable justification or excuse for Liberia's dreadful black-on-black abuses.

To compete or even inch toward parity with Europe and the United States, the neo-Marxist continued, Americo-Liberians needed to modernize and industrialize their country, and thus had to employ some sort of forced labor to vie with the Western powers on the inherently unlevel international playing fields. White people's condemnations of Liberia, Du Bois protested, were hypocritical, and its leaders had been wrongly singled out for censure. He viewed its indigenous workforce as a resource that must be developed in the context of a rising black modernity. Such advancements, he argued, would benefit the "darker races" in their entirety and prove that Negroes were capable of infinite progress, including successful self-government characterized by humane policies, fiscal responsibility, sound leadership and management — though racists and racism impeded such efforts both in the United States and wherever nonwhites tried to advance anywhere in the world. Du Bois's rhetoric implied that he equated any criticism, or even frank appraisals, by Negro Americans of the ruling Americo-Liberians with disloyalty to the race.

But one thing on which most black people in the United States and West Africa agreed was that whites, at home or abroad, within government and without, could and would manipulate the Christy Commission's findings to claim that people of color were inherently incapable of self-rule, and Liberia therefore should be deprived of its independence. Other than Haiti, which remained under American occupation, and Ethiopia, the Horn of Africa's feudal monarchy—incessantly eyed by covetous Italy—whose sovereigns blithely insisted that they really were not Negroes, Liberia was the world's only autonomous black nation. Du Bois argued that France and England, which had annexed great swaths of Liberia's borderlands that abutted their own colonies in the decades leading up to the Great War, hoped to overthrow and bring down any "independent government . . . on the west coast of Africa." He implied that although a distinguished African American social scientist researched and wrote the report, and humanitarian concerns for the indigenous people may have prompted it, it was driven by vested economic interests (the Firestone Company's) and white supremacist assumptions much like those that facilitated the repellent, ongoing segregationist practices within the United States.

Others in the black American press also made their voices heard, with several newspaper editors or columnists heading over to Liberia to observe firsthand and report on what all the commotion was about. First they tested the waters of public opinion at home, mulled over and responded to input from their African American readers, then tried to influence their government's policies toward the African republic. The NAACP's *Crisis*, the National Urban League's *Opportunity*, and several black-owned-and-operated weekly papers challenged the Christy Commission to investigate the venal forced labor practices that detrimentally affected Negroes within the United States—but that, of course, did not happen.

George S. Schuyler, an up-and-coming black journalist, wrote for the *Pittsburgh Courier*, and his columns ran elsewhere in the minority press as well. For the purpose of delving into the Liberian scandal, however, the *New York Post*, a major mainstream publication, put him on its hefty payroll. For more than a month early in 1931, Schuyler nosed around Monrovia and Liberia's hinterlands, in search of valid information as well as hearsay or gossip—and he ferreted out plenty of both. Schuyler's articles appeared that summer in the *Post,* and later in the year he published his inflammatory allegorical novel *Slaves Today.* With his muckraking journalism as well as his thinly disguised fiction, he excoriated the True Whig Party, including Edwin Barclay's new, "reformed" regime. Many of the republic's powerful men, Schuyler charged, tolerated or even participated in polygamy, made tribal women their sexual slaves, and otherwise abused them. Coercion, corruption, and vice, he wrote, flourished in Monrovia, and his own government's representatives sometimes acted in complicity with local administrators. His revelations roiled the muddy waters and escalated the rancor of an already bitter debate. The best solution, Schuyler contended, was for the United States to bite the bullet, act like the imperial power it already was, and assume full control over Liberia.

George Schuyler and William Henry Hunt may well have met each other in Liberia, but neither left a record of any such encounter. After their meandering voyage from the Azores, the Gibbs-Hunts disembarked in late March 1931, a few weeks after Schuyler and the new minister, Charles Mitchell, arrived and just as internal and international circumstances vis-à-vis the republic were tumbling into chaos — with worse to come. On a personal level, obviously expecting a warmer reception, Hunt fretted in his memoir that "no arrangements whatever had been made to receive me." In addition, despite his prior conversation with Consul Wharton in the Canaries and other preparatory boning up, the conditions that Hunt found truly shocked him.

Urban Monrovia, with its population barely topping ten thousand, had no sidewalks. Imposing boulevards, he observed, had been laid out, but "they are for the most part overgrown with grass or projecting rocks and too rough for the few cars in the town to pass over them." Its foremost avenue wound past the white-sided, red tile–roofed homes of the country's leaders, as well as the American, British, and other European (including the Vatican) legations, through verdant coastal slopes that plunged into the Atlantic, then petered out near a promontory marked by the Cape Mesurado lighthouse, amid squalid waterside ghettoes known as Vai, Kru, and Congo Towns. The official "Western" city had troubles aplenty of its own, but those settlements where many indigenous people dwelled had become especially fertile incubators for insect-, rodent-, and waterborne diseases, and were far more wretched than the Hoovervilles that sprang up like weeds on the fringes and parklands of many American cities as the Great Depression intensified. For both of the Gibbs-Hunts, even on its best days, Monrovia seemed a far cry from idyllic São Miguel.

While trying to obtain housing, they fell victim to a prevalent racket in which a property owner declared himself willing to rent out one of his run-down holdings, but the potential lessee had to pay in advance for exorbitant repairs. In this case, the needed renovations proved so extensive that Billy and Ida's new home remained uninhabitable for three months, but they finally set up and held sway over a sizable household. Like most others in the diplomatic community and the more affluent Americo-Liberians, in addition to a nonresident daily laundress, the Gibbs-Hunts employed at least five in help, including a cook, a night watchman, a yard man, and a "boy" named Ernest who served as their chauffeur, though automobiles in the entire country, with its total population approaching two million, numbered only a couple of hundred. Their live-in maid, who cleaned their quarters and attended to a variety of personal tasks, had accompanied them from the Azores. To live in such an apparently opulent fashion, the Gibbs-Hunts surely had to supplement Billy's meager government salary with some of Ida's carefully nurtured inheritance and investment income.

Consul Hunt groused about the distressing "light fingered propensities of the average Liberian boy." On a pitch black night — oil lamps lit most of Monrovia's private homes, and its public spaces had virtually no illumination at all — soon after establishing his residence, Hunt reported, one such youth "stripped stark naked, then jumped over the neighbor's fence and dived under [our] house to steal the clothing off the clothes line. . . . His purpose was to dress himself with as many tropical suits of clothing as possible and walk off with them." Although Hunt's sentry apprehended that one pint-sized and clownishly overdressed bandit, the consul petulantly continued, "I was obliged to contend with such petty annoyances constantly."

Billy Hunt described the prototypical brick or stucco residences "occupied by the whites" (like most longtime and new Monrovians, Hunt referred to the Americo-Liberians as well as all Westerners, himself and his wife included, as "whites") as being constructed atop pillars "three to six feet above ground." Despite some of the early Negro settlers' efforts to replicate for themselves in West Africa the columned porticos and broad verandas that characterized the southern United States' antebellum plantation mansions, the local elite seldom built their houses from wood anymore because it had become prohibitively expensive and also, wrote Hunt, provided "hiding places for the destructive pest known in those countries as the 'white ant'" — or termite. In addition, he went on, "a host of pests and constant irritants . . . squeeze the joy out of life."

Moths eat holes in all one's clothing, cockroaches devour your book bindings and make nests in the kitchen, enormous rats find their way to the most unheard of places . . . the redoubtable driver ants form a procession . . . on which occasions every other living thing . . . must vacate [the residence] on shortest notice, from the head of the house to the family angora. . . . Jiggers bore under the soles of the feet and lay their eggs, insect bites and heat produce a rash against which the most flimsy clothes feels like nettles, a very distressing itch called "dhobies" [a tropical ringworm] makes its appearance. . . . Other [vermin] are annoying under any circumstances, but when seen through the haze of a tropical "touch of sun" or the blur of a pernicious fever, they assume proportions out of all reason.

Supplementing those pestilent intrusions, Hunt recalled, "the bad odors, the mists and sounds get on one's nerves, the damp, silent, drooping, thick green forests on every side close in on one like a deep smothering sepulchre." "Under such circumstances," he glumly added, "the mind even grows sick, and the body quickly follows." The city had few sewerage facilities and little clean water, and telephone and electric services functioned haphazardly; the only bank was run by Firestone, in its own interests. The *New York Times* reported at the time that "heaps of refuse are allowed to accumulate all over the town," adding that "there is a shocking absence of sanitary arrangements and in consequence, outbreaks of yellow fewer are of constant occurrence." "Today in Liberia," the article concluded, "sanitation simply does not exist."

The "native" diet, Hunt recounted, was limited to peanuts, shreds of fish or poultry, "rice, manioc, palm oil, coffee, bananas, plantains, sugarcane, bread fruit, coconuts, and greens of different varieties." To those basics, Americo-Liberians and other "whites" added "beans, carrots, watermelons, turnips, corn," as well as staples that had to be imported from overseas, including "potatoes, sugar, flour, oats, milk, butter, salt, cheese, [and] canned fruits." Parasites infested the cattle and swine, so such meat was unsafe, expensive, and of inferior taste. Hunt suggested eating "more often and less heartily than in the homeland." And though he recognized that liquor could provide a dangerous and seductive relief (as exemplified by Vice Consul Henry Carter's boozy dependency, which must have been exacerbated by the State Department's blanket refusal to offer him any opportunities for career advancement) from Monrovia's pervasive tedium, Hunt insisted that the "moderate use of alcohol is not wholly harmful in the tropics," and also maintained that physical exercise was essential to one's health and well-being.

Monrovia, he reported, had "no theatres, movie houses or night clubs, [and] only occasionally a newspaper." "There is no railroad in Liberia," Hunt added, "the only country on the West coast [of Africa] without this form of transportation," but he failed to explain that elsewhere on the continent Europe's colonial overlords impressed "native" laborers to construct and maintain such rail lines. He recalled the challenges of traveling into the unwelcoming, almost impenetrable interior "by foot, hammock, or on horseback over narrow trails, sometimes leading through swamps, across rivers, or over steep hills" — something that most Americo-Liberians and outsiders were reluctant to do. Despite occasional balmy days, the weather usually was torrid. Pith helmets for the men and parasols for any and all "white" women were considered virtual necessities, as they had been in Madagascar, to protect them from the blazing equatorial sun, but every year the region also endured a wiltingly humid, seven-month wet season characterized by a drenching 175 inches of annual rainfall accompanied by formidable flooding.

Much that Consul Hunt encountered in the country distressed him, although he had, and expressed, great compassion for its travails. He had little sympathy with the Firestone company, but resigned himself to the fact that, for the foreseeable future, the United States' extensive financial interests guaranteed that "Firestone is in Liberia to stay." "Unless the League of Nations can suggest some practical plan of meeting the difficult clauses of the Firestone Loan Agreement," he added in his memoir, "there seems to be lots of future trouble in store." Absent the company's resumption and more rigorous execution of its "original program of planting and development, [any] dreams of a Utopian Negro Republic . . . would be further away than ever."

Hunt acknowledged the longstanding hopes of "devising a new civilization for Negro West Africa," but recognized that the Americo-Liberians antagonized and did little to encourage the "confidence of the hinterlanders, without which no constructive development can be accomplished." Lacking such cooperation, he wrote, "the native problem would remain as serious as ever." The administration needed critical infusions of "new blood [to maintain the] tottering state of Independence." "I venture to say," he continued, "that the natives, intelligently and humanely advised and directed, can do a great deal for the lasting benefit of both races [thereby again categorizing the Americo-Liberians as at least "nonblack," if not actually "white"] as has been shown in other parts of tropical Africa."

Hunt also (but only later, safely in retrospect) reproached his own country: "The United States Government has hindered other nations from interfering in Liberia's domestic affairs, but has done nothing whatever to remedy the internal abuses. . . . The American policy of hands off seems to imply that 'Uncle Sam' would gladly be relieved of his responsibility towards the little black Republic." Hunt sided with those who advocated some sort of external intervention, but wanted to see such efforts initiated only to reensure Liberia's long-term autonomy, and he cautioned that "European nations . . . interested in the development of West Africa would not sit idly by and see such a large area of Africa with its 350 miles of coastline, remain commercially stagnant and unproductive." He suggested that "an effective administration should be inaugurated by the appointment of . . . Commissioners and Military Instructors chosen by the United States Government," or failing that, by "the designation of European Commissioners under the League of Nations." Like many other Negroes, Hunt was torn between his devotion to the cause of an independent Liberia and a belief that the country required managerial and financial help, or even a total bailout, to achieve that ultimate objective.

Ida had her own difficulties during the Gibbs-Hunts' early months in Liberia, and the problems that plagued her sister Hattie and her husband back in the United States had not abated. Hattie, who remained in New York City, again divulged those agonies, this time telling Ida that "my legs already refuse to carry the body." A friend in Washington had written Hattie that Napoleon Marshall "was drinking altogether too much." "I know he is disgracing himself & me," she mourned, "but I can't help it."

And despite all that Ida Gibbs Hunt had learned in advance, and Liberia's history as the iconic site and supposed ancestral home where more than a century of Negro Americans' pan-Africanist hopes and ambitions had played (or fizzled) out, the firsthand reality of the country's wretched political, economic, and developmental predicament distressed her at least as much as it did her husband. She began thinking through and analyzing the formidable problems she observed, and started plotting out her own attempt to tackle them. In April 1931, weeks after arriving, and probably about the time that word reached her of the death in Chicago of the reformer Ida Wells-Barnett, she wrote Du Bois, "I take this opportunity to make a suggestion to you about the Pan African Congress." "Liberia is in dire straights and something must be done to save it," she went on. "No matter whose fault it is nor what the cause, it is no worse than others and not so bad as some. The point is that it must be helped. . . . It needs some strong and honest patriots (and it has some) and capital to finance the needed improvements."

Cutting to the chase, Gibbs Hunt continued, "I would suggest that the

P.A.C. adopt this country and try to help it," and she recommended renaming Du Bois's Pan-African Congress the Liberian Aid Society. Long before reaching Monrovia, in fact, she had already tried to stimulate interest in a new appellation for the congress — one that would be "less alarming to African exploiters." She, "of course," expected Du Bois to continue as president of any such reconfigured organization, but also envisioned her own pivotal role as one "which would enable me to surround myself with . . . competent persons to help carry out some construction ideas I have." Gibbs Hunt, who had received few thanks and little recognition for her efforts on behalf of the 1920s congresses, proposed that she be named "Chairman of the Executive Comm." "I want this not through ambition," she iterated (knowing that many contemporaries, possibly including Du Bois himself, considered "ambition" an unseemly attribute for a woman), "but as a means to help." "Financially we are weak," she admitted, yet she nonetheless firmly believed that "we can put into operation financial aid at a reasonable rate of interest." Given her affluent and savvy father's entrepreneurial tutelage, Gibbs Hunt probably had more financial expertise, understanding, and basic horse sense than did Du Bois. "I shall also write to Mr. Joel Spingarn [the NAACP's longtime Jewish benefactor and board chairman, and a supporter of the early Pan-African Congresses] about this," she added, but to date no such letter has turned up.

Gibbs Hunt clearly recognized that her recommendations were controversial, and feared, with good reason, that her correspondence might be intercepted, because she cautioned Du Bois to "keep this letter strictly private at present, make a copy of it and then destroy it. And let me know after talking over the idea with some others what you think. . . . You'd better answer in a plain white envelope." She felt the need to specify those apprehensions because even the new President Barclay's supposedly reformed regime in Liberia still often censored or seized personal mail — whatever its origin or destination.

Du Bois was loath to consider seriously any approaches other than his own, and Gibbs Hunt's, while perhaps impractical, were visionary and bold but benevolently interventionist. His reply (there's no telling if he followed her instructions about the "plain white envelope"), while less acerbic than his earlier communications regarding the Pan-African Congresses, nonetheless dismissed her core recommendation and did not address the option of renaming or realigning the extant but semidormant congress. "Any effort on the part of American Negroes to help or co-operate with Liberia must be taken with the greatest caution and delicacy," he began. "Liberia is naturally jealous of her history and accomplishments, and she has not in the past taken kindly to efforts which seem to assume that American Negroes can patronize and guide a country which after all belongs to its heritage." But he saw possibilities in one secondary implication he derived from Gibbs Hunt's proposal. "On the other hand," he added, deftly shifting gears, "I have always meant that the Pan-African Congress, if it should continue to exist, should be a means of helping colored countries. It would be a fine thing to have a really representative Congress meet in Monrovia.... Already there are some tentative suggestions that we should meet in Haiti." Although the embers of their old pan-African visions still glowed, Du Bois was not otherwise encouraging. "Outside of that," he concluded, "I do not see anything that we could do except at the specific request of Liberia, but if you have any suggestions, I should be glad to attempt to follow them."

Ida Gibbs Hunt's primary goal of bringing critical reforms to Liberia may have been implausible, but her approach differed from those of other interventionists. She alone, it seems, hoped to address the republic's ongoing difficulties by establishing a committed and benevolent but unaffiliated pan-African entity that was nonsectarian, nonpolitical, nonbelligerent, nonmilitary, noncorporate, non-League of Nations, non-American government, and predominantly nonwhite. But those suggestions, as well as Du Bois's vision of convening a reconstituted congress in Africa, soon became moot points, because an intervening personal crisis cut short their epistolary exchange, though she later rethought, reshaped, and tried to resuscitate those ideas.

In keeping with his upgraded status and expanded responsibilities in Monrovia, Consul Hunt quickly settled into the new job and, he later explained, "assumed the dual functions of Consul and Secretary of Legation." For the first and only time in his career, four men worked under him. Two were his compatriots — one of whom was the enterprising young African American William George — and two hailed from the neighboring colony of Sierra Leone. "It was impossible," Hunt ruefully observed, "to find a native Liberian ... qualified to fill the post of clerk." "The American government and the President of Liberia were 'en politesse diplomatique' [at a diplomatic impasse]" following the findings of the Christy Commission, he added, so "I never met President Edwin Barclay personally." But former presidents C. D. B. King, whom Ida first had encountered at the 1919 Pan-African Congress, and the decrepit Arthur Barclay (recently a member of the Christy Commission), the "Chief Justice of the Supreme Court, [and] some ... Cabinet Officers were occasional visitors at my home."

Charles E. Mitchell, the legation's new chief, preceded the arrival of Consul

Hunt by only a couple of weeks, so Mitchell was unfamiliar with the circumstances, protocols, and procedures in Monrovia. Hunt also found him insufferable. The experienced, circumspect, and otherwise tolerant consul complained in his revelatory chronicle that Mitchell "had no diplomatic training." Although the official relationship was such that he and Ida had little choice but to cloak their feelings and socialize with Mitchell and his wife, he labeled his superior a "consummate sycophant," then brusquely dismissed him as "one of the most shallow and tiresome 'hot air merchants' it has ever been my misfortune to know."

Nor did Liberia's citizenry fare much better in Hunt's estimation. The Americo-Liberians — still fewer than thirty thousand throughout the country by that time, with their numbers gradually increasing through intermarriage with select members of the indigenous tribes — he complained, "devote themselves solely to politics [and] as loyal party followers they all look forward to being appointed to some office by their President, take their turn as officials, and get rich." Although Hunt's memoir does not address gender issues, Charles Johnson characterized Liberia's men as the most sexist he ever encountered. "I know of no place where the unimportance of women, of all classes, is more marked," Johnson wrote. "They are not public figures. They are not leaders in church. . . . They are wholly unimportant except as breeders." As the educated, sophisticated wife of the new consul and secretary of legation, Ida Gibbs Hunt was a ranking ancillary distaff member of the diplomatic community, and also considered, by local standards, an elite "white" person. But because she was a childless older woman, few Liberians would have paid her much heed.

"Most of the educated [Americo-Liberian men]," Consul Hunt wrote, "pose as lawyers." Hunt culled some of his comments from a speech recently delivered in London by the supercilious Cuthbert Christy, who scoffed that despite those reputed lawyers' claims, their country had no law school. "[They] seem to be engaged in politics as a profession and belong to the 'Whig Party,' which has developed into more or less an oligarchy, and been handled with such ingenuity as to maintain the Whigs in power since the foundation of the Republic," Hunt reported. The corruption, inefficiency, and apparent enervation of that all-male ruling "oligarchy" appalled him, and he argued that "it would have been much better for the country if President King had not 'slammed the door to spurious patriots from across the Atlantic,' [and] permitted Marcus Garvey's contingent of handicraftsmen" to settle there. That was an astonishing assertion coming from a conservative, experienced diplomat like Hunt, and one who knew so well and greatly admired the Garvey-hating W. E. B. Du Bois, who, of course, had served as President C. D. B. King's and Minister Samuel Porter Hood's enthusiastic coconspirator in the successful 1924 exclusion of the Garveyites from Liberia.

As the wife of the proverbial "Yankee Consul," Ida Gibbs Hunt also, as the odious rhyme by Consul George Horton put it, "sizzle[d] in Liberia [where] Afric skeeters buzz." Unlike her husband, who had become quite ill at two previous posts, Ida had survived those years without contracting any serious maladies, but here she ran out of luck. She and Billy dutifully ingested their prophylactic quinine, drank no water other than bottled Evian or Perrier, and made diligent use of insect repellents. Servants doused their residence with bleach, "screened [it] in with fine wire mesh, and an equally fine mosquito net . . . cover[ed] each bed." Nonetheless, within five months of their arrival, like so many American representatives and their spouses who predated her, Ida fell victim to the ubiquitous *Anopheles* "skeeter" and contracted malaria —a much more serious case than Billy's in Madagascar or Guadeloupe. She tried to tough it out, but in August 1931 a letter from her brother Horace gently scolded, "I advise you to leave the Home of your Ancestors [as] soon as possible, be a live Coward rather than a dead Hero for your race."

Anopheles mosquitoes serve as malarial vectors, carrying parasites that penetrate the skin following a usually painless, even unnoticed, prick by the female's wiry proboscis. Falciparum malaria is the most lethal strain, and even today legions of its victims die. After the sting, which raises a small rosy wheal due to anticoagulants in the insect's saliva, protozoa swarm into the bloodstream, invade the red cells (some Mediterraneans, Middle Easterners, and Asians, as well as many Africans and their diasporic descendants, inherit a sickle cell trait that may cause pain and dire health problems but offers a degree of immunity to malaria itself), migrate to the prey's liver, then besiege other vital organs. Within a few weeks the compromised erythrocytes rupture, thereby infiltrating and destroying more such cells. If not treated aggressively, malaria can hang on indefinitely, become recurrent, or fatal. Ida suffered all the ghastly, familiar symptoms: uncontrollable icy shivers and hot sweats (agues, recurring in two-to-three-day cycles and thus called quotidian or intermittent fevers), headaches, throbbing joints and muscles, nausea and vomiting, jaundice, fatigue, delirium, an enlarged spleen or compromised kidneys, and anemia resulting from internal hemorrhaging. In a blow to her dignity and vanity, Ida's hair also fell out, leaving her almost as bald as an egg, although trauma from overly rigorous medication may have worsened that alopecia.

Despite her brother's exhortations, Ida yearned to stay with her husband, but that soon proved to be impossible. Although Firestone had brought over a few of its own white physicians, medical care in Liberia was chancy at best and difficult to obtain, with only six American- or European-trained doctors (some of whom Charles Johnson had found shockingly incompetent) in the whole country. Billy Hunt admitted that his wife's "condition was so serious at times that the attending physician was unable to decide whether it would be possible for her to return to America as she so much wished." Medicines and therapeutic supplies were hard to come by, overpriced, and often adulterated. Cuthbert Christy and Johnson both called the shabby government hospital a "farce." It only recently had been converted from an "old French cable station bombarded by a submarine during the war," and soon would be shut down altogether.

Finally, Billy explained, he and the servants strapped the ailing Ida, with her bare scalp most likely swaddled in protective silk scarves, into a "'Manny Chair' [which quite resembled one of Madagascar's ubiquitous *filanzanas*], the usual method of handling invalids along the west coast," and a team of porters delivered her to the Mesurado lagoon, whence a surfboat bore her out to an oceangoing vessel anchored a few miles at sea. In September 1931 the ship carrying her off from Liberia forever sailed for England. This time she and Billy would be separated for more than a year. "Accompanied by a private trained nurse and with the aid of the ship's doctor and nurses," her husband wrote, "she arrived safely at Liverpool." Britain's centuries of treating its countrymen who contracted malaria and similar maladies in equatorial colonies made that the venue in which to receive the most professional treatment, and once she got there, an English physician "transport[ed] her to a clinic specializing in tropical diseases."

Ida remained in Liverpool for several weeks, "awaiting the departure of a steamer for the United States," her spouse recalled, but still needed nursing care as she began her Atlantic journey's final leg. Billy kept relatives and friends like Hattie and W. E. B. Du Bois updated on Ida's condition, procured their support, and the word spread. A few weeks later, the State Department's Lillie Mae Hubbard, with whom the Gibbs-Hunts had spent time in the Canaries with Clifton Wharton, wrote to Du Bois, observing, much as had Consul Wharton's wife, Harriette, that she believed "it must have been against [Gibbs Hunt's] will to be in Africa, and that is the thing which worked most on her mind." As evidence of those sentiments, Hubbard (who in 1925 had experienced a comparably critical malarial episode herself and had also been shipped home for several months) said Gibbs Hunt's nurse disclosed "that after she began to get near the States, she was a different person. . . . I am very glad to hear that Mrs. Hunt is well again." Billy Hunt added that his wife's "long and expensive journey ended in a hospital in New York." There she rejoined Hattie, who despite her own ailments looked after her sister as best she could, and "after a few months," Billy concluded, Ida "was able to enjoy life again."

Two months after Ida Gibbs Hunt got back to the United States, Carter G. Woodson's Association for the Study of Negro Life and History (Ida was a dedicated charter member) held a fractious debate at its annual meeting in New York City about the ongoing controversies concerning Liberia. Most participants defended the country's autonomy, and some of them also assailed Charles S. Johnson's report to the League of Nations. Although Ida Gibbs Hunt loyally attended most of the association's conventions, no evidence confirms whether she or her sister went to that year's sessions, but the Gibbs ladies soon returned together to the nation's capital.

By late the following summer, Liberia came to play a role in the United States' presidential race. Harvey Firestone, who headed the company that bore his family name, was the Republican President Herbert Hoover's most bountiful campaign donor. Putting his own financial interests foremost, but supposedly with the goal of stabilizing the rubber-producing nation where the corporation had made sizable investments of money, equipment, and personnel, Firestone lobbied for an even more commanding American stance in Liberia. He wanted one of his white countrymen installed as a near-absolute dictator, with the extant Americo-Liberian administrators reduced to mere figureheads. As he envisioned it, that imposed Western regime would serve as a military occupation, much like the one that still dragged on in Haiti. By contrast, most African Americans, who saw this as one more attempt to destroy the sovereignty of the world's only fully self-governing black republic, demanded the maintenance of an independent state. A French-led League of Nations team arrived at much the same time to dictate further reforms, while State Department officials continued to vacillate in their counsel to the White House.

Opportunistic Democrats, in turn, began reshaping prevailing perceptions about the Republicans' imperialist-interventionist intents in Liberia, hoping to woo the expanding and increasingly restless and vocal northern Negro electorate, most of which in the past reliably, loyally, almost blindly, had supported any and all representatives of the "Party of Lincoln." That summer the Democrats selected Franklin Delano Roosevelt, New York's charismatic governor (whom Billy Hunt claimed to have met in the early 1890s in Groton, Massachusetts), as their presidential candidate. The Great Depression and the United States' internal economic plight would carry by far the greatest political heft in the upcoming election, but as that time approached, the Liberian issue, with its complex international permutations, assumed some importance as well. Which would weigh more heavily with Hoover's incumbent GOP administration: Harvey Firestone's personal clout and his very seductive, big corporate money, or hanging on to its traditional Negro votes?

On August 10, 1932, Charles E. Mitchell, the beleaguered envoy extraordinary and minister plenipotentiary, left Liberia for a brief home leave, and the State Department placed Second Secretary William Henry Hunt in charge of the increasingly hobbled legation. Hunt served in that capacity only through September 3, at which time a white department civil servant replaced him and took over the United States mission until Mitchell returned the next month.

Meanwhile, conditions in Liberia further deteriorated. It fell into financial default and suspended indefinitely any payments on the huge Firestone loan that had been secured six years before. Over the next few months Minister Charles Mitchell and President Edwin Barclay, who had started out as staunch allies, grew more and more at odds. Mitchell parroted others' proposals that his country should take total charge of Liberia's governance and reconfigure the nation as its dependent protectorate. The bitter policy and personal differences between them escalated amid accusations that, in collusion with Firestone, the State Department's ranking officials in Washington (all of them white men) actually wanted Barclay to fail, but then to stick around as an impotent black token of authority. With good reason, various observers suggested that, as his government's top representative to the African republic, Mitchell was slavishly following orders from the department, because more than ever, its bureaucrats disliked and distrusted all Liberians and considered them hopelessly incompetent.

Before 1932 ended, President Barclay refused to acknowledge Mitchell's presence and formally protested to State Department higher-ups that the American minister had "overstepped the bounds of courtesy in writing personal letters to the President of Liberia that were so offensive that they could not be overlooked." Officials in Monrovia and Washington soon came to share

Consul Hunt's assessment of Mitchell as an ineffective, gauche, ill-prepared blowhard. By the following February, Barclay demanded that the United States recall its chief of mission, the State Department acquiesced, and Mitchell had no choice but to return home the next month. Because he was a Republican appointee, however, his departure would have come about quickly in any case, as a result of the new administration in Washington. The Democrat Franklin Delano Roosevelt had been elected with the support of more "colored" voters than ever before.

When William George stepped in as the acting head of legation in Monrovia, his country sent no one to replace Mitchell, and did not restore substantive diplomatic contact with Liberia until 1935. It appointed the first American ambassador — an exemplary Negro lawyer with a broad global vision named Edward R. Dudley — only in 1949, in part because (at least in theory and often in fact) international protocols called for posting an African representative of the same elevated rank to the segregated District of Columbia. In addition, the actuality and actions of any "colored" ambassador might appear to repudiate white America's "appropriate" social order.

Hunt, however, had unobtrusively left Monrovia a few months before Mitchell's contentious downfall and withdrawal. He arranged to pack up and ship home his personal effects and those his wife had left behind. Replicating Ida's travel itinerary, the consul sailed from Liberia to England, thence to New York City. Ida and Billy Hunt were finally reunited in Washington, D.C.

On October 27 Hunt reported for duty at the State Department. Several years later, in response to a request for information from the historian Carter Woodson, a letter from the department's archival overseer confirmed that William Henry Hunt served at the secretariat for another two months as a key adviser on troubled Liberia until his official retirement on December 31, 1932. Hunt's remarkable, honorable, little known yet diverse, often frustrating career in diplomacy (the first such prolonged service for any African American in the State Department's employ), ended just one day shy of thirty-five years from his optimistic New Year Day's departure for Madagascar with his late father-in-law, Judge Mifflin Wistar Gibbs.

Fading Images

Washington, D.C., 1932–1957

When Consul Hunt arrived home late in 1932 to spend two final months of government service as an adviser on the morass in Liberia, he walked over every morning to the Department of State's rococo mausoleum across from the White House and a short distance from his stateside residence. After thirty-five years during which Billy in particular, but Ida too, lived half a world away from their homeland, his public role on the international stage began grinding to a halt.

In recent months, to the horror of many but with President Hoover's approval, armed troops had ruthlessly ousted from Washington the huge assembly of angry black and white World War I veterans known as the Bonus Army. They were petitioning their government for payment of promised dividends for honorable wartime service by staging the largest (at that time) protests in the nation's history — but also flouting the military's and the capital city's dedication to racial segregation.

For a while the Gibbs-Hunts faced a temporary financial crunch. Although in truth Billy Hunt was sixty-nine, according to his own assertions, backed up by myriad public records, he was six years younger than that. So he found himself in a bind: government pensions usually set in at sixty-five, but since he had falsified his age since the 1880s, it would have been embarrassing, not to say well nigh impossible, to change it back five decades later. His pension would kick in within a couple of years, but until then Ida's well-nurtured investment income helped to tide them over. William Yerby, who was a year or two younger and whose diplomatic career in many ways paralleled Hunt's, also retired from the State Department that fall. Yerby lived on in Chicago, where he died in 1950, at eighty-two.

In time, the Gibbs-Hunts gave to Howard University much of the artwork they had collected around the world, including the portrait of Billy in equestrian garb astride his mare near St.-Étienne. Many other possessions had been lost or destroyed during their intercontinental moves or reduced to sludge in Guadeloupe's 1928 *cyclone de la siècle.* They kept for themselves a modest assemblage of treasures, including photographs and other mementos of their African sojourns: an embossed dagger and jewel-toned silk saris from Madagascar, and a pair of handsome stools carved in the shape of elephants from Liberia.

As she often had done as a diplomat's wife, Ida still could set for her guests an elegant table. Although servants had performed most of the culinary chores while she and Billy lived abroad, after returning home she sometimes took to the kitchen to prepare favorite dishes herself, most of them mastered during two decades in France. A multicourse repast might include crocks of *soupe à l'oignon* made from sauteed onions simmered in *vin blanc* and *consommé* then ladled over croutons blanketed with grilled *fromage,* followed by a succulent *poussin rôti* accompanied by a side dish of *aubergines,* and climaxed with a *tarte tatin.*

During the years following Billy's retirement, a number of the Gibbs-Hunts' acquaintances passed away. Among them were the Senegalese politician and pan-Africanist Blaise Diagne, whom they first met in Madagascar at the turn of the century; Alice Dunbar-Nelson, Paul Laurence Dunbar's widow, who became a skillful writer herself; the expatriate African American painter Henry Ossawa Tanner, who never returned home from his extended residency in France; the Reverend Francis Grimké, who had officiated at the wedding of Frederick Douglass and his second wife as well as that of Ida and Billy; and the lyricist, Harlem Renaissance chronicler, and NAACP executive James Weldon Johnson, who spent six years overseas early in his career with the State Department, and whose ambitions to obtain a consulship in Europe almost scuttled Billy Hunt's career. All of them died in the mid-1930s.

Throughout their lives the Gibbs-Hunts had crossed paths with numerous other distinguished African Americans. They included the Kentucky Derby–winning jockey Isaac Murphy, the seminal pan-Africanist Reverend

Alexander Crummell, the congressmen John Mercer Langston and George White, Booker T. Washington, Frances Ellen Watkins Harper (author of the novel *Iola Leroy*), Ida B. Wells-Barnett (who, long before Ida Gibbs Hunt, had adopted the nom de plume Iola), former consul Archibald Grimké and his poet daughter Angelina, and of course Mollie Church Terrell, Anna Julia Cooper, and W. E. B. Du Bois. Like that diverse assembly, excepting the earliest among them, the Gibbs-Hunts began their adult lives as Republicans, as did most Negroes in those generations, but over time many of them became dismayed by the GOP's increasing arrogance and indifference about issues of racial inequity. So as Ida's late father Mifflin Wistar Gibbs, her brother-in-law Napoleon Bonaparte Marshall, and Du Bois had long since done, they bid a less-than-fond farewell to the Party of Lincoln. By the early 1930s, like a number of their colleagues, they saw themselves as at least incipient Democrats, although they and the rest of Washington's nearly six hundred thousand residents could not vote at all, even in presidential elections. Most African Americans greatly admired the new president, Franklin Delano Roosevelt, and his outspoken wife, Eleanor. Party politics aside, the Harlem Renaissance and the Jazz Age, replete with newly enfranchised women, hard-drinking, cigarette-puffing flappers, speakeasies and bathtub gin, had yielded to a more somber decade characterized by the dire economic circumstances generated by the Great Depression.

Those years nonetheless progressed fairly well for Ida Gibbs Hunt, who continued steering her venerable Book Lovers' Club, a strong intellectual sisterhood that had generated similar groups in various other cities with a critical mass of well-educated Negro women. Among its loyal members were the three Georgias — Ida's friend Georgia Lawson, the poet Georgia Douglass Johnson, and Georgia Bond, the mother of both Caroline Bond Day, the anthropologist who had corresponded with Consul Hunt in the Azores, and Ida's protégée Wenonah Bond. Ida still served on the board of her city's "colored" YWCA, worked with the Women's International League for Peace and Freedom, and supported her sister's efforts, including the Save Haiti League and the Washington Conservatory of Music and Expression.

In their new but old city of residence, the Hunts and Marshalls also sponsored a group called La Société des Amis de la Langue Française, a beefed-up successor to Ida's long-lived Cercle Français organized under the patronage of the Haitian Minister and Madame Dantès Bellegarde. The society's mission was, "To enter into relations with friends of French culture of whatever race, nationality or religion . . . to establish among them and its members ties of moral and literary sympathy." It convened twice monthly at Anna Julia Cooper's small, autonomous new college, and diplomats from the French embassy often participated in its diverse activities. Soon after returning home for good, Billy Hunt served as the master of ceremonies at the society's reception honoring Bellegarde when he stepped down (but only temporarily) from his post as Haiti's top diplomat in the United States. Among the gala's other patrons were William Jay Schieffelin, a (white) fellow officer with Captain Marshall in the 15th Regiment who also had been Hunt's wealthy first employer in New York in the 1890s; Charles Mitchell, Consul Hunt's bombastic nemesis at the ministry in Monrovia; several Howard University officials; and, of course, Dr. Cooper herself.

Napoleon Marshall, Hattie's husband of twenty-seven years, never recovered from his wounds inflicted during the Great War. He thoroughly disliked Washington's Walter Reed Army Hospital, the military never agreed to fully compensate him for his medical care, and with his wartime maladies exacerbated by diabetes and his struggles with alcohol, he finally left the nation's capital for good. On June 8, 1933, the *New York Times* reported:

> Captain Napoleon Bonaparte Marshall of the old Fifteenth Regiment, N. Y. N. G. [New York National Guard] will be buried today in Arlington Cemetery. He died Friday at the Veterans Hospital, Bronx, of bullet wounds received in the World War. He was cited for gallantry in action. Yesterday afternoon his body lay in state in the armory of the 369th Infantry, the name given the Fifteenth, a colored regiment, during the World War. . . . He was 57 years old, a graduate of Harvard and a lawyer.

Relatives, friends, fellow officers, and a contingent of the men whom he had defended in Texas and commanded in France drew near as a cadre of riflemen fired off memorial volleys and a solitary bugler played taps. Much like the West Point graduate and charismatic officer Colonel Charles Denton Young, Marshall was laid to rest beneath oaks and gnarled conifers on a shady hillside at Arlington National Cemetery. For years to come, the United States military continued to discriminate against its dedicated Negro personnel in life but, ironically perhaps, did not segregate Colonel Young, Captain Marshall, or a number of other African American heroes in death.

In the political arena, in 1934 a black Republican-turned-Democrat named Arthur Mitchell defeated the black Chicago congressman Oscar De Priest. Six years before De Priest had been elected as the country's very first Negro member of Congress since 1900, when, faced with rising intimidation from North

Carolina's white majority, the Gibbses' old friend George White had opted not to run again for his old seat. Owing to rampant disfranchisement, especially in the South, however, membership in that embryonic black congressional caucus started by DePriest expanded only at a snail's pace for decades to come, really until after implementation of the 1965 U.S. Voting Rights Act.

Charles S. Johnson, who had written the provocative 1930 report on Liberia for the League of Nations, returned to Fisk University. There he wrote prolifically about how economic forces shaped race relations, served as the school's chairman of social sciences, and eventually, in 1947, became its first Negro president. But in 1934 Johnson came to Washington as part of President Roosevelt's new "Black Cabinet," colloquially known as the Black Brain Trust but formally titled the Interdepartmental Group Concerned with the Special Problems of Negroes.

The oldest member of the Brain Trust was the erstwhile pan-Africanist Henry Alexander Hunt, principal of Fort Valley, a small, historically black institute, then a college that later became a cog in Georgia's huge university system. In 1930 the NAACP had bestowed on Hunt its prestigious Spingarn Medal for his achievements in education, and four years later the president persuaded him to relocate from the rural South to Washington, where he worked for the governor of the Farm Credit Bureau. But Charles Johnson, Henry A. Hunt, and the almost forty other Black Brian Trusters — among them its titular leader, Mary McLeod Bethune, a Florida educator who was Eleanor Roosevelt's crony at the Labor Department — did not hold cabinet rank. (The first "real" Negro cabinet member was Robert Weaver, another former Brain Truster who in 1965 became Lyndon Johnson's secretary of housing.) Those key advisers to Roosevelt's white movers and shakers also included William Hastie, a future appointed governor of the U.S. Virgin Islands then a renowned federal judge, and Ralph Bunche, another Spingarn medalist, PhD, Howard University professor, and an internationalist who served intermittently at the State Department. In 1950 Bunche would receive the Nobel Peace Prize for his efforts on behalf of the United Nations in negotiating a tenuous detente between Israel and the Arab states.

Members of the Black Cabinet have often been devalued and their effectiveness belittled, but they strove mightily to make Roosevelt's leading white New Dealers more responsive to race issues. They challenged governmental inequities and prompted modest progress in reducing federal job discrimination, expedited African Americans' involvement in New Deal programs, encouraged their participation in Democratic politics by making the party and the administration seem more concerned about their needs, and helped to build innovative cross-racial coalitions around issues of economic justice and social welfare. Their power clearly was limited, but this was the first time that Negroes had wielded any significant clout at all in their government's executive branch.

Whether Roosevelt's so-called Black Cabinet was a palliative political sop thrown out to assuage the Democrats' expanding northern Negro constituency, or whether it reflected the president's heartfelt commitment to racial equality, or even his wife's frequent prodding, matters little. That new group of African American federal officials came into play on Roosevelt's early watch, as he initiated numerous other major governmental reforms. The president's progressivism — compared to his predecessors — also led him to appoint the first female cabinet member, and Ruth Bryan Owen as the first woman (a well-connected white one, to be sure) to head a diplomatic mission. In 1936 Owen was appointed minister to Denmark. The first to hold the title of ambassador was Eugenie Moore Anderson, who served in that same European country from 1949 to 1953. The State Department nonetheless still promoted very few women, racial or religious minorities, or lower-class white men. Sexism, racism, and elitism severely restricted such groups' opportunities for advancement, and deprived the country of their considerable and diverse talents and acumen.

Few African Americans even managed to enter the career foreign service in the years after Billy Hunt's retirement. Between 1924, when the service hired Clifton Wharton, and 1951, only thirteen Negro men were among the thousands whom the State Department brought on in that capacity, and it employed that "baker's dozen" only following World War II. Edward R. Dudley, a lawyer and noncareer hire who, like William Hastie, had served as an appointed governor of the Virgin Islands, finally achieved another milestone. In 1949, prompted by mounting pressure from groups such as the NAACP as well as by many still often ambivalent Negro Democrats, President Harry S. Truman would upgrade the position Dudley already held in Liberia as minister plenipotentiary and make him the United States' first Negro ambassador.

Despite Roosevelt's efforts, the Great Depression dragged on, and Europe's imperialism continued. In 1935 and 1936 Benito Mussolini initiated the use of internationally banned mustard gas in Abyssinia (Ethiopia). The Italians ravaged Haile Selassie's feudal empire and Mussolini solidified control over his expanded colonial Italian East Africa. Selassie's forces, while ample in numbers, were armed only with spears and antiquated rifles, and they had just three decrepit biplanes. The Italians pitched African captives out of fighter planes, mutilated corpses, strafed villages, torched Ethiopia's capital city, set up forced labor camps, and imposed a rigid apartheid system. Such obscenities continued despite international opprobrium. Protests on the part of many Negro Americans soon became even more clamorous than those during the recent Liberian crises, as they tried to build transatlantic, transcontinental bridges of support to East Africa. These events led to an increasing sense of identity with the continent of (some of) their ancestors.

Italy's venality both portended and accompanied the world's headlong plunge into global warfare, epitomized by genocidal slaughters grounded in doctrines of racial supremacy. With Chancellor Adolph Hitler in full control, Germany's army began rolling over its neighbors, and the Nazis embarked on the extermination of millions of Jews, and countless gypsies, homosexuals, and the mentally and physically "imperfect" as well. Germany's *Führer* denigrated everyone who was not a "superior" Aryan — white, Protestant, and usually of northern European ancestry — contemptible policies that echoed Germany's early twentieth-century massacres of indigenous black people in its former colonial Southwest Africa.

Hitler's doctrines, which blatantly touted Aryan physical supremacy, went on international display at the "nonpolitical" 1936 Berlin Olympics. President Roosevelt officially stayed out of the debate, though his country briefly threatened to boycott that year's games because Germany excluded its own "non-Aryan" athletes. But ultimately the United States did participate, and its delegation included eighteen African Americans, among them the sprinter Ralph Metcalfe (a decade before, a French journalist had compared him to Consul Hunt), who ironically replaced a Jewish runner on the gold-medal medley team. In the 1970s Metcalfe became a distinguished Chicago congressman.

On one occasion Hitler heard the Negro American contralto Marian Anderson sing. He commented on how astonishing it was for such a gorgeous voice to emanate from the body of an ape (Mollie Church Terrell similarly observed that some white Americans seemed to regard her as "a gorilla in human form"), and he prevented Anderson from completing her scheduled concert tour in Germany. But problems generated by her race were not limited to the adversities she faced in Germany. The Daughters of the American Revolution (the DAR), an all-white, "patriotic" organization to which Eleanor Roosevelt belonged, canceled a 1939 recital by Anderson (because she was a Negro) at its Constitution Hall, Washington's most prestigious auditorium. The first lady resigned her DAR membership, then facilitated an alternate Easter Sunday concert by Anderson at the Lincoln Memorial. An interracial audience of seventy-five thousand attended that event, which the singer opened with a moving rendition of "My Country 'Tis of Thee." It is hard to imagine that the politically aware, music-loving Gibbs sisters failed to attend that landmark concert, performed by one woman they deeply admired and made possible by another.

In an unpublished essay titled "Our Duty to Liberia," written about this time, Ida Gibbs Hunt began wrestling anew with a nagging dilemma that harkened back to the measures for Liberia's salvation she had first outlined to Du Bois in 1931. Five years later, she once again laid out the African republic's troubled history, the grievous results of which she had seen firsthand. She delineated several ways in which American Negroes might assist it economically, including an ambitious proposal to establish a new black-owned United States to Liberia steamship line, quite like Marcus Garvey's earlier, ill-fated schemes.

"In this age of colonization and encroachment," Gibbs Hunt wrote, "now is the time to help establish more firmly the few governments which the African possesses." Liberia, she cautioned, "can never be a white man's country." She sharply enjoined members of her nation's white majority to "understand the brotherhood of man" and acknowledge "that the color of a man's skin does not prevent him from becoming as valuable and respectable a citizen as any other." And she exhorted her fellow African Americans to "read the signs of the times if we wish to be actors instead of spectators in the drama of nations."

On January 24, 1936, one of the Gibbs-Hunts' many acquaintances, Lucy Diggs Slowe, Howard University's dean of women, addressed a convocation at her school. Both Mordecai Johnson, Howard's president, the first person of color to hold that position, and its executive secretary Emmett Jay Scott, the late Booker T. Washington's right-hand man at Tuskegee Institute and a special assistant to the secretary of war during World War I, attended. Surprisingly, Slowe did not mention Ida Gibbs Hunt, her sister Hattie Gibbs Marshall, Mollie Church Terrell, or Anna Julia Cooper among Howard's "outside guests," who, she reported, included "visitors from the Conference on Cause and Cure of War." That larger gathering had been convened in Washington by several almost all-white women's organizations, but its sponsors had excluded the pacifist and borderline socialist Women's International League for Peace and Freedom (WILPF), with which Helen Curtis, Addie Waites Hunton, Georgia Bond, Gibbs Hunt, Church Terrell, and Dean Slowe herself were affiliated. Those six women, however, remained among its notably few Negro members.

Speaking to her mostly African American audience, Slowe shared her impressions of the recent conference in their city. She detailed how its white attendees had taken "back to their . . . communities valuable information on the economic, social, political, and cultural reasons for war, [and] methods of getting rid of war and promoting peace," yet she bluntly complained that "our Negro population is not connected up with this movement." Slowe thought that involvement in such efforts was vital for anyone who aspired to be a responsible citizen and believed "it was the duty of the women of the nation to educate public opinion against war," but protested that "even in matters which closely affect colored people in this country, . . . white women are far better informed than most Negro women." She cited the recently suspended military occupation of Haiti, the "Liberian question, and . . . the general question of the darker peoples of the world" as issues that ought to concern black women, and she urged them to emulate their white sisters and "use the same techniques for informing themselves on international matters and of making their voices heard." Dean Slowe wanted to stimulate debate and raise her listeners' consciousness, but she was wrong in part, and should have acknowledged that a good number of Negro women were already well schooled about and deeply involved in international affairs, although institutional discrimination often severely limited their participation. Many others, of course, had few material resources, different concerns, and onerous daily responsibilities, so they could not make such voluntary activities a priority.

Slowe's address at Howard predated by little more than a year the boldest treatise Ida Gibbs Hunt ever wrote: "The Price of Peace." She probably first delivered it at the fall 1937 convention of the Association for the Study of Negro Life and History (ASNLH). Carter G. Woodson's *Journal of Negro History* published it soon thereafter, and the *American Political Science Review* would include the essay on its prestigious annual list of "recent publications of political interest."

"Nearly two decades after the great holocaust to end war, we still have wars," Gibbs Hunt's piece began. "The new alignment of fascist nations against the Communist republics threatens the security of the entire world . . . there is no greater menace to world peace today than capitalistic imperialism." In respect to colonialism, little had changed: "Africa and all primitive countries [remain as] spoils to be divided among the nations of Europe either as mandates or colonies without regard for the wishes of the governed." Such colonies nonetheless "claim their right to . . . decide their own destinies. . . . The darker races are restless and seething, and realize as never before that their rights are not to be respected if they conflict with the greed or selfish interests of the white man." Europe was "watching with jealous eyes all tendencies to self-assertion or to independent government on the part of subject peoples," she continued. "France aids and encourages Spain to hold on to her possessions in Northern Africa (Morocco) and England encourages both, fearing for her passage to Egypt and India. Italy looks on . . . anxious to extend her territorial possessions in Africa. . . . War vessels hover like hawks over their prey, waiting to take advantage of any pretext to interfere." Her own ambivalent country "kept aloof from colonial entanglements for a long time, but since . . . her purchase of the Philippines and other territor[ies,] she seems to have become inoculated with this virus." And, Gibbs Hunt wrote, "During the [previous] war, secret agreements had . . . been made for dividing up the German colonies [that] left France and England ruling over by far the greater part of the Dark Continent. . . . Germany now is striving to get back these possessions."

What could and should be done about those looming geopolitical crises? "If the leading nations really desire peace and disarmament the world over," Gibbs Hunt argued, "they can have it by paying the price: 1st, by forgetting the hatred and repairing the faults of the late war; 2nd, by granting gradual independence and autonomy to the darker races now held subject against their wills in Africa, Asia, and elsewhere." Despite that dauntingly high "price of peace," she remained optimistic. "The peace sentiment is growing," she insisted. "In all countries a few brave souls are speaking out against imperialism and exploitation. Call them Pacifists, Bolsheviks, Communists, or what not, they are right in principle, in this respect, at least." All the world's people and nations, she concluded, must decisively "turn their backs on the dark crime of war." Although Gibbs Hunt and Slowe disagreed about black women's cognizance of and commitment to international issues, they agreed on the most pertinent focuses for such concerns.

Dean Slowe had another link to the Gibbs-Hunts as well. Not long after her address at Howard, she played a role in a personal encounter that significantly realigned Billy and Ida's priorities. A feminist playwright named Mary Burrill, who taught speech and drama at Dunbar High School and was the sister of Billy's onetime vice consul Edmond Burrill, brought over a talented student of hers to meet the Hunts. Mary Burrill and Lucy Slowe lived together in a dedicated partnership until Slowe's untimely death at the end of 1936. Their protégé, David Leer, a slender, light-skinned, fifteen-year old, probably quite resembled Billy Hunt at that age. He had lost his parents and needed affection, guardians, financial support, and a secure place to live. It also appeared evident that David was gay. Burrill and Slowe must have hoped that a well-situated, worldly couple such as the Hunts could provide him with guidance and a safe harbor, and accept his homosexuality without dismay or disapproval — as they did. It has been suggested to me that Mary's brother Edmond, who in 1909 abruptly left the State Department's employ under unexplained circumstances and later probably took his own life, may have done so because of personal anxieties, public anathema toward his own covert sexual orientation, or perhaps even threats of exposure.

Whatever circumstances aligned to steer David Leer to them, the Gibbs-Hunts welcomed him and forged a lasting relationship with the youngster, who became almost their adopted son. He often decked himself out in flamboyant garb, bowed down with a regal flourish as he playfully called Ida "Madame" and Billy "the Great Pasha," delighted their friends, and brought them gaiety and laughter before moving to New York City to forge a new life for himself on the stage. Billy, his "stepfather," sometimes visited him there. David then toured the world as the premier danseur (in some ways a cultural ambassador) with a Negro opera company. Providing a loving, nonjudgmental home for an uprooted youth who looked not unlike he may have imagined his own boyhood self must have meant a great deal to the solicitous retired consul, and David Leer thereafter remained an integral member of the Gibbs-Hunts' extended clan.

Attending Dunbar High School with David was Jean Bellegarde, a son of Ida Gibbs Hunt's Pan-African Congress colleague Dantès Bellegarde, who had also been a friend of the Gibbs-Marshalls in Haiti. In 1930 (four years later President Roosevelt suspended his country's long military occupation of the island nation), Minister Bellegarde left a lengthy diplomatic tour in Paris to represent his republic in the United States and at the Pan American Union. Bellegarde intermittently worked and lived in the nation's capital, sometimes accompanied by his wife and children. Unlike most others in his small delegation, his light skin allowed and occasionally led him to pass for white. He thus could patronize the city's "whites only" restaurants and hotels. His country's continuing rocky political circumstances and turbulent changes of administration, however, meant that he shuttled in and out of Washington for many years. In 1943, with World War II in full swing and needing to consolidate the United States' support throughout the Americas, the State Department upgraded the Haitian legation to an embassy, and President

Roosevelt accepted the credentials of its first ambassador, Joseph Charles, whom the Gibbs-Hunts' colleague Rayford Logan lauded as a "charming and dignified" dark-skinned diplomat who officially broke the color barrier (at least for a few distinguished "colored" foreigners) at some of the capital city's many segregated public facilities.

In 1940 another of the their longtime cohorts, Mary (Mollie) Church Terrell, published her spirited autobiography, *A Colored Woman in a White World*. It was one of only a handful of similar works by members of her race and sex, and its international perspective was unique, though the State Department's and the military's discriminatory policies had restricted her global initiatives to privately sponsored endeavors and work with nongovernmental organizations. Her book includes several anecdotes about her enduring bond with Ida Gibbs Hunt, and also reflects on her loyalty to, passion for, but often troubled relationship with the United States:

> "It's my country," I said indignantly, "I have a perfect right to love it and I will. My African ancestors helped to build and enrich it with their unrequited labor . . . while they were shackled body and soul in the most cruel bondage the world has ever seen. . . . [They] suffered and died for it as slaves, and they have fought, bled, and died for it as soldiers in every war which it has waged. It has been cruel to us in the past and it is often unjust to us now, but it is my country after all," I said aloud, "and with all its faults I love it still."

In addition to Logan, Bellegarde, and Church Terrell, the Gibbs-Hunts enjoyed a rousing group of friends from their city, country, and overseas, including many from both continental and colonial France, the Azores, and Liberia. They joined discussion groups with present and past State Department personnel, including William C. George, the man with whom Hunt had worked most closely in Monrovia. George became a full-fledged foreign service officer only in 1945, and he never achieved the rank of ambassador. The Gibbs-Hunts also exchanged visits with Lillie Mae Hubbard, whom they had met in 1929 with Consul Clifton Wharton in the Canary Islands. Wharton himself persevered and ultimately flourished. He took on a variety of assignments, even slogging around the Azores-Madagascar-Liberia circuit covertly designated for black emissaries and initially completed by Consul Hunt. He won over the grudging department with his diligence, acumen, tact, and other diplomatic skills, and in 1958 President Dwight D. Eisenhower promoted and appointed Wharton as his ambassador to Romania — the first such position in Europe granted by the United States to any person of color, and the first ambassadorship ever given to a Negro career foreign service officer.

After her early stints in Liberia and the Canaries, Hubbard remained with the consular service for decades, moving on to posts in the Azores, Lisbon, and Havana. Finally she became her country's first black female consul in 1956 when the State Department assigned her to multiracial Rio de Janeiro. The rest of her life, however, remains largely undocumented. Even Clifton Wharton Sr.'s equally distinguished son, Clifton Wharton Jr. (an eminent leader in education and an internationalist who served his nation as deputy secretary of state in the 1990s), for whom Hubbard was his "Aunt Lillie," cannot provide further information. The department hired no other woman of her race in any nonmenial category until shortly after World War II, when it brought in a few to fill clerical positions. The first to start out with a diplomatic appointment was probably Joyce Garrett, who came aboard in 1960, but she resigned in short order. The department ignored, demeaned, or suppressed most of its few professional women (even white ones), and the environment for a woman of color must have been poisonous.

By 1940 the country was edging ever closer to all-out war, especially in response to Hitler's rampages through Europe. Germany was joined by Italy, Japan, and several smaller nations, creating the infamous Axis. But only when Japan bombed Pearl Harbor on the island of Hawaii, a jewel in the United States' Pacific "empire," late in 1941, did the isolationist nation fully commit itself to defeating totalitarianism. Until then it had remained somewhat above the fray, serving only as the Arsenal (warped by the sassy black writer and anthropologist Zora Neale Hurston into the "Arse-an'-all") of Democracy. In response to fears of and disdain for its new Asian foe, the government confiscated the property of thousands of Japanese American — but not German or Italian American — citizens and confined them and their families in dismal internment camps. Most of the world's powers, later including Russia and finally even Italy, opposed Japan and Germany, but a number of others, authoritarian Spain and Portugal notably among them, remained neutral. They felt sympathetic toward Nazi Germany, hedged their bets, and at the war's end Portugal managed to retain most of its global empire.

During World War II, four decades after he had joined the military, the U.S. Army belatedly promoted to general the first Negro: Benjamin O. Davis. (The all-white, all-male Marines, however, Haiti's longtime occupiers, enlisted their first African Americans only in 1942, under force of federal law, and finally got their own first black general in 1979.) Davis had served in the

Philippines and Liberia in many capacities, then taught military science at several historically black colleges. The United States assigned the aging Brigadier General Davis to the European theater, largely thanks to first lady Eleanor Roosevelt's intervention and perseverance. Grateful Liberia and France, but not his own country, bestowed their highest military honors on him, and he retired in 1948 after fifty years of often unappreciated service to his nation.

The segregated United States military did recruit, train, and promote a few more black officers, and celebrated breakthroughs such as the Tuskegee Airmen (although those pilots had to train and serve in separate and very unequal facilities), who downed German fighter planes over North Africa and Europe, made white Americans somewhat more aware of their country's patriotic darker-skinned minority's overlooked and underappreciated contributions. The armed forces began to enlist increasing numbers of women, including some Negroes, who usually were discriminated against as much as were black men. Those Americans, and others, supported their country as best they could, but they also began speaking out ever more forcefully about the urgency of winning the "Double V": victory over fascism abroad, and victory over racial bigotry at home.

None of the Gibbs-Hunts' close friends died in battle, but they suffered a major personal loss in those years. Unhappily widowed, with her hands so gnarled by arthritis that she no longer could play the piano, walking with crutches, often in financial straits, and writing books she could not get published, Hattie Gibbs Marshall persevered, all the while nurturing Negro youngsters in her home and at her music school. In a reflection of her lifelong singularity, she forswore Christianity to join the Baha'i faith, an independent religion founded in nineteenth-century Iran. It was grounded in a commitment to racial and sexual equality and a belief that the world's people must unite to live in peace and harmony. Gibbs Marshall opened her conservatory for Baha'i meetings because most public facilities in the nation's capitol refused to accommodate such interracial gatherings. But her health continued to deteriorate, and she died late in 1941 at the age of seventy-three. Her simple marble headstone stands beside her husband's at Arlington Cemetery.

Ida Gibbs Hunt kept in touch with Addie Waites Hunton, who worked with the WILPF and with the NAACP on its efforts to secure black people's voting rights and end school segregation. Waites Hunton passed away two years after Hattie. Helen Curtis, their World War I and pan-Africanist colleague, returned from Liberia with four adopted children whom she raised to adulthood in New York. Another "colored" woman of their generation, Belle da Costa

Greene, the only daughter of the one time African American consul Richard Greener, mingled in that city's elite circles, where she passed for white — Portuguese white — and squandered an inheritance bequeathed by her legendary employer, J. P. Morgan. She ran the Morgan Library until shortly before her death in 1950. Greene associated with no Negroes whatsoever — her father had died in the 1920s, still shunned by his ambitious, racially ambiguous child — and the very few people who knew her dark secret never revealed her designated race. Like Belle da Costa Greene, Alice Jones Rhinelander also had tried to escape the Negro identity that she feared would disgrace her. Ida Gibbs Hunt had written about her notorious court case in the Paris edition of the *Tribune*. Alice's white former husband died in the early 1930s, but she lived (in near seclusion) for another four decades.

Germany meanwhile barreled through France and set up a new capital in Vichy, near St.-Étienne. But Paris did not burn, and in London, General Charles De Gaulle established the Free French government-in-exile. Reflecting her disgust with the United States' Jim Crow practices, Josephine Baker, who had performed so insouciantly at the Folies Bergère, became a citizen of France. She gathered intelligence for her new country's resistance movement, joined its Croix Rouge, and, proudly wearing her uniform, sang "La Marseillaise" as she entertained cheering Allied troops of all races and origins in North Africa.

Under Germany's aegis, that area and the proximate sub-Saharan regions remained war zones for several years, and only when the Axis powers' fortunes in Africa collapsed did Liberia join in on the side of its historic partner, the United States. Soon thereafter, Liberia's True Whig Party lost control over the government, and women and the indigenous people finally were given the right to vote. Madagascar seemed far removed from the hubs of military engagement, but the British, projecting an imminent Japanese invasion, assumed martial charge over the huge island in 1942, then ceded it back to De Gaulle a year later.

Consul James Graneth Carter, who had succeeded Billy Hunt in Tamatave, served in Madagascar for two decades, went to France from 1927 to 1940, and then was sent back again, this time to Tananarive, the old inland royal capital to which Hunt had made his historic overland trek with Governor General Gallieni at the turn of the century. Soon after British troops arrived in 1942, Carter left his longtime State Department post and returned to the United States, where he died seven years later.

Just after the war ended, France granted the Indian Ocean colony a partially self-elected legislature, but an armed struggle for full independence almost immediately erupted. It was the first significant indigenous revolt there since the *Menelamba,* or Rising of the Red Shawls, forty years before when Hunt was still consul. French forces brutally quashed those new uprisings at the cost of a hundred thousand Madagascan military and innocent civilian lives — another holocaust, devastating to the Malagasies, but virtually unacknowledged internationally. If the United States had lost a comparable percentage in World War II, its death toll would have been nearly four million instead of four hundred thousand.

By the late 1940s, using divide-and-conquer techniques by pitting one dark-skinned colonial ethnic group against another, France deployed its Senegalese troops across the African continent to reimpose order on the Malagasies by brutal means, some of which resembled, but were not yet called, "waterboarding." Those methods were quite like the "water cure" that the United States military had used on recalcitrant Filipinos in the early 1900s and that many law enforcement officers inflicted on black convict laborers in the American South. In 1950 France reluctantly acknowledged the Malagasies' arduous road to independence, completing the process a decade later. Retaining control over its rebellious colonial island no longer seemed worth the cost and bother.

Throughout Africa and much of Asia, similar devastating and interminable decolonization struggles ensued. Over the next thirty years, France, Britain, Italy, Spain, Belgium, and Portugal grudgingly granted varying degrees of autonomy to the colonies that had made up their vast "colored" empires. Yet political independence did not bring accord or prosperity to the world's darker races. Most of the new countries were and remained tragically impoverished and underdeveloped. Ancient but often unacknowledged ethnic, class, and religious feuds often bitterly fragmented them. In many instances these debilitating travails have carried over into the twenty-first century.

Ida and Billy Hunt would have attempted to keep informed about the struggles in Madagascar, but it was impossible to do so. Even though it had very limited resources, the United States' black press tried to follow and report that story, but the most influential internationally oriented white-owned-and-operated newspapers (the *Washington Post* and the *New York Times*) scarcely acknowledged Madagascar, and ran virtually nothing about colonialism's convulsive death throes in that presumably insignificant African outpost. The majority of Americans had no exposure at all to the Great Red Island. A division of the Smithsonian Institution mounted the first major exhibit of

Madagascan material culture a full century after Billy Hunt and M. W. Gibbs assembled at their consulate in Tamatave the raucous menagerie of indigenous animals designated for the National Zoological Park, which even now remains an integral part of the Smithsonian. And New York City's Bronx Zoo (which in the early 1900s had displayed a caged pygmy named Ota Benga kidnapped from the Belgian Congo) finally presented to the public the extraordinary panorama of Madagascar's unique flora and fauna only in 2008.

For five years World War II raged on land, at sea, and in the air, in Africa, the Pacific, the Middle East, and all across Europe. Finally, the tide turned, largely thanks to the United States' heroic sacrifices resulting from its bold and bloody invasion of France. Hitler took his own life, his generals surrendered, the Allies declared victory in Europe, and the former antagonists began negotiating the terms of peace, including a contentious division of vanquished Germany itself. Once those heated hostilities ceased, however, a treacherous cold war began. The increasingly powerful Soviets instituted and enforced a brutal hegemony over Eastern Europe, drew down an "iron curtain" between its new satellites and the (more) democratic, capitalist Western European nations, and the United States dedicated itself to resuscitating that region with the Marshall Plan.

The charismatic President Roosevelt, who had concealed his physical infirmities from the public, died in April 1945, and Truman succeeded him. Soon thereafter, purportedly to avenge Japan's residual belligerence and avoid further losses of American lives, the United States dropped its lethal new atom bombs on the cities of Hiroshima and Nagasaki, killing 150,000 civilians and debilitating far more than that. But despite costly triumphs on multiple fronts, throughout the war the country's military was almost completely segregated, and remained so until late 1947, when in response to ongoing provocation both from organizations like the NAACP and from "ordinary" African Americans who threatened to sit out the upcoming presidential election, Truman issued Executive Order 9981, which ostensibly integrated his nation's armed forces.

As for W. E. B. Du Bois, in the wake of Germany's defeat, the first Pan-African Congress since 1927 convened in Manchester, England, in 1945, but its leadership had definitively shifted from the United States to Africa, and the seventy-seven-year-old Du Bois was the only American citizen who attended. Amid bitter squabbles, he had left *Crisis* magazine in 1934 and returned to Atlanta University. He briefly went back again to the NAACP, then departed for good amid a hailstorm of controversy when he joined the

Socialist Party. With much of the country having succumbed to an apoplectic Red Scare, in 1950 Du Bois was indicted and tried — though acquitted — for treason. His ailing wife, Nina, with whom Ida Gibbs Hunt had collaborated in fund-raising for previous Pan-African Congresses, passed away that year, and the widower promptly married Shirley Graham, a dynamic writer and social activist who, like Ida Gibbs, had earned two academic degrees at Oberlin. The Du Boises renounced their American citizenship and moved to newly independent Ghana, the former British Gold Coast, where he died in late August 1963, on the eve of the great civil rights March on Washington for Jobs and Freedom. No letters between Du Bois and Gibbs Hunt after the early 1930s are known to have survived, and there is no telling what more those perhaps deliberately misplaced communications might have revealed about their intense, abstruse, long-lasting relationship.

In retirement, Billy Hunt often retreated to his study, bent over his papers, riffled through albums, clippings, letters, and photographs, and began working on a memoir about his incredible life around the world. Almost certainly through the ASNLH, Carter G. Woodson's organization, in which Ida remained active, the Hunts met a rising historian named Harold T. Pinkett. In 1940 Pinkett's first published article, "Efforts to Annex Santo Domingo to the United States, 1866 to 1871," which reveals his keen international knowledge and understanding, appeared in the ASNLH *Journal*. Before the war, Pinkett taught at Morgan State, his own alma mater and a historically black college in Baltimore, and he had already earned a master's degree in history when the National Archives hired him in 1937 as its first professional of his race. He then enlisted in the army and served three years in Europe, the Philippines, and Japan. Pinkett lectured at Howard University for many years, and in 1953 American University awarded him a doctorate. (Rayford Logan acerbically observed in his postwar diary that some students in the District of Columbia at that time transferred from American University to the still all-white George Washington University because they did not want to risk having to sit in classes with Negroes.) Soon after the war ended, Pinkett returned to his position at the Archives, where he long remained an eminent authority in matters pertaining to his country's natural resources and agricultural legacies.

In the late 1940s Harold Pinkett began dropping by to chat with Consul Hunt. The acolyte was short and brown skinned in contrast to the aging, tall, light-skinned former diplomat, and he became Hunt's amanuensis who helped to pull together his splendid memoir, "From Cabin to Consulate." Hunt chose to share little about his marriage, but provided ample details, some verifiable, others not, about his early escapades and especially his remarkable diplomatic life. A handful of black men before him (Frederick Douglass, John Mercer Langston, James Weldon Johnson, and Ida's father, Mifflin Wistar Gibbs) had published autobiographies that featured their experiences as American consuls who proudly and effectively (though briefly) represented their country abroad. William Henry Hunt hoped to see his own equally historic story appear in print — but that never happened.

Pinkett transcribed both Hunt's true accounts and his tall tales about buggy trips with Jesse James, swabbing out brothels, riding alongside Derby-winning jockeys, witnessing heinous murders, and dining with foreign ministers and Siamese royalty during an almost certainly fictitious global odyssey. Hunt claimed to have crossed paths with J. P. Morgan and Kaiser Wilhelm II (true), future president Franklin Roosevelt, Leon Trotsky, and Madagascar's Queen Ranavalona III (not true). He shot alligators with Governor General Joseph Gallieni, snatched a pistol from the hands of a potentially homicidal ex-consul, soared over France in a hot-air balloon, undertook covert diplomatic heroics on behalf of that nation during the Great War, and survived Germany's bombardments of Paris. He weathered near shipwrecks and the early twentieth century's most catastrophic hurricane. Over time, Pinkett must have decided that it was neither his role nor within his capacity to verify or document those intriguing stories. Rather, he stimulated the consul's memory, organized his sundry reminiscences, set them down, and typed them up. Together, the two men stitched a lifetime of patchwork anecdotes into a whole, vivid, kaleidoscopic quilt. With no apparent differentiation, Pinkett enshrined both Hunt's unvarnished truths and his glorious inventions. If Hunt resented the shameful reality that elitist politics and racial prejudice had kept him from achieving more than he did in his country's foreign service, or if he sensed that his wife's audacious feminism and her very public, black-identified pan-African activities might have scotched his career's further progress, he revealed no anger or bitterness.

In November 1946 Phyllis Gibbs, a young librarian who was a great-granddaughter of Thomas Gibbs, Ida's cousin with whom she had taught in Florida sixty years before, married a navy veteran, Washington lawyer, and future judge named John Fauntleroy. Although she was almost eighty-five, Ida stood in the receiving line and helped to greet the couple's guests. She seemed pleased and animated, wearing a coiffed wig (little of the hair she had lost during her near-fatal bout with malaria ever grew back), chic hat, opera gloves, and a satin gown overlaid with lace, perhaps created decades before by her French *modiste*. Soon thereafter, the newlyweds rented and settled into a cozy apartment that their relatives, whom they called "Cousin Ida" and "Cousin Billy," created for them on their home's top floor.

A year and a half later, the Gibbs-Fauntleroys' first child, Phylicia, was born. Both of the Gibbs-Hunts had loving relationships with the sparkling little girl, but Billy in particular served as a supplemental care giver. The elderly gentleman often pushed Phylicia's stroller on extended promenades, told her splendid stories (not unlike those in his memoir), and became her knight in shining armor when a childish prank might otherwise have evoked a scolding from her parents.

The older couple cherished their close ties to the Gibbs-Fauntleroys since their more immediate families had dwindled away. Ida and her siblings had no direct descendants whatever. Her brother Horace and his wife stayed on in Chicago after World War II, but efforts to learn more about them have failed. Billy's sister Maggie and brother-in-law Dallas Hughes had died in the 1920s. Fannie Hunt Murray, his other surviving sister, had two children. Fannie had come from Colorado to New York with her son, Walter, and daughter, Mary, whom she supported by working as a laundress — as had her slave-born mother in the South after the Civil War. By the time of the Negro Renaissance, Fannie and Mary had left the city, passed away, or changed their names and are now untraceable. Walter, however, became a waiter in Harlem, involved himself in Democratic ward politics, and sometimes took the train down to visit his Uncle Billy in Washington. One or both of Fannie's offspring reportedly moved to California at some point, married, and had children of his or her own, but that supposition remains unproven.

Daniel Hunt, Billy's youngest brother, most likely had first crossed the color line in the 1880s, become a farmer like his white, slaveholding father in their home state of Tennessee, and severed connections with his African American kin. If that is the case, the country's ingrained laws and prejudices prevented Daniel and Billy (who sometimes engaged in situational passing but never forswore his African roots) from keeping up with one another, and those kinship ties were irrevocably ruptured — one of many profound personal tragedies created by generations of governmentally sanctioned and socially reinforced racism in the United States. In Billy Hunt's case, the Gibbs-Fauntleroys, friends from the foreign service and the neighborhood, and folks such as David Leer and the Sheedys, with whom Billy had kept in touch for decades after boarding with them while attending Lawrence Academy in the 1880s, replaced his biological family.

Age began taking a toll, but the retired consul kept himself informed about world events. He listened to and expounded on radio news broadcasts during and after the war, but by the late 1940s he negotiated the household stairs only with difficulty. Nonetheless, on occasion he even cooked for the Fauntleroys, and pigs feet, Phylicia Fauntleroy later recalled, were one of his specialities. He may have conjured up skills he had learned from the black chef, whom he referred to in his memoir only as Cal, at the Nashville eatery where he had worked as a boy. Or perhaps he replicated a recipe shared by the expatriate bistro proprietors Louis and Antoinette Mitchell, who had served southern-style *pieds de cochon* to their black and white, European and American patrons in Paris during and after World War I.

But Billy's health continued to decline, and when his time came it was not dramatic. He was not shot by a demonic former consul, as he had feared long ago in Madagascar, or swept away to "Davy Jones's locker," as he twice thought might happen when the surfboats in which he and Ida were passengers almost capsized in the storm-wracked Atlantic. Rather, he died quietly at home in December 1951. He was eighty-eight years old — though officially only eighty-two.

Unlike his white former coworkers, Consul Hunt attended the "black" St. Mary's Church in Washington's Foggy Bottom neighborhood, several blocks from his and Ida's residence and just a bit farther than that from the State Department. Hunt professed to have little commitment to organized religion, but like St. George's, the "white" church in New York City where he had engaged with J. P. Morgan and met Teddy Roosevelt in the 1890s, St. Mary's also was Episcopal. Billy may have worshipped at both places because his white Hunt forebears had claimed a bygone affiliation with the Anglican Church that hailed back to the original North American British settlement at Jamestown. St. Mary's Chapel for Colored People, as it was often called, was established in 1867 as the District's first Negro Episcopal church. Its most renowned early pastor had been the late pan-Africanist Alexander Crummell (known primarily as a Baptist), with whom Anna Julia Cooper and Ida Gibbs had lived in the 1890s. Crummell was Du Bois's idol, and for years he had taught and preached in Liberia. Billy Hunt's service, however, was held not at St. Mary's but at a nonsectarian funeral home, and he was interred nearby at Lincoln Memorial Cemetery. His widow and all of the Gibbs-Fauntleroys grieved deeply, but they soldiered on.

Soon after her husband died, Ida sold her home and moved with the Gibbs-Fauntleroys to their new residence, also in the District of Columbia, where they became the first of their race to live on the pleasant 1200 block of Ingraham Street, Northwest. Many of their Caucasian neighbors welcomed them. One, however, painted his house's brick façade solid black in protest, as if announcing to passersby: "Beware! Negroes now live here."

Honoring their revered elder, the younger couple settled Ida into the best bedroom. She rarely ventured into the kitchen anymore, except in the late mornings when she prepared tea with milk, "in the English style," and made (deliberately) burned toast that infused the house with an acrid smell. Ida pored over the daily newspapers with a magnifying glass, checked on the status of her stocks, and always completed even the toughest crossword puzzles. She read the WILPF's journal, *Four Lights,* clipped and saved articles about the country's mounting debates over Negroes' civil rights, and remained an activist, a teacher by nature and training, and an accomplished polyglot. In addition to English, she was fluent in French, understood Antillean Creole, could read Portuguese, maintained some familiarity with several Malagasy tongues, and remembered bits of German, Latin, and Greek from college. In Phylicia Fauntleroy's preschool years, the older woman often would pull from her drawer a linen square embroidered with the words *mouchoir* (handkerchief) and *oiseau* (bird), with which she unsuccessfully tried *("répétez après moi!")* to teach the toddler French.

Ida Gibbs Hunt continued writing poetry and her opinionated letters, a number of which never got mailed, but the *Washington Post* published several of them, on topics as diverse as the city's unregulated truck traffic and the career of the internationalist Ralph Bunche. The most notable of these was her candid 1950 proposal to desegregate public education in the District, where she had begun teaching more than five decades before. As to the "school controversy," Ida exhorted the editors and their readers, "The true solution, of course, is ending segregation." She believed that such initiatives would encounter little resistance: "Most of the white students would remain if [it was] put before them [as a] *fait accompli.* Young people would probably accept it, . . . and if their elders would stop prejudicing them they would get along all right." "Several other States ended segregation by beginning in the high schools," she added. "Why not try that here, and at once? . . . Why not start by transferring a certain number of pupils from Cardozo ["colored"] to Central [white] . . . and thus make Central a nonsegregated school?"

That forthright epistle appeared almost two years before the U.S. Supreme Court received the NAACP's landmark cases known as *Brown v. Board of Education* and *Bolling v. Sharpe,* the companion pleading for the District of Columbia. With its subservient and uniquely bastardized political status, Washington, D.C., arguably was not covered by the Constitution's Fourteenth Amendment, which promises equal protection under the law for the citizens of all states. The Court's May 1954 decisions, essentially overturning *Plessy v. Ferguson* (from 1896), however, found that separate was inherently *not* equal, and prescribed school desegregation nationwide. Those critical rulings tortured much of the country for decades to come, as resistance by whites manifested itself in violent, self-destructive ways. The city of Washington, by contrast, opened its public schools to all races the next fall, with considerable resentment but minor overt conflicts, as Gibbs Hunt had predicted. Nonetheless, within a few years "white flight" set in and prevailed. With a few exceptions, the District's schools became resegregated — and almost entirely black.

The Supreme Court's decisions heartened the adults in the Fauntleroy–Gibbs Hunt household and their cohorts, but they feared that seven-year-old Phylicia might not receive the quality education that she had enjoyed at the impressive, uniquely well-funded and well-staffed all-black facility she formerly attended. They did not want her to think that because she had been transferred to a "better" school with white students and teachers, Negroes were in any way less intelligent or able. Many Americans knew about and were appalled by the results of the sociopsychological "doll tests" when the NAACP presented its cases to the Court. Black youngsters, deeply wounded by assumptions and practices that made them feel inferior, chose "colored" dolls (their synthetic melanin-tinted skins much the same hues as those of the children themselves) as the ones that were "stupid," "ugly," or "bad." The Court's cagey 1955 addenda to its prior decisions specifying that school desegregation should proceed only "with deliberate speed" would not have satisfied Ida Gibbs Hunt at all.

That year's mutilation and murder of fourteen-year-old Emmett Till, and his killers' vile gloating when they were acquitted, reflected many white southerners' beliefs that black males might not "know their place," and would feel free to initiate intimate sexual relations with white women. A few months later, spurred by Rosa Parks, a stalwart NAACP member, Montgomery, Alabama's black residents, fed up with segregation and ceaseless insults on their city's buses, organized an arduous, yearlong boycott that thrust a dynamic young minister named Martin Luther King Jr. into the public arena, and painfully began changing the face of the South.

In 1952 the *Washington Post,* which had reported in such detail about Ida Gibbs and William Henry Hunt's wedding almost half a century earlier, ran a charming photograph beside a feature article headlined "Three Oberlin 'Old Grads' Meet: Reunited Trio Blazed a Trail," about Mary (Mollie) Church Terrell, Ida Gibbs Hunt, and Anna Julia Cooper. Their rendezvous took place at Cooper's Le Droit Park home. At that time Church Terrell was eighty-eight, Gibbs Hunt ninety, and Cooper about ninety-two. "Sixty-eight years ago at Oberlin College in Ohio, three hopeful young women in ... caps and gowns became part and parcel of a social revolution," the story recounts. "[T]hey agreed that the difficulties they encountered as mere female members of a recently-freed race only made their triumphs sweeter."

With stunning understatement the *Post*'s white correspondent, Estelle Sharpe, wrote that "[a]nyone trying to analyze their lives in terms of [a] typical American success story [would] have to deal with contradictions." Church Terrell and Gibbs Hunt, Sharpe continued, explained that they had married "'poor guys' who later distinguished themselves": Robert Terrell as the country's first Negro federal judge, and Consul Hunt, of course, with his groundbreaking though uncelebrated career in the foreign service. But Cooper, "as she says facetiously, 'was always a poor boy' [herself]." "Everyone at that time in the South," Cooper recalled, referring to the 1860s, "thought a woman didn't need to know anything. No one willingly even taught me the alphabet." Because of the "lucky happenstance" of living not far from one another in the District of Columbia, the article concludes, "their friendship has continued to the present. Yesterday's reunion was an undoubted success." The piece says nothing about their activities on the world stage, but in different ways all three women became and remained dedicated internationalists and impeccable intellectuals, and all played significant roles in their city.

Church Terrell had led the National Association of Colored Women (NACW), served on the District of Columbia's board of education, traveled the world, and addressed international conferences in English as well as French and German — all before 1900. Half a century later, impeccably groomed, wearing a stylish though serviceable coat, hat, gloves, and elegant but sturdy shoes, she brandished both her cane and a protest sign as she first unsuccessfully requested service, then picketed Washington's segregated restaurants and theaters to spearhead the struggles against the city's Jim Crow practices. When she died in July 1954, at the age of ninety, her body lay "in state" at the NACW's headquarters, and several obituaries cited Gibbs Hunt and Cooper, both of whom attended her funeral, as the only persons still alive who had participated in that organization's founding caucus in 1896.

In 1925, when she was "only" sixty-five, Cooper had earned her doctorate at the Sorbonne in Paris, then returned home as the fourth female Negro PhD to teach at Dunbar High School. In later years she turned out pithy essays, expounded on education and politics, and extolled the import of women and black people telling their own stories. As she had written back in 1892: "What is needed, perhaps, to reverse the picture of the lordly man slaying the lion, is for the lion to turn painter." She taught for nearly eight decades, challenged local officials, several times was dislodged from her academic posts, raised five foster children, and founded, headed, and staffed Freylinghausen University, a small school of higher learning (the city rescinded its accreditation, but Cooper continued operating under the radar) situated in her home for older, nontraditional students who wanted to renew or complete their educations. Her pace slowed, but she remained dedicated to and involved in civic issues almost until her death in 1964 — at age one hundred and five.

Ida Gibbs Hunt entered her nineties living with the Gibbs-Fauntleroys and enjoying their second daughter, Jacqueline Ida. She adored, shrewdly observed, and chronicled the escapades of their first son, called Jackie, born several years later. In late November 1957, Ida's extended family and more than twenty friends and neighbors celebrated her ninety-sixth birthday with a festive gathering. The Fauntleroy girls gleefully confessed to the reporter who chronicled the party that they had eaten more than a dozen tea sandwiches, but when asked how old she was, Ida Gibbs Hunt vainly declined to answer.

Several times she had faced down death. She almost drowned in a rampaging river, then in the Atlantic, and was laid low by malaria, each time far from competent medical care and her home in the United States. Early in 1929, having survived Guadeloupe's deadly hurricane, she presciently wrote, "I've long had the impression or presentiment, that I was not due to die by violent means." She was right about that. On December 19, one month after her birthday gala and six years to the day after Billy's death, she simply failed to awaken.

Joined by family and friends, including David Leer, Harold Pinkett, and a few of Billy's former State Department coworkers, the Gibbs-Fauntleroys held a wake, then coordinated Ida's funeral observance on Christmas Eve. No one who had attended William Henry Hunt and Ida Alexander Gibbs's 1904 wedding was even alive when she died fifty-three years later, with the exceptions of Angelina Grimké, the Terrells' daughter Phyllis, and two cousins. The latter trio had been Ida's junior bridesmaids. After a subdued service, the cortege of autos drove a few miles southeast to Lincoln Memorial Cemetery, which stretches across acres of Suitland, Maryland's verdant hills just beyond the District of Columbia's southeast city line. As one enters the facility, the graves of whites are situated on the left side of the road, while the right side is mostly the domain of black people. And there, among the most comprehensive and diverse group of African American leaders interred anyplace in the country, Ida was laid to rest next to her husband.

Their unobtrusive twin grave markers are flat, embossed bronze plaques, now burnished and weathered by time and the elements to a soft verdigris. Situated on a grassy bank in a section evocatively called the Roosevelt Lawn, the Gibbs-Hunts, as overlooked in death as they were in life, lie side by side, deep in the shadow of the hulking, elaborate granite tombstone that specifies the adjoining resting places of the far more celebrated Robert and Mary (Mollie) Church Terrell. Others of Ida and Billy's neighbors at the cemetery include Georgia Douglas Johnson, lyric poet, Book Lovers' Club member, and one of Du Bois's amours; Georgia Bond, another old "book-loving" friend; Mordecai Johnson, Howard University's first Negro president, and its dean Lucy Slowe, who had carped about black women's ignorance of international affairs; the bibliophile Jesse Moorland, in whose acclaimed repository at Howard the Hunts' papers now are archived; Rayford Logan, with whom Ida Gibbs Hunt worked in the 1920s on behalf of the Pan-African Congresses; the onetime Black Cabinet member Judge William Hastie; the historian Carter G. Woodson, Ida's sometime editor who founded and led the ASNLH almost until his death shortly before Consul Hunt's, and many such others.

In 1945 Zora Neale Hurston had written to W. E. B. Du Bois, exhorting him to sponsor "a cemetery for the illustrious Negro dead." "Let no Negro celebrity," she passionately argued, "no matter what financial condition they might be in at death, lie in inconspicuous forgetfulness." Of course, there neither is, nor can there be, only one, single such site. But in death, much as in life, the permanent residents of Lincoln Memorial Cemetery, "no matter [their] financial condition," do indeed cluster together. And those members of that significant and intriguing though frustrating group that Du Bois called the Talented Tenth still may convene for what might be imagined as sepulchral intellectual, political, and cultural salons at which they endlessly discuss, debate, and celebrate the pain as well as the myriad wonders of African American and black diasporic life.

The Gibbs-Hunts' Stories and Mine

And now, patient reader, your reluctant author reveals herself. I first saw William Henry Hunt's photograph in my childhood. The identification under it reads "Former U.S. Consul at St. Etienne, France," and the racially ambiguous Hunt seems every inch the distinguished foreign service officer that he was for many years. The picture appears in a book titled *A Study of Some Negro-White Families in the United States,* by Caroline Bond Day. She had acquired the photo from Consul Hunt as a result of their correspondence when he and Ida were living in the Azores. Caroline was my aunt, my mother's older sister, and in 1932 Harvard University published her seminal study of mixed-race persons as part of its academic series called Varia Africana. Because my own hardworking, obstinately optimistic family of achievers insisted that despite my gender and designated race any career would be open to me, that citation of an early twentieth-century Negro consul did not surprise me. But it should have. Hunt's life on the world stage was groundbreaking and unique.

The world is infinitely large, yet also small. Since members of the Talented Tenth, so designated by W. E. B. Du Bois, moved in interlinked circles, many of my relatives knew him, as well as Langston Hughes, Mary Church Terrell, Zora Neale Hurston, Captain Matthieu Boutté, Ambassador Edward R. Dudley, the journalist George Schuyler, Marian Anderson, the black Brain Trusters Ralph Bunche, William Hastie, and Robert Weaver, and others who populate these pages. Much later, I interviewed the Church-Terrells' daughter, Phyllis Terrell Langston, who was born while Ida Gibbs lived in her parents' home and was a flower girl at Ida and Billy Hunt's wedding. Later, I came to know Terrell Langston's only child as well. When my husband and I were newlyweds, Charles S. Johnson's son was a good friend, and in the next generation, his son has become our son Mark's neighbor and political compadre. In addition, the descendants of Consul George H. Jackson, who served in France with Consul Hunt a century ago and who took part in several of Du Bois's Pan-African Congresses, have recently discovered their own Negro heritage. Coincidentally, in 2007 the Jacksons' foundation granted our daughter Elizabeth one of the country's premier poetry awards. And like Billy Hunt, my green-eyed, light-skinned, but resolutely black-identified father, Arthur Logan, who was born and lived for his first ten years at Booker T. Washington's Tuskegee Institute, also went to Williams College, still an all-male institution when I, Arthur's only daughter, finished high school. He received a superb education there and graduated with academic honors in 1930, but also faced considerable bigotry and discrimination, as well as incredulity and wonderment about his full racial identity.

When I met Rayford Logan, from an unrelated family but also a Williams alumnus, at a State Department reception in the 1960s, he looked up at me and archly observed, "Ah yes, you are one of the tall Logans, while I am one of the short ones." During my (belated) graduate studies at Howard University a few years later, I took a challenging seminar called United States Foreign Relations, taught by the peerless Professor Arnold H. Taylor. It dramatically widened the narrow lens through which I had previously viewed the black American experience. While researching a term paper, "Women of the World: African-American Women as Internationalists, 1890–1940," I came across the writings of Ida Gibbs Hunt, Harriet Gibbs Marshall, Helen Curtis, Addie Waites Hunton, and Lucy Slowe, and began looking at such individuals with new eyes, seeing them beyond the boundaries of what have usually been presumed to be their intellectually and geographically circumscribed lives and interests. Arnold Taylor began to badger me about expanding my paper into a larger work.

I arrived in Washington just as its residents were granted the right to vote in presidential elections. (Our majority-black city still does not enjoy full voting representation in Congress.) Here I came to know and admire new generations of estimable black diplomats, both career officers and political appointees, especially the indomitable Patricia Roberts Harris, whom in 1965

President Lyndon Baines Johnson appointed as the country's very first female African American ambassador. Clifton Wharton Jr. is the elder son of the country's first black career ambassador, who was Billy Hunt's State Department colleague from 1924 to 1932. The younger Wharton also has contributed greatly to his country's foreign and domestic policies, and he too has become a friend. And so has Phyllis Gibbs Fauntleroy, who still often wears the etched gold bracelets that her great-great-uncle Mifflin gave his daughter Ida.

John L. Waller, who died in 1927, was the contentious United States representative in Madagascar whose tenure there shortly preceded that of consuls Gibbs and Hunt. He has ties to my life as well. In years past, my husband, Clifford Alexander, and Waller's Malagasy-American grandson, the acclaimed lyricist Andy Razaf (born Andreamentaria Razafinkeriefo), always called each other "cousin," but whether that was a term of endearment or an acknowledgment of real kinship, we do not know. For decades Clifford's mother, Edith McAllister, was a neighbor of the Wallers and Razafs in Westchester County, New York. During one family visit, Andy Razaf gave his much younger "Cousin Cliff" an autographed copy of the illustrated sheet music for his new masterpiece, "We Are Americans Too," a fierce anthem celebrating Negro Americans' patriotism in World War II. He also composed the brilliant down-and-dirty verses for scores of Jazz Age classics such as "Ain't Misbehavin'" and "Honeysuckle Rose," "Stompin' at the Savoy" and "The Joint is Jumpin'."

In the mid-1960s Clifford Alexander, less wounded by the country's enduring racism than many of his predecessors, became one of President Johnson's counsels (his office was located in the mammoth building across from the White House that often is called "Old State," where Consul Hunt had reported for so many years), then chairman of the federal Equal Employment Opportunity Commission. During that stretch the president also named him ambassador to Swaziland, which had been Britain's last-surviving colonial outpost in Africa. From 1977 to 1981 he again served his country as secretary of the army under President Jimmy Carter. Clifford was the first of his race to hold that position, and he delivered the graduation address at West Point just two years after the military academy finally admitted women. He promoted to general more than thirty African Americans, including the first black woman, Hazel Johnson. Among those new generals was one who achieved far greater acclaim on the national and world stage. His name is Colin Powell, and two decades later he became the United States' first black secretary of state.

While compiling and shaping the Gibbs-Hunts' story, I often asked myself, who among their contemporaries might have been the Colin Powells of an earlier generation? To achieve their ambitions, Powell and his successor, Condoleezza Rice, both of them ambivalent about or opposed to affirmative action, discerned the importance of having influential white male mentors, to the near exclusion of others. But absent his era's pervasive racism, would Colonel Charles D. Young, a rare late nineteenth-century black West Point graduate who served his nation in four other countries, have risen as far as did Powell, or as General and President Dwight Eisenhower, or General George C. Marshall, whose humane leadership and confident visions rehabilitated Western Europe after World War II? (And, I wonder, might General Marshall even have been related to Captain Napoleon Bonaparte Marshall?)

Mifflin Wistar Gibbs, Archibald Grimké, George H. Jackson, James Weldon Johnson, James G. Carter, William Yerby, William Henry Hunt, and a number of other Negro men, all received early State Department appointments. They never could advance far, yet admirably represented their country abroad. But if they had enjoyed the privileges and opportunities granted many of their white male contemporaries, they would have contributed much more than they did in helping to improve or repair the United States' sometimes tarnished image overseas — especially, perhaps, among the world's vast nonwhite majority. Although the barriers they had to surmount were far more challenging, I believe without doubt that tough, diligent, far-sighted, well-informed women such as Mollie Church Terrell, Anna Julia Cooper, and especially Ida Gibbs Hunt, all of whom often had to forswear their own vigorous aspirations, would have made superb ambassadors, generals, or admirals. It is hard to know or say whether they or the United States suffered more from the cruelty and mind-boggling stupidity of racism and sexism.

Secretary Powell increased diversity in his by then huge State Department (its employees now exceed twenty-five thousand) by cautiously advocating the recruitment of minorities, women, and persons with physical disabilities. Despite such initiatives, most of the department's senior positions remain in the hands of heterosexual white men, though lateral entries into mid-to-upper-level posts have ameliorated the stark underrepresentation of nontraditional appointees in the higher ranks. Early in the twenty-first century, the appointment of a black woman, Condoleezza Rice, as secretary of state did little more to recalibrate the foreign service's overall demographics, and most of those officials closest to Secretary Rice were white and male. Only in late 2008 did she concede that she wished the foreign service better reflected the United

States' glorious heterogeneity. In addition, she and her predecessor, Secretary Powell, sometimes to his apparent chagrin, presided over one of the more disastrous periods in United States history in terms of its arrogant diplomatic and military blunders and its resultant tattered image in the world. To succeed on a truly grand scale, celebrity and equal opportunities always include the possibility of highly visible failures, but Rice and Powell alone can hardly be held responsible for their country's reckless misadventures.

And now, the world has taken yet another turn. For the first time the United States has elected a man of color as its president. Our secretary of state, Hillary Clinton, is a formidable woman, and our ambassador to the United Nations, Susan Rice, is African American. President Barack Hussein Obama's heritage, however, does not reflect this country's abysmal legacy of Negro slavery. Rather, he is the son of a black Kenyan and a white Kansan, and he was raised in Hawaii and Indonesia. We remain optimistic but are yet to see whether such expanded power sharing and inclusiveness at home will translate to more enlightened policies abroad. Nonetheless, at President Obama's January 20, 2009, inaugural ceremonies, Elizabeth Alexander, my daughter, delivered her original poem "Praise Song for the Day," evoking her country's diverse history and promise, and especially the haunting praise songs of African and African American tradition.

My aunt Caroline Bond Day's book, which focuses on Americans of mixed racial ancestry but insists that they had no innate superiority over their darker-skinned brethren, was published before any of these latter-day contenders were born. It touches on William Henry Hunt, and also on members of my father's maternal family, who bore that same surname. They were light-skinned African Americans, some of whom looked a lot like Consul Hunt; and they too were assumed to have both white and Native American "blood." My parents assured me that those two "Negro-White" Hunt families shared no common ancestry, but I since have learned that both Billy Hunt's and my father's Anglo-American Hunt forebears maintained that they could trace their origins back to the Reverend Robert Hunt, the Anglican clergyman who came to the New World's Jamestown settlement in 1607 with Captain John Smith. But that jointly held belief, it seems, was only a wishful attempt on the part of Billy's and my own white antecedents to ennoble their humble lineage. In the context of Jamestown's four hundredth anniversary, historians burst those aspirational bubbles and overwhelmingly concur now that the acclaimed Reverend Hunt had no direct, linear descendants at all in the United States.

Into the 1920s, and well beyond, segregation and restricted opportunities still ensured that the small cadre of well-educated, successful African Americans remained a close-knit group, in some ways much like a family. I recently discovered that Consul Hunt and my great uncle, the Black Cabinet's Henry Alexander Hunt, met at the 1921 Pan-African Congress in Paris. Their ties to the African motherland, frayed by centuries of the international slave trade, as well as by slavery itself and the United States' brutal ongoing segregation and racism, could have been rekindled by their mutual interest in and attraction to that movement. Like a number of others of his race who traveled to France in those years, Henry A. Hunt may have visited or stayed at the consulate in St.-Étienne, which Consul William Henry Hunt slyly designated his Ville Noir. And those men, about the same age (the latter born in 1863 in southern Tennessee, the former in contiguous Georgia in 1869), did indeed look enough alike to be related. Both of them also had black female antecedents who shared the unusual given name Annekee (or Anneky), and both of those women, reluctantly or not, had borne white men's children. Considering these coincidences, wouldn't those two gentlemen named Hunt have wanted, and tried, to figure out if they might be kin?

I also learned that in the 1930s members of Roosevelt's Black Cabinet, many of them, like Henry A. Hunt, permanent residents of other states and therefore feeling displaced or lonely while they worked far away from home, often drove an hour north from the District of Columbia to enjoy Sunday picnics with native Washingtonians at the Montgomery County, Maryland, farm of Georgia Lawson, one of Ida's dearest friends. (On one occasion, observers spotted Mary McLeod Bethune, and her benefactor and chum Eleanor Roosevelt, paddling their feet in the Lawsons' mill pond.) Billy and Ida Hunt may well have reencountered Henry A. Hunt on just such an occasion. I first heard these stories, and more, when Georgia Lawson's son Jimmy invited me out to visit him at his family's rural abode. Long before, Ida Gibbs Hunt had given young Jimmy the tall gilded trophy that members of Consul Hunt's sporting club had bestowed on him when he left France in 1927, as well as more than six hundred of the Gibbs-Hunts' picture postcards sent to them by a diverse group of correspondents around the world over a span of fifty years. Jimmy Lawson saved those keepsakes into his eighties, then shared them with me.

After Henry A. Hunt died in Washington late in 1938, Du Bois eulogized his beloved colleague by rhetorically asking why he had stayed so resolutely within the African American community, never taken the easier path and opted to become the white man that his physiognomy seemed to declare him, when "thousands of men and women like him have done so." Those "thousands" who passed for white included several members of both Henry Hunt's and Billy Hunt's families. "The overwhelming opinion of white Americans is that . . . one black ancestor in eight or sixteen makes [a] tremendous difference of identity, of treatment and opportunity," Du Bois added. To further explain Henry Hunt's rationale, he argued that "to take a stand in America as anything but a Negro would have made him supremely unhappy, because here was an opportunity for battle . . . on the highest plane." "Life is primarily family and friends," Du Bois concluded, and "one cannot lightly cast off this enveloping and intriguing bond of love and affection and seek to create a new place in a strange world." Those sage words, which still reflect the United States' racial enigmas and inequities, also could have applied to W. E. B. Du Bois's other longtime friend: Consul William Henry Hunt.

In 1922 an unknown photographer, probably my aunt Caroline Bond Day or my maternal grandmother, Georgia Bond, took a snapshot of Wenonah and Ida Gibbs Hunt that I came across many years later. The worldly sixty-year-old woman, dressed in an ankle-length dirndl, looking a trifle stiff because she was already suffering from the arthritis that afflicted both her and her sister, and the girl with long thick braids, wearing her sashed, pleated skirt and proper schoolgirl's black stockings, stand close together under a grape arbor in the Bonds' backyard. Smiling, with their arms linked, they seem fully attuned to one another. The identifying caption, written in my mother's familiar hand, says: "Mrs Hunt & I." About that time, Ida asked Wenonah Bond to spend a year with her at the consulate in St.-Étienne. Shortly before my mother passed away in 1993, she told me that she had yearned to go. My loving but unyielding grandmother, however, refused to let her precious, plucky teenager leave Washington for an unknown and presumably reckless life among "foreigners" thousands of miles from home.

After my mother died, a tiny envelope addressed with a spidery script turned up among her jumbled belongings. The circular postmark, next to a fading maroon three-cent stamp, reads: WASHINGTON D.C. 1938 FEB 28 5:30 PM. Ida Gibbs Hunt's elegant, engraved ivory notepaper folded inside reveals a warm message thanking "My dear Wenonah," who had sent the Gibbs-Hunts an announcement of her daughter's birth. Following her 1931–32 sojourn in Europe, Wenonah Bond earned a graduate degree at Columbia University, became a social worker, and married Arthur Logan. She remained in New York City, resisting race-, class-, and gender-based inequities of all sorts and maintaining her curiosity about the world and its diverse people, yet she never emerged as a significant internationalist. Ida wrote that at a recent tea party in Washington she had talked with her friend Georgia Bond, who shared a photo of Wenonah holding her baby, newly christened Adele Hunt Logan: my name, and that of my paternal grandmother. Ida Gibbs Hunt said that the infant looked "bright and lively." I'd like to report that she added that I was the prettiest little girl she ever saw, but in truth, she did not. "Mr. Hunt," she continued, joined her in extending congratulations to the new parents. She closed her missive "affectionately," with love from "uzzer muzzer" — other mother.

That same bleak winter of 1938, with the world increasingly in disarray, Ida Gibbs Hunt expounded in "The Price of Peace" on her aspirations for, yet dire concerns about, the darker races. "Soon they will be a mighty army marching to victory, or death, if need be," she wrote. "We little know what the future may bring. . . . Empires fall and crumble but the world goes on."

For several years I have explored the Gibbs-Hunts' stories to better understand how their commitments, ambitions, and intellects shaped their lives, as did their assessments of and dealings with the magnificent greater world. I also have tried to explain how prejudices and segregation both demarcated and distorted those worlds — yet they and a few others transcended those daunting barriers. To those complex ends, and to add their clarion voices to a select chorus, I extend this tribute to Ida Gibbs Hunt and William Henry Hunt.

Acknowledgments

As I worked on this book, I needed and received the support of many wise and generous people. I scarcely know where to begin, but never could have done it without all of them. The following have shared their insights and information, and have been of invaluable assistance in pulling together this work: Eleanor Alexander, Elizabeth Alexander, Rae Alexander-Minter, Onesimo Almeida, Louis Andrell, Esme Bahn, Patrick Bellegarde-Smith, Allison Blakely, Jane Bond, Andrew Brescia, Adrienne Brooks, Ronald Bruce, Gail Buckley, A'Lelia Bundles, Bea Clark, Maryse Condé, Paul Phillips Cooke, Maceo Dailey, Horace Dawson, Tom Dillard, Shireen Dotson, Sarah Fee, Richard Fox, Doug Frank, Ficre Ghebreyesus, Paula Giddings, Debra Newman Ham, Rosemary Hanes, David Hardy, Louise Hutchinson, Lester Hyman, Renee Ingram, Kenneth Janken, Ben Justesen, Trica Keaton, Christine Kraemer, Edgar Krebs, Ray and Jean Langston, Jimmy Lawson, David Levering Lewis, Peter Lewis, Becky Livingston, Alan McPherson, Edna Medford, Marly Merrill, Cliff Muse, Nick Nesbitt, Ronald Palmer, Sharon Patton, Joe Reidy, Midge Richardson, Brian Roberts, Janet Sims-Woods, Jean Strouse, Ibrahim Sundiata, Arnold Taylor, Rosalyn Terborg-Penn, Harry K. Thomas, Barbara Walker, Wendy Walker, Clifton Wharton, Greta Wilson, and last but hardly least, Michael Winston. As for the late Donna Wells, John Hope Franklin, and Walter Hill, I will treasure your help forever, but miss your presence among us even more.

As always, I am indebted to Willard Gatewood. Ages ago, he saw my master's thesis, and has remained my mentor and friend ever since. Willard read every chapter of this new effort with vision, understanding, and a careful eye. He encouraged me all along the line and pointed out my errors of syntax, fact, and interpretation, then insisted that I send him the (more or less) finished manuscript for yet another reading. His critiques mean the world to me and I remain eternally grateful.

At George Washington University, I thank both my frustrating yet irreplaceable students and my colleagues, especially Bill Becker, Allida Black, Nemata Blyden, Bob Cottrol, Vanessa Gamble, Jim Horton, Dane Kennedy, Jim Miller, (as always) Michael Weeks and Evelyn Williams, and Andrew Zimmerman (a truly discerning reader). At the University of Virginia Press thanks to Ellen Satrom, Ruth Melville (a priceless editor), Raennah Mitchell, Morgan Myers, and especially Dick Holway, who told me eighteen years ago that he'd like to do a book with me someday. It took a long time but that day has come. I hope it was worth the wait.

Archival research has been essential. I thank the experts at Oberlin College, particularly Roland Bauman and Tammi Martin, and the attentive historians in Mason County, Kentucky. A number of folks at the National Archives and Records Administration, and at Manuscripts and Special Collections in the Library of Congress, have helped me as well, especially in leading me to and through the Kendrick-Brooks collection. I am infinitely grateful to Joellen ElBashir, among others, at Howard University's Moorland Spingarn Research Center. I received welcome guidance from many patient professionals and caretakers at Yale's Beinecke Library, Lincoln Memorial Cemetery, the American Geographical Society, Lawrence Academy, Princeton University, Williams College, and Harvard's Peabody Museum. All of them helped to make this work as complete and accurate as possible.

Others have held my hand, solved computer problems, fed and clothed me, kept mind, body, and home in order, and listened to retellings of "the life and times . . ." A big shout-out and hugs to those who helped to hold everything together. This group includes Andrea, Angela and Jim, Arica, Arlette, Barbara and David, Beckie, Bob, Brenda, Camille and Bill, Charity, Christian, Christine, Claudia and Fede, Colleen, Conxita and Richard, Cris, Dee, Dega, Deneen, Elinor, Eve, Evelyn, Grae, Hanna, Heidi, Janet and Bill, Janet and Calvin, Janice, Janice, Jean and Dan, Judy, Kim and Juan, Linda, Lonnae, Lucy, Maria, Maureen, Nan, Nancy and Ray, Paolo and crew, Ruth and LaSalle, Ruth Ann, Sandra, Scott, Sharon, Skip, Stephanie, Sununtha, T, Tamara and Gregory, Toni and Bob. Forgive me if your name is missing. My mind has become a sieve. You know who you are, and know that I remain ever grateful.

I also must express my personal and political pride and joy in our new first family. We all worked hard, and so did you. What a difference an election makes! Our country and the world feel different.

Ida Gibbs and William Henry Hunt have no direct descendants, but Phyllis Gibbs Fauntleroy and her daughters, Phylicia Fauntleroy Bowman and Jacqueline Ida Fauntleroy Long, as well as the late David Leer, helped me enormously, even when they feared I might not be getting it all quite right. I have respected both you and the Gibbses', Hunts', and Marshalls' legacies to the very best of my ability. Thankfully, almost everything you shared with me has been documented through independent sources.

Most important to me is my own family. In her final years, my mother, Wenonah Bond Logan, shared intriguing stories about her long relationship with and deep affection for Ida Gibbs Hunt. (How I wish I had known her!) As for today's and tomorrow's generations, big bouquets for Mark and Amy Alexander, Elizabeth Alexander and Ficre Ghebreyesus, and especially for Jonah, Maya, and Calvin, and Solomon and Simon — the amazing younger ones to whom I dedicate this book and whose respect I cherish. Lotsa, lotsa love and kisses, and never forget these stories.

Finally, there's my fabulous Clifford. He shared with me everything he could recall about his parents' ties to the Razafs and the Wallers, read every draft chapter, both praised my work and told me (with tactful honesty) when it was unreadable — and did the grocery shopping and much more. His love, support, patience, and enthusiasm have kept me going through this and many such projects, even when I have been a less than stellar companion. (Once again, wow! and a miraculous happy anniversary, my dear.)

These relatives and friends, supporters and colleagues have helped to make this book possible, but for any errors, omissions, and mistakes of fact or interpretation, I am responsible.

Notes on Sources

My last book had more than one hundred pages of endnotes. That falls into a category of "more information than one needs to know." Here, I pare that down as much as possible, avoiding repetition, yet providing curious readers with adequate data to further pursue lines of inquiry and curiosity suggested in the text without interrupting the story's flow. Traditional notation forms have been simplified, reconfigured, or even laid aside. I provide some sources in a paragraph at the start of each section of chapter notes, followed by the notes themselves, keyed to pages. Those give citations for specific quotations and unfamiliar information. I do not include notes when the sources are clearly indicated in the text and additional citations would be redundant. The material's variety and complexity, however, results in occasional exceptions and segues that represent my musings.

The following key provides abbreviations or acronyms for names (personal and institutional) and sources referred to more than a couple of times in the notes. The selected bibliography offers full citations that can provide the reader with information that may not appear elsewhere. I have not divided this list into books, articles, or journals, primary and secondary, published or unpublished sources, one reason being that in some cases I use a book or article as a primary source, but on other occasions as a secondary one. I also like to find all of an author's work situated in one place. And really, what difference does it make if a source has been published or not? I belong to a senior generation, but researching with and through Google has become almost second nature. I have not, however, included data here that were not confirmed in two or more electronic sources. Unless this material includes specific quotations, I generally do not provide the source, since it is widely available online.

To compensate for aberrant filing, my notes usually indicate correspondence and the like from specific collections by name and date, either in addition to or instead of the usual box or folder numbers. Less frequently cited manuscript collections, journals, and the like appear only in the notes.

Acronyms, Abbreviations, and Short Titles
Used in the Notes and Selected Bibliography

Manuscript Collections

AGS	American Geographical Society Archives
BTW, LOC	Booker T. Washington Papers, Library of Congress
FD, LOC	Frederick Douglass Papers, Library of Congress

Hunt, MSRC	William Henry Hunt–Ida Gibbs Hunt Papers, Howard University, Moorland Spingarn Research Center
K-B, LOC	Kendrick-Brooks Family Papers, Library of Congress
MCT, LOC	Mary Church Terrell Papers, Library of Congress
MCT, MSRC	Mary Church Terrell Papers, Howard University, Moorland Spingarn Research Center
NARA	National Archives and Records Administration
RWL, LOC	Rayford W. Logan Papers, Library of Congress
WEBD, LOC	W. E. B. Du Bois Papers, Library of Congress

Newspapers and Journals

CAM	*Colored American Magazine*
CAN	*Colored American* (newspaper)
Crisis	*The Crisis: A Record of the Darker Races*
JNH	*Journal of Negro History*
NYAN	*New York Amsterdam News*
NYT	*New York Times*
Opportunity	*Opportunity: A Journal of Negro Life*
WES	*Washington Evening Star*
WP	*Washington Post*

Individuals and Organizations

AJC	Anna Julia Cooper
FD	Frederick Douglass
HG or HGM	Harriet Gibbs Marshall
IG or IGH	Ida Gibbs Hunt
JML	John Mercer Langston
JWJ	James Weldon Johnson
MCT	Mary (Mollie) Church Terrell
MWG	Mifflin Wistar Gibbs
NBM	Napoleon Bonaparte Marshall
PAC	Pan-African Congress
RMJ	Richard Mentor Johnson
WEBD	William Edward Burghardt Du Bois
WHH	William Henry Hunt
WILPF	Women's International League for Peace and Freedom

Prologue

The epigraph from Henry James's *Washington Square* epitomizes the late nineteenth century's social ambience and societal mores as applied to class among the United States' elite, and specifically their attitudes toward gender and marriage. The articles about the Gibbs-Hunt wedding appeared in *WES* and *WP*, April 14, 1904.

Here and elsewhere, I rely heavily on Appiah and Gates, *Africana;* Hine et al., *Black Women in America;* and Logan and Winston, *Dictionary of American Negro Biography,* for background information about African American leaders and events.

2   *a noted scholar:* I urge the reader not to look for the title or author of the "mystery novel" until this chapter's end. To do so would eliminate the surprise of discovery.

3   *performed the ceremony:* In addition to the *WES* and *WP* articles on the indicated dates, *CAN,* April 15, 1904, also ran a detailed description of the Gibbs-Hunt nuptials.

3   *had made great strides:* Details of WHH's background from the first chapter of his "Cabin to Consulate."

5   *encaged Congolese pygmies:* On the captive Congolese pygmies here and elsewhere, see Bradford and Blume, *Ota Benga.*

7   *amendment to the Constitution:* Kristof, "Marriage," cites the constitutional amendment that Georgia representative Seaborn Roddenberry introduced in Congress in December 1912.

7   *"Indians, Chinese, Filipinos":* MCT, *Colored Woman,* 383.

8   *"peau rouge":* WHH, "Cabin to Consulate."

12   *"brilliant social function":* CAN, April 15, 1904.

12   *"Memory fails":* WEBD, *Autobiography,* 12.

13   *the audacious teacher:* Descriptions of Caroline Wynn and suppositions that she was modeled on IGH first suggested to me by David Levering Lewis, and found in WEBD, *Quest,* 253–54, 258, and throughout chap. 24.

14   *"overlord of the county":* WHH, "Cabin to Consulate," 3.

16   *"Being an Alexander":* IGH to "L.E.," May 1926, Hunt, MSRC, box 1, folder 37.

1. The Vice President's Daughters

Frances Ellen Watkins Harper's novel *Iola Leroy,* quoted in the epigraph, is a touchstone throughout this book. MWG knew Harper in Philadelphia during his youth. Her novel's title is arguably one source of the pseudonym that IGH adopted in the 1920s. Harper's focus on racial complexities and insistence on more privileged African American women's responsibility to less fortunate members of the race who needed "uplift" inspired and shaped IGH's life. Meyer's biography of RMJ, while written from a traditional white male perspective in the 1930s, provides ample details about Vice President

Johnson's "life and times." Also helpful is John Cooper's "When No One Won." Since RMJ was a public figure, numerous Web sites provide similar details about him. Much information in this chapter comes from the U.S. censuses for Tennessee's Scott and Mason counties, 1820 through 1860, and for Oberlin, Ohio, in 1850, 1860, and 1870. For Oberlin, my primary sources have been Bigglestone's *They Stopped in Oberlin*, JML's autobiography, and Oberlin College's archival records. Marlene Merrill has my thanks for her prior research on women and African Americans at Oberlin, especially in Lawson and Merrill, "The Antebellum 'Talented Thousandth.'"

19   *"Rumpsey Dumpsey"*: This phrase is found in virtually every account of RMJ's life. It supposedly first appeared in a poem by Richard Emmons. See J. S. Cooper, "When No One Won," part 2.

19   *"civilize" and "socialize"*: Ibid., part 3.

20   *"illustrated abolitionist principles"*: Meyer, *Life and Times,* 413.

21   *"No one can more sincerely"*: Ibid. 211, 313.

21   *"chief manager of the domestic concerns"*: Ibid. 317.

23   *Some of his white critics:* J. S. Cooper, "When No One Won," part 2.

24   *one critic said:* Meyer, *Life and Times,* 413.

24   *Another fellow observed:* Ibid.

24   *a political cartoon:* "An Affecting Scene in Kentucky," *Harper's Weekly,* n.d., in http://loc.harpweek.com/LCPoliticalCartoons.

24   *A smutty pun:* Meyer, *Life and Times,* 422, 466.

24   *a patron at Johnson's tavern:* Ibid., 340.

26   *Uncle Tom's Cabin:* Stowe's book first appeared in serial form in 1852 and 1853, then the next year as a novel.

27   *"a negro girl named Maria"*: Weld, *American Slavery,* 166.

29   *"my dear colonel"*: J. S. Cooper, "When No One Won," part 2.

29   *"rare intellectual achievements"*: From thebgs2@home.com. Other information about the Johnson-Pence family in http://www.pipeline.com/~richardpence/bibles.

29   *Those same records show:* "Slavery in Mason County, Kentucky," Deed Book 37, 233–34.

30   *mama's baby:* Spillers, "'Mama's Baby.'"

32   *"peddling goods, wares"*: "Slavery in Mason County, Kentucky," Judgements, November 1, 1855, Case 19824.

34   *their oldest girl:* "Mary Jane Patterson," in Hine et al., *Black Women in America,* 911–12; and Lawson and Merrill, "Antebellum 'Talented Thousandth.'"

34   *"the education of people of color"*: "Oberlin College," in Hine et al., *Black Women in America,* 897.

34   *"not the pool of Bethesda"*: Ibid., 898.

35   *"for future usefulness"*: Bigglestone, *They Stopped in Oberlin,* 1.

36   *"Lady Gibbs"*: Mentioned several times in WHH, "Cabin to Consulate."

36 *"I hate to say these things"*: Egypt, *Unwritten History of Slavery,* 169, 174.

37 *"I have had a model wife"*: MWG, *Shadow and Light,* 64.

2. *Mirror of the Times*

MWG's autobiography, *Shadow and Light,* is the primary source for this chapter. His words on autobiography in the epigraph carry weight beyond their specific application here. Other background sources include Dillard's "Black Moses of the West," his "Golden Prospects and Fraternal Amenities," and Woodson's "The Gibbs Family." Also see Stanley, *Hurry Freedom;* Killian, *Go Do Some Great Thing;* and Winks, *Blacks in Canada.* Concerning early African American State Department consuls, the most comprehensive source is Justesen's "African-American Consuls Abroad." In the early 1990s, Professor Arnold H. Taylor provided his students (including me) with a copy of a typescript from the State Department titled "Negroes Employed at Officer Levels in the Department of State," and Ambassador Ronald D. Palmer shared similar information that he has compiled. Biographical entries for a number of Negro consular officers also appear in the *Dictionary of American Negro Biography* and *Africana.* These sources have been compared and culled for the information at this chapter's end. Charles Kennedy's *The American Consul* details the consular service in its entirety before World War I.

39 *"I still see"*: MWG, *Shadow and Light,* 17–18.

40 *"go do some great thing"*: Ibid., 36–37.

42 *"Indians, Africans"*: Dillard, "Black Moses," 28.

42 *"the first periodical in the state"*: Ibid., 31.

42 *"Truth, crushed to earth"*: From the few extant copies of *Mirror of the Times,* LOC, Newspapers and Periodicals Division.

42 *"We will never willingly pay"*: Dillard, "Black Moses," 34.

43 *Archy Lee was different*: A synopsis of the Archy Lee case and Peter Lester's beating in ibid., 35–36.

44 *Gibbs's farewell message*: Ibid., 39.

44 *"Now and always"*: FD quoted in Bell, "Negro Nationalism," 42.

45 *"On account of the salubrity"*: MWG, *Shadow and Light,* 60.

45 *"An important step"*: Ibid., 63–64.

46 *"rich planter who died"*: Ibid., 228–29.

46 *"resisting expulsion"*: IGH, "Recollections of Frederick Douglass," 203.

46 *"pulsebeat of the great national heart"*: MWG, *Shadow and Light,* 64.

47 *Just two years earlier:* The political efforts of black Americans in Vancouver are detailed in Dillard, "Black Moses," 58–59; and throughout Killian, *Go Do Some Great Thing.*

47 *But the election's sore losers:* Killian, *Go Do Some Great Thing,* 121–23.

48 *"Whatever the future may have"*: FD quoted in Bell, "Negro Nationalism," 42.

48 *Colonial hosted a gala:* For the Colonial Opera House incident, see Killian, *Go Do Some Great Thing,* 116–26; and Dillard, "Black Moses," 53–55.

50 *"I had left politically ignoble":* Killian, *Go Do Some Great Thing,* 144.

51 *"it was not without":* Ibid.

51 *"sits like a nightmare":* Dillard, *Black Moses,* 69.

51 *"revolutionary change":* Ibid., 70.

52 *"Ku Klux":* MWG, *Shadow and Light,* 112.

53 *"carpetbag Negro":* Dillard, "Golden Prospects," 308.

54 *"I take the first opportunity":* MWG to FD, April 5, 1884, and July 19, 1889, FD, LOC, reels 4 and 5. The MWG-FD correspondence stretched at least from 1884 until 1895. See FD, LOC, reels 4, 5, 6, 8, and 9, much of which is undated.

54 *"No one that I could":* MWG to FD, n.d., FD, LOC, reel 6.

55 *"wants white representation":* FD to MWG, 1895, ibid., reel 8.

55 *"[i]f we were only united":* Ibid.

55 *"was the grand old man":* MWG to HGM, November 11, 1912, Washington Music Conservatory Papers, MSRC, box 1.

55 *cablegram of condolence:* MWG to Helen Pitts Douglass, February 24, 1895, FD, LOC, reel 8.

56 *U.S. Constitution:* Article 2, Section 2(2).

57 *"Liberia-Madagascar-Azores circuit":* This phrase appears in many places, including Palmer's "Black Pioneer Officers."

59 *"Madagascar had not come":* MWG, *Shadow and Light,* 223.

3. Ida Alexander Gibbs's Pictures from a Well-Spent Youth

MCT's *Colored Woman,* 32, is the source of the epigraph. In addition to the sources about Oberlin mentioned above, I also use JML's autobiography, *From the Virginia Plantation.* On African American leaders and their lives in Washington, D.C., I rely greatly on Gatewood's *Aristocrats of Color* and Moore's *Leading the Race.* Giddings has an excellent description of the 1893 Chicago Exposition in *Sword among Lions,* as does Larson in *Devil in the White City* and Levy in *James Weldon Johnson.* Most information here about Paul Laurence Dunbar and Alice Moore Dunbar derives from Eleanor Alexander's riveting dual biography, *Lyrics of Sunshine and Shadow.*

62 *John Mercer Langston:* Quotations from JML, *From the Virginia Plantation,* 101, 97, 159.

62 *She was born:* AJC's year of birth is variously reported as 1858 or 1859.

63 *"the first institution of learning":* JML, *From the Virginia Plantation,* 100.

63 *"You learned another thing":* Ibid., 138.

63 *Mollie Church . . . commented:* Quotations from MCT, *Colored Woman,* 45, 47, 33.

63 *"if there is an ambitious girl":* Lemert and Bhan, *Voice of Cooper,* 87.

63 *"College-bred women"*: MCT, *Colored Woman,* 120.

64 *"Teaching had always seemed"*: Hutchinson, *Ann Julia Cooper,* 38.

64 *beribboned parchment diplomas:* IGH's diploma in Hunt, MSRC, box 6.

64 *"'real ladies' did not work"*: MCT, *Colored Woman,* 59.

65 *Molly boarded:* Ibid., 85–87.

65 *"shy of women"*: Ibid., 32.

65 *"guiding star"*: This phrase appears several times in WHH, "Cabin to Consulate," and in his letters to IG.

66 *"Negro melodies"*: HGM, "Music as a Proffession."

69 *embroidered silk streamer:* In Hunt, MSRC, box 2, folder 49.

69 *spoke "so enthusiastically"*: MCT, *Colored Woman,* 64.

69 *"Mr. Terrell . . . used to go"*: Ibid., 102.

70 *"In five years"*: Ibid, 106. Photograph of Phyllis Terrell (Langston) in Hunt, MSRC, box 2, folder 69.

70 *"[W]e both believed"*: IGH, "Recollections," 202.

71 *"[I]t is rumored"*: CAN, September 1, 1900.

71 *Du Bois described:* Quotations from WEBD, *Quest,* 253–54, 258.

72 *"my wife's life-long training"*: WEBD, *Autobiography,* 281.

74 *"He isn't so bad as a lover"*: IG to HG, January 15, 1898, Hunt, MSRC.

74 *"there is no need"*: CAN, October 27, 1900.

74 *"such a high toned place"*: MWG to WHH, January 26, 1903, Hunt, MSRC.

74 *"Although seventy-eight"*: CAN, March, 1901.

74 *"brainy . . ."*: WHH to IG, January 12, 1901, Hunt, MSRC, box 1, folder 16.

75 *admiring reporter wrote:* CAN, May 21, 1898.

75 *"Mrs. Mifflin Wistar Gibbs"*: Ibid., March 24, 1901.

75 *"carry out our intentions"*: WHH to IG, March 18, 1903, Hunt, MSRC, box 1, folder 16.

75 *"We are not growing any younger"*: WHH to IG, January 12, 1901, ibid.

76 *"supposed to be worth"*: CAN, September 7, 1901.

76 *"giving it a good send off"*: MWG to IG, March 1902, Hunt, MSRC.

76 *"there is much dissatisfaction"*: MWG to BTW, January 31, 1902, BTW, LOC, reel 197.

76 *"I have your and Ida's letters!"*: MWG to WHH, January 26, 1903, Hunt, MSRC, box 1, folder 1.

76 *"here I speak only French"*: WHH to IG, February 24, 1902, ibid.

77 *"When Paul Dunbar married"*: MCT, *Colored Woman,* 111.

78 *a chatty news item:* CAN, May 14, 1904.

78 *"alarming growth of color prejudice"*: Ibid., February 1, 1902.

79 *engraved invitations:* Gibbs-Hunt wedding invitation in Hunt, MSRC, box 2, folder 36.

79 *"the appointment of Mr. Hunt"*: CAN, September 4, 1901.

79 *"the present of $1,000"*: Ibid., April 16, 1904.

81   *"most brilliant social function":* Ibid.

81   *one of which was signed:* Dated April 12, 1904, in WHH, MSRC, box 2, folder 69.

4. "From Cabin to Consulate"

Much of the information in this chapter is derived from WHH's manuscript memoir, first shared with me by Ambassador Palmer. A copy resides in Hunt, MSRC. One of my greatest challenges has been to sort truth from fiction in this memoir. I think I have it right, but who really knows? Hunt had good reason to reshape data about his early life for expediency's sake, and also for posterity. The Horatio Alger aspects of his story are so remarkable that I have included several references from *Risen from the Ranks, or Harry Walton's Success.* As to Alger's homosexuality, see especially Salmonson, "The Dark Side of Horatio Alger, Jr." In my efforts to verify and detail various aspects of WHH's stories, I have accessed Franklin County, Kentucky (free, slave, and agricultural), and the Missouri and Minnesota censuses from 1860 until 1900, as well as city directories from Nashville, St. Louis, and Minneapolis–St. Paul. Child's memoir, *The Pearl of Asia,* gave me insights into his life as a diplomat in Siam and provided comparisons to WHH's statements in "Cabin to Consulate." I was struck by my own memories of Verne's *Around the World in Eighty Days* and its similarities to WHH's stories. Rereading it reinforced my belief that it provided the inspiration for WHH's account of his two-year circumnavigation (real or fabricated) of the world. (I provide no page numbers here because *Around the World* has appeared in so many versions.) Andrew Brescia and Doug Frank at Lawrence Academy and archivists at Williams College have shared with me information they had about Billy Hunt's tenure at their schools.

82   *"Youth is hopeful":* Alger, *Risen from the Ranks,* 13.

83   *"an American colored youth":* WHH, "Cabin to Consulate," 1.

84   *"overlord of the county":* Ibid., 3.

86   *"attachment to the straggling village":* Ibid., 7.

86   *"ever-ready rattan cane":* Ibid.

87   *"found it quite impossible":* Ibid., 8.

87   *"Great Magician Heller":* Ibid., 9.

88   *"I blossomed out":* Ibid., 14.

88   *"life was considered too cheap":* Ibid., 15.

88   *"had no children":* Ibid., 17.

89   *"a house of ill fame":* Ibid., 19.

89   *"Republican State Convention":* Ibid., 20.

89   "Wanderlust *claimed me":* Ibid., 21.

90   *"staggered me beyond all else":* Ibid., 23. The story of WHH's purported travel around the world in ibid., 22–44.

90   *imperial city of Siam:* Quotations about WHH's stay in Siam, ibid., 29–33.

91 *"We dined together"*: Ibid., 37.

92 *"dreamland of waltz"*: Ibid., 42.

92 *"unable to reach his bedside"*: Ibid., 44.

93 *von Munchausen:* WHH to Robert Terrell, June 1898, MCT, LOC. I thank Allison Blakely for sharing a copy of this letter, which mentions WHH's interest in Baron von Munchausen.

94 *"Most Magnificent Hotel"*: Advertisement in Minneapolis *City Directory,* 1889.

94 *"[D]uring my residence"*: WHH, "Cabin to Consulate," 44.

95 *"the school-maggot"*: Ibid., 46.

96 *"explained fully my situation"*: Ibid., 49.

96 *"heard it said"*: Ibid., 50.

96 *"a place where we were taught"*: Quoted in Frank, "First Black Students." Most of the school's older archives were lost in two early twentieth-century fires.

97 *"swanky and aristocratic"*: WHH, "Cabin to Consulate," 52.

98 *"On completion"*: All quotations in paragraph from WHH, "Cabin to Consulate," 56–57.

99 *"Freshman Editorial"*: Williams College *Yearbook,* 1895, Archives of Williams College.

99 *tenth reunion snapshot:* Shared with me by Jimmy Lawson. All of this material awaits cataloguing in Hunt, MSRC.

99 *"I have realized since"*: WHH, "Cabin to Consulate," 57.

100 *"there was no future for me"*: Ibid.

101 *Hunt boasted:* Ibid., 61, 62.

101 *"when the time arrived"*: Ibid., 64.

102 *"had no previous experience"*: Ibid.

102 *"all barriers were swept"*: Ibid.

102 *"being firm in the belief"*: Ibid., 65.

103 *"I have made a good beginning"*: Alger, *Risen from the Ranks,* 13.

5. The Madagascar Portfolio

Various authors have chronicled the Waller incident: Ambassador Skinner, historians Woods and Blakely, anthropologists Walker and Krebs, and Singer, in his book on Andy Razaf. (Razaf, the Malagasy-American jazz lyricist formidably named Andreamentaria Razafinkeriefo at birth, was John Waller's grandson.) I read everything I could find on Madagascar. My Eritrean-born son-in-law, Ficre Ghebreyesus, made it a mission to educate me more fully about the continent of his birth. Priestley's *France Overseas* has been especially helpful on French colonialism. "Despatches from United States Consuls in Tamatave, 1853–1906" (NARA, Record Group 59, roll 11, vol. 11) includes the State Department's official Madagascar correspondence from that period. MWG's *Shadow and Light* and WHH's "Cabin to Consulate" document those men's personal experiences.

108 *Hunt reported:* WHH to Robert H. Terrell, June 1898, MCT, LOC, box 1.

108 *"it was a mistake":* Quoted in Krebs and Walker, "Madagascar," 130.

110 *"red hot iron":* WHH, "Cabin to Consulate."

110 *One article asserted:* Krebs and Walker, "Madagascar," 130.

110 *"I would rather die":* Ibid.

112 *Hunt's analysis:* WHH, "Cabin to Consulate," 66–67.

112 *Hunt glibly wrote:* WHH to Robert H. Terrell, June 1898, MCT, LOC, box 1.

112 *Hunt later wrote:* WHH, "Cabin to Consulate," 69, 73. Also see WHH, "Inauguration of a Railway."

113 *Gibbs and Hunt were greeted:* Quotations from WHH, "Cabin to Consulate," 70, 71; and WHH to Robert H. Terrell, June 1898, MCT, LOC, box 1.

114 *Madagascar:* Most background information about the island from Brown, *History of Madagascar.*

114 *coral and silver necklace:* MCT, *Colored Woman,* 3. MCT heard her grandmother identified as a "Malay princess." Malaysia was the geographic origin of many Madagascans, so this more or less confirms the story shared with me by MCT's grandson, Ray Langston, who describes the necklace in his possession as coming from Madagascar.

114 *Tamatave's climate:* WHH, "Cabin to Consulate," 70.

115 *"difficult to forget":* Ibid., 71.

115 *"indigenous population":* WHH, "Medical Work in Madagascar."

116 *Hunt staunchly defended:* WHH, "Cabin to Consulate," 103. The anthropologist Sarah Fee explained to me the Académie Malgache's past and present significance.

116 *"je serais heureux":* All quotations from these cards (mistakes included) from uncatalogued Lawson postcards, Hunt, MSRC.

116 *"[I]t is unnecessary to say:* WHH to IG, March 18, 1903, Hunt, MSRC, box 1, folder 16.

117 *the generic Malagasy:* WHH, "Cabin to Consulate," 90.

117 *"High Commissioner for the French":* Ibid., 86.

117 *"a man is judged":* Ibid., 73.

117 *reported in his autobiography:* MWG, *Shadow and Light.* Details about the menagerie also from NARA, RG 59, roll 11, vol. 11, May through October 1899.

118 *Hunt later wrote:* WHH, "Cabin to Consulate," 75–76.

119 *his follow-up cable:* MWG to David J. Hill, Assistant Secretary of State, June 30, 1899, NARA, RG 59, roll 11, vol. 11; and MWG, *Shadow and Light,* 308–11.

119 *"the animals be returned":* WHH, "Cabin to Consulate," 76.

119 *"The Doctor tells me":* WHH to IG, January 12, 1901, Hunt, MSRC, box 1, folder 16.

120 *"brave, capable":* WHH, "Cabin to Consulate," 80.

120 *Gibbs lamented:* MWG, *Shadow and Light,* 284.

120 *series of articles:* WHH, "Inauguration of a Railway" and "Population of Mada-gascar." See also "Chemin de Fer de Tananarive à la Mer," Hunt, MSRC, box 3, folder 80.

121 *"I had no more chance":* WHH, "Cabin to Consulate," 78, 79.

121 *"They might see":* MWG to WHH, January 16, 1902, Hunt, MSRC, box 1, folder 28.

121 *"One of the Professor's friends":* WHH, "Cabin to Consulate," 80.

122 *"blend in":* My thanks to Louis Andrell, who has several of the "other" William Henry Hunt's papers, for sharing his understanding of Roosevelt's purported statement. Letter from President Theodore Roosevelt to the white William Henry Hunt on his gubernatorial appointment, September 26, 1901, in http://www.gilderlehrman.org/collection.

122 *"barriers such as differences":* WHH, "Cabin to Consulate," 77.

122 *solicited the new consul:* Ibid., 78. WHH reported this invitation to the Department of State on December 4, 1901.

122 *Their trek:* WHH's descriptions of this trip from ibid., 78, 81–84.

124 *"keep your head cool":* Ibid. See Pieterse, *White on Black,* 195–98, for a discussion of this fear of the possible transference of melanin, or blackness.

124 *active social life:* WHH, "Cabin to Consulate," 113.

125 *he again crossed paths:* WHH's quotations about this episode from ibid., 93–95.

126 *"I have at last brought":* WHH to IG, October 19, 1903, Hunt, MSRC, box 1, folder 16.

126 *"Spider Spun Silk":* Hunt, MSRC, box 3, folder 82.

126 *he noted:* WHH, "Cabin to Consulate," 88–90.

127 *he later insisted:* WHH, "Cabin to Consulate," 107.

127 *"Among the cherished memories":* Ibid., 110.

127 *"Nobody took a livelier interest":* CAN, March 22, 1905.

128 *"BH improves with age":* IGH to HG, August 15 and 17, 1904, and February 18, 1905, Hunt, MSRC, box 1, folder 28.

128 *"high class Indians":* IGH to HG, August 15, 1904, ibid.

128 *"loose and flowing":* IGH to HG, n.d., Hunt, MSRC, box 3, folder 79.

129 *"suited Ida's temperament":* WHH, "Cabin to Consulate," 110.

129 *"I am not overburdened":* IGH to HG, July 31 and August 17, 1904, and February 18, 1905, Hunt, MSRC, box 1, folder 28.

129 *Gibbs Hunt wrote:* Ibid., and IGH's undated manuscript re Thomas Nelson Page, folder 29.

131 *"Life in the tropics":* WHH, "Cabin to Consulate," 104, 111.

131 *death of one such person:* WHH described the circumstances surrounding Dennis Sullivan's death in several letters to the State Department in January and June 1906, "Despatches," NARA, RG 59, roll 11, vol. 11.

131 *informational broadside:* Hunt, MSRC, box 2, folder 42. For details about the Niagara Movement, see esp. D. L. Lewis's *Du Bois: Biography,* chap. 12, "Going

over Niagara." Documents concerning the first and second Niagara conferences and detailing IGH's involvement in the movement are grouped together, alphabetically and by date, in WEBD, LOC.

133 *"Because of the subjugation":* IGH quoted in Rouse, "Out of the Shadow," 40.

133 *The controversy began:* A number of sources reference the Brownsville debacle, including my own *Homelands and Waterways,* 387–89.

134 *Another event:* For AJC's removal from the principalship of the M Street School, see esp. Hutchinson, *Anna Julia Cooper,* 66–83.

135 *"If you hear from Pa":* IGH to HG, February 18, 1905, Hunt, MSRC, box 2, folder 28.

135 *"to some other post":* Alvee A. Adee, Department of State, to MWG, March 29, 1905, Hunt, MSRG, box 2, folder 3.

135 *"I am glad to be able":* Third Assistant Secretary of State (name illegible) to IGH, November 11, 1906, ibid., box 1, folder 25. St.-Étienne is the preferred form, but when quoting from original documents, I use the differing spellings, accents, and hyphenations for such names as they appear in those sources.

136 *"the wheaten loaf":* WHH, "Inauguration of a Railway," MSS in AGS Archives. Invitation from Libbey to Gallieni, Libbey to WHH, August 1, 1905, Hunt, MSRC, box 1, folder 1.

137 *a new typewriter:* Carter's request, January 29, 1907, NARA, RG 59, State Department 1906–1910, "Minor Files," reel 1228.

137 *"There is an idea":* C. S. Osborn, *Madagascar,* 375.

6. France, 1907–1918

Among the best sources concerning France, race, and expatriate black Americans are Archer-Straw, *Negrophilia;* Bernard, *Afro-American Artists in Paris;* Dunbar, *Black Expatriates;* Edwards, *Practice of Diaspora;* Pieterse, *White on Black;* and Stovall, *Paris Noir.* James Weldon Johnson's authobiography *Along This Way,* the source of this chapter's epigraph, epitomizes the overromanticized vision that some African Americans had of France in this era. For the significance of Africa and Africans in the Great War, see esp. Crowder and Osuntokun, "First World War." Significant secondary sources on African Americans in that conflict include Barbeau and Henri's *Unknown Soldiers* and Buckley's *American Patriots.* Also see my chapter "Captains' Tales," in *Homelands and Waterways.* Scott's *Official History* is probably the best overall contemporary account. Badger chronicles James Reese Europe during and after World War I in *A Life in Ragtime,* while Mathews's biography does the same for Henry Ossawa Tanner.

138 *"empty champagne bottles":* WHH, "Cabin to Consulate," 118.

139 *the city where he would be stationed:* Ibid., 119–24.

139 *George H. Jackson:* U.S. Department of State, "Negroes Employed at Officer Levels"; and Palmer, "Black Pioneer Officers."

140 *"some new coon"*: Blakeley, "Richard T. Greener," 314, quoting a State Department memorandum from July 1907.

140 *convivial Billy Hunt:* Quotations in this paragraph from WHH, "Cabin to Consulate," 121, 122.

141 *"My appointment as Consul"*: Ibid., 123.

141 *"the biennial inspection"*: Ibid., 124–26.

142 *"I am very satisfied"*: Gallieni to WHH, February 24, 1907, Hunt, MSRC, box 1, folder 1; dinner by WHH honoring Gallieni, ibid., box 3, folder 88.

142 *thorny issue:* WHH, "Lunacy in France," NARA, RG 59, State Department 1906–1910, "Minor Files," reel 1228, May 20, 1907.

143 *"prolong her stay"*: WHH, "Cabin to Consulate," 126.

143 *"royally received"*: My thanks to Ben Justesen for sharing this tidbit he found about IGH in the *Indianapolis Freeman,* August 10, 1907.

143 *"St. E. is not"*: IGH to William Wilson, October 3, 1907, Hunt, MSRC, box 2, folder 38.

143 *"The weaver of St. Etienne"*: WHH, "Cabin to Consulate," 128.

143 *Billy's . . . pen pals:* Uncatalogued Lawson postcards; similar quotations are found in letters throughout Hunt, MSRC, box 1.

144 *that treacherous plot:* For details of the Johnson-Anderson-Washington plot against WHH, see Levy, *James Weldon Johnson,* who mentions "You're All Right, Teddy," 102. In *Booker T. Washington Papers,* see esp. 9:256, 257, 276–77, 403, 10:494–95, and 11:380. Nothing about the incident appears in JWJ's autobiography, *Along this Way,* and WHH mentions it not at all, leading to the supposition that he never knew what was transpiring.

144 *"free from the conflicts"*: JWJ, *Along This Way,* 207–9.

146 *"Many thanks"*: WHH to JWJ, December 1911, JWJ Papers, Beinecke Library Archives, Yale University, consular letters, series 1, box 5.

147 *"handsome silver trophy"*: *Washington Bee,* March 20, 1914.

147 *Its problems surfaced:* Dillard details MWG's misfortunes concerning the bank in "Black Moses," 104–10.

149 *Four years later: Washington Bee,* May 23 and October 17, 1908.

149 *"An honor rarely bestowed"*: CAM, October 1909, 299.

149 *a unique assignment:* WHH, "Cabin to Consulate," 133–35.

150 *"the blue manufacture"*: Uncatalogued Lawson postcards, Hunt, MSRC.

150 *"would alienate Dr. Washington"*: MCT, *Colored Woman,* 194.

150 *"that my experience"*: MWG to WEBD, January 14, 1910, WEBD, LOC, reel 1.

151 *"great brains"*: WEBD, *Autobiography,* 280, 282.

151 *conference on textiles and tariffs:* Hunt, MSRC, box 6, album.

151 *reported to the State Department:* Ibid., box 3, folder 81.

151 *Other involvements included:* WHH, "Cabin to Consulate," 129, 138–40.

152 *similarly thrilling escapade:* Ibid., 167.

153 *occasions to speak in public:* Ibid., 131.

153 *"located on a wooded hill":* Ibid., 148.

153 *"he realized that he was not":* Ibid., 165.

153 *Reverend Frank Nelson:* Account of their reunion in Rome in ibid., 151, 152.

154 *"Senator and Mrs. Willard Saulsbury":* Ibid., 168.

154 *Union Française:* Undated pamphlet, Hunt, MSRC, box 2, folder 60.

155 *"the vacation months of July":* Lemert and Bhan, *Voice of Cooper,* 321, 327–28.

155 *wrote his older daughter:* Dillard, "Golden Prospects," 333; and MWG to IGH, January 24, 1913, Hunt, MSRC, box 1, folder 13.

156 *William Libbey:* My thanks to Princeton University's archivists for providing biographical information, including an obituary, on Professor Libbey, and to David T. Hardy for informing me about Libbey's tenure at the National Rifle Association and his interactions with President Wilson between 1916 and 1918.

156 *"I haven't heard from Pa":* IGH to MCT, April 20, 1915, Hunt, MSRC, box 1, folder 13.

157 *laudatory obituary: Crisis,* October 1915, 274.

158 *President Wilson:* Wilson's racism has been extensively documented. See esp. O'Reilly, *Nixon's Piano,* 85, for Wilson's "darky" stories.

158 *"Fate of the 'Darker Races'":* Hunt, MSRC.

158 *"I don't have to do anything":* IGH to MCT, April 20, 1915, ibid.

159 *"fratricidal war":* IGH to MCT, ibid.

159 *Billy Hunt admitted:* WHH, "Cabin to Consulate," 153, 154.

159 *Ida's report:* IGH to MCT, April 20, 1915, MCT, MSRC.

160 *From the first encounters:* Quotations in next three paragraphs from WHH, "Cabin to Consulate," 155, 157, 163, 164.

161 *"Who could have imagined":* WHH, "Cabin to Consulate," ibid.

162 *memorial carte postale:* This and additional cards mentioned below in uncatalogued Lawson postcards, Hunt, MSRC.

162 *"Europe is suffering":* IGH to MCT, April 20, 1915, MCT Papers, LOC, reel 4.

163 *"with a few notes about my life":* WHH to WEBD, January 19, 1916, WEBD, LOC, reel 5.

163 *"a member of one of the first":* WHH, "Cabin to Consulate," 159, 160.

164 *"must change things":* IGH to MCT, April 20, 1915, MCT, LOC, reel 4.

165 *her equivocal review: JNH,* October 1918, 444–45.

165 *"knitting and crocheting":* IGH to MCT, April 20, 1915, MCT, LOC, reel 4.

165 *Hunt gradually came to believe:* Following quotations all from WHH, "Cabin to Consulate," 170–80.

166 *French press applauded:* D. L. Lewis, *WEBD: Biography,* 565; WHH, "Cabin to Consulate," 173.

167 *poem . . . sketch:* Hunt, MSRG, box 3, folder 77; and WHH, "Cabin to Consulate," 144.

167 *"Our Government's patience"*: Hunt, "Cabin to Consulate," ibid.

167 *Du Bois urged:* "Close Ranks," *Crisis,* July 1918, 111; WEBD, *Autobiography,* 274.

169 *"Tho The Crisis"*: IGH to WEBD, July 12, 1918, WEBD, LOC, reel 6.

169 *"dirty nigger"*: In several sources, including Buckley, *American Patriots,* 197.

170 *"St. Etienne machine guns"*: Little, *Harlem to the Rhine,* 317.

170 *"As the first American officer"*: Ibid.

170 *"Your little friend"*: Uncatalogued Lawson postcards, Hunt, MSRC.

170 *"the cannonading"*: Little, *Harlem to the Rhine,* 57.

171 *"he was wounded"*: Scott, *Official History,* 262.

171 *"Three times"*: *Crisis,* February 1918, 168.

171 *"one of the strange coincidences"*: IGH to WEBD, November 23, 1918, WEBD, LOC, reel 6.

172 *"Into this maelstrom of war"*: Scott, *Official History,* 375.

172 *Henry Ossawa Tanner:* For details of his painting and other work during World War I, I thank Ray Alexander-Minter. Also see my *Homelands and Waterways,* 414, 486.

173 *"England had Canadians"*: *Crisis,* December 1918, quoted in Buckley, *American Patriots,* 221.

174 *Du Bois set sail:* See esp. D. L. Lewis, *Du Bois: Biography,* chap. 19, "The Wounded World."

174 *"questions which you and I"*: IGH to WEBD, November 23, 1918, WEBD, LOC, reel 6.

175 *"To France"*: K-B, LOC, box 13, folder 8.

7. France, 1918–1927

Contee, Edwards, Geiss, and Janken have written effectively on various aspects of pan-Africanism. For WEBD, nothing comes close to Lewis's biographies, and pan-Africanism's role in his life spans vols. 1 and 2. Logan lays out his personal involvement in "Historic Aspects of Pan-Africanism," which I thank Michael Winston for sharing with me. Also helpful in compiling this chapter have been Benson's *Battling Siki,* Rose's *Jazz Cleopatra,* and Josephine Baker's autobiography. And see notes here for chapter 5 on Andy Razaf, and for chapter 6 on black American expatriates in France. D. L. Lewis details the intricacies of Du Bois's and Gibbs Hunt's sojourns in Paris, especially during the 1919 PAC, and other incidents retold here. His earlier study, *When Harlem Was in Vogue,* in my estimation, is the best history to date of the Harlem Renaissance. WEBD, LOC, includes every known document pertaining to the PACs of the 1920s. IGH's memorabilia from those PACs is in Hunt, MSRC, box 2, folder 56. Several sources about the Garvey movement also appear in the bibliography. The epigraph for this chapter comes from an untitled, undated essay by IGH in K-B, LOC, box 13, folder 8; and Hunt, MSRC, box 3, folder 76. Given the references therein, there is little question as to when she wrote it.

176   *they both arrived:* Lewis points to the detailed documentation of IGH and WEBD's mutual activities in Paris in this period as evidence of their intimate personal and physical relationship. I am convinced only of their intense intellectual intimacy.

176   *That month's report:* Quoted in Lewis, *Du Bois: Biography,* 561.

176   *"the problem of the twentieth century":* Lewis, *Du Bois: Biography,* chap. 11, "The Souls of Black Folk."

177   *Paris itself intoxicated:* WEBD quotations from Lewis, *Du Bois,* chap. 19, "The Wounded World."

177   *"watched as if":* Ibid., 569.

178   *pan-Africanist interests:* Little, however, has been investigated or written about the critical but constrained roles women and gender played in the 1920s pan-Africanism.

180   *advocates claimed:* Van deBurg, *Modern Black Nationalism,* 12, gives this alternate explication of UNIA.

183   *Attired in a modest:* A blurred photograph of the PAC in *Crisis,* May 1919, 32, unfortunately could not be adequately reproduced for this book.

184   *James Reese Europe:* In addition to Badger's *Life in Ragtime,* my own *Homelands and Waterways,* 538–40, documents his story.

184   *"We are both sorry":* IGH to WEBD, March 6, 1919, WEBD, LOC, reel 4.

185   *"I am full of regret":* WEBD to IGH, April 17, 1919, ibid., reel 7.

185   *but she did go:* Quotations on MCT's travels to Zurich and St.-Étienne from *Colored Woman,* 338–54.

186   *she incredulously asked:* IGH to MCT, 1919, in MCT Papers, LOC, reel 4; MCT, *Colored Woman,* 341. Schaffer's "Lost Riot" provides an excellent account of Washington's disturbances in 1919.

187   *"well-merited recognition":* IGH to Archibald Grimké, July 31, 1919, Grimké Papers, MSRC, box 5, folder 95.

187   *Boisneuf:* Buckley details the incident in *American Patriots.*

189   *"How is the Pan-African":* IGH to WEBD, June 7, 1921, WEBD, LOC, reel 9.

190   *"I am counting on your presence":* WEBD to IGH, June 23, 1921, ibid.

190   *"of which Mr. Logan":* IGH to WEBD, September 11 and 16, 1923, ibid., reel 11.

190   *"I hope that you will agree":* WEBD to IGH, August 28, 1923, ibid.

190   *"I read with great interest":* Isaac Béton to IGH, n.d., and IGH to Béton, ibid.

191   *"tho I had made all preparations":* IGH to WEBD, August 22, 1921, ibid., reel 9.

191   *she may have read:* IGH's presentation is not mentioned by Lewis or in WEBD's papers concerning the 1923 PAC, but the information does appear in an article in the *Chicago Defender,* November 14, 1925.

192   *their poetry:* Cf. IGH's "To France" (quoted in chap. 6), with Fauset's "The Negro Soldiers" and "Christmas Eve in France."

192   *"On that platform":* Fauset, "Impressions of the Second Pan-African Congress," *Crisis,* November 1921, 15.

192 *Logan recalled:* Logan, "Historical Aspects," 94.

193 *"As experience and knowledge grow":* in Lewis, *Du Bois.*

193 *"Civilization, civilization":* Quoted in Stovall, *Paris Noir,* 32.

194 *From his hotel:* All quotations about this trip from WHH, "Cabin to Consulate," 144–47.

194 *Italian-made movie:* Rosemary Hanes at the LOC's Moving Images Section ferreted out this information for me.

195 *that he was a Negro:* Years ago the historian Jane Bond heard this comment from Rayford Logan and shared it with me.

195 *Ida also purchased: NYT,* February 21, 1922.

195 *she delivered a lecture:* The *Washington Tribune,* May 22, 1922, mentions IGH's lecture "The Women of France," presented at Dunbar High School. I found the manuscript of her speech titled "The New Sphere of Woman" in K-B, LOC, box 13, folder 8, but it clearly provides the gist of her talk at Dunbar, then later revised. I have not been able to determine how some of IGH's oeuvres and memorabilia came to reside in these papers, but assume that she became a friend of Antoinette Brooks Mitchell in Paris in the 1920s. The photo of Wenonah Bond and IGH, in my possession, was taken during IGH's 1922 visit to Washington.

196 *leave the country:* Wenonah Bond Logan shared this incident with me in 1990.

196 *in a letter:* Wenonah Bond's letter reprinted in *New York Age,* 1932.

197 *"Iola Gibson":* The use of literary aliases by African American women is cited in several entries in Hine et al., *Black Women in America;* MCT mentions using Euphemia Kirk in *Colored Woman,* 222.

198 *sleight of hand:* Brian Roberts shared with me this interpretation of the "Iola Gibson" pseudonym. For an insightful reading of IGH's work, see his "Artistic Ambassadors," chap. 5, "Diplomats but Ersatz."

199 *"doesn't understand your brief":* Quotations in the following paragraphs from IGH's argument with WEBD throughout September and October 1923 are from WEBD, LOC, reel 12, Pan-African Association Congress and their personal correspondence.

200 *"strictly private":* IGH to WEBD, 1931, ibid.

200 *self-serving response:* Béton's message concerning IGH was enclosed in WEBD's letter back to her.

202 *"to prevent another holocaust":* IGH, "New Sphere of Women." In the absence of a full transcript of her talk at the 1923 Pan-African Congress, I assume that these words on the same subject reflected her views on women's rights at that time.

202 *"back to Africa":* Logan, "Historical Aspects," 97.

202 *internecine squabble:* For the quarrel between Diagne and Maran, see Edwards, *Practice of Diaspora,* 188; Egonu, *"Les Continents";* and Janken, "African American and Francophone Black Intellectuals."

203 *"I came to Lisbon": Crisis,* January 1924, 170.

203 *"the most popular man"*: Ibid., March 1924, 202.

204 *"Africa is at once"*: Ibid. Van DeBurg, *Modern Black Nationalism,* 47–50, and others, quote Du Bois's flowery writing during this, his first trip to Africa.

205 *"Diagne is a Frenchman"*: WEBD, "The Negro Mind Reaches Out," in Alain Locke's *The New Negro,* quoted in Janken, "African American," 503.

205 *Nardal sisters:* In addition to Edwards, *Practice of Diaspora,* see Boittin, "In Black and White," which focuses on the Nardals.

205 *postwar journals:* See Janken, Edwards, Boittin, and Stovall on French colonial journals in the 1920s.

206 *familiarity with American consular activities:* Edwards, *Practice of Diaspora,* 226, 367; Wayne Cooper, *Claude McKay,* 225, 235.

207 *defend her PhD dissertation:* Edwards, *Practice of Diaspora,* 126–28; Lemert and Bhan, *Voice of Cooper,* 320–30.

207 *number of female PhD's:* The others were Eva B. Dykes, Otelia Cromwell, and Georgianna Simpson.

208 *notorious legal case:* The Rhinelander story is fully detailed in Earl Lewis and Ardonizze, *Love on Trial;* and see my "Color of Blood."

209 *letter to the editor: International Herald Tribune,* December 10, 1925. Responses appeared in the *Tribune* on December 12, 15, and 23. The Rhinelander controversy continued for some time. See IGH to WEBD, January 4, 1926, WEBD, LOC, reel 20; and WEBD, *Crisis,* December 1926.

210 *"vogue for Negroes":* Quoted in Boittin, "In Black and White," 125. See Archer-Straw, *Negrophilia,* for black women's skin-lightening and hair-straightening efforts.

210 *Battling Siki:* The French also glorified yet tried to dismiss as a savage the ill-fated Siki, whom gangsters in New York City shot and killed that same year.

211 *letter to her brother:* IGH to "L.E.," May 1926, Hunt, MSRC, box 1, folder 37. It is a bit confusing that, though clearly written to her brother Horace, the greeting is to "L.E."

211 *"Rallye Passe Partout":* WHH, "Cabin to Consulate," 243.

212 *Croisière Noire:* Archer-Straw, *Negrophilia,* 67–70. An earlier Croisiere Noire took place in 1923.

212 *"I am not a Bolshevik":* IGH to Addie Hunton, enclosed in a September 1927 letter Hunton forwarded to WEBD, in WEBD, LOC, reel 1.

213 *"ship the archives":* WHH, "Cabin to Consulate," 169.

213 *French sportwriter:* Quoted in ibid., 143.

213 *downcast members:* Following quotations from ibid., 136, 142, 143, 175–77.

214 *Hunt later reminisced:* Ibid., 178.

214 *René Maran:* Quoted in Stovall, *Paris Noir,* 32.

8. Snapshots from Guadeloupe

Older as well as recent Anglophone materials on Guadeloupe in this period are sparse. I found several articles, including IGH's "The Hurricane," in *Crisis;* one in *Opportunity;* and another in Cunard's *Negro: An Anthology* — and that only in the rare, unedited first edition at MSRC. Kleinberg's *Black Cloud,* about the hurricane of 1928, provides in-depth information on Atlantic storms and cites WHH's memoranda to the State Department in his chapter "The Islands," 35–46, but he focuses more on Florida than the Caribbean. His chapter "Zora," 205–11, however, led me to Zora Neale Hurston's *Their Eyes Were Watching God,* the source of the epigraph. Additional information about Guadeloupe has been gleaned from travel brochures, encyclopedias, Web sites, general histories of the Caribbean, and WHH's memoir. The American Red Cross documents at NARA include detailed information about the damage inflicted during the 1928 hurricane in Record Group 2, boxes 709 and 750–54. My friendship with Bea Stith Clark led me to Maryse Condé and her extensive work about her home island. During a discussion with Condé in April 2005, she generously assessed and corrected a draft of this chapter.

215 *"I've worked hard"*: IGH to Addie Waites Hunton, September 1927. Waites Hunton enclosed this letter in one of her own to WEBD, in WEBD, LOC, reel 1.

217 *"What a curious way"*: *Crisis,* May 1927, 105, and October 1927, 374.

219 *"do not consider themselves"*: *Time* magazine, January 9, 1928.

219 *Once ashore:* Following quotations from WHH from "Cabin to Consulate," 179–83.

220 *Ida drily commented:* IGH to WEBD, January 19, 1928, WEBD, LOC, reel 27.

221 *Maillard . . . wrote:* Maillard, "In the French West Indies."

222 *"the language of their parents"*: Here and in next paragraph, Flavia-Leopold, "Child in Guadeloupe," 497, 498.

222 *retold in* Crisis: Cook, "Would You Like?" 382.

223 *"Is the life blood"*: Here and next paragraph: WHH, "Cabin to Consulate," 183.

224 *"to show where they came from"*: Condé, "Role of the Writer," 697.

224 *"Practically all social functions"*: Cook, "Would You Like?" 383.

224 *"Surprised to find"*: IGH to WEBD, January 19, 1928, WEBD, LOC, reel 21.

224 *"Unique brotherhood"*: Condé, "Role of the Writer," 697.

225 *"sale nègre"*: Bea Stith Clark clarified for me the heavily freighted significance of this phrase in the French Caribbean.

225 *"the child"*: Maillard, "In the French West Indies."

225 *Baker's first motion picture: NYT,* June 28, 2005.

226 *"about the French colonies"*: Baker and Bouillon, *Josephine,* 84.

226 *"today a foreign power"*: Balch, *Occupied Haiti,* 157; and see Plummer, "Afro-American Response."

227 *denigrated the local people:* Plummer, "Afro-American Response," 130.

227 *"fear the American": Opportunity,* December 1927.

228 Dark Princess: For some reason, William Yerby, one of Hunt's few African American foreign service colleagues, became incensed when he heard that the book was circulating among his consular staff in Portugal.

228 *"Just a word of congratulations":* IGH to WEBD, July 5, 1928, and WEBD's response, August 3, WEBD, LOC, reel 25.

229 *Writing the following winter:* Unless otherwise attributed, quotations in the ensuing pages from IGH, "Hurricane."

229 *"The scenery is wild":* IGH to Addie Hunton, September 1927, WEBD, LOC, reel 1.

230 *"tropical storm of considerable intensity":* Kleinberg, *Black Cloud,* 37.

230 *"negro huts of no particular value":* Ibid., 38.

232 *In his own account:* Unless otherwise attributed, quotations in the ensuing pages from WHH, "Cabin to Consulate," 184–88.

236 *"In view of the rottenness":* Kleinberg, *Black Cloud,* 41.

236 *"Perhaps you know that":* IGH to WEBD, October 25 and 26, 1928, WEBD, LOC, reel 27.

236 *"We have lost so much":* IGH to WEBD, October 26, 1928, ibid.

237 *"Thank you very much":* WEBD to IGH, November 7 and December 6, 1928, ibid.

238 *"Captain Marshall's article":* IGH to WEBD, February 12, 1929, ibid., reel 29. I found several references to this piece by Marshall in the "Sunday 'World,'" but was not able to locate the article itself.

238 *"with the supremacy":* WHH, "Cabin to Consulate," 189.

238 *"a thunder storm in comparison":* Ibid., 191.

9. Odysseys through the Portuguese Atlantic

Anglophone sources about the Portuguese Atlantic are even sparser than those on Guadeloupe. Onesimo Almeidō, a scholar of the Azores, tells me that more is available in Portuguese, but not much. For background information on Portugal and its empire, I relied on a combination of encyclopedias. The Web site http://www.usconsulateazores.pt/ historyoftheconsulate is an informative electronic source about the American presence there. While browsing the Internet I came across Dames and Seeman's article "Folklore of the Azores," which was helpful concerning the islands' cultural heritage. It includes the translated Azorean *fado* which opens this chapter. It seemed especially fitting in characterizing the evanescence of the Gibbs-Hunts' two years in São Miguel.

240 *Hunt later described it:* WHH's account of the journey in "Cabin to Consulate," 191–94.

242 *"nothing more or less":* WHH's description of the Azores in ibid., 191–96.

243 *"Mother of Navigators":* Ibid., 205.

243   *"peasant crop"*: Ibid., 196.

245   *Hunt flatly declared:* Following quotations from ibid., 197.

246   *"Azores-Madagascar-Liberia circuit"*: Palmer, "Blacks Pioneer Officers," 263.

247   *Consul Hunt's exequatur:* November 1929, Hunt, MSRC, box 3, folder 40.

247   *he later wrote:* Quotations in next three paragraphs from WHH, "Cabin to Consulate," 196–99, 201.

248   *chatty epistolary relationship:* WHH and WEBD corresponded several times early in 1930, and the photo of WHH appeared in *Crisis* that January.

248   *"Harriet Beecher Stowe"*: *NYAN,* June 6, 1929.

249   *"limited knowledge of the language"*: WHH, "Cabin to Consulate," 192.

249   *Hunt also corresponded:* Caroline Bond Day to WHH, June 2, 1930, Caroline Bond Day Collection, Correspondence, 1926–1931, Peabody Museum Archives, Harvard University. The photograph appears in Day's *A Study of Some Negro-White Families.*

250   *a contentious gathering:* An account of the Foreign Service Association meeting on Haiti, and Du Bois and Marshall's roles in it, in "Our Policy on Haiti."

250   *"south as far as Tuskegee"*: HGM to WEBD, February 25, 1930, WEBD, LOC, reel 33.

251   *"with the powers"*: HGM to IGH, December 25, 1930. Hunt, MSRC, box 1, folder 20.

251   *"I am glad to hear"*: WEBD to NBM, August 12 and 14, 1930, WEBD, LOC, reel 31.

251   *Marshall told Du Bois:* NBM to WEBD, January 1 and 18, 1931, ibid., reel 35.

252   *Hattie meanwhile:* HGM to IGH, September 29, October 20 and 22, 1930, Hunt, MSRC, box 1, folder 20.

252   *"the first time he has had"*: HGM to IGH, December 25, 1930, ibid.

252   *Hattie informed Ida:* HGM to IGH, October 20 and December 28, 1930, ibid.

253   *"I have never been the same"*: Horace E. Gibbs to HGM, October 15, 1930, ibid., folder 12. I have been unable to determine when his accident occurred or what it entailed.

253   *"the very movements"*: WHH, "Cabin to Consulate," 198–201.

254   *"advanced to the grade"*: Following quotations from ibid., 200, 202.

254   *Ida wrote Du Bois:* IGH to WEBD, January 24, 1931, WEBD, LOC, reel 34.

255   *a seriocomic odyssey:* Following account from WHH, "Cabin to Consulate," 203–10.

258   *"What a shame"*: Clifton R. Wharton Jr., who is preparing to publish his memoirs, found these quotations about the Gibbs-Hunts' brief visit to the Canaries in his mother's 1929 diary and generously shared them with me.

258   *"a number of educated Senegalese"*: WHH, "Cabin to Consulate," 211.

258   "Great iron canoes": Quoted in Putnam, "'Modern Slaves,'" 244.

259   *Hunt later recalled:* WHH, "Cabin to Consulate," 210–11.

10. Liberia

In contrast to the sparse materials about Guadeloupe and the Portuguese Azores, scholars and sojourners have written a lot about Liberia, much of it dealing with the turmoil there during the 1920s and 1930s. Until the modern era, those were the most fractious years in Liberia's history, especially concerning its often ambivalent relationship with the United States. See especially the works by Taylor and Sundiata listed in the bibliography. Liberia has also inspired an eclectic mix of writings by a variety of African Americans, from the nineteenth-century consul Henry F. Downing's *The American Cavalryman: A Liberian Romance* (his fictionalized take on Charles Denton Young's first assignment in that country, which Ida Gibbs Hunt reviewed in 1917), to Bundy's "Folk-Tales from Liberia," Schuyler's histrionic novel *Slaves Today,* and Charles S. Johnson's posthumously published memoir, *Bitter Canaan.* Also see Christy's "Liberia in 1930," a somewhat racist but detailed account. During the period in question, contributors to the foremost Negro American journals, *Crisis* and *Opportunity,* frequently opined about the black African republic. In addition, Padgett's "Ministers to Liberia" proved invaluable to me, as did Putnam's "'Modern Slaves'" and Phillip Johnson's dissertation, "Seasons in Hell." I thank former U.S. Ambassador to Liberia Lester A. Hyman for his insights about the diplomatic reciprocity requiring that a black Liberian ambassador would come to this country's segregated nation's capital if we sent someone of that same rank to Liberia. A clipping of the distasteful ditty by Consul Horton, used as the epigraph to this chapter, was found in the Hunts' papers, MSRC, box 6, clippings album.

260 *ample fanfare: Crisis,* April 1931, 132.

260 *"Only in Liberia": Opportunity,* May 1931.

261 *an array of African Americans:* The succession of official American diplomatic representation in Liberia is admirably laid out in Padgett, "Ministers to Liberia." The men who preceded Owen Lun Smith are specified here in chap. 2.

262 *"swore like a trooper":* RWL Diary, 1950, RWL, LOC, container 3. RWL's diaries run chronologically but are minimally dated.

262 *"You should never curse":* Bundy, "Folk-Tales from Liberia," 447.

263 *"working for the overthrow":* WHH, "Cabin to Consulate," 212.

264 *"Officials of the Liberian Government":* quoted in Taylor, "Involvement of Black Americans," 61.

264 *"anomalous position":* A sentiment slightly revised from ibid., 74.

265 *"none but Negroes":* From the Liberian constitution, quoted in WHH, "Cabin to Consulate," 215.

267 *dispatch a delegation:* Phillip Johnson's "Seasons in Hell" provides excellent details about the Christy Commission and Charles Johnson's 1930 sojourn in Liberia, including the description of Henry Carter as "half tanked," 204.

268 *"U.S. Negroes were a hundred years":* Christy, "Liberia in 1930," and similarly in WHH, "Cabin to Consulate," 203.

269 *On reviewing Johnson's account:* WEBD details the debate over Charles Johnson's report to the League of Nations in several articles that appeared in *Crisis,* March through July 1931.

271 *"missionary enterprise as the hand-maiden":* WEBD, *Crisis,* March 1931, 101–2.

271 *"Liberia is no more guilty":* Ibid., May 1931, 172.

272 *"independent government":* Ibid.

272 *nosed around Monrovia:* Schuyler's trip to Liberia is detailed in his articles in the *New York Post,* June and July 1931, and he fictionalized a lot of data from that sojourn in *Slaves Today.*

273 *"no arrangements whatever":* Quotations in this and next three paragraphs from WHH, "Cabin to Consulate," 212–13.

274 *a sizable household:* Photographs of the Gibbs-Hunts' household staff and other associates in Monrovia in Hunt, MSRC, box 2, folder 70.

274 *"occupied by the whites":* Following quotations from WHH, "Cabin to Consulate," 217–21.

275 *"heaps of refuse":* NYT, January 11, 1931.

275 *"rice, manioc, palm oil":* Quotations in following paragraphs from WHH, "Cabin to Consulate," 217–21.

277 *"my legs already refuse":* HGM to IGH, July 9, 1931, and August 17, 1931, Hunt, MSRC, box 1, folder 20.

277 *"I take this opportunity":* IGH to WEBD, April 21, 1931, WEBD, LOC, reel 34.

278 *"Any effort on the part":* WEBD to IGH, May 20, 1931, ibid.

279 *"assumed the dual functions":* Following quotations from WHH, "Cabin to Consulate," 213.

280 *"I know of no place":* Quoted in Phillip Johnson, "Seasons in Hell," 189.

280 *"Most of the educated":* WHH, "Cabin to Consulate," 213, 215.

281 *"screened [it] in":* Ibid., 218–19.

281 *Ida fell victim:* For the following description, I accessed numerous Web sites on malaria, its symptoms, course, and treatment. Horace E. Gibbs to IGH, August 9, 1931, Hunt, MSRC, box 1, folder 12.

282 *"condition was so serious":* WHH, "Cabin to Consulate," 219.

282 *"hospital a 'farce'":* Phillip Johnson, "Seasons in Hell," 209.

282 *"'Manny Chair'":* WHH, "Cabin to Consulate," 219.

282 *"it must have been against":* Lillie Mae Hubbard to WEBD, September 1931, WEBD Papers, LOC. Hubbard's letter also discussed the careers of William Yerby and Carleton Wall.

283 *"long and expensive journey":* WHH, "Cabin to Consulate," 219. IGH's hospitalization in New York mentioned in "Society," *NYAN,* November 25, 1931.

284 *"overstepped the bounds of courtesy":* Quoted in Taylor, "Involvement of Black Americans," 74.

285 *in response to a request:* Letter from State Department to Woodson concerning WHH reprinted in Padgett, "Ministers to Liberia," 92.

11. Fading Images

Distilling a quarter century of world history into one chapter that also details the private lives of IGH, WHH, and their associates has been daunting. What is relevant, what is not? How deeply should I delve? Much of the information here is available in encyclopedias, history texts, newspapers, or journals, and I have benefited by talking with several people who knew the Hunts, including my late mother, Wenonah Bond Logan, Jimmy Lawson, and David Leer. Phyllis Gibbs Fauntleroy shared her memories and memorabilia, then hesitated about having much of what she told me concerning the family be attributed to her or appear in print. I assured her that I would be discreet and only do honor to her relatives. Fortunately, other sources and public records have reconfirmed what she told me. Useful descriptions of President Franklin Roosevelt's "Black Cabinet" appear in Weiss's *Farewell to the Party of Lincoln*, Sitkoff's *New Deal for Blacks*, and O'Reilly's *Nixon's Piano*.

287   *much of the artwork:* Archivists at Howard University find no records of the artwork that the Gibbs-Hunts donated, but Gibbs Fauntleroy told me about and confirmed that gift, as did the late David Leer.

287   *an elegant table:* Jimmy Lawson and Phylicia Fauntleroy Bowman mentioned in interviews the foods that IGH and WHH prepared for family and friends.

288   *"To enter into relations":* "La Langue Française," *WP,* November 13, 1932.

289   *Relatives, friends:* There is no extant description of NBM's funeral and its attendees. His grave and HGM's, however, appear as described, as does Colonel Young's, and there are accounts of other military funerals at Arlington Cemetery in that era.

291   *the first woman:* On the first women foreign service officers, see Foley, "Diversity in Diplomacy."

292   *"gorilla in human form":* MCT, *Colored Woman,* 47. References comparing black people to monkeys still appear with appalling frequency, as in the *New York Post*'s February 22, 2009, cartoon that portrayed a dead animal, with observers commenting, "They'll have to get someone else to write the next stimulus bill," an obvious reference to President Barack Obama and the recent incident when a gorilla was killed after mauling its owner's friend. *Post* spokespersons first denied culpability, but then conceded that the portrayal was (at the least) ill advised.

293   *"Our Duty to Liberia":* Hunt, MSRC, box 3, folder 55.

293   *Marcus Garvey's earlier:* Following his release from a federal prison and deportation from the United States, Garvey returned to his native Jamaica for several years, then relocated to London, where he died in 1940.

293   *Lucy Diggs Slowe:* "Luncheon: January 24, 1936 — Crandall Hall," MSRC, Slowe Papers, box 20, folder 7.

295   *David was gay:* Everyone with whom I spoke who remembered David Leer agrees that he was gay. The intimate relationship between Slowe and Mary Burrill was and is well known, while several scholars have speculated on an earlier

romance between Burrill and Grimké. Little is known about Edmond Burrill, but one member of the family suggested that, like Mary, he too probably was homosexual. The "nature vs. nurture" debate about the determinants of sexual orientation continues.

296 *playfully called:* David Leer's use of those terms of endearment first shared by Gibbs Fauntleroy but substantiated by Phylicia Fauntleroy Bowman, Jimmy Lawson, and Leer himself. I spoke by telephone with Leer in Palm Beach, Florida, in 2005, shortly before his death the next year.

297 *"charming and dignified":* RWL Diary, January 1948, RWL, LOC, container 3.

297 "It's my country": MCT, *Colored Woman,* 99.

297 *Joyce Garrett:* Palmer's "Black Pioneers." Brian Roberts shared with me the April 1960 *Ebony* magazine article about Lillie Mae Hubbard.

298 *Arse-an'-all:* Quoted in Roberts, "Artistic Ambassadors," 221.

301 *interminable decolonization struggles:* I appreciate my colleague Dane Kennedy's observations in "Decolonization and Disorder," on the multidimensional chaos generated by the legacies of imperialism as the European nations granted independence to their various African and Asian colonies.

301 *ran virtually nothing:* I was astounded to find that the *WP* and *NYT*'s exhaustive indexes turned up only brief paragraphs on this major postwar colonial confrontation. Those few came from French news services, but at least one longer account appeared in the *Chicago Defender,* a major "black" newspaper.

301 *first major exhibit:* The Smithsonian has had a collection of Madagascan silks and artifacts, however, for many decades. See Kraemer and Fee, *Objects as Enigmas.*

303 *Pinkett:* My thanks to John Hope Franklin, Deborah Newman Ham, Arnold H. Taylor, and Michael Winston for sharing remembrances of Harold T. Pinkett. Franklin and Pinkett were great friends and frequent travel companions. My conversation about Pinkett with Franklin in spring 2008 was the last I had with him. When I told him about this book, what most intrigued him was the Madagascar story line, because that island was the world's most abundant source of orchids, which he lovingly cultivated.

303 *Logan acerbically observed:* RWL Diary, January 1945, RWL, LOC, container 3.

305 *Fanny Hunt Murray:* In "Cabin to Consulate" WHH states that his sister Fannie had children and grandchildren in California. I have not been able to fully track them down, however, since the only clue to their identities is a single reference to Walter Murray in the *NYAN* "Society" column, August 11, 1934, which mentions a visit to his "uncle and aunt, Mr. and Mrs. William H. Hunt," in Washington. That led me to his mother's and sister's names in the U.S. censuses for New York City in 1900 and 1910.

306 *died quietly at home:* Obituaries for WHH in, e.g., *Atlanta Daily World,* December 28, 1951. Death had already come, two years before, to another man who shared that name. As recounted in chapter 5, the white William Henry Hunt served as governor in the American territory of Puerto Rico from 1901 through

1904. He may have become entangled in some unspecified misconduct there, but thanks to his influential family and solid political affiliations, he was relocated to Montana, where he became a respected federal district judge. He retired to California, then to Virginia, not far from Washington, D.C., where he died Nothing suggests that Governor and Judge William Henry Hunt and Consul William Henry Hunt ever actually met.

307   *"Beware!":* This is my interpretation of Phylicia Fauntleroy Bowman's account of the "black house" on their block. She also told me about IGH trying to teach her French by using the embroidered *mouchoir*.

307   *candid 1950 proposal:* IGH, letters to the editor, *WP,* March 4, 1950. An earlier letter about truck traffic in Washington, ibid., May 26, 1936.

309   *"Three Oberlin 'Old Grads'":* Estelle Sharpe, *WP,* April 4, 1952. Sharpe writes about the graduates' "caps and gowns," but the only photo I have seen of the class of 1884 shows the young women wearing dresses, and MCT, *Colored Woman,* 48, mentions the "jet black dress" purchased and sent by her mother for that occasion.

310   *"What is needed":* AJC, *Voice from the South,* 225.

310   *ninety-fifth birthday:* IGH's birthday party reported in Pearl Cox, "Pearlie's Prattle," *Afro-American,* November 28, 1957.

310   *"I've long had the impression":* IGH, "The Hurricane," *Crisis,* January 1929, 26.

311   *Lincoln Memorial Cemetery:* My visits to this cemetery have been eye-opening. Its dignity and beauty, and the remarkable number of distinguished African Americans interred there, astounded me.

311   *"illustrious negro dead":* I thank my daughter, Elizabeth Alexander, for remembering this quotation from Hurston, which is accessible at http://www.zoranealehurston.com/biography.

Epilogue

314   *I met Rayford Logan:* This encounter occurred in a reception room at the "New" State Department around 1965, when my husband, Clifford Alexander, was working for President Lyndon Baines Johnson.

315   *Andy Razaf gave:* This copy of the sheet music is fading, but framed and ensconced in our home.

317   *is a formidable woman:* The country's first female secretary of state was Madeleine Albright.

318   *son Jimmy:* My thanks to Louise D. Hutchinson, who introduced me to Jimmy Lawson, and to Jimmy himself for sharing stories about his mother's friends the Hunts, and showing me the sports trophy from St.-Étienne, as well as hundreds of the Gibbs-Hunts' postcards that he had carefully stashed away but not revisited for decades. Happily, he then donated all of them to MSRC.

318   *"thousands of men and women":* WEBD, "Significance of Henry Hunt," 6, 7.

319   *snapshot of Wenonah:* Both the photograph of Wenonah Bond and IGH and IGH's February 27, 1938, note to her are in my possession.

Selected Bibliography

Abajian, James de T. *Blacks in Selected Newspapers, Censuses and Other Sources: An Index to Names and Subjects.* Boston: G. K. Hall, 1977.

Ajayi, J. F. Ade, and Michael Crowder. "West Africa 1919–1939: The Colonial Situation." In *History of West Africa,* ed. Ajayi and Crowder, 2:578–607. Essex, England: Longman, 1974.

Alexander, Adele Logan. "The Color of Blood." *Savoy,* August 2001, 58–62.

———. *Homelands and Waterways: The American Journey of the Bond Family, 1846–1926.* New York: Pantheon, 2000.

Alexander, Eleanor. *Lyrics of Sunshine and Shadow: The Tragic Courtship and Marriage of Paul Laurence Dunbar and Alice Ruth Moore.* New York: New York University Press, 2001.

Alexander, Elizabeth. *Praise Song for the Day: A Poem for Barack Obama's Presidential Inauguration, January 20, 2009.* St. Paul: Graywolf Press, 2009.

Alger, Horatio, Jr. *Risen from the Ranks, or Harry Walton's Success.* 1874. New York: Media Books, 1972.

Allen, Philip M. *Madagascar: Conflicts of Authority in the Great Island.* Boulder: Westview, 1995.

Appiah, Kwame Anthony, and Henry Louis Gates Jr., eds. *Africana: The Encyclopedia of the African and African American Experience.* New York: Oxford University Press, 2005.

Archer-Straw, Petrine. *Negrophilia: Avant-Garde Paris and Black Culture in the 1920s.* London: Thames and Hudson, 2000.

Badger, R. Reed. *A Life in Ragtime: A Biography of James Reese Europe.* New York: Oxford University Press, 1995.

Bahn, Esme, and Charles Lemert, eds. *The Voice of Anna Julia Cooper.* New York: Rowman and Littlefield, 1998.

Baker, Josephine, and Jo Bouillon. *Josephine.* New York: Harper and Row, 1967.

Balch, Emily Greene. *Occupied Haiti.* Compiled by the WILPF. New York: Writers Publishing Company, 1927.

Barbeau, Arthur E., and Florette Henri. *The Unknown Soldiers: African-American Troops in World War I.* New York: Da Capo, 1974.

Barclay, Charles. "The Case of Liberia." *Crisis,* April 1931.

Bell, Howard H. "Negro Nationalism: A Factor in Emigration Projects, 1858–1861." *JNH* 47 (January 1962): 42–53.

Bellegarde-Smith, Patrick. *In the Shadow of Powers: Dantès Bellegarde in Haitian Social Thought.* Atlantic Highlands, NJ: Humanities Press, 1985.

Benson, Peter. *Battling Siki: A Tale of Ring Fixes, Race, and Murder in the 1920s*. Fayetteville: University of Arkansas Press, 2006.

Bernard, Catherine. *Afro-American Artists in Paris: 1919–1939*. New York: Hunter College Art Galleries, 1989.

Bigglestone, E. William. *They Stopped in Oberlin*. Oberlin, OH: Oberlin College, 1981.

Billington, Monroe Lee, and Roger D. Hardaway. *African Americans on the Western Frontier*. Boulder: University of Colorado Press, 1998.

Blakely, Allison. "The John L. Waller Affair, 1895–1896." *Negro History Bulletin* 37 (February 1974): 216–22.

———. "Richard T. Greener and the 'Talented Tenth's' Dilemma." *JNH* 59 (October 1974): 305–21.

Boittin, Jennifer Anne. "In Black and White: Gender, Race Relations, and the Nardal Sisters in Interwar Paris." *French Colonial History* 6 (2005): 120–35.

Bradford, Phillips Verner, and Harvey Blume. *Ota Benga: The Pygmy in the Zoo*. New York: St. Martin's, 1982.

Brown, Mervyn. *A History of Madagascar*. London: Marcus Werner, 2002.

———. *Madagascar Rediscovered: A History from Early Times to Independence*. Hamden, CT: Archon, 1979.

Bryson, Robin. *The Azores*. London: Faber and Faber, 1963.

Buckley, Gail. *American Patriots: The Story of Blacks in the Military from the Revolution to Desert Storm*. New York: Random House, 2001.

Buell, Raymond Leslie. *Liberia: A Century of Survival, 1847–1947*. Philadelphia: University of Pennsylvania Press, 1947.

Bundy, Richard C. "Folk-Tales from Liberia (in Abstract)." *Journal of American Folk-Lore* 32 (1919): 406–27.

Bussey, Gertrude C., and Margaret Tims. *The Women's International League for Peace and Freedom, 1915–1965: A Record of Fifty Years' Work*. London: Allen and Unwin, 1965.

Calkin, Homer L. "Early Appointments of Blacks to the Foreign Service." Department of State *Newsletter,* February 1979, 30–32.

Campbell, Gwyn. "Madagascar and the Slave Trade, 1810–1895." *Journal of African History* 22 (1981): 203–27.

Child, Jacob T. *The Pearl of Asia: Reminiscences of the Court of a Supreme Monarch*. Chicago: Donahue, Henneberry, 1892.

Christy, Cuthbert. "Liberia in 1930." *Geographical Journal* 77 (June 1931): 515–40.

Cole, Jennifer. *Forget Colonialism? Sacrifice and the Art of Memory in Madagascar*. Berkeley: University of California Press, 2001.

Condé, Maryse. "O Brave New World." *Research in African Literatures* 29 (Fall 1998): n.p.

———. "The Role of the Writer." *World Literature Today* 67 (Autumn 1993): 696–98.

Contee, Clarence G. "Du Bois, the NAACP, and the Pan-African Congress of 1919." *JNH* 57 (January 1972): 13–28.

Cook, Mercer. "Would You Like a French Island?" *Crisis,* December 1939, 363, 382.

Cooper, Anna Julia. *A Voice from the South.* 1892. Edited by Mary Helen Washington. New York: Oxford University Press, 1988.

Cooper, John S. "When No One Won: Richard Mentor Johnson." Parts 1–3. http://www.suite101.com/article.cfm/4996/106608.

Cooper, Wayne F. *Claude McKay: Rebel Sojourner in the Harlem Renaissance.* Baton Rouge: Louisiana State University Press, 1987.

Cronon, Edmund David. *Black Moses: The Story of Marcus Garvey and the Universal Negro Improvement Association.* Madison: University of Wisconsin Press, 1966.

Crowder, Michael, and Jide Osuntokun. "The First World War and West Africa, 1914–1918." In *History of West Africa,* ed. J. F. Ade Ajayi and Michael Crowder, 2:546–77. Essex, England: Longman, 1974.

Cunard, Nancy. *Negro: An Anthology.* 1934. New York: Frederick Ungar, 1970.

Dames, M. Longworth, and E. Seeman. "Folklore of the Azores." *Folklore* 12 (June 1903): 125–46.

Darton, Nelson Horatio. "Memorial of William Libbey." Geological Society of America *Bulletin* 39 (March 1928): 35–40.

Davidson, Eugene. "The Black Cabinet in the New Deal, Henry A. Hunt, Farmer." *Atlanta Daily World,* April 20, 1934.

Davis, Allison. *Leadership, Love and Aggression.* New York: Harcourt, Brace, Jovanovich, 1983.

Dawson, Horace G., Jr. "First African-American Diplomat." *Foreign Service Journal,* January 1993, 42–45.

Day, Caroline Bond. *A Study of Some Negro-White Families in the United States.* With a foreword and notes by Earnest A. Hooten. Cambridge: Peabody Museum of Harvard University, 1932.

Dickson, Paul, and Thomas B. Allen. "The Legacy of the Bonus Army." *Washington History* 19–20 (2007–8): 87–96.

Dillard, Tom W. "The Black Moses of the West: A Biography of Mifflin Wistar Gibbs, 1823–1915." MA thesis, University of Arkansas, 1975.

———. "Golden Prospects and Fraternal Amenities: Mifflin W. Gibbs's Arkansas Years." *Arkansas Historical Quarterly* 25 (Winter 1976): 307–33.

Du Bois, William Edward Burkhardt. *The Autobiography of W. E. B. Du Bois.* New York: International Publishers, 1968.

———. *Dark Princess: A Romance.* 1928. Jackson: University Press of Mississippi, 1995.

———. *Dusk of Dawn: An Essay toward an Autobiography of a Race Concept.* New York: Schocken, 1968.

———. *The Quest of the Silver Fleece.* Chicago: A. C. McClurg, 1911.

———. "The Significance of Henry Hunt." *Fort Valley State College Bulletin: Founders and Annual Report,* October 1940.

———. *The Souls of Black Folk.* Chicago: A. C. McClurg, 1903.

———. *The World and Africa.* New York: International Publishers, 1965.

Dunbar, Ernest. *The Black Expatriates.* New York: Dutton, 1968.

Dunbar-Nelson, Alice. "Negro Women in War Work." In Scott, *Official History,* 372–97.

Edwards, Brent Hayes. "Pebbles of Consonance: A Reply to Critics." *Small Axe* 17 (March 2004): 134–49.

———. *The Practice of Diaspora: Literature, Translation, and the Rise of Black Internationalism.* Cambridge: Harvard University Press, 2003.

Egonu, Iheanachor. "*Les Continents* and the Francophone Pan-Negro Movement." *Phylon* 43 (Fall 1981): 245–54.

Egypt, Ophelia Settle. *The Unwritten History of Slavery: Accounts of Negro Ex-Slaves.* Nashville: Social Science Institute, Fisk University, 1945.

Fabre, Michael. *From Harlem to Paris: Black American Writers in France.* Urbana: University of Illinois Press, 1991.

Fauset, Jessie. "Impressions of the Second Pan-African Congress." *Crisis,* November 1921, 12–18.

"Final Rites Paid William H. Hunt." *Atlanta Daily World,* December 38, 1951.

Fish, Hamilton. *Memoir of an American Patriot.* Washington, DC: Regnery, 1991.

Flavia-Leopold, E. "The Child in Guadeloupe." In Cunard, *Negro: An Anthology,* 497–500.

Fletcher, Marvin E. *America's First Black General: Benjamin O. Davis, Sr., 1880–1970.* Lawrence: University Press of Kansas, 1989.

Foley, Corazon Sandoval. "Diversity in Diplomacy: Trailblazers Corridor." Exhibition notes, U.S. Department of State, n.d.

Frank, Douglas Alan. "The First Black Students at Lawrence Academy." In *The History of Lawrence Academy at Groton, 1792 to 1992,* 151–57. Groton, MA: Lawrence Academy, 1992.

Franklin, John Hope, and Alfred A. Moss. *From Slavery to Freedom: A History of African Americans.* New York: McGraw-Hill, 1994.

Gabel, Leona C. *From Slavery to the Sorbonne and Beyond: The Life and Writings of Anna J. Cooper.* Northampton, MA: Department of History, Smith College, 1982.

Gallieni, Joseph. *Neufs ans à Madagascar.* Paris: Librairie Hachette, 1908.

Gatewood, Willard B. *Aristocrats of Color: The Black Elite, 1880–1920.* Bloomington: Indiana University Press, 1971.

Geiss, Immanuel. *The Pan-African Movement: A History of Pan-Africanism in America, Europe and Africa.* New York: Africana Publishing, 1974.

Gibbs, Mifflin Wistar. *Shadow and Light: An Autobiography with Reminiscences of the Last and Present Century.* Washington, DC, 1902. New York: Arno Press, 1968.

Giddings, Paula. *A Sword among Lions: Ida B. Wells and the Campaign against Lynching.* New York: HarperCollins, 2008.

Gilroy, Paul. *The Black Atlantic: Modernity and Double Consciousness.* Cambridge: Harvard University Press, 1993.

Guill, James H. *A History of the Azores Islands.* Tulare, CA: Golden Shield, 1993.

Ham, Debra Newman, ed. *The African American Mosaic: A Library of Congress Resource Guide for the Study of Black History and Culture*. Washington, DC: Library of Congress, 1986.

Hannau, Hans W. *Guadeloupe*. Garden City, NY: Doubleday, n.d.

Harlan, Louis R. *Booker T. Washington: The Making of a Black Leader, 1856–1901*. New York: Oxford University Press, 1975.

———. *Booker T. Washington: The Wizard of Tuskegee, 1901–1915*. New York: Oxford University Press, 1983.

Harper, Frances E. W. *Iola Leroy, or Shadows Uplifted*. 1893. New York: Oxford University Press, 1988.

Heinl, Nancy Gordon. "America's First Black Diplomat." *Foreign Service Journal*, August 1973, 20–22.

Henle, Ellen, and Marlene Merrill. "Antebellum Black Coeds at Oberlin College." *Oberlin Women's Studies Newsletter*, Spring 1979, 8–11.

Heseltine, Nigel. *Madagascar*. London: Pall Mall, 1971.

Hine, Darlene Clark, Elsa Barkley Brown, and Rosalyn Terborg-Penn, eds. *Black Women in America: An Historical Encyclopedia*. 2 vols. Brooklyn: Carlson Publishing, 1993.

Howay, F. W. "The Negro Immigration into Vancouver Island in 1858." *British Columbia Historical Quarterly* 3 (October 1968): 110–13.

Hughes, Langston. *The Big Sea*. 1940. New York: Hill and Wang, 1979.

———. *I Wonder as I Wander: An Autobiographical Journey*. New York: Hill and Wang, 1993.

Hunt, Ida Gibbs. "The Hurricane." *Crisis*, January 1929, 24–26.

——— [Iola Gibson, pseud.]. "The New Sphere of Woman." K-B, LOC, box 13, folder 8.

———. "The Price of Peace." *JNH* 23 (January 1938): 79–86.

———. "To France." K-B, LOC, box 13, folder 8.

———. "Recollections of Frederick Douglass." *Negro History Bulletin* 16 (1953): 202–3.

Hunt, William Henry. "From Cabin to Consulate." Introduction by Harold T. Pinkett. MS, n.d., Hunt, MSRC.

———. "Geodetic Surveying, Topographical Work, and Map Making in Madagascar, 1903." *Bulletin of the AGS* 36, no. 9 (1904): 561–63.

———. "The Inauguration of a Railway in Madagascar." MS, October 1904, AGS.

———. "Madagascar Roads, Railway and Transport Systems." MS, n.d., AGS.

———. "Medical Work in Madagascar." MS, September 1904, AGS.

———. "The Tananarive Observatory." *Bulletin of the AGS* 33, no. 3 (1901): 204–6.

Hunton, Addie W., and Kathryn M. Johnson. *Two Colored Women with the American Expeditionary Forces*. Brooklyn, NY: Brooklyn Eagle, 1920.

Hutchinson, Louise Daniel. *Anna Julia Cooper: A Voice From the South*. Washington, DC: Smithsonian Institution, 1981.

Ingram, E. Renée. "Reverend Dr. Owen Lun West Smith: From Minister to Minister Resident and Consul General." *Journal of the Afro-American Historical and Genealogical Society* 20, no. 1 (2001): 1–16.

Janken, Kenneth R. "African American and Francophone Black Intellectuals during the Harlem Renaissance." *Historian* 60 (1998): 490–91, 503–4.

———. *Rayford W. Logan and the Dilemma of the African-American Intellectual.* Amherst: University of Massachusetts Press, 1993.

Johnson, Charles S. *Bitter Canaan: The Story of the Negro Republic.* New Brunswick, NJ: Transaction Books, 1987.

———. "Liberia." *Crisis,* April 1931.

Johnson, G. Wesley. "African Political Activity in French West Africa, 1900–1940." In *History of West Africa,* ed. J. F. Ade Ajayi and Michael Crowder, 2:608–34. Essex, England: Longman, 1974.

Johnson, James Weldon. *Along This Way.* 1930. New York: Da Capo, 2000.

———. *The Autobiography of an Ex-Colored Man.* 1912. In *Three Negro Classics.* Introduction by John Hope Franklin. New York: Avon, 1965.

———. *Black Manhattan.* New York: Knopf, 1930.

Johnson, Phillip James. "Seasons in Hell: Charles Spurgeon Johnson and the 1930 Labor Crisis in Liberia." PhD dissertation, Louisiana State University, 2004.

Justesen, Benjamin R. "African-American Consuls Abroad, 1899–1909." *Foreign Service Journal,* September 2004, 72–76.

Kennedy, Charles Stewart. *The American Consul: A History of the United States Consular Service, 1776–1914.* Westport: Greenwood, 1990.

Kennedy, Dane. "Decolonization and Disorder." Lecture presented at the National History Center, Washington, DC, July 2008.

Kent, Raymond K. *From Madagascar to the Malagasy Republic.* New York: Praeger, 1962.

———, ed. *Madagascar in History: Essays from the 1970s.* Albany, CA: Foundation for Malagasy Studies, 1979.

Killian, Crawford. *Go Do Some Great Thing: The Black Pioneers of British Columbia.* Vancouver: Douglas & McIntyre, 1978.

Kirby, John B. *Black Americans in the Roosevelt Era: Liberalism and Race.* Knoxville: University of Tennessee Press, 1980.

Kleinberg, Eliot. *Black Cloud: The Deadly Hurricane of 1928.* New York: Carroll and Graf, 2003.

Kraemer, Christine Mullen, and Sarah Fee, eds. *Objects as Envoys: Cloth, Imagery, and Diplomacy in Madagascar.* Washington, DC: National Museum of African Art, Smithsonian Institution, 2002.

Krebs, Edgar, and Wendy Walker. "Madagascar in the Minds of Foreigners: The Case of United States Consul John Lewis Waller, 1891–1895." In Kraemer and Fee, *Objects as Envoys,* 121–47.

Krenn, Michael L. *Black Diplomacy: African Americans and the State Department, 1945–1969.* Armonk, NY: Sharpe, 1999.

Kristof, Nicholas D. "Marriage: Mix and Match," *NYT,* March 3, 2004.

Lacascade, Suzanne. *Claire-Solange, âme africaine.* Paris: Eugéne Figuière, 1924.

"Lady Vice Consul." *Ebony,* April 1960, 43–46.

Lambek, Michael J. *The Weight of the Past: Living with History in Mahajanga, Madagascar.* New York: Palgrave, 2002.

Lane, Ann J. *The Brownsville Affair.* Port Washington, NY: Kennikat, 1971.

Langley, J. Ayodele. "Pan-Africanism in Paris, 1924–46." *Journal of Modern African History Studies* 5, no. 1 (1969): 69–94.

Langston, John Mercer. *From the Virginia Plantation to the National Capital; or, The First and Only Negro Representative in Congress from the Old Dominion.* Hartford: American Publishing Co., 1894.

Lanting, Frans. *Madagascar: A World Out of Time.* New York: Aperture, 1990.

Lara, Oruno. *Histoire de la Guadeloupe (1491–1920).* Paris: Nouvelle Librairie Universelle, 1923.

———. *Question de couleurs (blanches et noirs).* Paris: Nouvelle Librairie Universelle, 1923.

Larson, Erik. *The Devil in the White City.* New York: Crown, 2003.

Lawson, Ellen N., and Marlene Merrill. "The Antebellum 'Talented Thousandth': Black College Students at Oberlin before the Civil War." *Journal of Negro Education* 52, no. 2 (1994): 142–55.

Lemert, Charles, and Esme Bhan, eds. *The Voice of Anna Julia Cooper.* New York: Rowman and Littlefield, 1998.

Lerner, Gerda. *Black Women in White America.* New York: Random House, 1972.

Levy, Eugene D. *James Weldon Johnson: Black Leader, Black Voice.* Chicago: University of Chicago Press, 1973.

Lewis, David Levering. *W. E. B. Du Bois: Biography of a Race, 1868–1919.* New York: Henry Holt, 1993.

———. *W. E. B. Du Bois: The Fight for Equality and the American Century, 1919–1963.* New York: Henry Holt, 2000.

———. *When Harlem Was in Vogue.* New York: Knopf, 1981.

Lewis, David Levering, and Deborah Willis. *A Small Nation of People: W. E. B. Du Bois and African American Portraits of Progress.* New York: Amistad, 2003.

Lewis, Earl, and Heidi Ardizzone. *Love on Trial: An American Scandal in Black and White.* New York: Norton, 2001.

Little, Arthur W. *From Harlem to the Rhine.* New York: Covici-Friede, 1936.

Livermore, Seward W. "The Azores in American Strategy-Diplomacy, 1917–1919," *Journal of Modern History* 20 (September 1948): 197–211.

Locke, Alain. "The Colonial Literature of France." *Opportunity,* November 1923, 331–35.

Logan, Rayford W. *The Betrayal of the Negro: From Rutherford B. Hayes to Woodrow Wilson.* New York: Macmillan, 1965.

———. "Confessions of an Unwilling Nordic." *The World Tomorrow,* July 1927, 297–300.

———. "The Historical Aspects of Pan-Africanism: A Personal Chronicle." *African Forum* 1 (Summer 1965): 90–104.

Logan, Rayford W., and Michael R. Winston, eds. *Dictionary of American Negro Biography*. New York: Norton, 1982.

Louis, Wm. Roger. "The United States and the African Peace Settlement of 1919: The Pilgrimage of George Louis Beer." *Journal of African History* 4, no. 3 (1963): 413–33.

Maillard, Filogenes. "In the French West Indies." *Crisis* 23, January 1922, 126.

Maran, René. *Batouala*. New York: Thomas Seltzer, 1922.

Marshall, Harriet Gibbs. "Music as a Profession." *Negro Music Journal* 2 (November 1903): 55–59.

———. *The Story of Haiti: From the Discovery of the Island by Christopher Columbus to the Present Day*. Boston: Christopher Publishing, 1930.

Marshall, Napoleon Bonaparte. *The Providential Armistice: A Volunteer's Story*. Washington, DC: Liberty League, 1930.

Martin, Tony. *Race First: The Ideological and Organizational Struggles of Marcus Garvey and the U.N.I.A.* Westport, CT: Greenwood, 1976.

Mason, M. "Women's Contribution to the Pan-African Struggle: Revisited." March 1997. Hartford Web Publishing, http://www.hartford-hwp.com.

Mathews, Marcia M. *Henry Ossawa Tanner, American Artist*. Chicago: University of Chicago Press, 1969.

Matthews, T. T. *Thirty Years in Madagascar*. London: Religious Tract Society, 1904.

McCollum, Obie. "Royalty and Rhythm," *NYAN,* October 6, 1934.

McFeely, William S. *Frederick Douglass: A Biography*. New York: Norton, 1991.

McKay, Claude. *A Long Way from Home*. San Diego: Harvest/HBJ, 1957.

Meier, August, and Elliott Rudwick, eds. *The Making of Black America,* vol. 2, *The Black Community in Modern America*. New York: Atheneum, 1971.

———. "The Rise of Segregation in the Federal Bureaucracy." *Phylon* 28 (Summer 1967): 178–84.

Meriwether, James H. Meyer. *Proudly We Can Be Africans: Black Americans and Africa, 1935–1961*. Chapel Hill: University of North Carolina Press, 2002.

Meyer, Leyland Winfield. *The Life and Times of Colonel Richard M. Johnson of Kentucky*. New York: Columbia University Press, 1932.

Moore, Jacquelyn M. *Leading the Race: The Transformation of the Black Elite in the Nation's Capital, 1880–1920*. Charlottesville: University Press of Virginia, 1999.

Moses, Wilson Jeremiah. *The Golden Age of Black Nationalism, 1850–1925*. Hamden, CT: Archon, 1978.

Moss, Alfred A., Jr. *The American Negro Academy: Voice of the Talented Tenth*. Baton Rouge: Louisiana State University Press, 1981.

Nardal, Paulette. "La Guadeloupe." Guides des colonies françaises. Paris: Société d'Editions Géographiques, Maritimes et Coloniales, 1931.

O'Brien, Robert W. "Victoria's Negro Colonists, 1858–1866." *Phylon* 3 (1942): 15–18.

O'Reilly, Kenneth. *Nixon's Piano: Presidents and Racial Politics from Washington to Clinton*. New York: Free Press, 1995.

Osborn, Chase Salmon. *Madagascar, Land of the Man-Eating Tree*. New York: Republic, 1924.

Osborn, Henry Fairfield. "A Thrilling Life Story: The Travels and Adventures of William Libbey, '77." *Princeton Alumni Weekly*, October 28, 1927.

"Our Policy on Haiti Scored in Debate." *NYT*, December 29, 1922.

Oxley, Howard W. "The Crisis in Liberia." *Crisis*, December 1932, 373–74.

Padgett, James A. "Diplomats to Haiti and Their Diplomacy," *JNH* 25 (July 1940): 265–330.

———. "Ministers to Liberia and Their Diplomacy." *JNH* 22 (January 1937): 50–92.

Palmer, Ronald D. F. "Black Pioneer State Department Foreign Service Officers, 1869–2000." Photocopy of a typescript, n.d.

———. "Blacks in the Foreign Service of the United States, 1848–1994." Photocopy of a typescript, n.d.

Paterson, Thomas G. "American Businessmen and Consular Service Reform, 1890 to 1906." *Business History Review* 40 (Spring 1966): 77–97.

Pieterse, Jan Nederveen. *White on Black: Images of Africa and Blacks in Western Popular Culture*. New Haven: Yale University Press, 1992.

Plummer, Brenda Gayle. "The Afro-American Response to the Occupation of Haiti, 1915–1934." *Phylon* 43, no. 2 (1982): 125–43.

———. *Rising Wind: Black Americans and U.S. Foreign Affairs, 1935–1960*. Chapel Hill: University of North Carolina Press, 1996.

Priestley, Herbert Ingram. *France Overseas: A Study of Modern Imperialism*. New York: Octagon, 1966.

Putnam, Aric. "'Modern Slaves': The Liberian Labor Crisis and the Politics of Race and Class." *Rhetoric and Public Affairs* 9, no. 2 (2006): 235–56.

Rabearivelo, J. J. "A Historical Survey of Madagascar." In Cunard, *Negro: An Anthology*.

Rawick, George P., ed. *The American Slave: A Composite Autobiography*. 16 vols. Westport, CT: Greenwood, 1972–77.

Redkey, Edwin S. *Black Exodus: Black Nationalism and Back-to-Africa Movements, 1890–1910*. New Haven: Yale University Press, 1969.

Richardson, Joe M. "Jonathan C. Gibbs: Florida's Only Negro Cabinet Member." *Florida Historical Quarterly* 42 (April 1964): 363–64.

Roberts, Brian Russell. "Artistic Ambassadors and African American Writing at the Nation's Edge, 1893–1940." PhD dissertation, University of Virginia, 2008.

Roberts, Stephen H. *The History of French Colonial Policy, 1870–1925*. 1929. New York: Archon, 1963.

Rogers, Francis M. *Atlantic Islanders of the Azores and Madeiras*. North Quincy, MA: Christopher, 1979.

Rose, Phyllis. *Jazz Cleopatra: Josephine Baker in Her Time.* New York: Doubleday, 1989.

Rothfield, Otto. "Liberia and the League of Nations." *Crisis,* April 1931, 121–22.

Rouse, Jacqueline Anne. "Out of the Shadow of Tuskegee: Margaret Murray Washington, Social Activism, and Race Vindication." *JNH* 81, no. 4 (1996): 31–46.

Salmonson, Jessica Amanda. "The Dark Side of Horatio Alger, Jr." http://www.violetbooks.com/alger.html.

Schaffer, Michael. "Lost Riot." *Washington City Paper,* April 3, 1997.

Schuyler, George S. *Slaves Today: A Story of Liberia.* New York: Brewer, Warren, Putnam, 1931.

Scott, Emmett J. *Scott's Official History of the American Negro in the World War.* 1919. New York: Arno, 1969.

Sharpe, Estelle. "Three Oberlin 'Old Grads' Meet." *WP,* April 4, 1952.

Sharpley-Whiting, T. Denean. *Negritude Women.* Minneapolis: University of Minnesota Press, 2002.

Singer, Barry. *Black and Blue: The Life and Lyrics of Andy Razaf.* New York: Schirmer, 1992.

Sitkoff, Harvard. *A New Deal for Blacks: The Emergence of Civil Rights as a National Issue,* vol. 1, *The Depression Decade.* Oxford: Oxford University Press, 1981.

Skinner, Elliott P. *African Americans and U.S. Policy toward Africa, 1850–1924: In Defense of Black Nationalism.* Washington, DC: Howard University Press, 1992.

Smith, Jessie Carney, ed. *Notable Black American Women.* Detroit: Gale, 1972.

Smith, John David. *Black Judas: William Hannibal Thomas and "The American Negro."* Athens: University of Georgia Press, 2000.

Spillers, Hortense V. "'Mama's Baby, Papa's Maybe': An American Grammar Book." *Diacritics* 17 (Summer 1987): 64–81.

Stanley, Jerry. *Hurry Freedom: African Americans in Gold Rush California.* New York: Crown, 2000.

Stovall, Tyler. *Paris Noir: African Americans in the City of Light.* Boston: Houghton Mifflin, 1996.

———. "Harlem-Sur-Seine: Building an African American Diasporic Community in Paris." *Stanford Electronic Humanities Review* 5, no. 2 (1997).

Stratton, Arthur. *The Great Red Island.* New York: Scribner, 1964.

Strouse, Jean. *Morgan, American Financier.* New York: Random House, 1999.

Sundiata, I. K. *Black Scandal: America and the Liberian Labor Crisis, 1929–1936.* Philadelphia: Institute for the Study of Human Issues, 1980.

———. *Brothers and Strangers: Black Zion, Black Slavery, 1914–1940.* Durham: Duke University Press, 2003.

Sweeney, W. Allison. *History of the American Negro in the Great World War.* 1919. New York: Negro Universities Press, 1969.

Taylor, Arnold H. "The Involvement of Black Americans in the Liberian Forced Labor Controversy, 1929–1935." In *Proceedings: Conference on Afro-Americans. Afro-*

Americans and Africans: Historical and Political Linkages, 59–83. Graduate School of Arts and Sciences, Howard University. June 1974.

Terrell, Mary Church. *A Colored Woman in a White World.* Washington, DC: Ransdell Publishers, 1940.

———. "The International Congress of Women Recently Held in Berlin, Germany." *Voice of the Negro,* October 1904.

Tyson, Peter. *The Eighth Continent: Life, Death, and Discovery in the Lost World of Madagascar.* New York: William Morrow, 2000.

U.S. Department of State. Historical Office, Bureau of Public Affairs. "Negroes Employed at Officer Levels in the Department of State and the Foreign Service, 1869–1969." February 1969.

———. Office of Equal Employment Opportunity. "A Chronology of Key Negro Appointments in the Department of State and the Foreign Service, 1869–1969." May 1969.

Van de burg, William L., ed. *Modern Black Nationalism, from Marcus Garvey to Louis Farrakhan.* New York: New York University Press, 1997.

Vandercook, John W. "Whitewash." *Crisis,* October 1927, 289–93.

Verne, Jules. *Around the World in Eighty Days.* Paris, 1872.

Walters, Ronald W. *Black Presidential Politics in America: A Strategic Approach.* Albany: State University of New York Press, 1988.

Washington, Booker T. *The Booker T. Washington Papers.* Edited by Louis R. Harlan and Raymond Smock. 14 vols. Urbana: University of Illinois Press, 1972–89.

Weaver, John D. *The Brownsville Raid.* New York: Norton, 1970.

Weiss, Nancy. *Farewell to the Party of Lincoln: Black Politics in the Age of FDR.* Princeton: Princeton University Press, 1983.

Weld, Theodore Dwight. *American Slavery as It Is; Testimony of a Thousand Witnesses.* 1839. Salem, NH: Ayer, 1991.

Wells, Ida B. "The Reason Why the Colored American Is Not in the World's Columbian Exposition." 1893. Reprinted in Trudier Harris, *Exorcizing Blackness: Historical and Literary Lynching and Burning Rituals.* Bloomington: Indiana University Press, 1984.

Wilson, Edward E. "The Joys of Being a Negro." *Atlantic Monthly,* February 1906, 245–50.

Winks, Robin W. *The Blacks in Canada: A History.* Montreal: McGill-Queens University, 1997.

Wolf, Eric. *Europe and the People without History.* Berkeley: University of California Press, 1982.

Wolgemuth, Kathleen Long. "Woodrow Wilson and Federal Segregation." *JNH* 44 (April 1959): 158–73.

———. "Woodrow Wilson's Appointment Policy and the Negro." *Journal of Southern History* 23 (November 1958): 457–71.

Woods, Randall Bennett. *A Black Odyssey: John Lewis Waller and the Promise of American Life, 1878–1900.* Lawrence: University Press of Kansas, 1981.

Woodson, C. G. "The Gibbs Family." *Negro History Bulletin,* October 1947, 3–22.

Young, James C. "Liberia and Its Future." *Opportunity,* November 1928, 327–31.

Zabilba, Gladys. *Welcome to the Azores.* Jefferson, IA: Bee and Herald, 1963.

Additional Archival Collections

Cooper, Anna Julia. Papers. Howard University, MSRC.

Day, Caroline Bond. Collection. Harvard University, Peabody Museum Archives.

Grimké, Archibald. Papers. Howard University, MSRC.

Johnson, James Weldon. Papers. Yale University, Bienecke Library.

Madagascar Collection. Eliot Elisofon Photographic Collection, National Museum of African Art, Smithsonian Institution.

Oberlin College Archives. "Pioneer Database" and Group 28, Alumni Records.

Slowe, Lucy Diggs. Papers. Howard University, MSRC.

Washington Music Conservatory Papers. Howard University, MSRC.

Index

In subheadings and qualifiers, personal names of the Gibbs and Hunts families are abbreviated (e.g., Ida Gibbs Hunt [IGH] and William Henry Hunt [WHH], etc.).

Douglass, Frederick (*continued*)
movements and, 44, 48; foreign service career of, 8–9, 54, 56; friendship with MWG and, 40, 46, 54–55, 156; marriage to Pitts of, 7; memoirs of, 12, 83; pan-Africanism and, 179; World's Columbian Exposition and, 68
Douglass, Sarah Mapps, 197
Downing, Henry Francis, 57–58, 165, 228
Dred Scott case, 43, 46–47
Du Bois, Nina, 72, 151, 212, 303
Du Bois, Shirley Graham, 303
Du Bois, W. E. B.: on colonialism, 164, 173–74, 184; death of, 303; differences with Washington and, 11, 73, 132; Fisk University upheaval and, 161; friendship with H. A. Hunt and, 318–19; friendship with IGH and, 2, 13, 71–73, 80, 150–51, 176, 179, 200, 228–29, 248, 288, 303, 338; friendship with WHH and, 97, 163, 203, 216–17, 248, 288; Liberia and, 203–4, 263, 268–69, 271–72, 277–79, 281; memoirs of, 12; military service and, 167–69; Niagara Movement and, 131–32; occupation of Haiti and, 216, 250; on pawning, 269; on segregated/inferior education, 134; Socialist Party and, 251, 302–3; Spingarn award and, 187; Versailles Peace Conference and, 173–74, 181, 183–84; women's suffrage and, 154–55. Writings and lectures: "The Black World at Present," 202; *Dark Princess,* 228; Harvard University dissertation of, 56; "The History of the Pan-African Movement," 202; "On the Damnation of Women," 27–28; *The Quest of the Silver Fleece,* 2, 13, 71–72, 150–51, 229; *The Souls of Black Folk,* 11, 73; *The Star of Ethiopia,* 157. See also *Crisis*; National Association for the Advance-

ment of Colored People; Pan-African Conference/Congresses
Du Bois, Yolande, 213, 228–29
Dudley, Edward R., 9, 285, 291
Dunbar, Paul Laurence, 68, 77, 135
Dunbar (Paul Laurence) High School (Washington, D.C.), 70, 135, 154, 188, 191, 197, 207, 295–96, 310
Dunbar-Nelson, Alice, 77, 172, 287
Durham, John S., 56

educational opportunities, 27, 38, 52, 69, 86, 123; school desegregation and, 307–8
Eisenhower, Dwight D., 297, 316
Emancipation Proclamation (1863), 50, 84–85
Episcopal Church, 100, 153, 306. *See also* St. George's Episcopal Church; St. Mary's Church
Ethiopia, 272; Italy's atrocities in, 111, 291–92; U.S. representatives to, 56, 217
Europe, James Reese, 168, 172, 184
Europe, Mary, 184, 196
Evening Star (newspaper), 1–2, 12, 79
expatriation movements, 44, 47–50, 199, 265. *See also* "back to Africa" movements

Fairchild, James, 62, 64
Fall, Louis M'barick, 164, 199
"Fate of the 'Darker Races,' The" (I. G. Hunt), 158
Fauntleroy, Jackie, 310
Fauntleroy, Jacqueline Ida, 310
Fauntleroy, John, 304–5
Fauntleroy, Phylicia, 305, 306, 307
Fauntleroy, Phyllis Gibbs (IGH's cousin), 304–5, 315
Fauset, Jessie, 154, 189, 191–93, 205
15th New York State Army Reserve Regi-

ment, 168, 184, 289. *See also* 369th Infantry Regiment, U.S. Army

Fifteenth Amendment (U.S. Constitution), 50

Firestone, Harvey, 283–84

Firestone Plantations Company, 267–70

Firestone Tire and Rubber Company, 264, 267, 276, 284

Fish, Hamilton, 168

Fisk University, 87, 161, 290

Flavia-Leopold, Emmanuel, 222

Florida, race relations in, 52

Fourteenth Amendment (U.S. Constitution), 50, 308

Fragoso Carmona, António Óscar de, 247

France: race relations in, 10, 140–41, 188–89, 199, 205–6, 211; U.S. representatives to, 58; women's suffrage in, 154, 195–96

Francis, William Treyanne, 263–64

Fredericks, Edmund Fitzgerald, 183

free people of color, antebellum, 32, 43

French, J. P. D., 80

Freylinghausen University, 310

"From Cabin to Consulate" (W. H. Hunt), 12, 83, 103, 107, 250, 303–4

Fugitive Slave Act (1850), 32, 42–43

Gallieni, Joseph Simon, 5–6, 80, 115–16, 122–24, 128, 142, 161–62, 222

Garfield, James, 53

Garner, Margaret, 26, 32, 35

Garnet, Henry Highland, 57

Garrett, Joyce, 297–98

Garvey, Marcus, 10, 157–58, 180–81, 192, 202–4, 237, 263, 280–81, 346

George, William C., 264, 279, 285, 297

Gerard, James, 163

Gerbinis, Louis, 221, 236

Germany: colonies of, 184, 295; Mandates Commission and, 184, 193. *See also* World Wars I and II

Gibbs, Donald (IGH's brother), 47, 74

Gibbs, Francis (IGH's brother), 47

Gibbs, Harriet ("Hattie") Aletha (IGH's sister). *See* Marshall, Harriet ("Hattie") Gibbs

Gibbs, Horace (IGH's brother), 29, 47, 147, 181, 253, 281, 305

Gibbs, Ida Alexander. *See* Hunt, Ida Alexander Gibbs

Gibbs, Jonathan (IGH's uncle), 39–40, 52–53, 66

Gibbs, Rev. Jonathan (IGH's paternal grandfather), 38

Gibbs, Maria (IGH's paternal grandmother), 38–39, 45

Gibbs, Maria Ann Chinn Alexander (IGH's mother): ancestry of, 14, 25, 27–31, 36, 46, 71; California visit of, 42–43; courtship/marriage of, 35, 45–46; death of, 16, 127; education of, 1, 34; enslavement of/Tennessee youth of, 37; religious affiliations of, 47, 61; return to Ohio of, 51–52, 61; Vancouver years of, 47, 49; Washington years of, 71, 74–75, 79

Gibbs, Mifflin Wistar (IGH's father): Arkansas years of, 52–54; bank scandal and, 147–49; California years of, 40–44; childhood of, 38–39; citizenship of, 47–48, 50, 59; on colonialism, 120, 179; community/philanthropic activities of, 53–54; courtship/marriage of, 35, 45–46; death of, 156–57; education of, 38–39, 52; elected public office and, 48, 53; in Florida, 52; foreign service career of, 4, 8, 54–56, 58, 74, 101–2, 107–8, 119–20; friendship with Douglass and, 40, 46, 54–55, 156; friendship with Washington and, 11, 76, 145, 147, 156; later years of, 127–28, 147–49, 155–57; Madagascar years of, 58–60, 113–20; memoirs of, 11, 16, 38,

Hughes, Langston, 206, 254, 313

Hughes, Margaret ("Maggie") Hunt (WHH's sister), 85–86, 100, 157, 213, 305

Hunt, Annekee (WHH's grandmother), 85–86, 318

Hunt, Clinton (WHH's uncle), 84–85

Hunt, Daniel (WHH's brother), 85, 94, 305

Hunt, Elizabeth (WHH's sister), 85–86

Hunt, Frances ("Fannie") (WHH's sister). See Murray, Frances ("Fannie") Hunt

Hunt, Henry Alexander, 191, 290, 318–19

Hunt, Ida Alexander Gibbs: "adoptions" by, 295–96; ancestry of, 14–15, 24–25; Arkansas years of, 54, 65; background of, 1–2, 10–11, 78, 95; "back to Africa" movements and, 10; birth of, 47, 61; cooking skills of, 287, 307; courtship/marriage of, 1–5, 11–12, 65, 73–76, 78–81, 94–96, 127; death of, 310–11; education of, 1, 9, 62–64, 66, 179, 309; finances of, 130; friendship with Du Bois and, 2, 13, 71–73, 80, 150–51, 176, 179, 200, 228–29, 248, 303, 338; health of, 66, 281–83, 305; later years of, 307–10; marriage of, 11, 81, 211, 304; Ohio childhood of, 61; organizational affiliations of, 70, 74–75, 131–33, 150, 165, 226, 288, 293, 310; pan-Africanism and, 176, 178–79, 181–83, 189–92, 199–202, 215, 218, 277–79, 293; pen name of, 13, 197–98, 209, 254–55; possessions/artwork of, 220, 232, 259, 287; relationship with others' children and, 70, 77, 305; religious affiliations of, 80; social issues/internationalism and, 10, 129–32, 133, 164, 174–75, 179, 195, 197–98, 206, 209, 293–95, 307; sources for biography of, 12–13, 200, 254; stateside respites of, 130–31, 143, 150, 169, 237; teaching career of, 5,

64–66, 69–71, 74, 80–81; travels of, 54, 65, 67, 133, 179; women's suffrage and, 64, 70, 154–55, 195–96. Writings and lectures: "The Coloured Races and the League of Nations," 202; "The Fate of the 'Darker Races,'" 158; "Harriet Beecher Stowe and the Woman Suffrage Movement," 248; "Imperialism and the Darker Races," 191; "The New Sphere of Women," 197; "Our Duty to Liberia," 293; "The Price of Peace," 286, 294–95, 320; "To France," 175; "The Women of France," 195–96, 339

Hunt, John (WHH's brother), 85, 88, 94

Hunt, Margaret ("Maggie") (WHH's sister). See Hughes, Margaret ("Maggie") Hunt

Hunt, Rev. Robert, 3, 84, 317

Hunt, Sophia (WHH's mother), 84–87, 89

Hunt, William B. (WHH's father), 84–86

Hunt, William Henry ("Billy"): "adoptions" by, 295–96; ancestry of, 14–15, 83–86; "back to Africa" movements and, 280–81; birth/birthdate of, 83, 92, 95, 286–87; childhood/youth jobs of, 86–92, 94, 96, 101; colonialism and, 130–31, 203, 214, 223–24, 228; conspiracy against European posting of, 12, 144–46; cooking skills of, 306; courtship/marriage of, 1–5, 11–12, 65, 72–76, 78–81, 94–96, 127; education of, 65, 86–87, 95–101, 116; fabulous stories of, 3, 88–94, 97, 102–3, 124, 304, 330; foreign service career of, 4, 8, 60, 73, 101–2, 121, 135–36, 195, 212–14, 216, 218, 238, 241–42, 246, 254, 259–61, 284–85; friendship with Du Bois and, 97, 163, 203, 216–17, 248; health of, 124, 232, 238, 240, 306; marriage of, 11, 81, 211, 304; memoirs of, 12, 83, 103, 107, 250,

malaria, 124, 131, 232, 240, 262, 281–83, 305, 310

Mandates Commission (League of Nations), 184, 193

Manuel II, King of Portugal, 246

Maran, René, 193, 204, 214

Marshall, George C., 302, 316

Marshall, Harriet ("Hattie") Gibbs (IGH's sister): birth of, 47; conversion to Baha'i faith of, 299; courtship/marriage of, 78, 133; death of, 299; education in Haiti and, 227; education of, 3, 54, 65; finances of, 251–53, 299; health of, 252, 277, 299; pan-Africanism and, 181, 191; philanthropic work of, 237, 251; sources for life of, 13; teaching career/conservatory of, 65–66, 71, 74, 133, 227, 251, 288, 299; wedding of IGH and, 3; woman suffrage and, 154. Writings: *The Story of Haiti*, 227, 250–51

Marshall, Napoleon Bonaparte "Nap," 316; Brownsville (Tex.) racial conflicts and, 133–34, 145, 148–49; courtship/marriage of, 78, 133; death of, 289; finances of, 251–53; health of, 237–38, 251–52, 277; memoirs of, 251–52; as military attaché to Haiti, 195, 226–27; military service of, 168–71, 184; on occupation of Haiti, 250; pan-Africanism and, 191; philanthropic work of, 237–38, 251. Writings: *The Providential Armistice*, 251–52

Marshall Plan, 302

Martinique, 230

Maxwell, Campbell, 57

Maysville, Kentucky, 31

McAllister, Edith, 315

McCarthy, "Spot," 87–88

McClure's (magazine), 129–30

McCoy, William, 57

McKay, Claude, 114, 206

McKenzie, Fayette Avery, 161

McKinley, William, 55, 58, 75, 101, 122, 261

Metcalfe, Ralph, 213, 292

Meyer, Leland, 20

Mirror of the Times (newspaper), 15, 42–43

miscegenation, 6–7, 14, 22, 26, 63, 83, 85; legal cases on, 7, 208–9. *See also* race relations

Mitchell, Arthur, 289

Mitchell, Charles E., 237, 260, 264, 273, 279–80, 284–85, 289

Mitchell, Louis and Antoinette, 199, 206, 211, 306

Mitchell, Sanford, 29

Monroe Doctrine, 3, 226

Moorland, Jesse, 311

Morgan, J. Pierpont, 100, 147, 153–54, 300, 304, 306

Morrison, Toni, 26

Mortenol, Sosthène H. C., 117, 161, 164, 182, 192–93, 222

Munchausen, Friedrich Hieronymous von, Baron, 93

Murphy, Isaac, 88, 287

Murray, Frances ("Fannie") Hunt (WHH's sister), 85–86, 89, 94, 157, 305

Murray, Mary (WHH's niece), 305

Murray, Walter (WHH's nephew), 305

Mussolini, Benito, 291

NAACP. *See* National Association for the Advancement of Colored People

NACW. *See* National Association of Colored Women

Nardal, Jane, 205, 206, 207, 210, 225

Nardal, Paulette, 205, 206

National American Woman Suffrage Association, 70

National Association for the Advancement of Colored People (NAACP), 9, 132, 150, 308; boycotts of *Birth of a Nation* and, 158; discrimination in the military and, 168–69, 302; Du Bois's split from, 302–3; pan-Africanism and, 173–74, 179, 202, 215; Spingarn awards of, 187, 290. See also *Crisis*

National Association of Colored Women (NACW), 70, 132–33, 198, 201, 309–10

National Negro Business League, 76, 145

National Urban League, 164, 206, 260, 268, 272

National Zoological Park (Washington, D.C.), procurement of animals for, 118–19

Native Americans, 7–8, 19, 25, 42, 84

Navy, U.S., racism in, 118

Negro (Cunard), 222

Negro World (journal), 206

Nelson, Frank, 100–101, 153–54

New Negro, the, 188, 210

"New Sphere of Women, The" (I. G. Hunt), 197

New York (N.Y.), 150, 157, 169, 188, 237, 252, 277. *See also* Harlem (N.Y.)

New York Age (newspaper), 146

New York Post (newspaper), 272

New York Times (newspaper), 251, 275, 289, 301

Niagara Movement, 131–32

Obama, Barack Hussein, 317

Oberlin, Ohio, 33–35, 62–63

Oberlin College (Ohio), 9, 63–65, 155

Oberlin Music Conservatory (Ohio), 54, 65

Oberlin Preparatory School (Ohio), 34

"Of Mr. Booker T. Washington" (Du Bois). See *Souls of Black Folk, The*

Ohio, race relations in, 33–35, 62–63

Olympics (Berlin, 1936), 292

"On the Damnation of Women" (Du Bois), 27–28

Opportunity (journal), 164, 206, 257, 260, 272

"Our Duty to Liberia" (I. G. Hunt), 293

Owen, Ruth Bryan, 291

Page, Thomas Nelson, 129–30, 132

Pan-African Association, 183, 193, 199, 212

Pan-African Conference (1900), 10, 73, 150, 183

Pan-African Congresses, 10, 13, 150; First (1919), 176–78, 181–83, 279; Second (1921), 189–93, 318; Third (1923), 199–203, 244; Fourth (1927), 212, 215–16, 227; Fifth (1945), 302; Liberia and, 271, 277–79

pan-Africanism, 176–81, 338

Paris (France): race relations in, 10, 140–41, 188–89, 211; World War I and, 160

Parks, Rosa, 308

Parsons, Eben, 98

Patterson, Henry, 34

Patterson, Mary Jane, 34, 69

Pearl of Asia, The (Child), 90–91

Pence, Daniel, 23

Pence, Imogene Chinn Johnson, 22–24, 28–29, 31

pen names, use of, 13, 197–98, 209, 254–55

Pennsylvania, race relations in, 38, 40–41

Perse, Saint-John, 225

Peterson, Jerome, 144, 146

Philadelphia (Pa.), 38, 40–41

Pinchback, P. B. S., 79

Pinkett, Harold T., 303–4, 310

Pitts, Helen, 7

Plessy v. Ferguson, 101, 134, 308

Polk, James K., 55

Porter, Horace, 107–8

Portugal, 242–43, 245–47, 255–56

postcard exchanges, 116, 143, 162, 318

Powell, Colin, 9, 315–17

Powell, William F., 57

"Price of Peace, The" (I. G. Hunt), 286, 294–95, 320

primitivism, 10, 141, 167, 210–12, 226, 292

Princeton University and seminary, 50, 52, 156

Providential Armistice, The (N. B. Marshall), 251–52

Puerto Rico, U.S. territory, 122, 156

Pullman, George, 67, 89

Pullman car porters, 89, 95–96, 100, 102

Purvis, Harriet, 39, 47

Purvis, Robert, 39

Quarles, John, 57–58

Quest of the Silver Fleece, The (Du Bois), 2, 13, 71–72, 150–51, 229

Race Nègre, La (journal), 205

race relations, 6–8, 188, 316–17, 319; in Arkansas, 53; in California, 41–44; in Florida, 52; in France, 10, 140–41, 188–89, 199, 205–6, 211; in Kentucky, 27, 31; in Ohio, 33–35, 62–63; in Pennsylvania, 38, 40–41; in Tennessee, 86; in Vancouver, 44–45, 47–51; in Washington, D.C., 6–7, 71, 78, 186–87, 292–93, 299, 307–10

racial conflicts: in Brownsville, Tex. (1906), 133–34, 145, 148; in Washington, D.C. (1919), 186–87

racial identities, 76–77, 92, 94, 167, 179, 208–9, 224–25, 274, 300, 305

racial stereotypes, 346; in *Birth of a Nation,* 158; misconceptions and, 8, 63; primitivism and, 10, 141, 167, 210–12, 226, 292; sexuality and, 7, 22, 209–10; World's Columbian Exposition and, 67

Ranavalona III, Queen of Madagascar, 5, 108, 110, 115, 123–24, 194, 304

Razaf, Andy (Razafinkeriefo, Andreamentaria), 110, 184, 206, 315

Reber, Samuel, Jr., 264

Red Cross (Croix Rouge), 152, 162, 165, 172–73, 235–36, 300

Red Shawls rebellion (Madagascar), 131, 136, 301

Regan, Caroline Dudley, 209–10

Republican Party (U.S.) and politics, 2, 58, 89, 120, 145, 148, 288–89

Revue des Deux Mondes (journal), 225

Rhinelander, Alice Jones, 208–9, 225, 300

Rhinelander, Leonard, 208

Rice, Condoleezza, 9, 316–17

Rice, Susan, 317

Roberts, Joseph J., 265

Rollin, Frances, 197

Roosevelt, Eleanor, 288, 290, 292, 299, 318

Roosevelt, Franklin D., 97, 284, 288, 290–92, 296, 302, 304

Roosevelt, Theodore, 5, 76, 97, 100, 122, 133–34, 145, 148, 226, 306

Root, Elihu, 135

Rosso, Stéphane, 205–6, 225

Ruffin, John N., 59

safaris, 122–23, 212

St.-Étienne (France): commerce/industry of, 143, 149–50, 151, 159–60; consulate inspection in, 141–42; geography/climate of, 143; society/culture in, 140, 151–53; U.S. representatives in, 135, 139, 212–13, 218; World War I and, 159–61, 163, 165–67, 170

St. George's Episcopal Church (N.Y.), 100, 153

St. Louis World's Fair (1904), 4–5, 133

St. Mary's Church (Washington, D.C.), 306

St. Michael's. *See* Azores, Portuguese

Salazar, António de Oliveira, 247, 256

San Francisco (Calif.), race relations in, 41–44

Santo Domingo, 56–57, 97

São Miguel. *See* Azores, Portuguese

Satineau, Maurice, 205, 225

Washington, D.C.: education in, 69; race relations and segregation in, 6–7, 71, 78, 186–87, 292–93, 299, 307–10

Washington Bee (newspaper), 12, 75, 148–49, 195

Washington Conservatory of Music and School of Expression, 74, 251, 288, 299

Washington Post (newspaper), 1, 12, 79, 186–87, 301, 307, 309

Washington Square (H. James), 1, 325

Watkins, Frances Ellen. *See* Harper, Frances Ellen Watkins

Weaver, Robert, 290, 314

Weld, Theodore Dwight, 27

Wells-Barnett, Ida B., 13, 68, 173, 198, 202, 277, 288

West Indians and West Indies, 10, 45, 181–82, 191, 203. *See also individual countries and islands*

Wetter, Edward Telfair, 59, 109–11, 113, 125–26

Wharton, Clifton, Jr., 9, 298, 315

Wharton, Clifton R., Sr., 9, 207, 257, 259, 263–64, 273, 297–98

Wharton, Harriette, 258, 282

White, George, 79, 288, 290

Wilhelm II, Emperor of Germany, 153, 159, 304

Williams, John T., 59

Williams College (Mass.), 98–100, 122, 144, 189, 314

WILPF. *See* Women's International League for Peace and Freedom

Wilson, Edward Everett, 98

Wilson, Woodrow, 13, 155–56, 158, 167, 186, 189, 226, 262

Winters, Lewis, 88

women: black feminism and, 209–10; cult of True Womanhood and, 36; education for, 63–64; military service by, 165, 172, 299; slavery's oppression of, 35–36; State Department roles for, 291, 298; stereotypes of black, 7, 22, 209–10, 226; voting rights for, 47, 64, 195–96. *See also* miscegenation

"Women of France, The" (I. G. Hunt), 195–96, 339

Women's International League for Peace and Freedom (WILPF), 10, 185, 226, 288, 293–94, 307

Woodson, Carter G., 165, 171, 186, 283, 311

World's Columbian Exposition (1893), 5, 67–69, 198

World's Congress of Representative Women from All Lands (1893), 9

World War I (WWI), 159–63; African American nurses and, 165; African American soldiers in, 167–73, 184, 187–88; Bonus Army aftermath of, 286; colonial/African soldiers in, 163–64, 173, 222; colonialism and, 164–65; women's service in, 165, 172. *See also* Mandates Commission; Versailles Peace Conference

World War II (WWII), 292, 298–300, 302

Wynn, Caroline (protagonist in Du Bois's *Quest*), 2, 13, 71–72, 151, 229

Yancy, Allen, 269–70

"Yankee Consul, The" (Horton), 260

Yerby, William, 140, 155, 247, 250, 287, 341

Young, Andrew, 9

Young, Charles D., 9, 52, 165, 168, 191, 195, 262–63, 316

Young Women's Christian Association (YWCA), 131, 175, 288

Zeppelins, 152, 160, 228